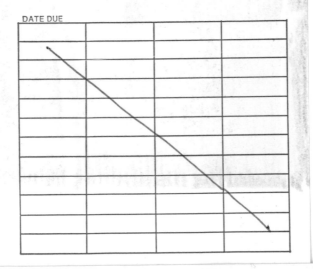

AMBROSE
BIERCE

"*I doubt if anything is really irrelevant. Every-thing that happens is intrinsically like the man it happens to.—In some indescribable way the event's modified, qualitatively modified, so as to suit the character of each person involved in it. It's a great mystery and a paradox.*"

Spandrell in POINT COUNTER POINT

AMBROSE BIERCE
A BIOGRAPHY
BY CAREY McWILLIAMS

....

WITH A NEW INTRODUCTION BY THE AUTHOR

....

ARCHON BOOKS   1967

Library of Congress Catalog Card Number: 67-25641
Printed in the United States of America

DEDICATED

TO

VINCENT O'SULLIVAN

PREFACE

T HE limitations of a biography are largely determined by the extent and availability of information about the subject of the biography at the time it is written. When this volume was begun, no biography of Ambrose Bierce had been written. The available information about Bierce consisted, for the most part, of a brochure by Mr. Vincent Starrett and certain autobiographical portions of the "Collected Works." Upon these slender pillars an enormous pyramid of conjecture had been erected. My efforts, therefore, have necessarily resulted in a volume which is as much a source book as it is a biography. It was necessary to read the entire body of Mr. Bierce's journalism, from 1868 to 1909, in which much autobiographical information is to be found. To make this material readily available has required more frequent and extended quotations than would otherwise be necessary. No critical analysis of Bierce's writings has been attempted, with the exception of one chapter, in which his stories are studied in the light of the biographical information now made available. Because of the wild and fantastic rumors that have circulated unchallenged about Bierce's life for so many years, it has been neces-

*sary to emphasize deliberately certain phases of his ex·
perience. It has been impossible to escape, at times, a contro-
versial attitude which has been personally distasteful and
unpleasant. Some misstatements have been refuted with a
rudeness the only justification of which is the malice that
inspired the misdeeds of which complaint is made.*

*Much of the information used in this volume was ob-
tained by personal interview. Hence it is extremely difficult
to make appropriate acknowledgments, a difficulty which I
can only trust will be appreciated by the many friends and
acquaintances of Mr. Bierce who have been so generous
with information and assistance.*

*There is no way in which I can summarize my indebted-
ness to George Sterling for his friendship, encouragement
and assistance. Always the most generous of friends, he
placed every one who knew him in an embarrassing position,
as one is invariably embarrassed who has received unexpected and undeserved gifts that, in the very nature of things,
cannot be repaid. If, in the pages that follow, George Sterling's name is treated with apparent sevcrity, it is only upon
the strength of information which he himself gave me and
upon the inclusion of which he would have insisted. I most
certainly have had no intention or desire to belittle the memory of a man for whose memory I entertain only the kindest
affection.*

*Helen Bierce Isgrigg has been most generous with in-
formation about her father. Her patience under an interminable interrogation has been miraculous. Several of Mr.
Bierce's biographers, whose names were unknown to Mrs.
Isgrigg, have complained of her severity. As a matter of
fact, her good humor in the face of the constant indignities
of the press has been nothing less than admirable. It is diffi-*

*cult to adequately acknowledge the assistance which she has
so generously given me in connection with the preparation
of this volume. It should not be inferred, however, that she
is in any manner responsible for the statements made in this
book, unless I have specifically mentioned her name.*

*Mrs. Milton E. Getz and Mr. Willard S. Morse have
kindly permitted me to make use of their excellent and in-
valuable collections of Bierce material, as has Mr. Robert
Cords. Dr. Max Farrand and Miss Dorothy Lehmann of the
Huntington Library, San Marino, have been of great assistance. Mr. Jackson Berger of the Los Angeles "Times" has
my thanks for several personal courtesies. I am indebted to
D. J. H. and H. McW. for assistance in connection with the
preparation of this manuscript.*

*The bibliography at the end of the book will supply
specific references to most of the quotations. Where letters
of George Sterling are mentioned they have invariably been
taken from "The Letters of Ambrose Bierce," published by
the Book Club of California. The letters of Bierce to S. O.
Howes, Charles Warren Stoddard and Walter Neale are to
be found in the collection of Bierce material in the Huntington Library, San Marino.*

CAREY MCWILLIAMS

*Los Angeles, California.
August 23rd, 1929.*

INTRODUCTION—1967

Writing a new introduction for *Ambrose Bierce: A Biography*, first published in November, 1929, presents a problem. There would be little point in attempting to re-evaluate or tamper with what I wrote about Bierce thirty-eight years ago. I am, and in a sense I am not, the same person I was then. A thorough re-evaluation would be unfair to the person I then was and it would be a bit absurd to impose on that person's limitations and enthusiasms a retrospective point of view. So what I have decided to do is simply to explain how I happened to write the book, to say something about the circumstances under which it was written and to offer a few brief comments on some of the major insights and new findings that others have contributed to the Bierce canon in the intervening years.

As I wrote in 1929, the reputation of Ambrose Bierce has gone through some strange transmutations. Overlooked for long periods, he has been enthusiastically "discovered" and "rediscovered" at intervals. Several explanations can be offered for this peculiar fate, but the most persuasive is that for many years is was difficult to get copies of his books. In one sense it could be fairly said that he was never really "published" until the Neale Publishing Company brought out the *Collected Works* in twelve volumes. But this pretentious edition came too late and included too much. Today, however, Bierce has come into his own. While the once familiar question, "Who was Ambrose Bierce?"—which later became "Whatever happened to Ambrose Bierce?"—is still heard occasionally, Bierce has finally been given a secure, if not clearly defined, position in American letters. Even so it is not uncommon to read, every now and then, an article or essay on Civil War fiction or some kindred theme which fails to mention his work. For example, in the *Sewanee Review* (Spring 1961) one learns from a piece by James M. Cox that of the American writers of the 19th century only two, Walt Whitman and Mark Twain, had directly participated in the Civil War. But despite an occasional aberration of this sort, no one disputes the proposition that Bierce deserves a permanent niche in the annals of American writing. If the time for breathless "rediscoveries" is over, individuals will continue to discover him and usually with a sense of shock and surprise. A majority of these will reject him—the majority always has—but a minority will become Bierce addicts. Not merely as a writer, but as a person—as a presence—Bierce becomes very much a part of the lives of those who identify with his point of view.

I discovered Bierce quite accidentally. In the early 1920s my family had moved from Colorado to Southern California. I was going to college at the time (the University of Southern California) and holding down a job at the *Los Angeles Times*. The municipal library of the City of the Angels was then located on the top floors of the old Metropolitan Building. As I was prowling through the stacks one day, I happened to come on the impressive *Collected Works*—forbidding, austere, and unread (some of the pages were uncut). As a devoted reader of *The Smart Set* and an avid fan of H. L. Mencken, I had, of course heard of Bierce. Taking down a volume, I found myself staring at the handsome pencil drawing of Bierce by Miss F. Soule Campbell which he had selected as the frontispiece to the first volume. I was "hooked"; I became and still remain a Biercian.

The immediate difficulty was, of course, that I could not find out very much about Bierce. I read what there was to read but it failed to satisfy my curiosity. So I began to dig around; after all, Bierce had lived in California for many years, so there must be many people still living who had known him. But I was handicapped by the lack of any plausible credentials; I was a sophomore in college, I held a full-time job, I had no money for travel, or to purchase materials, or to conduct investigations. So my research had to go forward slowly, laboriously, with long interruptions and many frustrations. It was an after-hours process, mostly nights and vacations and weekends; a matter of accumulating information item by item.

The first real break came when I saved enough money to finance an initial exploratory trip to San Francisco. There, on February 11,

1925, in J. J. Newbegin's Post Street bookstore, I met George Sterling, the poet, for the first time. We became close friends, then and there. On that first visit, I had several long sessions with him at the Bohemian Club and we remained in almost continuous contact, by correspondence and visits north and south, from that time until his death (he committed suicide in his room at the club on November 17, 1926, on the eve of a meeting, which he had keenly anticipated, with Mencken). A more generous person than Sterling I have never met. He was not at all shocked by my absurd ambition to write a biography of Bierce; on the contrary, he was most enthusiastic and, in addition to long hours of talk, he put me on to some of the prime sources. The deeper I became involved in the research, the more fascinated I became not merely with the subject but with those who had known him. The cast included: Fremont Older, William Randolph Hearst, Roosevelt Johnson (boyhood friend of Sterling's from his Sag Harbor days, a fabulous eccentric), James Tufts, one-time editor of the San Francisco *Examiner* and proud possessor of a fine collection of Bierce's "Prattle" columns, Gertrude Atherton, James Hopper, Willard S. Morse (retired mining engineer for the Guggenheim interest; he had a splendid library of Western Americana with many rare Bierce items), Sterling's charming sisters, Mary Austin, E. H. ("Ned") Hamilton, Elizah Brooks (a delightful old gentleman who lived in the Napa Valley; he had worked with Bierce at the Sub-Treasury in San Francisco), Col. Charles Erskine Scott Wood and his wife Sara Bard Field, the poetess (the Colonel received me, one warm summer day, at his beautiful home on a hilltop near Los Gatos overlooking the Santa Clara Valley; he was attired at the time in the toga of a Roman Senator, complete with gilt sandals!), any number of beautiful ladies who had known, loved and admired Bierce (where Walter Neale got the notion that only ugly ladies loved Bierce, I can't imagine). Of all those I met, Sterling was the most helpful. Our friendship was not, unfortunately, to last very long but I got to know him very well indeed (I did the notice about him which appears in the *Dictionary of American Biography,* Vol. XVII, p. 585). And finally, of course, I came to know Bierce's daughter, Helen, who, when I first met her, had been recently divorced from Francis Isgrigg.

The story of my friendship with Helen Bierce would make a full-length memoir. Of all the "characters" I met in piecing together

Bierce's story, she was easily the most preposterous and improbable. I had tried long and hard to locate her but without success and then, of course, I discovered by chance that she was living in Los Angeles! At first she put me off but later consented to see me and we became, and until her death remained, great friends. Physically she resembled her father; she had his head, his bearing, his carriage. Even when I first knew her, when her fortunes were at low ebb and she was no longer young, she was a very handsome woman, bouncy and exuberant, with more than her share of vitality. But in mind and temperament she was quite unlike her father. She was, for example, a devoted Christian Scientist with a strong predisposition to believe in almost any "new thought" notion that came along if it promised new hope and good cheer. She had been badly spoiled as a girl and as a young lady and was improvident to a degree that caused me endless concern and inconvenience. For years, I loaned her money, when I could, paid her bills, stalled off collection agencies, helped find her places to live, and ran errands for her. She was a hard person to help. There was her extravagance, for one thing. Then, too, she was accident-prone; she was always breaking a leg or an arm, and every accident was, of course, an economic disaster. Like most "new thought" true-believers, she not only insisted on taking a rosy view of the future but she insisted that you share her optimism. She was generous to a fault; if you gave her $10, she was very likely to hand it over to the first person she met who needed help. Just as it was next to impossible to get her to focus on reality—any reality— so it was almost impossible to get her to concentrate on any particular incident or to recall a name or date or place. I never succeeded in getting from her a clear picture of her mother, of the kind of person she was or what her interests were. Intellectually the daughter did not understand her father because, intellectually, she did not understand anything. She referred to him as "popsy" and he to her as "Bib." But she had strong emotions and deep feelings and, at this level, in her own way, she did "understand" her father and was deeply attached to him. But she was not a good informant even about him; illuminating, yes, reliable, no. She was difficult to pin down, her recollection was faulty, her attention-span was limited, and she was always more interested in something other than what I was trying to quiz her about at the time.

Two of the many letters I received from her suggest quite vividly and accurately what she was like as a person. One is dated April 19, 1934: "Carey dear—Just got a 'job' from Jensen out in County Welfare and here I am! Thank the Gods! Now will you leave me a couple of dollars at your office so I can eat until I am *rich?* I got a delightful letter from Starrett [Vincent Starrett, of Chicago, who prepared a bibliography of Bierce's writings—C. McW.], the other day and he asked to be remembered to you 'very muchly.' O, am I a busy child! *I am.* This is written in between *breaths.* Love from Little Helen." The job did not last long. The other, undated, reads: "Dear Carey—Enclosed is the first payment and every Monday I shall endeavor to see payments reach you if you will be kind enough to see the proper party receives them [one of her numerous creditors—C. McW.]. I won't even try to tell you how much your loyal friendship has been to me in these troublesome times—I am just praying with all my heart and soul to be given the great privilege of *proving* my gratitude, and some way I know that time will come! I have found out that a truly great desire indicates the possibility of its fullfilment [*sic*] in your life. I only wish I had known that truth 20 years ago. God bless you—Sincerely, Helen B."

Almost from the moment of our meeting, Helen had told me of a trunk which her father had left with her in Bloomington, Illinois (she was then Mrs. H. D. Cowden), before leaving for Mexico. It contained letters, clippings, papers, photographs, books, etc. Naturally I was aquiver to see this material. But the trunk, I soon found out, was never available; it was in "storage", she didn't want to get it out until she was properly "settled"—there was always some excuse. In due course it dawned on me that she was jealously guarding the trunk and its contents as her one solid resource, which indeed it was. She liked me, she trusted me, but I could sense that she somehow felt that once I had seen the material I might be less attentive to her needs and problems. In an effort to help her, I had tried to get her to tell me enough about her parents and her brothers (both dead) so that I might ghost a piece for her which might be sold for a good price to, say, one of the women's magazines with some such title as "My Father, Ambrose Bierce." But I never succeeded in getting her to be specific; she was too breezy, too full of bounce, much too prone to talk about herself, her romances and adventures, and, of course, her great expectations. Months passed and the mysterious trunk still eluded me.

Finally I induced her to permit me to negotiate a sale, sight unseen, of the trunk and its contents. I worked out the details with my good friend, Jake Zeitlin, the Los Angeles book dealer. Jake got Mrs. Milton E. Getz, whose husband was a top official of the Union Bank and Trust Company, to offer what was then a good sum—as I recall it was $7,500—for the trunk and contents and a portrait of Bierce by J. H. E. Partington. But Mrs. Getz had been buying rare books somewhat in excess of her allowance for such purposes and so the purchase price had to be paid in installments. In the meantime, the trunk was to be kept in storage as security against the sums she was paying over each month. I insisted that the monthly payments should be paid to me as trustee for Helen Bierce, as some protection against her extravagance and, also, because she had creditors. The sum enabled her to get along fairly well for a couple of years. Most of the time, of course, she was out of work, for there was nothing much she could do. Now and then she toyed with the idea of opening a shop or something of the sort but nothing much ever came of these notions. When the proceeds from the sale were exhausted, her life went from bad to worse. There were accidents and other calamities and misfortunes too numerous to mention. And then she became seriously ill and was taken to the Los Angeles County Hospital, where I visited her as often as I could. The last time I saw her she was propped up in bed, a bit shaken by adversity but still cheerful and thoroughly convinced that things would soon take a turn for the better. Despite the trials and tribulations she caused me, I remember her with great warmth and affection. (Helen Bierce died in Los Angeles County December 16, 1940.)

But the sale of the "trunk" did not solve the problem of access to the contents. First of all, I had to wait until the full purchase price had been paid. The agreement of sale contained a provision, on which Mrs. Getz had insisted, that I was to have access to the material once it had been delivered to her but only at "the convenience of the buyer." This seemed fair enough at the time. But like most collectors, Mrs. Getz had a strong proprietary feeling about her acquisitions. The trunk, I discovered, contained some real treasures. I should have been able to make a leisurely exploration of the contents, item by item. I should have been able to prepare copies or make photostats. But I discovered that I was to be given only a limited time to inspect the contents. Going over the material proved to be a nerve-wracking, frustrating, utterly exasperating experience, the more so as by then I had a deadline to meet for delivery of the manuscript. I made the most of my limited right of inspection despite the fact that I could not devote full time to it. Later—so I have been told—Mrs. Getz got "tired" of the Bierce collection and broke it up. The hurried hours I spent looking through the material were for me a nightmare; when I think back upon the experience, even after all these years, I still feel cheated.

By the time I graduated from the University in 1927, I had been working on the Bierce book for five or six years, devoting as much time to it as I could spare from a crowded school-and-work schedule. After graduation, I was able to devote a little more time to the project. At college, one of my first published articles was about Bierce (it appeared in *The Wooden Horse,* March, 1924, the college literary magazine I was later to edit); and the first article I ever sold to a magazine—price, $10.00—was about Bierce (it appeared in *The Argonaut,* March 14, 1925). Not long after I got out of school, I did a piece about Bierce, summarizing some of the research I had been doing, and Mencken accepted it for publication in *The American Mercury* (February, 1929). As soon as it appeared, I received a letter from Albert Boni offering a contract for a book, which, of course, I promptly accepted. The advance was $250.00—which, although I did not know it then, was to represent my total earnings from the book.

From what I have said about the circumstances under which *Ambrose Bierce: A Biography* was written, several conclusions can be drawn. First of all, it is the work of a young man; most of the research and a large part of the writing were done while I was still in college. Second, the book was researched and written under harassing circumstances; indeed as I look back I wonder that it ever got written. As published, the book represented a great deal of hard work, and much original research; it was the first serious attempt to dig out the facts about Bierce. Prior to the appearance of the book, it had been much more fun to write "about" Bierce, as many people had done, than to take the trouble of checking such mundane matters as vital statistics or to scratch for leads and sources. After 1929, critics and biographers at least knew the main facts of his life and could easily identify the areas and issues that required further study and investigation. Precisely because the book was written under the circumstances I have outlined, I feel that the text should stand as it was published.

And besides, I stand by the essential theme—the basic interpretation. In a sense the theme is that Bierce was not essentially a cynic or skeptic but rather an idealist, more accurately perhaps a moralist, who, at an early and impressionable age had been exposed to a frightful baptism of fire—an ordeal of suffering and horror—that had shaped his character and outlook. In an introduction that I did for a paperback edition of *The Devil's Dictionary* in 1957, I tried to suggest what Bierce was really like by comparing him with Oliver Wendell Holmes, Jr. (William McCann, in his introduction to *Ambrose Bierce's Civil War,* and Edmund Wilson in *Patriotic Gore,* have made the same comparison). Bierce and Holmes were both born in 1842. Both were exposed to the fires of a cruel and horrendous Civil War when they were young men. Both participated in some of the heaviest fighting of the war and both were wounded. Both were intense idealists when they enlisted; they emerged from the war in a different mood. Neither ever forgot or, for that matter, fully recovered from the effects of the war. Both were proud, sensitive, and extremely intelligent; after the war both took a frosty and detached view of human affairs and were somewhat olympian in outlook. Both were men of rare courage; both looked out at life in a clear-eyed way. Both took an extremely bleak view of the corruption of the post-1865 decades and yet, as Edmund Wilson notes, were too much old-fashioned Americans to identify with the ideals of social justice which began to be voiced near the the turn of the century. Both held their heads high. Holmes was the more favored; he was able to make a much better adjustment than Bierce. He had a name, family position, a sound education, connections, a measure of inherited wealth. Bierce had none of these. "Bierce's mind," Van Wyck Brooks once wrote in *The Freeman,* "had nothing upon which to feed but the few books, old and well tried, that had nourished his youth. One can only guess how much more effective his life would have been if it had been passed in a congenial atmosphere of living ideas. While his interests were parochial, his outlook . . . was broadly human. He was a natural aristocrat"—like Holmes—"and he developed a rudimentary philosophy of aristocracy which, under happier circumstances, might have made him a great figure in the world of American thought. . . . No man was ever freer of personal bitterness. It is impossible to read his letters without feeling that he was a starved man; but certainly it can be said that, if his generation gave him very little, he succeeded in retaining in his own life the poise of an Olympian."

Both Holmes and Bierce were enormously sensitive to human suffering, to injustice, to cruelty, but at the same time both took a cool view of the universe and cherished few illusions about it. A lonelier man than Bierce, as Van Wyck Brooks noted, never existed. But he was a Stoic, or, rather, he became one. Bierce's "nothing matters" was not a counsel of despair; quite the contrary. What he meant was that everything mattered so much that life would be unendurably cruel if pain and memory lasted forever. But pain does lessen. Anguish does abate. Memories do fade. And because, in the end, nothing matters, life can be endured. Shortly before he disappeared into Mexico, he wrote Nellie Sickler, a young girl that he never met but with whom he corresponded, off and on, for many years, a letter in which he said: "But you are happy; and that is all that it is worth while to be. Nothing else is of any value— just happiness. The difference between a good person and a bad one is that one finds happiness in goodness, the other in badness; but, consciously or unconsciously, happiness is all they seek or can seek. Even self-sacrifice is a species of indulgence. And at the end of it all we see that nothing matters. No, my child, we shall never meet; and even that will not matter." ("A Collection of Bierce Letters," University of California *Chronicle,* January, 1932.)

Since 1929 a good deal of research and commentary has been devoted to Bierce—the man and his work—and some of it has real value. In this section I want to touch on some of the highlights.

First—because it came first—I want to mention some material that I brought to light. Publication of my book brought the usual flow of mail, some of it important. It enabled me, for example, to clarify a point or two about Bierce's disappearance ("The Mystery of Ambrose Bierce," *The American Mercury,* March, 1931). It was in this way, too, that I unearthed the interesting letters Bierce wrote Mrs. Allen Sickler ("A Collection of Bierce Letters," University of California *Chronicle,* January, 1932). In one of these letters, dated September 21, 1913, Bierce explained why he was leaving for Mexico and South America. "My plan, so far as I have one, is to go through Mexico to one of the Pacific ports, if I can *get* through without being stood up against a wall and shot as an American. Thence I hope to sail for some port in South America. Thence go across the Andes and perhaps across the continent. . . . Naturally, it is possible—even probable—that I shall not return. These be 'strange countries,' in which things happen; that is why I am going. And I am seventy-one!" Even more important than these letters was the material on which I based "Ambrose Bierce and His First Love, An Idyll of the Civil War," which appeared in *The Bookman* for June and July, 1932. It included a photograph of Bierce just after he had enlisted, a photograph of his childhood sweetheart, Fatima Wright, some poems that she had inspired, and a most revealing letter he wrote Clara Wright dated June 8, 1864, from Ackworth, Georgia, in which he said that his brigade had lost nearly a third of its members killed and wounded since leaving Cleveland, Tennessee. So far as I know this is the only letter Bierce wrote while in the service of which there is any record. The material touched on a period, in January, 1864, when Bierce was recuperating at the home of his parents, in Warsaw, Indiana, from a wound he had received in action. In the letter of June 8 he had said, "my turn will come in time," and it nearly did. For on June 23 he was severely wounded—a head wound—at Kenesaw Mountain (The *Columbia Encyclopedia* gives the spelling as Kennesaw, and fixes the date of the battle as June 27, 1864. Kennesaw is doubtless correct but it is a later spelling; as to the date, the battle may have extended over a period of days. (Of this wound, Bierce once said that his head had been "broken like a walnut." Following a period of hospitalization, he returned to Warsaw for a long furlough in the summer of 1864, but this time there were no long walks and buggy rides with the Wright sisters; just why, no one knows. In September, he rejoined his regiment and, the war over, he received his discharge in Huntsville, Alabama, on January 10, 1865.

Still another find I turned up was a long letter dated October 1, 1904, which Bierce wrote on the occasion of the 24th Annual Reunion of the Ninth Indiana Volunteers, first published as a Reunion Pamphlet at South Bend, October 7, 1904. I turned it over to James Hart—a devoted Biercian—who published it under the imprint of The Harvest Press in 1931 with the title "Battlefields and Ghosts." A fine letter, it closes with a passage inspired by a visit

Bierce had made to the scene of the regiment's old fort in the Cheat Mountains. "The whole region," he wrote, "is wild and grand, and if any one of the men who in his golden youth soldiered through its sleepy valley and over its gracious mountains will revisit it in the hazy season when it is all aflame with the autumn foliage I promise him sentiments that he will willingly entertain and emotions that he will care to feel. Among them will be, I fear, a haunting envy of those of his war comrades whose fall and burial in that enchanted land he once bewailed." (As is well known, Bierce had a splendid war record. He enlisted on April 19, 1861, when he was nineteen—the second person in the county to enlist after the firing on Fort Sumter—and was assigned to Company C, Ninth Indiana infantry. Known as "The Bloody Ninth," it participated in front-line combat at Shiloh, the first major battle of the war, and suffered the highest casualties of all Union regiments engaged. In the entire Rolls of the regiment, there is not one mark against Bierce. He was cited for gallantry and efficient service fifteen or sixteen times in the dispatches. (See "Ambrose Bierce and the Civil War," Napier Wilt, *American Literature,* November, 1929.)

Of the more recent research, George W. Knepper's publication of the journal of Lucius Verus Bierce—*Travels in the Southland, 1822–1823,* Ohio State University Press, 1966, with an introduction and map—is of major importance. I had turned up much material about General Lucius Bierce (see pp. 17–22) and was aware, as anyone familiar with the facts would be, that he must have been a major influence in the life of his nephew. General Bierce, who died on November 11, 1876, was one of the best known public citizens of northern Ohio during his lifetime (he once served as Mayor of Akron). But I had not fully appreciated the commanding position he occupied in the community until I had occasion to visit Akron in 1961. On this visit, Mr. Knepper made it possible for me to read the journal General Bierce had kept of his travels in the Southland— from Athens, Ohio, where he had attended the University of Ohio, along the Kanawah River in West Virginia, from Sweetsprings to Roanoke, from there to Winston Salem and on to Spartanburg, then through a portion of the Cherokee Nation to Rome, Georgia, then to Gadsden and Huntsville, and finally back to Athens through Kentucky and Tennessee. I also visited the General's handsome residence on a hill overlooking the Ohio Canal (it is today the art museum—a gift from the General), and drove out to see the John Brown farm near Akron. I had a chance also to see the old prints of Buchtel College (now the University of Akron), a small Universalist school chartered in 1870 to which General Bierce had given his library. Unfortunately the library was destroyed by fire in 1899, so that it is impossible to get any precise idea of the extent of the collection, but considering the fact that it served as *the* college library, it must have been—for the time and place—a very fine private library.

One of the aspects of Bierce's life that has always presented a real puzzle is how this largely self-educated Indiana farm boy acquired his aristocratic bearing, his general "stance" and style, his fierce independence, not to mention the rudiments of a classical education and, from an early age, a keen interest in literature. Bierce's father, a not-too-successful farmer who served as county assessor, overseer of the poor and vice president of the local agricultural society, had a fairly good small library by the standards of the time and place, but he, too, was largely self-educated. The influence of General Bierce, the uncle, provides a key to the puzzle. Mr. Knepper reports that "family tradition maintains that Ambrose modeled himself upon his purposeful, active, and opinionated Uncle Lucius, possibly even to the extent of copying and improving upon his style." The exact extent of this influence cannot be determined despite the new, confirming details that Mr. Knepper has unearthed. Did Bierce visit his distinguished uncle? did he read in his library? did they correspond? General Bierce was not survived by any sons or daughters, and his books and papers were destroyed in the Buchtel College fire. But the uncle's fame throughout northern Indiana and northern Ohio, his general prominence in the anti-slavery agitation, as well as the fact that he was a man of education and considerable learning in a variety of fields, must have made him a vivid figure in the early life of his nephew.

Anti-slavery agitation was, of course, strong throughout the Western Reserve, and General Bierce was a major spokesman for the anti-slavery forces. He knew John Brown very well. On the evening of Brown's execution, General Bierce delivered an oration in the course of which he said: "Thank God I furnished him arms—as did others in Akron—and right good use did he make of them." Tradition has it that the swords which Brown and his sons carried at the time of the Kansas raids had been presented to Brown by General Bierce. Sanborn, in his book about Brown, said that the swords used were "not sabers exactly, but weapons made like the Roman short-sword, of which six or eight had been given to Brown in Akron, Ohio, just before he went to Kansas, by General Bierce of that city, who took them from an armory there." Oswald Garrison Villard, in his memorable biography of Brown, stated that "General Bierce's title came from a northern Ohio secret society, the 'Grand Eagles' organized to attack the Canadian government. The arms given John Brown by Bierce belonged to this society, and included artillery broadswords that bore either on the hilt or the blade the device of an eagle, and which were the identical weapons used in the Potta-watomie killings." Actually the society was called the Hunters, not the Grand Eagles. Truman Nelson, a great authority on Brown, tells me that the Foot Artillery Sword, Model 1833, answers the assorted descriptions, even to the design of an eagle on the pommel (I am indebted to him and to Boyd B. Sutler, of Charleston, West Virginia, for details). But I have a letter from Nyle H. Miller, of the Kansas State Historical Society, dated February 12, 1960, in which he informs me that the museum has only one sword, and that the details of the gift do not clearly establish whether it was one of the swords which Bierce gave to Brown. The records merely indicate that the former secretary of the association wrote a label for the sword which reads: "This sword, with other arms, was brought to Kansas by Capt. John Brown, from Akron, Ohio, in 1855 or 1856."

The question about the swords is primarily of interest, of course, to Civil War buffs, but it is not without relevance to Bierce buffs. For it demonstrates how close General Bierce was to Brown and it gives some indication of how intensely the agitation of that period must have been reflected in the Bierce family. But the journal of General Bierce's travels in the South is much the best evidence of the extent to which the family was involved in the anti-slavery agitation. The General was a young man, just out of college, when he made this extensive trip, mostly on foot, through the slave territory. What he saw, and experienced, is vividly described in the journal. Immensely readable, there are passages in the journal which have the same force and clarity that characterized the nephew's style. Most travelers in the South, of that period, visited the cities of the coastal areas and seldom got into the heart of the slave territory. General Bierce did. He was one of the rare anti-slavery spokesmen who had seen slavery at close range; he really knew something about it. It was this tradition of intense personal involvement in the anti-slavery agitation to which Ambrose Bierce was exposed as a young man. His father, Marcus Aurelius, was an early subscriber to *The Northern Indianan,* an anti-slavery paper founded in Warsaw, Indiana, in 1856. For some years Ambrose, then in his teens, worked as a printer's devil on this paper.

Another item of importance in the latter-day research is Miss M. E. Grenander's study of the unpublished correspondence which passed between Bierce and Charles Warren Stoddard (*Huntington Library Quarterly,* May, 1960). Not only does this study provide interesting insights into Bierce's character and temperament but it also sheds light on his experiences as a journalist in London. Bierce looked back on his stay in England from 1872 to 1875 as the happiest period of his life. He had married the beautiful Mollie Day in San Francisco on December 25, 1871, and Capt. H. H. Day, the father-in-law, a wealthy mining engineer, gave the couple a trip abroad as a wedding present. A first son, Day, was born in December, 1872, and the second son, Leigh, was born in Leamington April 29, 1874. The Bierces seem to have moved about a great deal and, for part of the time, the mother-in-law, Mrs. Day, was with them. When she returned to the States, Mrs. Bierce was left with the care of the two infant sons and, as Miss Grenander notes, "with a husband submerged by a flood of journalistic hackwork." In 1874, Bierce wrote Stoddard that he had more work than he could do— "I have been, and am, up to my ears in work, grinding stuff for five publications, one semi-weekly, two weekly, one monthly, and one 'occasional'—a *pizen* thing for which I write every line. If some of these don't die of me I shall die of them." In May, 1875, Mrs. Bierce left England with Day and Leigh to return to the States for a visit with her parents. Although Bierce was not aware of the fact, she was then pregnant with her third child. In June, Bierce wrote Stoddard that he was lonely "without the wife and babies" and that he was "struggling with more work than I can manage and that is partly what has made me ill—for I am ill, though I keep pegging away, somehow." And then he added: "I live precariously and abominably." When Bierce learned of his wife's pregnancy, he left England (September, 1875) and back in San Francisco got a job in the

Assay Office of the Branch Mint. The third child, Helen, was born in San Francisco on October 30, 1875.

From this study it would appear that while Bierce probably did enjoy his years in England, they were by no means carefree. He was burdened with hackwork. He was often ill. Miss Grenander notes (p. 264) that the damp London climate aggravated his chronic asthma. This in itself is an interesting detail, for it is one of the first references to this condition. Chronic asthma, of the type from which Bierce suffered throughout his entire adult life, dates in most instances from early childhood. William McCann, in his introduction to *Ambrose Bierce's Civil War,* suggests that it is quite possible that "something prior to the war and the later unhappiness of his personal life, perhaps a congenital defect," tainted the stream of life for Bierce at its source. Edmund Wilson points out that Bierce "seems to have been haunted by the idea of death before he had even enlisted." He then observes that something seems to have "hobbled his exceptional talents—an impasse, a numbness, a void, as if some psychological short circuit had blown out an emotional fuse. The obsession with death is the image of this: it is the blank that blocks every vista; and the asthma from which Bierce suffered was evidently its physical aspect" (*Patriotic Gore,* p. 632). Psychoanalytic and psychosomatic studies indicate that chronic asthma, dating from infancy, tends to be related to a feeling that the mother's love has been withdrawn, leading to feelings of rage and resentment that can, in certain circumstances, be "reproduced" in the patient. The wheezing, the gasping, the feeling of suffocation probably reflect, and stimulate, a fear of death. In retrospect, I believe that this aspect of Bierce's life should have received greater stress than I gave it. (See *American Handbook of Psychiatry,* Vol. I, 1959, Chapter 35, "Psychophysiologic Aspects of Respiratory Disorders" by Eric D. Wittkower and Kerr L. White, p. 690.)

Bierce's years in England, as Miss Grenander makes clear, broadened his outlook, enriched his experience, and gave him an intensive training in a special style of journalism—the satirical journalism of *Figaro* and *Fun.* Out of this experience came the two "Dod Grile" books—*The Fiend's Delight* and *Nuggets in Dust,* to which Miss Grenander devotes some fascinating literary detective work (see *Huntington Library Quarterly,* August, 1965). It was good training for Bierce and it sharpened his pen, but his satirical talent was apparent before he left for England. His early satirical work in *The Overland Monthly* and the San Francisco *News Letter* had prompted the admiration of *The Nation* (June 17, 1869). The extraordinary ferment of the gold-rush years in California had made for a special kind of humor and wit. In a later comment, *The Nation*—which promptly spotted Bierce as "Dod Grile" (an anagram for God Rile)—observed that his wit was "as unlike that of any other American humorist as the play of a young human merry-andrew is unlike that of a young and energetic demon whose horns are well-budded" (November 21, 1872).

It should be stressed that the California to which Bierce returned in the fall of 1875 was not the California he had left in 1872. The gold-rush ferment had subsided; the great upsurge of exuberant prosperity was over—for the time being. The following year, 1876, marked a climax in American life, and there was more cause for unrest and discontent in California than elsewhere (see my *California: The Great Exception*, 1949, p. 172). The famous Compromise of 1876 marked the end of the attempts to "reconstruct" the South; by then the fervor of the anti-slavery cause had disappeared and the long dark night of "separate but equal" had begun. It marked, for all practical purposes, the end of the Civil War period and the rise of industrial America. "Violence flickered incessantly on every man's horizon that year," writes Robert V. Bruce (*1877: Year of Violence*, 1959, p. 10). "The youth of the American Republic is over," wrote Goldwin Smith. Back in San Francisco, with a wife and three children to support, Bierce was forced to take a job which he could hardly have found congenial after his years in England. He must have felt that life had closed in on him—that he was trapped. If this was his mood, it was matched by the violence and corruption of the new period that opened in American life, ironically enough, after the celebration of the centennial of the Republic.

A critical period in Bierce's life, about which I could learn very little, was his brief experience in the Black Hills as general agent for a mining company (see Chapter XVIII). Paul Fatout's *Ambrose Bierce: The Devil's Lexicographer*, (University of Oklahoma Press, 1951) is a fine study, particularly valuable for its research on Bierce's early years in Indiana. A later study by Mr. Fatout, *Ambrose Bierce and the Black Hills* (University of Oklahoma Press, 1956), is a superb piece of original research on this critically important episode in Bierce's life. After he had returned to San Francisco, Bierce had taken a job in the Assay Office of the Branch Mint (he had worked for the Sub-Treasury when he first arrived in California). How long he held this job I don't know, but the first issue of *The Argonaut*, March 25, 1877, carried Bierce's column "The Prattler," and thereafter he did a great deal of work for it. Nominally, Frank Pixley was the editor, but Bierce was the editor de facto. In May, 1879, Bierce's copy disappeared from the publication. The Black Hills were opened to unrestricted immigration on February 28, 1877. Because of his work in the Assay Office of the Mint, Bierce had occasion to follow the news about mining strikes and mining developments. In addition, of course, his father-in-law was a prominent mining engineer. In 1877, A. L. Bancroft & Company, in San Francisco, published a new *Map of the Black Hills Region Showing the Gold Mining District and the Seat of the Indian War*, drawn by A. G. Bierce, from surveys ordered by the War Department. I mention the map but it was Maurice Frink who finally turned up a copy of it (see *The Brand Book*, December, 1952). The surveys mentioned were those which Bierce had helped prepare as a member of General Hazen's expedition (see p. 70). It would appear that after Bierce's copy began to disappear from *The Argonaut* he became interested in the possibility of a career in mining. Throughout the summer and fall of 1879, he was interested in—at least to the extent of investigating—several mining operations. It was at this time—perhaps in the early part of 1880—that Bierce became involved in the Black Hills Mining Company (incorporated on December 8, 1879).

It is not clear just how Bierce became interested in this company. But during the war he had known S. B. Eaton—Sherburne Blake Eaton—a fellow officer on the staff of General Hazen. In the postwar period, Eaton had become a well-known corporation lawyer in New York, and along with some Eastern men of affairs had formed the Black Hills Mining Company. At some point, Bierce was asked to join the venture and on June 1, 1880, he appeared in Rapid City under the impression he was to take charge of the company's affairs at Rockerville. The immediate project was to construct a bedrock dam across Spring Creek near Sheridan, and from that point to build a huge wooden flume, tunneling through hills and winding across and around the gulches, 18 miles to the rich, but dry, diggings at

Rockerville (see Maurice Frink, *supra*). Prior to the time that Bierce appeared on the scene, the work had been in charge of a contractor named Capt. Ichabone M. West. The implications are clear that he had diverted a great deal of the company's money to his own uses, and that in collusion with him was the company's president, Gen. Alexander Shaler. At the time Bierce arrived, to take charge as general agent, things were in a mess and the directors of the company were divided about what should be done. From the outset, Bierce was involved in incredible difficulties. The company was virtually bankrupt. He was constantly fighting off creditors. He could not get clear instructions from New York. The construction project itself was extremely difficult. The experience was a ghastly, uninterrupted nightmare. It proved to be too much for him and he finally resigned—on September 24, 1880.

Against this background, it is interesting to note that Mr. Fatout, by painstaking research, demonstrates that Bierce proved to be a superb man of affairs and that he turned in a truly remarkable performance under the most trying circumstances. Moreover, by following the subsequent careers of Captain West and General Shaler, Mr. Fatout proves that Bierce was almost certainly right about them. This is the way Mr. Fatout sums up the Black Hills episode: "Here for a few devilish months in 1880 a good man worked very hard at a thankless job. He was industrious, loyal, and honest, and he was defeated. But in defeat he was a better man than the victors, a better man than he himself was at almost any other time in his life. Such behavior is worthy of remembrance. His name was Bierce—Major A. G. Bierce, General Agent."

Back in San Francisco in January, 1881, Bierce did not return to *The Argonaut*. There were stories that Frank Pixley refused to take him back and that this was the origin of the celebated quarrel in which they engaged for many years. But Bierce had never liked Pixley or his politics. In any case, he began to write for—and edit—*The Wasp*, a rival paper. "The bitter, sardonic Bierce of *The Wasp*," writes Mr. Fatout, seemed "a different person from the serious business agent" of the Black Hills. By comparison with his earlier work, the tone of his writing had become more bitter and more sardonic. Clearly, the collapse of the Black Hills venture must have been a severe blow, the more so since it left Bierce with a feeling—quite justified—of having been misused. He had reason to be disappointed in Eaton, who had been one of his closest friends. Mr. Fatout notes that "a curtain descends on the friendship after 1881." Eaton went on, of course, to become vice president of the Edison Electric Light Company and president of the company that later became General Electric; he served, also, as counsel for Thomas Edison. Samuel Insull once described him as a "pompous little man of military bearing, who strutted about his office at 65 Fifth Avenue, 'holding forth like a great mogul'" (see *Edison* by Matthew Josephson, 1959, p. 294). The Black Hills venture, brief as it was, marked a turning point in Bierce's life; never again did he try to escape from journalism. The Black Hills venture was thoroughly typical— it could serve as a symbol—of the corruption and general disorder and economic turbulence of the period. To Bierce's wartime disillusionment was now added a deep and abiding disgust with the society that had emerged after 1865.

No one, I think, need now fear that Bierce will be neglected, much less forgotten. At long last, the main facts of his fascinating life have been established; the man stands forth from the myth. Then, too, two world wars have stimulated interest in his work; he does not seem quite as "sardonic" and "bitter" as he once did. His general revulsion from the society that emerged after the Civil War will not strike most readers today as extreme. The paperback revolution has brought his work to the attention of a wide audience. In addition, modern critics have identified qualities in his stories that earlier critics had ignored. In the introducton that I wrote for *Bierce and the Poe Hoax* (Book Club of California, 1934), I tried to point up some of the differences between Bierce's stories and those of Edgar Allan Poe. With few exceptions, I wrote, Bierce's stories are "not concerned with terror so much as they are with a sort of mocking and ironic fright." And I quoted what Bierce himself had said: "When terror and absurdity make alliance, the effect is frightening." Miss Grenander, building on these comments, has given a new—and most revealing—reading to Bierce's "civilian" stories (see "Bierce's Turn of the Screw: Tales of Ironical Terror," *The Western Humanities Review,* Summer, 1957).

Of the war stories, the most perceptive recent criticism is that offered by David R. Weimer (see "Ambrose Bierce and the Art of War" in *Essays in Literary History,* Rutgers University Press, 1960).

Mr. Weimer notes Bierce's "marked interest in light, shadow, and color and in exact, sparing description"; he notes, too, that all the elements seem to work directly toward "the creation of a single, vivid, static scene." Particularly perceptive is Mr. Weimer's reference to the "pictorial focus" of the stories. I had pointed out that Bierce had the eye of an artist and some of the skills. How, for example, did this young Indiana farm boy, without special training, become the efficient map-maker and topographer on the staff of General Hazen? Joseph Nolan, who went to school with Bierce, told Maurice Frink that Bierce was a natural artist whose pencil sketches had been a source of delight to other youngsters (Elkhart, Indiana, *Truth,* October, 1922). The sketches, maps and drawings that Bierce made during the Civil War, and on the expedition with General Hazen, are expertly done. Mr. Fatout has given us a fine special study of Bierce's work as a war topographer (*American Literature,* November, 1954), which sheds new light on the "pictorial" element so strikingly apparent in the stories. It should be noted, also, that Leigh Bierce was a talented artist (see p. 267).

As a final item in the later research, I should like to mention Lawrence Berkove's dissertation "Ambrose Bierce's Concern with Mind and Man," a brilliant exposition of Bierce's thought, of his ideas, of his way of looking at life. When this dissertation is published—or the book based on it, which Mr. Berkove is now doing— it should help to convince the unconverted that there is depth and consistency to Bierce's thought and that Edmund Wilson's application of Voltaire's phrase "a chaos of clear ideas" does Bierce less than justice.

Only one thing, then, is needed to insure Bierce's place in American and world literature: a one- or two-volume edition of the best of his writing, rigorously selected, with all marginal items eliminated. Wilson Follett was quite correct when he said of Bierce that in the period 1870–1900 "there was but one possible way" for a serious writer to make his works count for a fraction of their worth. "That was by an unbroken association of decades with an established publishing house which could understand him, have faith in his long-range importance, and work and plan with him year in and year out for an indefinitely delayed reward." (*The Atlantic Monthly,* July, 1937.) Bierce never found such a publisher, and his long residence in the West only complicated the problem. His books were published, as Follett notes, at "capricious intervals," in small editions often sponsored by friends, and, as I have indicated, the *Collected Works* merely added to the confusion by including far too much of his less distinguished work. The best of Bierce—of the stories, the battle pieces, the satire, the memoirs, the epigrams, the letters, the journalism—is of timeless value, and this "best" would show to much better advantage if it could be removed from the rest of his work. Wilson Follett would have been the person to edit Bierce. But now perhaps the task should wait until publication of the edition of Bierce's letters on which Miss Grenander is now engaged. Follett thought that a "Selected Bierce" would probably contain "more than the English-speaking part of the New World has yet had from any other one pen." I am not prepared to say that, but I will say that there is far more of the "best" Bierce than even Bierce fans realize, and that this "best" is timeless.

CAREY MC WILLIAMS

New York, April 4, 1967.

CONTENTS

AMBROSE
BIERCE

INTRODUCTION

THE BIERCE MYTH

IT WAS the unique distinction of Ambrose Bierce to be referred to as dead when he was living, and to be mentioned as living when he was indubitably dead. His reputation is based on a series of elaborately interwoven paradoxes. Even to attempt a biographical study of his life requires a preliminary analysis of this critical confusion. His name is already a legend and his reputation is almost mythical so far has it been divorced from the central values of his work. Time has crystallized the mistaken opinions of his contemporaries into a generally accepted theory of his work. Such is the fate that befalls the "obscure" type in letters. Myth becomes imposed on myth, legend is interlaced with legend, so that in the course of time it becomes necessary to remove one layer of misunderstanding after another until at least the outline of the original may be traced over the pattern of errors that time has somewhat erased. Perhaps the "myth" is already a tradition and that a dissociation of ideas is impossible. It is a doubt which has often troubled me.

Some men are predestined to be the subject of misunderstanding, as though some quality about their lives invited absurd comment and irrelevant observation. Such a man was Ambrose Bierce. It is seriously to be doubted if there exists another figure in American literature about whom as much irregular and unreliable critical comment has been written. He has been characterized as great, bitter, idealistic, cynical, morose, frustrated, cheerful, bad, sadistic, obscure, perverted, famous, brutal, kind, a fiend, a God, a misanthrope, a poet, a realist who wrote romances, a fine satirist and something of a charlatan. Surely such misunderstanding is not an inevitable condition of fame. There exists no such wildness about the literature on Emerson, on Melville, or on Twain. If his admirers had realized that Bierce was a complex figure and that only by the use of paradox could they make any progress in definition, much confusion might have been avoided. Had his critics been able to move in both directions, first into his work and then back to the facts of his life, they might have succeeded in arriving at a more intelligent appreciation of his work.

To suggest the quality of this bulky literature devoted to a consideration of Bierce's writings, a few illustrations will suffice. J. S. Cowley-Brown wrote that "Bierce is as interesting as a kangaroo"; while Mr. Laurence Stallings has announced that "he has the kick of a zebra mule." Franklin H. Lane spoke of him as "a hideous monster, so like the mixture of dragon, lizard, bat, and snake as to be unnameable," but to William Marion Reedy he was "a man of silent generosities, a fellow of tenderness." One journalist in San Francisco always referred to him as "that rascal of the sorrel hair," but to Mrs. Ruth Guthrie Harding, who perhaps may be pardoned a sentimental tear or two, "Mr. Boythorn-Bierce" was always "a childlike person." Bierce has been listed by such critics as Alfred C. Ward and Harold Williams exclusively as a writer of the short story; others have considered him solely as a satirist. He has been named as a propagandist against war and as a friend of war; as an aristocrat with principles that were fundamentally democratic; as a satirist of great powers who was at the same time a hired libelist. To some his political views are impossibly trite while others think he was a philosopher of great acumen.

It is amazing to find even such an able journalist as George West writing in *The American Mercury*, July, 1926, that "Bierce, a veteran of the Civil War, came to California with his bent fixed and his talent developed. . . . With his negative answers he was a death-man, a denier of life, of a genuine but slight talent, and hence the last writer in the world to inspire others." Bierce had not written a line for print when he came to California; he actually learned to write in San Francisco, and as to inspiring others, he was the direct inspiration for many of the men Mr. West proceeds to list in his catalogue of California literati. How account for such writing? Bierce seems to have always inspired such inaccuracy, even from writers with such fine opportunities for observation as Mr. West.

In an effort to prove that the motivation for his short stories was subconscious, Dr. Isaac Goldberg has spoken of Bierce as "sadistic-masochistic!" Dr. Louis J. Bragman finds indications of the abnormal in all his work and sums him up as "a purveyor of morbidities." Mr. Walter Neale, with malicious ingenuity, discusses at length *the possibility* that Bierce may have been a sexual pervert! Of course, with elaborate precaution against criticism, Mr. Neale comes to the conclusion, as well he might, that there was no basis whatever for such a thought. But the list of absurdities does not cease here. Perversion and sadism are rather fashionable nowadays and Mr. Neale was probably clever to spice his book with such hypothetical misdemeanors. The suggestion has even been made that Bierce was a lunatic! Whispers to this effect circulate in the west to-day, because Bierce was known to visit a sanitarium at Livermore, California, and it has actually been rumored that he never went into Mexico at all but died in an asylum at Napa. What, one may well inquire, inspired all this nonsense, this pyramiding of misinformation, this repetition of error, this maze of conjecture and hearsay?

In attempting an explanation one must be patient and begin as far back as 1868 and gradually work forward through the veils of comment to 1913, and then a coroner's inquest must be conducted on the even more ludicrous situation since that date. In 1868 a young writer who conducted a page called "The Town Crier" on *The San Francisco News Letter and California Advertiser* began to acquire considerable fame in the west. He was, of course, quite a character in San Francisco. But in the east the New York journals began to quote his comments and to speculate as to his identity. Finally it became known that the Town Crier was a young fellow whose name was A. G. Bierce. At this early date there was little misunderstanding. Bierce was just a witty young journalist who wrote original copy. Some shrewd newspaper men began to note that his journalism was occasionally great satire, possessing peculiarly personal qualities and animated by great force and energy. But just when his reputation was beginning to be established on an understandable basis, the Town Crier left San Francisco and went to London.

It is of the first importance in dealing with the Myth to keep in mind the interruption in Bierce's career occasioned by this early change of residence. While Bierce was in England he was forgotten in this country and only a few journalists, such as James Watkins and Mr. Laffan, kept in touch with his work and knew that the Passing Showman of *Figaro* was the former Town Crier of the *News-Letter*.

But during these years, Bierce was making a reputation for himself in England. He published three books during his residence in London and became a well-known literary figure. His fame was considerable and he was remembered by many writers and critics who were able, in 1892, to associate Ambrose Bierce, the author of "Tales of Soldiers and Civilians," with the immensely interesting and provocative A. G. Bierce who was a friend of James Mortimer, Tom Hood, and Henry Sampson. Robert Barr, of *The Idler,* made this association very quickly and his comments stirred the recollections of his countrymen. But it was a long span of years from 1872 to 1892, so that England had to rediscover Bierce, and in the process many errors of perception occurred. This slight blur began to color the otherwise shrewd comment of the English critics. During Bierce's entire career, he was constantly being the subject of little flurries of critical comment in the English press, at intervals of from ten to fifteen years. Mr. Gladstone picked up a copy of "Cobwebs from an Empty Skull" one day and announced in an interview that he remembered the sensation the book had made on its first appearance and the pleasure its reading had given him. Such incidents, occurring at irregular intervals through the years, kept Bierce's reputation alive but imperfectly understood. Then, too, he wrote under the name of "Dod Grile" in England and this came to cause no little confusion and error. Every time he published a book in this country, the press of England would dig back into old files and there would be another series of reminiscent paragraphs and letters to the editor about this fellow who had once lived in London. The American press would occasionally notice these comments in the English papers and would only become more confused as to who Bierce really was and what he had written. The situation was an international complication and was the beginning of a Myth.

On his return to America, Bierce was made the subject of
elaborate discoveries and had to reëstablish his reputation on the
Pacific Coast. But the reputation which he soon acquired on
The Argonaut was checked before it could attain national significance by his mining expedition into the Black Hills. After
this venture, he was lost until his emergence as author of
"Prattle" in the San Francisco *Examiner*. With the first issues
of the *Examiner* containing "Prattle" he began to be recognized
as one of the most unique figures in American journalism. The
New York *Sun* would frequently quote his comments and the
Australian newspapers, notably the Sydney *Bulletin,* followed
his work with great interest. But as yet he had published no
books in America; his reputation was merely that of a brilliant
journalist.

With the publication of "Tales of Soldiers and Civilians"
in 1891 a new situation arose. Contrary to many dearly cherished illusions the book was not "neglected," but was the subject
of a great deal of critical comment which was, with scarcely a
single exception, enthusiastic. The author of any book in a new
genre is immediately the subject of speculation, inquiry and comment. Novelty always provokes uneven critical comment and
Bierce's book was shockingly different. It surprised critics; they
were taken aback by its excellence. But they were uncertain
what to write about it or its author. At this time, as is generally
the case with a new author of originality, a few left wing
critics, with a great preliminary blaring of trumpets, began to
proclaim the new God. Percival Pollard and Walter Blackburn
Harte, who were both familiar with Bierce's work in *The Examiner* and thus had an advantage over other eastern critics,
sounded their praise at least three octaves too high. Rather, I
should say, they were uncritical and struck the wrong note of
praise. They could not, as a matter of fact, have praised the
book too highly, *at that time,* for its appearance in 1891 was as
phenomenal as the appearance in *Graham's Magazine,* April,
1841, of "The Murders in the Rue Morgue." The critical situation that existed in 1891 remained essentially the same throughout Bierce's lifetime, that is, excessive praise on the left and a
long swing of the pendulum through intervening nuances of
opinion over to the sharp disapproval at the right.

This tangential situation was one that naturally fostered

misunderstanding. Bierce's personality was warped to fit the critical opinion of his various commentators. Those who liked his work manufactured a God; those who disapproved had no difficulty in imagining a Devil. What they wanted to believe they created, and when meeting Bierce in the flesh they found at least sufficient justification for their views to warrant their confirmation. Reading this body of literature, which for scientific purposes should be gathered into a Library of Error, one cannot help being vastly amused with the entire affair. There are elements of the farcical in the Bierce Myth; the thing takes on the aspects of high comedy. But, amusing as the situation most assuredly is, there is grave danger that Bierce's reputation may be sacrificed by it. Readers become confused; they sense a hoax and then hastily conclude that Bierce was a second-rate individual and a hack journalist.

Various minor elements have colored the legend. The "collectors" adopted Bierce at an early date, bidding high prices for his books and quarreling in angry voices, the strident notes of which reached general circulation, over debated points of authorship. The literary magazine on the fringe of the intellectual world always makes a fetish of figures which its editors think are "obscure" and which, by the very fact of their mention in such journals, could not be other than notorious. Bierce has always been a favorite of local reviews and "quarterlies." The articles published in these esoteric journals have been uniformly misleading and have spread confusion about his work like a fatal contagion. There has been much shrewd comment about Bierce's work, as I will have occasion to show, but it usually has come from unexpected sources and has been dismissed as incredible by the few who noticed it.

In the course of a Fourth of July oration in 1898, a western statesman invoked "the shades of Ambrose Bierce" to support some point in his argument. Referring to this inaccuracy the ghost wrote in his column of "Prattle" that "I am still on this side of the Styx. Moreover, I do not expect, even when reposing on beds of amaranth and moly, to have more than one shade." Arthur Conan Doyle made a similar contribution to the legend in "Through the Open Door" (1908), when he ended an interesting paragraph with the phrase that Ambrose Bierce *"was a great artist in his day."* The comment of such men as Conan

Doyle and Arnold Bennett, while sound enough as criticism, could not be other than inaccurate as to Bierce's life. These men belonged to another generation and did not remember Dod Grile of *Fun.*

And it must be borne constantly in mind that there was not a sound magazine article in print about Bierce's life until George Sterling's, "The Shadow Maker," appeared in *The American Mercury,* in September of 1925. Mr. Vincent Starrett's little book published in 1920, while interesting and valuable, did not contain much biographical information. Practically the entire body of criticism devoted to Bierce was written before the facts of his life and experience were known. When biographical information did not appear it was partial and fragmentary, and, while clearing up some points, left others in darker confusion than before the momentary illumination. Many people, for example, accepted all that George Sterling wrote about Bierce as true, when, as a matter of fact, Sterling's article left much to be desired, even as a magazine summary. The new interest in Bierce, the interest of the present generation, rests on two pillars of comment: Mr. Mencken's in this country and Arnold Bennet's, written under the nom de plume of Jacob Tonson for *The New Age,* in England. This modern interest is sound and genuine and any book about Ambrose Bierce should be primarily addressed to the audience it represents.

There are many other factors that require analysis. The geographical isolation of Bierce (and to be an author in San Francisco in the seventies virtually amounted to exile), is important. Bierce was never present where he was being discussed. Critics seldom saw him and it is not surprising to find newspaper articles and stories that question his very identity and which suggest that Ambrose Bierce was a Myth and his reputation a hoax. When his name was a byword in San Francisco, he was living at San Rafael, or St. Helena, or Auburn, so that he was read but not seen. Once his reputation as a satirist on the *Examiner* began to assume national proportions, Mr. Hearst very cleverly took advantage of the situation by sending him East. There his comment was read by people who were already familiar with his work as it had been reprinted in the eastern papers for some time, but they continued to associate him with San Francisco, even when he was living in their midst. When he was available for inspection, so to speak, at Washington, the sound modern interest in his work had not been born, and, as a result, he was merely a curiosity for such men as Mr. Mencken and Mr. Horton who were delighted with his wit and amused by his cynicism.

Just as Bierce's literary career was interrupted because of his untimely changes of residence, so were his books published. They never could be obtained when they were in demand. The three English volumes soon became collectors' items, and, while they were frequently mentioned by Bierce's admirers, they were never available, so that one could whisper that they were prodigious masterpieces without fear of refutation. His two volumes of verse and his most important collection of stories were published in the West in editions that were, more or less, limited and that were virtually destroyed by the great fire. These volumes were always difficult to obtain and when small eastern houses attempted to re-issue them, they failed and nothing came of their efforts. "The Monk and the Hangman's Daughter" was hailed as a masterpiece by scores of critics whose familiarity with it must have been vicarious. This condition resulted in uncertainty and doubt. It was not until Mr. Neale brought out the handsome "de luxe" edition that Bierce's writings became definitely available in the libraries. Even then the very appearance of such an edition was a source of mystery. There was absolutely no demand for a collected edition at the time it was published; it was out of all relation to Bierce's fame or importance and remained a publishing curiosity for years. Who was this magnificently printed author? He must be some one, a person of transcendent importance. Professor Fred Lewis Pattee, whose frankness must have characterized the silent doubt of many, wrote to Mr. Neale asking: "Is Bierce really a great writer?"

So far only those elements which might be termed "impersonal" have been considered. But an equally important element in the creation of the Myth was the purely personal. Bierce was a master of gestures and his mockery was compound of echoes and shadows. He was regarded as something of a *poseur;* his downright candor was mistaken in some quarters for unnecessary arrogance. Just as Baudelaire did little to correct the legends current about his life, so would Bierce, with

perverse satisfaction, permit the shadows to deepen. He became the phantom figure in some epic yarns: he slept in ceme-
teries; exhumed cadavers; spent long hours in the morgues
studying the features of the disintegrating; hated dogs; loved
reptiles; fought duels; and struck down his friends with great
cruelty. He was so vital a personality, such an extraordinary
man (and this is one point on which all forces converge in
agreement), that he provoked an inordinate amount of comment
and interest. Some people very shrewdly sensed that his writings
inadequately expressed his personality, not in the sense that he
was "frustrated by his environment," but that he could find no
subject adequate for his purposes. This disparity was of itself
a source of mystification. The so-called "gloomy" stories were
not subconsciously motivated, as I will have occasion to prove,
and were written deliberately with an eye on a carefully established formula and with a definite end in view.

Then, too, from 1881 until his disappearance into Mexico
he was always "the master" of a group of young writers. After
the work of these pupils began to appear in print, thanks to
Bierce's interest and tutelage, they never lost an opportunity to
sing their Master's praise in strophes that were as far off-key as
the early criticism had been. Just as Percival Pollard and Walter
Blackburn Harte had overpraised the greatness of Bierce's art, so
these pupils excessively extolled his personality. This condition
must have puzzled many readers for it was difficult to understand
at the time. There was no comparison too grandiose for these pupils; Bierce was verily their God. George Sterling's last letters to
Bierce, written after an intimate acquaintance of twenty years,
were still addressed to "Mr. Bierce" or "Dear Master" and
written in the formal style of one accepting an invitation to appear before omnipotence itself. When Gertrude Atherton announced, at a time when she had a considerable reputation in
England and France, that Bierce had "the best brutal imagination of any man in the English-speaking race" (whatever "best"
and "brutal" may mean), it naturally provoked considerable
commment and ultimate dissension.

Then, to seal the "mystery" of his life, Bierce made that
dramatic exit into Mexico. Psychologically, nothing he ever did
was more fortunate so far as his fame was concerned. Here
was a man who not only wrote of mysterious disappearances

but was one. Here was a cynic who yawned with disdain and had become so disgusted with his countrymen that he ventured south to escape boredom. A great silence engulfed his name and his fate was the subject of endless speculation. Every time a new story entitled "What Became of Ambrose Bierce?" would appear in print, it would release the pent-up imaginations of innumerable critics who would flounder anew in a problem that was not a problem and attempt to solve doubts that were certainties. The bibliography of the wild yarns attendant on his disappearance is reserved for a later section. But it is apparent, without an examination of them at this time, that they only spread confusion upon confusion so far as arriving at an sensible understanding of Bierce's personality was concerned. His work was broken up into contradictory fragments and his personality became a Faust or Hamlet for any one to play improvisations upon. As George Sterling melodramatically remarked : Bierce's enemies went into Mexico to feast on his bones.

In the wake of the War came the wave of disillusion that brought Bierce's work into exact focus with public opinion, for he anticipated modern thought at many points. A later chapter has been added with the publication of volumes by C. Hartley Grattan, Dr. Danzinger, and Walter Neale, along with Vincent Starrett's bibliography which, had it appeared years earlier, might have done much to avoid misunderstanding. These volumes are adequate testimony of the extent of Bierce's latter-day fame and reputation, and, whether they succeed in throwing much light on his life or not, they at least emphasize an important consideration, although tacitly and by indirection, that he was much more interesting as a personality than he was important as a writer. To this one might add, as a corollary, that his personality was itself of the first importance; that the very appearance of such a man in America during his lifetime was an anachronism and a promise. His was a personality strangely prophetic of what one might expect from the America of another generation, in its rebellion under the leadership of Mr. Mencken. And, with the course of time, it can be hopefully forecast that the Myth surrounding his career will be dissolved, that his writings will be appreciated for their inherent values, and that the hard, bright, shining core of his illumination will become a part of our tradition.

CHAPTER I

MOSTLY GENEALOGICAL

ONE would imagine that the easiest task in connection with writing a biography about even so "mysterious" a character as Ambrose Bierce would be to state the pronunciation and spelling of his name with unqualified accuracy. And such is the case, if one is not too curious, but, historically, the name is shrouded in uncertainties. The first Bierce to arrive in this country was not a "Bierce" but was Austin Bearse, who sailed in the "Good Shippe *Confidence*" in 1638 from Southampton and landed at Barnstable (Cape Cod), Massachusetts.*

According to ancient records, Austin Bearse was a small land owner. His farm consisted of twelve acres of very rocky land, which was bounded "easterly by John Crocker's land, northerly by the meadow, easterly by Isaac Robinson's land, and southerly into ye woods." A road from his home to Hyannis is still known as "Bearse's Way." He was quite religious, having joined "Mr. Lothrop's" church in 1643. His name stands at the head of the list of those converted after the church moved to Barnstable. He was very exact in the performance of religious duties, and insisted that children be baptized on the day of their birth, if Sunday, or on the next Sabbath. His son Joseph was born on a Sunday, and Austin carried him two miles to the church through a snowstorm so that he might receive a scriptural baptism. There is no record, unfortunately,

* For much of the information in this chapter, I am indebted to Miss J. M. Ames of Cleveland, Ohio, and Mrs. Fanny L. S. Meadows of Farmington, Utah.

whether Joseph survived his father's act of faith, but if he died of exposure it was a holy and orthodox death.

So far as the records may be checked and verified, all members of the family in this country who spell their names Bearse, Bearce, Barss or Bierce, are descendants of Austin Bearse. But no two of these factions can agree on the correct spelling or pronunciation of what is admittedly a common family name. This condition of uncertainty is not, of course, an unusual occurrence with family names in America, where many of the early settlers were so illiterate that they could only remember the sound of their names, and had no knowledge of spelling. Some branches of the Bierce family pronounce the name as though it were spelled "Beerce"; another group spell the name "Bearse" and pronounce it as though it were spelled "Burse"; and there is even some authority for the theory that it is a derivative of "Pierce." Originally the name was pronounced as if spelled "Barse" and many of the descendants still pronounce it in the ancient manner, even those who spell it "Bearss." One branch of the family that lived at New Fairfield and New Milford, Connecticut, changed the spelling to "Barse," while a group that emigrated to Canada changed the spelling to "Barss," and still another branch residing at Port Clinton, Ohio, spell it "Bearss" but pronounce it as if spelled "Barse." Such, then, is the history of the name.

As to the history of the family and its origin, a state of similar uncertainty prevails. Miss J. M. Ames, one of the family's genealogists, believes there is some basis for the theory that the Bierces originally came from Holland. But the better hypothesis, since it bears substantiation by a prominent member of the family who had a personal flair for historical vanities, would indicate that the family was of ancient Norman-French lineage. Such was the conviction of General Lucius Verus Bierce, and, from a sketch of his life by L. Moore, published at Akron, Ohio, in 1874, this information may be gleaned: "The family were originally Norman French, but long ago emigrated to, and settled in, England. The earliest historical account of the family and name that is accessible, is found in an old family Bible, printed in 1599, and still in the possession of General Bierce, in which is recorded on a fly-leaf the following incident:

" 'Marquis,' said Louis XIV to Marquis de Bierce, 'you make puns upon all subjects, make one on me.'

" 'Sire,' replied the courteous Marquis, 'you are *no subject' !* "

Wit and repartee would thus seem to be ancestral traits.

Coupled with this Norman-French verve and wit and mental agility, there was a strong strain of the proudest Highland blood in the later Bierces. The wife of William Bierce was Abigail Bell, and she was the grandmother of Ambrose. Abigail was the daughter of Ketchal and Sarah (Whitney) Bell of Cornwall, Connecticut. The Bells were an old, proud, arrogant Scottish family. They were famous in Scotland and in Britain during several generations for their eminence as physicians and surgeons, numbering among their better known members, Sir Charles Bell, the distiguished anatomist, who enjoyed considerable fame and reputation in his day. Whatever ability Bierce inherited, it is quite apparent that it came to him from his father's side of the family, for very little is known of Laura Sherwood, his mother. This inference is fortified by the fact that in Bierce both dominant ancestoral traits, wit and arrogance, came to a fine flower.

One of Austin Bearse's sons, whose name was James, moved from Pembroke, Massachusetts, to Connecticut, in 1739, and settled on the road east of Burnham Place, afterwards known as Cornwall Bridge.* James' name appears in the old records and documents of the period as "Bierce" and it is probable that he was the first of the family to adopt this spelling. It seems to have been definitely adopted by all his descendants. Cornwall, in Litchfield County, was the center of this branch of the family for many years and some members of the family still reside there. The old Revolutionary War records contain numerous references to Bierces in the Connecticut regiments, and James (the younger), William, Ezekiel, Nathan and Stephen were prominently figured in the local annals of Connecticut's participation in the War of Independence.

The lineage of Ambrose Bierce may be traced directly back to Austin Bearse, the succession running: Austin, James, Shubael, Hezekiah, William, Marcus Aurelius. William Bierce was the son of Hezekiah Bierce and Deborah Sturtevant. He

* "Genealogical and Family History of Connecticut."

was born at Halifax, Massachusetts, March 26, 1753, and married Abigail Bell. The records show that he belonged to Col. Herman Swift's regiment of Connecticut troups during the Revolutionary War, and Henry Newell Bierce has in his possession a powder horn on which is carved the following inscription: "William Bierce's horn, made at Ticonderoga, April 27, 1775." The soldierly tradition in the family was unbroken for three generations and it is interesting to note that William was an orderly sergeant at Ticonderoga, and fought in the battles of Monmouth, White Plains, and Fort George. During the dreary winter spent at Valley Forge, every officer in his company higher than himself was either killed or died of starvation or disease, leaving him in command. It is said that during his years in the service, William clothed himself and laid by all his pay, including the amount paid him for clothing, so that he might have a competence to start life anew when the war was over. But, with the inevitable disillusion that came *après le guerre,* he found that he had nothing but a considerable pile of worthless Continental bills. He finally gave these bills to his children for playthings and forgot the frugality of seven years of soldiering. This circumstance probably tinged the minds of both William and his son, Lucius Verus, on the subject of paper money. It was always a red flag to General Lucius Bierce, and he never lost an opportunity to flay its advocates. He once remarked, with characteristic Biercian terseness, "If we must have monied incorporations to control the currency, and regulate the exchanges of the country, let us have a United States Bank. For my part, I had rather be swallowed by a whale than nibbled to death by minnows." * However, it should be noted that William did receive some compensation for his services, for along with his honorable discharge he was given a hundred acres of land in Muskingum, Ohio, which he later sold for two dollars an acre.

William Bierce had quite a large family. His children were: Lucretia, Hanna Bell, Columbus, William Whiting, Lucinda, and the two favorites, Lucius Verus and Marcus Aurelius. These two sons were born in Cornwall, Marcus Aurelius on August 16, 1799, and Lucius Verus on August 4, 1801. They

* "Historical Reminiscences of Summit County," by General L. V. Bierce. H. T. and H. G. Canfield, Akron, 1854.

were the bright particular stars of the family and were, moreover, inseparable companions. Where one went, the other followed. They were of nearly the same age and both seemed to
have possessed a flair for the grand manner, particularly Lucius
Verus, who was destined to be referred to as "illustrious" from
early manhood. His life was a succession of orations, presentation speeches, and memorial odes. Marcus Aurelius was of a
more somber disposition and lacked the verve of his younger
brother. Both received a rather good education, for those times,
at Litchfield, but they were not destined to follow in the same
lines of quiet activity that characterized the lives of their
brothers and sisters, and in this they foreshadowed the parallel
situation of Ambrose and Albert.

Even before finishing his rudimentary schooling, Lucius
Versus had his eyes trained on the broad horizon of the West.
This was but natural. His father owned land out in Ohio.
Moreover, Connecticut at that time was making rather pretentious claims to all the lands, parallel with its boundaries, to
the west. This far outpost of Litchfield was called the Western
Reserve and Connecticut's more adventuresome sons were looking to it as their future home. When Lucius Verus was only
fifteen years of age, he journeyed west to Nelson, Portage
County, Ohio. Marcus Aurelius remained at Cornwall until
he could receive news of his brother's fortune, particularly as
he had married Laura Sherwood. (Feb. 26, 1822.) But it was
not long until he, too, was en route for the Western Reserve.*

Lucius, however, lost no time in going west and in becoming a famous character. He decided to go to Ohio University,
and arrived at Athens ill and possessed of only one-fifth of a
quarter of a dollar (this was during the "cut" money days).
He prepared for the University by studying under the Rev.
Jacob Lindley, President of Ohio University for many years,
and he soon matriculated, and by 1822 had received his degree.
He then decided to seek his fortune in the South, and persuaded
the Hon. Amos Crippen, a prominent citizen of Athens, to
loan him the money for his journey. He went south to York-
ville, South Carolina, and then to Lancaster, where he studied
law in the offices of Robert J. Renill, and later, in Alabama,
with Dr. Sterne Houghton, being admitted to practice in 1823.

* "Ohio and the Western Reserve," by Alfred Mathews (1902).

He soon returned to Ohio and entered the practice of the law at
Ravenna, in Portage County. He had only been admitted to the
bar a year when he was elected district attorney, an office which
he held for eleven years, resigning at the end of that period to
move to Akron. There he quickly became the town's "leading
citizen" and remained such until his death. His activities were
so numerous and varied that it is difficult to summarize them,
but a few of his exploits will be mentioned because of the
important influence he was to exercise on his nephew, Ambrose
Bierce.

In 1837 the "Patriot War," so-called, was organized by a
firebrand whose name was William McKenzie. It was a movement intended to free the Canadians from the despotic government headed by Sir John Colburn. McKenzie soon counted
among his most ardent supporters, Lucius Verus Bierce of
Akron. With Colonel Von Schultz, a Polish officer, who was a
refugee in America and along with some three hundred veterans who had been ordered from their country for participation
in a revolution, Bierce organized the "Grand Eagles," a secret
society designed to give McKenzie military support in his movement.

While the work of organization was being perfected, the
British struck Col. Von Schultz and his force at Detroit. The little band of liberators was annihilated and Von
Schultz met death on the scaffold. Bierce, who was now "General," hastened to the assembled refugees at Swan Creek and
told the remnant of the army that the fate of Canadian liberty
depended on them. Would they disband, after this reversal by
the tyrant, or would they fight on to the bitter end? One can
imagine that the oration was accompanied with appropriate gestures. The appeal, however, was not an unqualified success, for
all but 180 of the liberators fled to their homes. With the
remaining "army," General Bierce left Detroit for Windsor,
captured the town, and burned the barracks. Just as the revolution was getting into full swing, Col. John Prince arrived with
a company of British regulars and decimated the "Grand
Eagles" with a few rounds of musket fire. Most of the remaining rebels were killed, many of them being stood against a wall
at Windsor and shot down, and only about thirty escaped.
Among this group was "General" Bierce. His troubles were

not yet at an end, for on returning to Ohio he was called before the United States Court at Columbus to answer for a violation of the Neutrality Law of 1818. But Judge McLean was virtually forced to direct the grand jury not to bring in a free bill, so great was the popular sentiment in favor of General Bierce. The authorities, however, summoned him again before the court, but between that date and the day of the hearing an old friend of Bierce's was appointed by Van Buren as district attorney, and through his agency the matter was dismissed. The General was, of course, a great popular hero in Ohio.* He later organized the "Bierce Cadets" and was, for several years, Grand Master of the Masonic Lodge in Ohio.†

When the Mexican War broke out, the General volunteered for service, but his company disbanded soon after its organization, as the government did not desire further troops after the first call. He then devoted himself to public works, being on the board of education and mayor of Akron. Among his literary "masterpieces" was the composition of an ode which he read on the occasion when he presented a sword, which he had captured from a Britisher during the Patriot War, to Buchtel College. The grandiloquent lines of this ode were only slightly more rhetorical than his nephew's "Invocation." To have heard the General declaim these lines must have been a memorable experience:

THE BATTLE OF WINDSOR

The sun had set on Erie's wave,
The snow-clad hills on which the brave
Reposed, were silent as the grave,
    Or Soldiers' Sepulchre.

No martial sound, nor busy hum,
No clarion clang, nor rattling drum,
Gave signal that the time had come
    For daring feats of chivalry.

* "Fifty Years and Over of Akron and Summit County," by ex-Sheriff Sam Lane, 1892.
† "The Biographical Cyclopedia and Portrait Gallery of Ohio," edited by J. Fletcher Brennan. Cincinnati, 1880.

The soldier took his hasty meal,
Then fixed the deadly burnished steel,
Which soon the tyrant's fate would seal,
    When joined in war's dread revelry.

The Patriot band was soon arrayed,
Their hearts beat high, but none dismayed,
As each one drew his battle blade
    And shouted "Death or victory!"

Then foe to foe, in contest view;
Fierce flashed the fire, the rockets flew
And death was revelling 'mid the few
    Who bared their breast courageously.

The Patriot cry of deadly war
"Remember Prescott!" sounds afar,
And lurid flames and crashing jar,
    Push on the dreadful tragedy.

The warrior foe in contest slain,
The wounded strewed upon the plain,
Make fuel for the burning claim
    Of Barracks burning rapidly.

Now fiercer grew the dreadful fight,
Now fiercer rose the lurid light,
And shouts, and groans, as morning light
    Appeared, were mingled horribly.

Ah, dreadful sight! as morn arose,
The mingled corpse of friends and foes,
Bestrewed the ground amid the snows
    That formed their only sepulchre.

Among the General's other literary efforts were "An Epitome of the History of the Western Reserve from 1862 to the
Formation of the State Constitution in 1802," written expressly
for the Akron *Daily* and *Semi-Weekly Argus;* "Home Reminiscences for the Portage County *Democrat,*" including data about
the towns of "Atwater, Aurora, Deerfield, Freedom, Hiram,
Mantua, Palmyra, Randolph." This material, published in the
newspapers, was designed as a history of the Western Re-

serve, but was never compiled in book form. Among the numerous addresses of the General, the following were printed as pamphlets: "Centennial Historical Address delivered at Ravenna, Portage County"; and an address delivered before the Historical Society of Tallmadge, Ohio, Oct. 6, 1868, published by Fairbank, Benedict & Company in 1872 at Cleveland.

But during this period when Lucius Verus Bierce was entertaining his fellow citizens with fine orations and presentation speeches, Marcus Aurelius was lost in obscurity. It is difficult to trace his movements. It seems that he first came to Meiggs County, and located at a settlement of emigrants known as Horse Cave. There was never a town in Ohio by this name and none exists to-day. "Horse Cave" was simply the name of a settlement of very religious and pious emigrants from Connecticut, and got its name from the fact that the settlement was located on the "Horse Cave" stream, which is a tributary of Shade River, and has three branches—Gilmore Fork, Aumiller Fork and the main branch. The Horse Cave settlement, so-called, was about eight miles from the mouth of the stream, and it was here that Marcus Aurelius settled, and it was here, on the site of many a revivalist meeting, where prayers for the riddance of demon spirits made the nights vociferous, that Ambrose Bierce was born, on June 24, 1842. It was a strange circumstance that out of this settlement of the pious should come the scourge of piety, the arch-enemy of reverence and the author of a devil's dictionary.

Marcus Aurelius, following the herculean example set by his father, had a large family of children. Possessed of the same fondness for alliteration that graced his brother's orations, and, incidentally, not without a modicum of wit, he gave his children names the first letter of which began with "A." They were named: Abigail Bell, Amelia Josephine, Ann Maria, Addison Byron, Aurelius, Almeda Sophia, Albert Sherwood, Augustus, and Ambrose Gwinett. Marcus Aurelius, with his innumerable brood of children, moved from place to place in an effort to find a community so fertile that labor would be superfluous. They went from Meiggs County to a farm near Circleville, Ohio, where they lived for several years, and then finally drifted to Indiana, where they lived, first at Warsaw, and later at Elkhart. Marcus Aurelius died in 1876, and was buried at Elkhart.

It is apparent from even a casual examination of the history of the Western Reserve that its community life, particularly around Tallmadge and Akron, was intensely religious. To read such a volume as "Life in the Western Reserve" with its reiterated emphasis on missionary work and experience in salvation, would alone sufficiently indicate the evangelical tone of the community. To fortify this premise, one need only look at the harsh-featured faces, outlined in the old daguerreotypes, to know the character of the people who chanted their catechisms with the same high seriousness that they broke the soil. Little need be said of the early colonies at Pembroke and Cornwall. They were outposts of puritanism, and it was probably of some of his own ancestors that Ambrose Bierce wrote the lines:

> "My country, 'tis of thee,
> Sweet land of felony,
>   Of thee I sing;
> Land where my fathers fried
> Young witches and applied
> Whips to the Quaker's hide,
>   And made him spring."

The Western Reserve was merely a replica of Connecticut. Its favorite university was modeled after Yale and its theology was that of the Connecticut divines. Not only was General Bierce typical of the military daring of his family, and its ardent espousal of the cause of popular liberty, but he was also representative of its deep religious convictions. The General would often cease his deliverance of patriotic orations long enough to drop a tear or two, and an hour of rhetoric, anent a fallen drunkard. In March of 1848, early in his forensic career, he delivered two orations at Akron over the remains of a drunkard, Peach, who was frozen to death on the banks of a canal. Another victim of demon rum who was also the victim of General Bierce's flowery periods was a wretch by the name of Horace Darby, who died (God rot the thought!) of *delirium tremens* at Akron. Both of these discourses are in the archives of the Western Reserve Historical Society, and they would have furnished Ambrose great reading in the days when he lived within a hundred yards of the Graystone Winery at St. Helena, California, where the enormous vats were always redolent of that which the Crime Commission has now decreed is unfit for man to drink. Poor Bierce! his satire and wit, and taste for good Napa County wines, were forgotten with his disappearance, and the shadowy outline of General Bierce's ghost must bow with approval when modern statesmen echo his words delivered over the bodies of Peach and Darby.

Ambrose Bierce's first experiences were those of a boy on a Middle Western farm. He was on more intimate terms with his brother Albert than with any of his other brothers and sisters. He seems to have shown no feeling for the other members of his family, and to have made no pretense whatever of keeping in communication with them after leaving home. Consequently, very little is known of the other brothers and sisters. "Gus," or "Dime" as he was called, stayed on the farm at Elkhart. One sister died in far-away Africa, where she was a missionary. The cause of her death is unknown, but it is altogether likely that some one may have given her a copy of "Fantastic Fables." Addison, another brother, was a veritable colossus. He could perform great muscular feats, and was the "strong man" in a circus for some time. Albert alone was a congenial companion for Ambrose. They were inseparable during their boyhood and always entertained a genuine affection for each other, although in later years they quarreled.

Both Albert and Ambrose rather resented the religious atmosphere in which they were reared, and two more confirmed agnostics never came out of Indiana. Albert used to tell a story about how he and his brother took an old white horse down to the edge of a camp ground where a revival meeting was in process of generating considerable spiritual steam. They wrapped the old horse in straw, set it afire, and headed the blazing animal in the direction of the seekers for salvation. Perhaps this was the singular "white horse" apparition that Bierce wrote about * and that Flora MacDonald Shearer made the subject of a poem in "The Legend of Aulus."

Bierce was troubled in early life by fantasies, or apparitions, that passed darkly across his dreams. Some of them dated

* "Collected Works" (Vol. X, Page 131).

from childhood. One in particular that haunted his memory had
the following setting: it was night; he was traveling in darkness through a fire-swept region. Pools of water occupied shal-
low depressions, as if the fire had been followed by rain. Dark
clouds passed and revealed stars glittering in the sky. A crimson
light burned in the West, which reminded him in later years of
one of Doré's paintings. As he approached this light, battle-
ments loomed up on the horizon. Within this monstrous building, desertion reigned. Wandering around the building, he
finally came to a large room where the same phantasmagorical
light was gleaming. He sensed eternity in the light and tried to
express the feeling later in the lines:

> "Man is long ages dead in every zone,
>   The angels all are gone to graves unknown;
>   The devils, too, are cold enough at last,
> And God lies dead before the great white throne!"

Upon a bed in the room a figure lay. He gazed down into
its staring eyes and found that the eyes and features were his
own! It was a singular experience and troubled him by its
recurrence.

His early schooling was very rudimentary. With his
brother Albert he attended a rural school where education
was an improvised process. Each pupil was supposed to bring
a book; seldom was a student able to bring more than one book,
and it mattered not at all what type of volume he brought. It
was from the library, gathered in this haphazard manner, that
education was doled out to the pupils. The Bierce brothers
contributed a volume, significant in the light of the younger
Bierce's writings in later years: "The Three Spaniards." Both
brothers, however, remembered that their father was a rather
well read man and that he possessed a good library for a man
of his circumstances.

But the influence of their father was always secondary to
that of General Lucius Verus Bierce, their "illustrious" uncle,
with his military gestures, gorgeous rhetoric, and fiery idealism.
He it was who inspired Ambrose Bierce. In later years Bierce
frankly admitted that he had modeled his career after that of
his uncle. Marcus Aurelius, the father of the boys, was dogged

by a remorseless fate and a prolific spouse. Undoubtedly a man of native intelligence, courage and ability equal to that of his brother Lucius, he was never other than a poor farmer. His career, after leaving Connecticut for Ohio, might be summed up as consisting of meager acres and many children. Ambrose naturally resented this state of affairs; he was proud and haughty, even as a boy, and was rather contemptuous of his parents. This natural bent was fostered by the days which he spent with his uncle, who was interested in him. Later, when Ambrose was about seventeen, his uncle arranged for his attendance at Kentucky Military Institute. It is impossible to verify the duration of Bierce's stay at Kentucky, for the early records of the institute have been destroyed by fire. But that he did attend during the year 1859 is borne out by correspondence in my possession with a former classmate of Bierce's, William E. Guy.

It is scarcely necessary to point out the character of Kentucky Military Institute, particularly during the years immediately following its establishment in 1847. It was one of the highest class institutions of its kind in this country, and it was there that Bierce acquired his fine military bearing, always so impressive, and it was there that he was drilled in military fundamentals. Those who have had occasion to examine the maps that Bierce prepared during the Civil War have invariably been amazed by their fine draftsmanship. The maps were not the work of a novice, and it is apparent that he acquired at least the first principles of topographical engineering while at the academy. The years at the school only emphasized Bierce's sense of superiority; they only alienated him further from his family and early life. When he returned to Indiana in 1860, he was charged with impatience and eager for adventure.

Bierce always resented the limitations of his youth, although he never wasted much time over the incidents of fate. After the war he became a new individual and determined to forget the squalid landscape of his youth. During the summer months, and at odd moments, he had worked on the farm, in a saloon, and in a brickyard. This brickyard story was one that Joaquin Miller had heard and he would occasionally repeat it to people in the West, much to Bierce's annoyance. Some suggestion of the privations and meagerness of Bierce's early life

may be found in the memoirs collected by Mr. Maurice Frink.
("A Sidelight on Ambrose Bierce," *Book Notes*, August-September, 1923.) Bierce never hesitated to speak spitefully of his
boyhood, and never loathed anything quite so much as the horrors of a small, rural community, encased, as such Middle Western communities are, in a cocoon of finely spun, impenetrable
limitations. Such a life was provincial to an almost unbelievable
degree, and it left its imprint on American character of the
period. The war came just in time for Bierce. He was fortunate
in escaping so soon to the war and in leaving immediately for
California at its close, for whatever may have been the limitations of San Francisco in the sixties, it must be conceded that
the life there was infinitely more interesting than the life at
Elkhart, Indiana, *circa,* 1850.

Bierce's own record of his boyhood is perhaps best summed
up in some lines, taken from *The Wasp,* November 3, 1883:

> "With what anguish of mind I remember my childhood,
>   Recalled in the light of a knowledge since gained;
> The malarious farm, the wet, fungus grown wildwood,
>   The chills then contracted that since have remained.
> The scum-covered duck pond, the pigstye close by it,
>   The ditch where the sour-smelling house drainage fell,
> The damp, shaded dwelling, the foul barnyard nigh it,"
>   etc.

The specific character of the images, the sharpness of the
recollection after a period of forty years, sufficiently show the
repellence which he felt for every vestige of that early experience that lingered in his memory.

His attitude towards his youth was characteristic of the
man: he calmly decided to forget about the experience, and not
to mention or refer to it again. It was a closed chapter. He did
not whine or sniffle about early limitations; he ignored them
and went his way. Of course, in later years, he was rather bitter about his entire life. He once remarked to George Sterling
that his parents had been "unwashed savages." This opinion was
undoubtedly a passing irritation. But however unpleasant and
uninteresting the early days may have been, the war was to
destroy all memory of them, and the trip across the plains was
to mitigate their recollection. The dazzling, shimmering splen-

dor of the Shoshone falls and the swift, sharp beauty of the Golden Gate, would obliterate these images of farmyards. It was a fortunate escape. Whatever the horrors of the war may have been, they were nothing when compared with the horrors of an Indiana farm in 1850.

CHAPTER II

WAR DAYS [1861]

"1861—
Armed year! year of the struggle!
—Hurrying, crashing, sad, distracted year."
                                        —WHITMAN

THERE was indeed something sad and distracted about the year 1861. All the wild, hurried rumors that had been gathering force and momentum during the preceding years broke with a resounding roar in the firing on Fort Sumter. Throughout the late fifties, abolitionist propaganda had been actively circulated in the North, and it is not surprising to find that General Lucius V. Bierce, who had so vigorously championed the patriots of Canada, was in the vanguard of the movement to strike the shackles from the slaves. John Brown was a friend of General Bierce and had gone to Akron to receive arms and supplies for his expeditions in Kansas. General Bierce managed to gain possession of the arms and ammunition of a disbanded company of militia of the State of Ohio. He turned these supplies over to Brown, and, as a personal talisman, gave to Brown the pistols and broadswords which he had used in the "Grand Eagles" and on which were engraved the emblem of that organization.* These were the identical weapons used in the Pottawatomie affair. The violence of General Bierce's abolitionist sentiments must have reached the ears of his admiring nephew, for the General left doubt in the minds of none as to where he stood on the issue of slavery. As an attorney he had occasion, not infrequently, to confer with aboli-

* "John Brown," by Oswald Garrison Villard, page 85.

tionists, and he participated, as counsel, in several of the leading
cases involving the status of fugitive slaves. He was known
throughout the Middle-West as a fearless abolitionist.

On the fatal 2nd day of December, 1859, when John Brown
was executed, General Bierce appeared before the Court of
Common Pleas at Akron, Ohio, and moved its adjournment.
Court adjourned forthwith. At twelve o'clock noon all the
stores were closed, bells tolled for an hour, and a flag, draped
in mourning, was suspended from Empire Hall. That evening
an enormous mass meeting was held in the Hall, at which General Bierce delivered an oration on the death of John Brown.
His impassioned, violently emphatic denunciation of the events
which had preceded the Harper's Ferry tragedy left nothing
to be desired. Aside from its rhetorical manner, the address
shows careful preparation and no little skill in the art of mob-
baiting. The General could be as brusque and harsh in his utterance as his nephew came to be cruelly satirical. In exposing the
so-called "valor" of the Virginians, the General said, during the
course of his oration: "The dead of Brown's army lay unburied,
and the citizen soldiery exhibited their feats of valor on the dead
bodies. The head of one seen floating in the Potomac drew a
general fire from a Volunteer Company of the 'first families,'
exhibiting a surplus of heroism conclusively proving that they
feared no foe more than three days after he was dead." In red-
white-and-blue periods that waved and almost fired, the General
swept forward to the climax of his plea. Partisan in his viewpoint, bitterly unjust and dogmatic in certain passages, the old
warrior was undeniably eloquent in his vehement demand that
justice be done. He closed his oration with these lines:

"The tragedy of Brown's is freighted with awful lessons
and consequences. It is like the clock striking the fatal hour
that begins a new era in the conflict with slavery. Men like
Brown may die, but their acts and principles will live forever.
Call it fanaticism, folly, madness, wickedness, but until virtue
becomes fanaticism, divine wisdom folly, obedience to God
madness, and piety wickedness, John Brown, inspired with
these high and holy teachings, will rise up before the world
with his calm, marble features, more terrible in death, and defeat, than in life and victory. It is one of those acts of madness

which history cherishes and poetry loves forever to adorn with
her choicest wreaths of laurel." *

Whether it was with a sense of the impending catastrophe in
mind or not, Ambrose left military school, as nearly as can be
ascertained, during this same year, 1859. His early, pre-war
state of mind was entirely idealistic. What boy would be other
than idealistic with an uncle making fervid speeches to excited mobs who seemed to sense that the clouds of war were
inevitably gathering? The fiery zeal of the old General was reflected in the boy of nineteen, who thought that the war was
utterly a war of ideals and that the might of right was invin-
cible.

Nor was the General entirely a forensic patriot. On April
15, 1861, when President Lincoln rather calmly announced that
the enforcement of the laws of the Union was meeting with
some opposition in the states of South Carolina, Georgia, Alabama, Florida, Mississippi, Louisiana, and Texas, and requested
a volunteer force of seventy-five thousand to secure respect for
the Union of the states and its laws, General Bierce was one
of the first to respond. Although he was over sixty years of
age, he organized and equipped two companies of marines at
his own expense, supervised their drill work himself, and personally delivered them over to the government officials at the
Washington navy-yards. On returning to Ohio, he organized
two companies of artillery and would have led them into action
himself but for his appointment as assistant adjutant-general
of volunteers by President Lincoln.

The interest with which his nephews were following his
work is attested by the fact that Albert Bierce enrolled in the
18th Ohio Field Artillery, one of the companies organized by
General Bierce. Ambrose, however, had not waited for his
uncle to return from Washington, but had enlisted immediately
upon the call for volunteers, the date of his enrollment being
April 19, 1861. He volunteered for the "three months" service
at Elkhart and was assigned to Company C, 9th Indiana Infantry. His regiment trained at Camp Colfax and drilled in
civilian clothes. It was a flushed and feverish period of pre-war

* *The Summit Beacon,* Akron, Ohio, December 7, 1859.

activity. Hostilities had broken out, to be sure, but no one realized the consequences; it was a period of bugles and drums, flashing colors, and the high promise of glory. It was confidently boasted that three months alone would suffice to down the rebel. The young men of the 9th Indiana were still raw recruits, when, in May of 1861, they were ferried across the Ohio River and received their baptism of fire at the engagement of Philippi under Capt. George McClellan.

At the end of the three months' period of service the Confederates were still at large. It was then rather somberly forecast that three years would be required for the task of subduing the rebellion. Accordingly, Bierce reënlisted at LaPorte, Indiana, on August 27th, 1861, in the same company he had joined in April. He was enrolled this time, however, as sergeant of Company C. The date of his actual muster into service was September 5, 1861. He was to remain sergeant until one year later, when he was infinitely promoted to the rank of sergeant-major.

During the three months' service, the 9th Indiana was sent into Virginia. Years later Bierce spent a summer at Aurora, West Virginia, near the Maryland line, overlooking the Cheat River Valley in the Allegheny Mountains. He wrote an account of the experience which was read to the veterans of his regiment who assembled at Logansport, Indiana, October, 1904, in reunion. Of this Cheat River Valley, the scene of their early soldiering, he wrote: * "That region had ever since been to me, as I suppose it has to you, a kind of dreamland. I was reluctant to descend into it for fear of dispelling the illusion, but finally I did so, and passed a few of the most interesting weeks of my life, following the track of the Ninth, visiting its camps, the forts that it helped to build, those that it assisted to take, or try to take, the graves of the fallen and those of the misguided gentlemen whom it sent to their long rest, and who, doubtless, sleep not less soundly than the others." It was an enchanted land for Bierce, and he often revisited the scenes of his first soldiering. It is the background for two of his stories: "A Horseman in the Sky" and "The Story of a Conscience."

* Twenty-fifth Annual Reunion Pamphlet, Ninth Indiana Veteran Volunteer Infantry Association.

If, years later, it was still so fascinating, what must have been its charm at nineteen?

The first engagements of the war were sham battles; *opéra bouffe* affairs. At Philippi the Ninth came charging down a road into the little town, thinking it had the enemy surrounded, when, as a matter of fact, it was charging into his arms. A battery of guns posted on a hill began to shell the town, and, incidentally, to shell its own men. This was an incident that Bierce was later to use in a dramatic story: "One Kind of Officer." About the only effect the shelling had, however, in real life, was to take the leg off a Confederate. Bierce found the gentleman in 1903 still living near Philippi, but, as he added, "still minus the leg; no new one had grown on."

In this region, too, was the town of Belington, then just a village crossroads with a blacksmith shop. Two or three miles out from this town the regiment engaged in a sharp exchange of arms known as the Battle of Laurel Hill. Garnett, a Confederate officer, had erected some breastworks and the Union forces peppered away without any definite plan of attack, and, for the most part, without orders. It was in a forest, and Bierce found a clump of trees where, "just before nightfall one day occurred the one really sharp little fight that we had. It has been represented as a victory for us, but it was not. A few dozen of us, who had been swapping shots with the enemy's skirmishers, grew tired of the resultless battle, and by a common impulse, and I think without orders or officers, ran forward into the woods and attacked the Confederate works. We did well enough, considering the hopeless folly of the movement, but we came out of the woods faster than we went in, a good deal. This was the affair in which Corporal Dyson Boothroyd of Company 'A' fell with a mortal wound. I found the very rock against which he lay. *Our camp is now a race track.*" Bierce never failed to record the ironies that time invariably worked. The field of a heroic battle in ten years became a race track. Where monuments marked the graves of fallen heroes, cowards had fled the ground. Time was an echoing irony.

Bierce's account of the engagement at Belington was written, however, with his customary modesty, for it omitted an act of heroism on his part. It seems that during the fighting, which lasted for several days, Company C charged forward and took an advanced position known as Girard Hill, where they were exposed to a deadly fire. When about fifteen steps from the fortifications of the enemy, Corporal Dyson Boothroyd was shot through the neck and fell, unable to move. Bierce was near, picked Boothroyd up and carried him more than one hundred yards in the open under a galling fire, and succeeded in getting to safety. No officer was in sight to report the rescue, and Bierce always refused to mention the occurrence, but it was recorded in an Indiana history of the War, and was remembered by his old friend, Judge C. F. Moore.*

Upon the reorganization of the regiment for the three years' service, it returned to the same region. The Cheat River Valley was a strategic point and both armies guarded the old Staunton and Parkersburg turnpike, the Confederates at the southern outlet and the Union forces at the north. The young soldiers of the Ninth were so anxious lest they be encircled that they built their camp and fortress straddling the road. Here, during the months of '61, they could gaze across the valley and watch the blue smoke of Confederate camp fires curling lazily towards heaven in a perfect sky.

It was on the return of the Ninth, after the three months' service, that the affairs of Green Brier and Buffalo Mountain occurred. Green Brier was fought while they were encamped at Huttonsville, near the foot of the Cheat Mountains. The Confederates had erected breastworks near Green Brier River and an attack was planned which resulted in the Union forces being repulsed with heavy losses. These early years of the war were not entirely a matter of pleasant marching through forests, for Green Brier took the first heavy toll of the war. Then, too, Buffalo Mountain was a sharp battle. It occurred at the southern end of the valley. "Here," as Bierce wrote, "the regiment had its hardest fight in Western Virginia, and was most gloriously thrashed. When I saw the place (with better opportunities for observation than we had then), I knew why. The works are skillfully constructed and nearly a half mile in length, with placements for several batteries. They are built on a nar-

* For further details see: Charleston, West Virginia, *Gazette*, March 10, 1929, article by Andrew Price, head of West Virginia Historical Society. The matter was once the subject of a paragraph in the New York *Graphic*.

row ridge and are hardly more than one hundred and fifty yards wide at any point. At the rear, where our attack was made, (after the garrison having defeated our coöperating force in front, and got 'good and ready' for us to surprise them), there was but one approach and that by way of a narrow road, through acres of slashed timber, impenetrable to a cat. The trunks of the trees are still there, all pointing away from the fort, all decaying and none of them having even their largest branches. A big head-log across the embrasure commanding the road is so rotten that one can pick it to pieces with the fingers. I fancy the Yankee bullets have all been picked out of it; I found none. The slashed timber, which prevented us from attacking in line, saved our lives,—most of them—when we attacked in column. We took cover in it and pot-shotted the fellows behind the parapet all day, as I recollect it, and then withdrew and began our long retreat in a frame of mind that would have done credit to an imp of Satan. The road that penetrated the slashed timber is easily traced; I recognize the spot where Capt. Madden fell, at the extreme head of the column. Lord! how close to the works it was—I had thought it farther away." Always something of a professional militarist, as well he might be with such a soldierly tradition, Bierce took a keen interest in recounting manœuvers, attacks, strategies and campaigns. The memories of action were always more vividly recalled, in later years, than the impressions of the imagination. Strange as it may seem, his war writing grew more concerned with the details and mechanics of war the older he grew. His best imaginative work about the war was done early in his career.

It was a magical interlude for these young soldiers, this year among the pines and firs. Full of the dreams of valorousness inspired by a not-too-dangerous war (they were to know a very different form of fighting at Shiloh), they talked excitedly of promotion, honor and glory. It was an almost idyllic period. The setting was perfect and life was charged with a pleasant anticipation of danger. Bierce always referred to the Cheat Mountains as the "Delectable Mountains" and they were touched in his imagination with the bright colors of romance. Life was an unsheathed sword, brilliant in the sun with its sharp edge cutting the blue of the sky. How could he have helped being romantic, this nineteen-year-old sergeant? To these

young farmer boys (and the men of his company were quite
young), fresh from the low, flat regions of Indiana and Ohio,
there was magic in the mountains. Many of them had never
seen a mountain before, and now they were perched at the crest
of the Alleghenies watching the "faint graying of the blue
above the main range—the smoke of an enemy's camp." As
Bierce wrote of the experience later (*Collected Works,* Volume
I, Page 228) : "The flatlanders who invaded the Cheat Mountain country had been suckled in another creed, and to them
western Virginia—there was, as yet, no West Virginia—was
an enchanted land. How we reveled in its savage beauties!
With what pure delight we inhaled its fragrances of spruce and
pine! How we stared with something like awe at its clumps of
laurel!—real laurel, as we understood the matter, whose foliage
had been once accounted excellent for the heads of illustrious
Romans and such—mayhap to reduce the swelling. We carved
its roots into finger-rings and pipes. We gathered spruce-gum
and sent it to our sweethearts in letters. We ascended every
hill within our picket lines and called it a 'peak'."

Throughout the winter of '62, they stayed on in this Enchanted Land, hunting and drilling and playing at war. There
were bear and deer in quantity and the snow came in flurries
about the pines. It was not entirely a desultory winter. To make
a little excitement, the regiment would occasionally engage in
"affairs of outposts." They would make miniature "campaigns"
against the enemy, and were invariably driven back across the
snow-carpeted valley. Bierce wrote an account of their return
from one of these periodic forays for his *Collected Works*
(Volume I, Page 232). "All one bright wintry day we marched
down from our eyrie; all one bright wintry night we climbed
the great ridge opposite. *How romantic it was;* the sunset valleys full of visible sleep; the glades suffused and interpenetrated
with moonlight; the long valley of the Green Brier stretching
away to we knew not what silent cities; the river itself unseen
under its 'astral body' of mist!" (The italics are mine.) This
is a typical bit of Biercian reminiscence; flooded with romantic
sentiment for the "glad" days of the war, when the quality of
life was pitched higher and there was a spice of danger and
daring and romance to life. But it was not all romance, even
during the halcyon days of the war. On returning from one of

these expeditions, they found that the faces were gone from
the dead bodies of their fallen comrades—eaten away by the
wild swine of the mountains!

*   *   *

WITH the coming of spring, the regiment was ordered west,
and it said farewell to the Enchanted Land for many a day,
some to see it never again. Sergeant Bierce was not to see it
until nearly fifty years later, when all life had swept past and
he romantically wished that he had fallen with the brave chaps
like Captain Madden and Corporal Boothroyd, who met violent
deaths and escaped the "contracting circle" of boredom and
spiritual disintegration. Gone were the beautiful days in the
mountains and in their stead:

> "By Pittsburg Landing, the turbid Tennessee
> Sucks against black, soaked spiles with soil-colored waters.
> Country of muddy rivers, somber and swollen,
> Country of bronze wild turkeys and catfish-fries
> And brushpile landings going back to the brush."

The face of War was no longer averted. The hour of reveal-
ment had struck.

Camped on a triangle of land was General Grant's Army
of the Tennessee. Eight or ten miles distant at Savannah was
General Buell with the rest of the Union forces of the West,
and attached to his division was the Ninth Indiana. Grant had
not waited for Buell to arrive from Savannah, but had impa-
tiently crossed the river at Pittsburg Landing and was camped
on the enemy's side of the river, with his army backed against
the rushing, turbulent waters of the Tennessee. It was spring-
time and the river was roaring to its banks. Thus the scene.
The date was April 6, 1862, and it was Sunday morning, but
no church bells were ringing at Shiloh Chapel. The sky was
still indolent with sleep when General Johnston's swarming
hordes of gray Confederates, furious with recent defeats, fell
upon Grant's slumbering army. Men rushed out naked from
tents to die on waiting bayonets; a roaring confusion supplanted
the tranquillity of an April dawn.

Far away at Savannah, General Grant realized his folly

and rushed to join his men huddled up against the banks of the Tennessee. That morning at Savannah, Bierce noted that "the flag hanging limp and lifeless at headquarters was seen to lift itself spiritedly from the staff. At the same instant was heard a dull, distant sound like the heavy breathing of some great animal below the horizon. The Flag lifted its head to listen." Men instinctively rushed to arms; mess-cooks lifted camp kettles off the fire before breakfast; mounted orderlies disappeared in the distance; headquarters was a swarming hive of activity. Within a few seconds General Buell's army was running, actually running, the eight miles to Pittsburg Landing. As they approached they heard "the strong, full pulse of the fever of battle," the "assembly call of the bugles" which "goes to the heart as wine and stirs the blood like the kisses of a beautiful woman. Who that has heard it calling to him above the grumble of great guns can forget the wild intoxication of its music?" They were nearing Shiloh. Such a race was not to be run again during the war. Some regiments lost a third of their number from fatigue. As they rushed nearer and nearer the Landing, the rumble of the guns shook the earth with a slow, terrific energy.

Rushing breathless, arms flying, they topped the last intervening hill and a strange sight met their gaze. "Before us ran the turbulent river, vexed with plunging shells and obscured in spots by blue sheets of low-lying smoke. The two little steamers were doing their duty well. They came over to us empty and went back crowded, sitting very low in the water, apparently on the point of capsizing. The farther edge of the water could not be seen; the boats came out of obscurity, took on their passengers and vanished in the darkness. But on the heights above, the battle was burning brightly enough; a thousand lights kindled and expired every second of time. There were broad flushings in the sky, against which the branches of the trees showed black. Suddenly flames burst out here and there, single and in dozens. Fleeting streaks of fire crossed over to us by way of welcome." It was dusk now. Buell's forces had arrived just in time. Left alone for two hours more, the remainder of General Grant's army would have been annihilated. Against the red flare at the bluff's edge "could be seen moving black figures, singularly distinct but apparently no longer than

a thumb. They seemed to me ludicrously like the fingers of demons in old allegorical prints of hell." This, then, was Bierce's
first glimpse of Shiloh. The quotations are taken from "What
I Saw of Shiloh," a paper that he began in England, printed
in *The Wasp,* reprinted in *The Examiner,* and later carried
over into his "Collected Works" (Volume I, page 234). It represents some of his best war writing, although it is slightly
marred by that elegant diction which he inherited from a pompous age and just succeeded in saving from the purple emptiness
of the rhetorical flourish.

At night "we could just discern the black bodies of the
boats, looking very much like turtles. But when they let off
their big guns there was a conflagration. The river shuddered
in its banks, and hurried on, bloody, wounded, terrified." The
regiment was ferried across the river on board a little steamboat. Crossing the river in the rays of a "sad, red, splendid
sunset," Bierce noticed the figure of a woman standing on the
upper deck. "She stood on the upper deck with the red blaze
of battle bathing her beautiful face, the twinkle of a thousand
rifles mirrored in her eyes; and displaying a small ivory-handled
pistol, she told me in a sentence punctuated by the thunder of
great guns that if it came to the worst she would do her duty
like a man! I am proud to remember that I took off my hat to
this little fool."

Such was the sense of battle that Bierce knew and loved.
The sketch was written prior to the series of war stories that
were to make his fame as a "realist." Whether it was a result
of his military training, or whether the idea was simply a part
of the times, Bierce firmly believed in a universe of rigid and
immutable law. The principles of morality were to be determined
with mathematical certainty, and since they could be calculated
with such certainty, their violation would not be tolerated.
Poetry was to be written only in accordance with the strictest
"laws" of prosody. Art was a matter of fixed principles. The
writer must hue to the formula. He must create a "dominant"
impression; he must be dramatic. It was a theory of life and
art that emphasized the formal; existence was a pattern that
could be unerringly traced. There was no understanding of
convictions as merely psychological states of mind; the world
was a hard and fast equation and the idea of its appearance as

WAR DAYS [1861]

stories are warped to fit a pattern. The very meagerness of his
work is attributable to the fact that he could obtain few incidents sufficiently dramatic to fit his theory. His war stories are
seldom realistic. But so great was his force as a personality,
that one can almost *feel* him trying to escape from the hard
framework of his stories. Thus it becomes necessary to turn to
such pieces as "Shiloh" to get his genuine reaction to war; the
stories are misleading, colored as they are by artifice and made
to a pattern.

Reverting to his picture of Shiloh, he noticed the thousands
of men huddled under the bluff on the other side of the river
as the boat neared the shore. These men who huddled in abject
terror were beaten and cowed. They were paralyzed by the shock
of that early morning attack; no force could have driven them
up the bluff and onto the fatal plateau above. When the boat
landed, the disembarking Ninth had to beat these poor devils
back with rifle stocks. By the time the regiment reached the
plateau, the firing had largely ceased for the day. Occasionally there would be a blaze of firing or a shell would pass over-
head. The gunboats continued to shell the enemy. The regiments
marched through the night, shifting position, not knowing where
they were going, hearing much whispering from the smoke-
grimed faces of the men who had been on the plateau during
the day. And then it began to rain. They marched through a
rain-drenched forest, and at dawn were arrayed in battle formation facing a clearing. Then came "assembly." "It was directly before us. It rose with a low, clear, deliberate warble,
and seemed to float in the gray sky like the note of a lark.—
As it died away I observed that the atmosphere had suffered a
change; despite the equilibrium established by the storm, it was
electric. Wings were growing on blistered feet. Bruised muscles
and jolted bones, shoulders pounded by the cruel knapsacks,
eyelids leaden from lack of sleep,—all were pervaded by the
subtle fluid, all were unconscious of their clay."

The last vestiges of the forest were passed and they came
upon the open fields where the battle had raged the previous
day. It had been a clearing, slightly forested, but the battle had
stripped it of vegetation; not a tree had escaped. Pools of rainwater filled the depressions of the earth, "discs of rainwater

tinged with blood." The force of the battle was shown by the
leafless trees, the blackened stumps. Knapsacks were strewn
about and the débris of battle littered the field. The bodies of
dead horses were pitched against trees and cannon cases; ammunition wagons were capsized; and broken timbers dotted the
ground as though thrown about by the wind of a hurricane.
Men? "There were men enough; all dead, apparently, except
one, who lay near where I halted my platoon to await the slower
movements of the line—a Federal sergeant, variously hurt, who
had been a fine giant in his time. He lay face upward, taking
in his breath in convulsive, rattling snorts, and blowing it out
in sputters of froth which crawled creamily down his cheek,
piling itself alongside his neck and ears. A bullet had clipped a
groove in his skull, above the temple; from this the brain pro-
truded in bosses, dropping off in flakes and strings."

Still they encountered none of the enemy; the word ran
along the line that the Confederates had left in the night. The
line surged forward across the clearing. "Then,—I can't describe it—the forest seemed all at once to flame up and disappear with a crash like that of a great wave upon the beach—a
crash that expired in hot hissings, and the sickening 'spat' of
lead against flesh." Back across the clearing they retreated,
spattered with the mud tossed up by bullets and shells. Some
field pieces were rushed into position and had to be guarded.
No more charges into the smoking jungle of the battle, but a
seemingly interminable period of crouching beside the guns that
roared away with unabating fury. Finally, when the last of the
guns had been demolished by the fire of the enemy, Bierce's
company moved into a nearby wood.

He obtained leave to visit a ravine where a company of
Illinois soldiers had been surrounded, and, refusing to surren-
der, had been shot to the man. The woods had caught fire and
the bodies had been cremated. "They lay, half buried in ashes;
some in the unlovely looseness of attitude denoting sudden
death by the bullet, but by far the greater number in postures
of agony that told of the tormenting flames. Their clothing was
half burnt away—their hair and beard entirely; the rain had
come too late to save their nails. Some were swollen to double
girth; others shriveled to manikins. According to degree of
exposure, their faces were bloated and black or yellow and

shrunken. The contraction of muscles which had given claws
for hands had cursed each countenance with a hideous grin.
Faugh! I cannot catalogue the charms of these gallant gentlemen who had got what they enlisted for."

When he rejoined his company, his "reprehensible curiosity" satisfied, he found that the battle raged on, with charge
after charge rolling in irregular waves across the field only to
be driven back by deadly rifle fire. It was always to be so: the
heroic giving way to the prosaic. Suddenly a great lull came.
"Had we become stone deaf? See; here comes a stretcher-
bearer, and there a surgeon! Good heavens! a chaplain! The
battle indeed was at an end." Thus closed the day at Shiloh.

Bierce never forgot that first major battle. It was imper-
ishably etched in his memory. He never could shake the grip
that those fifteen hours had on his soul. He made war story
after war story based on some incident garnered from his experience at Shiloh. The battle meant something more to him
than just a shocking experience. He had participated in many
engagements before and the following years were replete with
battles equally severe. But Shiloh came to signify the turning
point in his life. He wrote of it sadly, lovingly, as though upon
its blood-drenched fields he had lost the perishable illusion of
youth. In those hours of battle he saw the pageantry of the
heroic go down to unutterable defeat before the ruthless idiocy
of chance. The dark rioting forces of an unseen fate rolled
across that plateau. Men and mules were reduced to a mass of
burning and indistinguishable flesh; arms and legs, bits of steel,
smoked-grimed rifles, and blood-soaked uniforms, were covered
with the ashes of a great, blind impartiality. The experience
seared a white-hot streak across his memory, like the trace of
the scalp-wound he received at Kenesaw Mountain.

Whatever he was to do or be, the memory of Shiloh would
not fade. It would serve forever as a token to his mind that
forces were at work in the world, subtle elements of the tragic,
that spelt the inevitable and eternal undoing of the brave, the
valiant and the heroic. It might mean the sharp, swift, accidental
thrust of a bayonet, or the malice of a friend, the embittering
meagerness of experience, or the shocking loneliness of death.
But it was all a game dealt out by this hand unseen, this face
averted, that mocked at animate and inanimate alike. It was not

the thought of Death, for its image was lovely and kind. It was the sense of an indescribable malevolence that was mixed up in a strangely inseparable manner with the good and beautiful. Life was a battle of imponderables in which nothingness triumphed. Here was the "waste land" that he could never cross; this was the experience that wedded horror and beauty forever and inseparably in his thoughts. No matter what historians might say, Confederate victory or Union triumph, Shiloh meant to Bierce the triumph of chance. As he wrote years later in *The Examiner,* (Aug. 31, 1889): "I believe that in the word 'chance,' we have the human name of a malign and soulless intelligence bestirring himself in earthly affairs with the brute unrest of Euceladus underneath his mountain."

Later Bierce transposed the experience. In the course of time the war became a pleasant memory. Wearying of thrusting at shadows, he waxed poetical over Shiloh and saw in it the trivial lifted to the grandeur of tragedy. The recollection of it tasted sweet and he could write:

> "O days when all the world was beautiful and
> strange; when unfamiliar constellations burned
> in the Southern midnights, and the mocking-bird
> poured out his heart in the moon-gilded magnolia;
> when there was something new under a new sun;
> will your fine, far memories *ever cease* to lay
> contrasting pictures athwart the harsher
> features of this later world, accentuating
> the ugliness of the longer and tamer life?
> Is it not strange that the phantoms of a
> blood-stained period have so fair a grace and
> look with so tender eyes?—that I recall
> with difficulty the danger and death and
> horrors of the time, and without effort all that
> was gracious and picturesque?"

It was ever so, this recollection of the war typified by "Shiloh," that tormented ("will your memories *ever cease*") his thoughts with contrasting images of horror and beauty. He never thought of the one without thinking of the other. Then, too, the memory created through the years an ever present consciousness of death, a mocking well of echoes that belittled every effort to which he turned his hand. What mattered ambitions, love, honor, gratitude, friends? Is it to be marveled by any sane or thoughtful person, that this man was something of a cynic? Must the eminent doctors of abnormal psychology make a "sadist" of this man who sometimes thought of severed limbs, broken skulls and the agonies of death? In his experiences during the war, prior to his majority, may be found the origin of his sense of an engulfing futility, a belittling fate, of the horrible allied with the beautiful. He was shocked into an attitude which became a habit. He could no more relax the tension of his mind, after that experience, than he could remove the scar from his scalp. If Dr. Goldberg had suggested that he was a "poet" instead of a sadist, he would have come much closer to the facts.

*　　*　　*

FAR down the Tennessee River a woman was seeing something of Shiloh. Josephine Clifford, the "Jo" of those most charming of Bierce letters, was on board a steamer which her brother, Albert, piloted up and down the river, bringing the wounded from Shiloh. Of these scenes, she wrote to Bierce in later years: "it was a long procession of litters and stretchers moving from the steamer lying at the levee at St. Louis to the hastily erected military hospital farther uptown. Most of the wounded soldiers had their faces covered; but wherever a hand was seen, the skin on it was shriveled and wrinkled, from the rain that had fallen on these poor fellows so long." She wrote this long afterwards, when these two strange souls came to know each other in the twilight of their lives at Wrights. They met and talked in the deep quiet of the Santa Cruz Mountains, when they were white with age. He argued to her, with studied disdain and implacable certainty, that nothing mattered, but he could never shake her beautiful belief that tenderness would have its triumph. It was a far cry from Shiloh to Wrights, as though the currents that had so nearly touched in 1862 were finally to drift close enough together in 1898 to permit of a final and belated whispering. But by 1898 they were both victims of the tragedy of time and rather regretted that they had survived Shiloh, for it had touched them deeply and unforgetably.

CHAPTER III

W A R   D A Y S   [1862 – 1865]

AFTER Shiloh both armies were shocked into a state of watchful waiting, with minor engagements throughout the summer. In the fall of 1862, General Beauregard was removed from command of the Confederate forces in the West and the energetic Braxton Bragg replaced him. General Bragg immediately carried into execution the campaign which resulted in the sacking of Kentucky and the determination, on the part of the North, to close up the west. The Ninth Indiana participated in the severe fighting around Corinth and Perryville, leading up to the fall of Nashville. When Thomas and his army were besieged in Nashville, General Hood's army was in the precarious position of having to shell a Southern city. Every shell fired might mean the demolition of the gunner's home. That Bierce appreciated the horror of the situation is shown by "The Major's Tale" ("Collected Works," Vol. VIII, page 65), and by "The Affairs at Coulter's Watch."

Shortly after the Battle of Corinth, Bierce had been commissioned Second Lieutenant (November 25th, 1862), and during the Nashville campaign he was assigned to the staff of General Sam Beatty of Ohio. One day while Beatty's forces were scattered in pursuit of the enemy, it was discovered that a detached brigade held a peculiarly exposed position some ten miles from headquarters. General Beatty saw that the brigade was imperiled, or so he thought, and dispatched some reserves to its assistance. Bierce was directed to pilot this expedition to the rescue. As he told the story:

"I never felt so brave in all my life. I rode a hundred yards in advance, prepared to expostulate single handed with the victorious enemy at whatever point I might encounter him. I dashed forward through every open space into every suspicious looking wood and spurred to the crest of every hill, exposing myself recklessly to draw the Confederate fire and disclose their position. I told the commander of the relief column that he need not throw out any advance guard as a precaution against the ambuscade—I would myself act in that perilous capacity, and by driving in the rebel skirmishers gain time for him to form his line of battle in case I should not be numerically strong enough to scoop on the entire opposition at one wild dash. I begged him, however, to recover my body if I fell." *

When the reserves arrived, however, it was found that the danger was over and that their heroic movement had been in vain. Despite the superfluous heroism, Bierce was mentioned in general orders for his gallantry on this occasion. It is interesting to note that out of this incident he evolved, "A Son of the Gods," perhaps his most popular story. But with what changes! The story is romanticized to an unbelievable degree; the young officer who rides in advance of the command to draw the enemy's fire is shot down and rises to salute his comrades while two armies stand breathless and agog at his heroism! The gallant fellow then dies and our hearts are broken. It is a good illustration of how Bierce invariably chose the wrong incident for his stories. To see his great energy and vitality being cramped and beaten into the obsolete riggings of the story form is a pitiful sight. After Poe the story must be "unusual"; it must be weird. All of Mr. Bierce's western imitators, W. C. Morrow, R. D. Milne, E. H. Clough and Emma Frances Dawson, were of the same opinion. The short story became a mechanical toy, devoid of grace, ease and charm. The characters spoke with an elegance not of this earth. There was never a more flagrant offender on the score of unnatural dialogue than Bierce. In his fanatical effort to escape the commonplace, he made his characters talk in a diction that suggests nothing so much as the sepulchral conversation of very elegant and romantic ghosts.

* *The Wasp*, July 14, 1883.

The day after Christmas, having permitted his soldiers to muse over the birth of their Lord and Savior twenty-four hours, General Rosecrans left Nashville with a large force and set out to drive Bragg south. The movement culminated in the Battle of Stone River, which proved to be one of the fiercest battles of the year. Towards the end of that day of hard fighting, the Ninth Indiana was stationed behind a railroad embankment. As dusk descended on the scene, Major Braden, who was commanding the regiment, fell seriously wounded. Sergeant N. V. Bowers remembered that it was Bierce who caught the Major in his arms and carried him back to a place of safety. Stone River, or Murfreesboro, as it was sometimes called, was a holocaust of slaughter: General Breckenridge lost two thousand men in the space of a few minutes. It became a dark memory for Bierce.

He revisited the scene in the winter of his life, and was amazed to stand in the enveloping and unbelievable silence of the night on a ridge that had once been trampled with the feet of marching armies. He could read, through the dim unreality of twilight, the inscription on an elaborate monument in the center of the field: "Hazen's Brigade, To the Memory of Its Soldiers Who Fell at Stone River, December 31, 1862." It was like reading the inscription on his own tomb. It was such an amazing experience to stand on this field of death alone, that he suddenly felt all the sensations of the battle come surging upon him. Had it actually happened? But this period of fifty intervening years, was it not really the part that was grotesquely unreal? He could not be sure about these shifting scenes, and he wrote "A Resumed Identity." It is the story of a lieutenant on Hazen's staff, who awoke on the battlefield years later and thought that the fighting still raged. That the experience, with its feeling of a lost reality, was genuine and personal is borne out by the fact that the story did not appear in the early editions. It was written after his residence in Washington and after he had made his first visit to the old battlefields. Time had strange gaps, there were air pockets in its continuity, and those years after the war seemed as unreal as a nightmare. He had seen the face of death with the mask removed at Stone River in 1862, and the years that followed failed to impress him with even the substantiality of a dream. Such experiences

are not forgotten: they become more vivid with time and blot
out the meaningless. The story closes with this sentence: "His
arms gave way; he fell, face downward, into a pool and yielded
up *the life that had spanned another life.*"

It was at Murfreesboro that an incident occurred which
Bierce often related. The army was paraded to witness a hanging. Two men had committed a particularly atrocious murder
outside of the issues of war; they were all murderers, but
whether they were publicly shot as such depended on whether
they were obedient assassins or free lances. These gentlemen
were free lances. To instil in the soldiers a proper fear of the
consequences of such irregular murders, the army was assembled to witness the punishment. At the critical moment, as one
of the men mounted the scaffold, he began to shout that he was
"going home to Jesus." As the words left his mouth, the engineer on a nearby railroad track emitted a loud, unmistakably
derisive, "Hoot! Hoot!" It expressed, as Bierce remarked, "the
sense of the meeting better than a leg's length of resolutions;
and when the drop fell from beneath the feet of that picnic assassin and his mate, the ropes about their necks were practically
kept slack for some seconds by the gusts of laughter ascending
from below. They are the only persons I know in the other
world who enjoyed the ghastly distinction of leaving this to the
sound of inextinguishable merriment." *

It was in the same issue of *The Argonaut* that he told the
incident of the cavalry officer who was to be shot for desertion.
The man was blindfolded and placed astride his own coffin. The
firing squad was ready to fire the fatal volley, when the doomed
man spoke to the officer in charge of the execution. No one
heard what was said. Later Bierce questioned the officer and
was informed that the unfortunate deserter had requested that
a saddle be placed on the coffin!

On February 14th, 1862, Bierce was commissioned First
Lieutenant of Company C, Ninth Indiana. His fellow officers
and comrades said that they remembered the date because he
was commissioned shortly after Captain Risley, who had mustered Bierce into the service, was captured. During the confusion that followed, Bierce commanded the company with precision and competency. It was for his courage and resourceful-

* *The Argonaut,* December 21, 1878.

ness on this occasion that he was made a first lieutenant at
twenty-one. But he was not long for Company C, as he was
soon transferred to General Hazen's staff to act as topographical
engineer. The Ninth Indiana had been assigned to Hazen after
Nashville.

General W. B. Hazen became more than just Bierce's chief:
he was another hero, a model, such as General Lucius V. Bierce
had been. Hazen and Bierce were close personal friends during
the war, crossed the plains together, and in after years always
corresponded. The two figures who most influenced Bierce during his twenties, Hazen and General Bierce, were soldiers and
such ardent, bellicose militarists at that! The early ideal with
Bierce was the military; the pen did not supplant the sword
until he was nearly thirty. This matter of heroes is not unimportant and it is doubtful if Bierce had even heard of Swift or
Voltaire until he reached San Francisco. Hazen lacked the
poetic, idealistic cast of General Lucius Bierce. He was taciturn,
grim, and adamant. Famed throughout the service as a great
disciplinarian, he was feared and respected wherever he was
known. He was proud and sensitive and suspicious. His
career was blotched by bad luck, his ugly disposition, and
the jealousy of rivals. Instead of turning politician and getting
better opportunities, he cursed darkly to himself and became
more saturnine. As a strategist and commander, he was probably
the equal of Sherman or Thomas, but he was always falling
into unfortunate quarrels. His junior officers felt, and with
some justification perhaps, that other Generals who knew and
feared his ability, deliberately forced impossible tasks upon him
to ruin his chances of promotion. His habit of bickering did
not cease with the war, as he became involved in a rather
notorious dispute with a "brother" officer in later years. It is
altogether likely that this old campaigner rather disillusioned
Bierce about the integrity of generals and the altruism of
brother officers who have relatives in politics.

Bierce was serving on Hazen's staff in the fall of 1863, at
the Battle of Chickamauga. This was another ghastly battle
which, like Shiloh, could have been avoided if the Union commander had been more alert. It was a battle for a road, and for
years the argument raged among strategists as to whether it
was necessary for Rosecrans to offer battle or not. The better

opinion seems to be that the battle could have been avoided, if he had used his wits. The battle occurred Sept. 20, 1863, and was, of course, one of the great engagements of the war. Shortly after the firing began, the Union force was cut in two. Bierce happened to be in the middle of the line when the Confederates came crashing through. He rushed to the left and joined General Thomas' brigade which was holding the ground with that remarkable tenacity which made for its commander the title of "rock of Chickamauga." Not having sufficient troops to sustain a general attack, General Thomas withdrew his right wing and was in danger of being completely surrounded. Bierce noticed the gleam of arms in the distance, and called Thomas' attention to the fact. He was dispatched to ascertain what force approached. He dashed off and soon reported back that it was General Gordon Granger with his brigade. Granger, alone of the Union field commanders, had kept his senses. Without waiting for orders, he had moved to join Thomas on the left at a time when Rosecrans had fled the field, wiring complete defeat to Washington. The discussion of such costly blunders as Chickamauga must have dealt Bierce's fine anti-slavery idealism a severe blow.

But if the blunders were appalling, incidents occurred which served to restore one's sense of humor. In reporting back to General Hazen's headquarters later in the day, Bierce noticed General Negley in hot retreat, and volunteered to escort him back to the scene of battle. The General indignantly refused the assistance and rushed to the rear. Bierce said that there was something absent-minded about Negley on this occasion, as though his mind were back in Chattanooga behind a breastwork!

While Bierce was cut off from Hazen's staff, he galloped away to visit his brother Albert, who was now a first lieutenant in the 18th Ohio Field Artillery in Granger's command. Chatting quite casually while the battle raged—Ambrose astride his horse and Albert directing the fire of the field pieces —their visit was momentarily interrupted by a rebel bullet that killed one of Albert's gunners. Not at all daunted, these young veterans propped the dead man up against a tree and went on talking, probably observing that it was a rather warm day. Albert's battery was to perform gallant service for the Union before the day was over, as will be noted in "The Truth About Chickamauga," (Archibald Gracie, Houghton Mifflin & Company, 1911). Old "Sloots," as Ambrose called his brother, was rather shy about relating his feats of gallantry, but he finally wrote an account of what he saw of Chickamauga for Mr. Gracie, who was his brother's friend. Ambrose was rather shocked at the document and forwarded it to Mr. Gracie with a word of apology for the style!

The battle raged all day. Towards evening General Brannan was in dire need of assistance on the left of Thomas' line, near what came to be called Snodgrass Hill. In response to his call for help, General Hazen detached the Ninth Indiana under the command of Colonel Suman, along with the 18th Ohio Field Artillery in which Albert Bierce was an officer. The fighting that took place late that evening at Snodgrass Hill was perhaps the bitterest of the day. It occurred in a cornfield at the crest of a hill, and the fighting was at close range, without orders, and with no opportunity for formations. It degenerated into a regular gang fight in the dark. Colonel Suman was momentarily captured and it looked like the entire regiment had surrendered, when, upon the magical reappearance of Suman in their midst again, they took up the fight anew. The Confederates later indignantly argued that the Ninth Indiana had actually surrendered and then, when they saw they had a chance to win, had picked up their arms and caught them off guard. In any event, the Ninth was the last regiment to leave the field that day, and the two brothers must have exchanged some great yarns next morning. The Park Commission allowed the Ninth Indiana to mark five places on the field at Chickamauga, and it was there, too, that a statue was erected in honor of General W. B. Hazen. Years later Major Henry S. Foote, a Confederate, author of "Recollections of the Chickamauga Campaign," and Bierce incarnadined the walls of Judge Boalt's law offices in San Francisco with their tales of gory Chickamauga. The Judge finally silenced the debate by remarking that they would both be talking about Chickamauga when he was a "celestial musician."

It is interesting to compare Bierce's description of Chickamauga, written in 1898, with his account of Shiloh, which was begun as early as 1875. The difference in time had a marked

effect on Bierce's attitude. The trembling indignation, the flashes
of poetry, that make Shiloh a fine bit of writing, are absent
from Chickamauga. In the latter piece he merely set down the
facts with yawning indifference. It is in even sharper contrast
with his story about Chickamauga, to be found in "Tales of
Soldiers and Civilians." This story is one of the most successful of all Bierce's fiction pieces, if only for the reason that it
manages to escape, after a fashion, from his conception of the
short story as an iron corset with dramatic buckles,—something
that fitted together like the parts of a puzzle, a matter of manufacture rather than of imaginative creation. It is the story of
a child who is playing in the woods at Chickamauga, or "river
of death," as it is called in the Indian language. The child en-
counters the wounded and dying remnant of a regiment, creeping away to the rear, and struts in front of this grotesque army:

> "Instead of darkening, the haunted landscape began to
> brighten. Through the belt of trees beyond the brook shone
> a strange red light, the trunks and branches of the trees making
> a black lacework against it. It struck the creeping figures and
> gave them monstrous shadows, which caricatured their move-
> ments on the lit grass. It fell upon their faces, touching their
> whiteness with a ruddy tinge, accentuating the stains with
> which so many were freaked and maculated. It sparkled on
> buttons and bits of metal in their clothing. Instinctively the
> child turned toward the growing splendor and moved down the
> slope with his horrible companions; in a few moments he had
> passed the foremost of the throng,—not much of a feat, consid-
> ering his advantages. He placed himself in the lead, his wooden
> sword still in hand, and solemnly directed the march, conform-
> ing his pace to theirs and occasionally turning as if to see that
> his forces did not straggle. (Surely such a leader never before
> had such a following.)"

In 1898 Bierce could only sigh, after the manner of a Reunion
Day Orator, with the veteran's professional sadness: "God's
great angels stood invisible among the heroes in blue and the
heroes in gray, sleeping their last sleep in the woods of Chickamauga."

It was shortly after this engagement, in fact on October
13th, 1863, that General Hazen wrote a note to Colonel Starling, requesting that M. G. Sherman, surgeon, and Ambrose

Bierce, topographical engineer, be allowed to remain on his staff where they had been serving for some time. After considerable meandering, the order was returned with the notation of Starling: "I am instructed by General Palmer to say that he has a high appreciation of both officers named, considering them among the very best in the service, yet entertaining a sincere desire to gratify and accommodate both them and you your request is most cheerfully complied with." Old Hazen probably chewed his mustache and cursed the "highfalutin" rhetoric of certain "damned smart-alecks," when he read that order. In any event, his young lieutenant got the order and filed it away among his papers. He was apparently not altogether displeased with its tone.

It is remarkable to observe the accuracy, fine detail, and general competency of the maps that Bierce made during the Civil War. His early training must have been very thorough, or else he picked up the art of cartography with amazing facility after his enlistment. His topographical map of the Battle of Brown's Ferry, which is the largest and most elaborate of the maps that he saved, reveals the hand of a highly skilled draftsman. His two Civil War notebooks, although meager in detail, are yet remarkably neat, precise and orderly. It is interesting to note that many of the Bierces were engineers. Bierce himself always had a feeling for order, outline and proportion. Engineering met his innate insistence upon precision. He could draw and sketch with considerable skill and his handwriting was always a model of neatness and accuracy. His favorite sciences were astronomy, logic and engineering.

On May 27th, 1864, General Hazen was ordered to lead his brigade through an almost impenetrable forest against a strongly entrenched division of General Johnston's army. He swore very elaborately to his staff, mentioned the rotten souls of certain jealous rivals, and then ordered his men forward in a charge that he knew was suicidal. The engagement was known as "Pickett's Mill." None of the major texts on the war refer to it, and it is just a note in the reports,—yet it was a battle of great fury and vigor. The entire dead numbered fourteen hundred, of whom nearly one-half fell killed and wounded in Hazen's brigade in less than thirty minutes of actual fighting. Yet of this arduous afternoon, nothing remains, save these scat-

tered notes in the official volumes. Later Ambrose Bierce came
to feel that life was a rather futile enterprise, full of mocking
events and absurd ideals. He has been charged with being superficial for entertaining such heretical notions. Perhaps an
afternoon at Pickett's Mill might have convinced his specious
critics that there was more to his cynicism than the attacks of
asthma, or the loss of a sweetheart or two, would explain. Men
fought bravely, and honorably, for an ideal. They were snuffed
out in a wood to abate the jealousy of an ambitious commander
and history forgot their dying. There was really something
rather fatuous in the working out of an omnipotent will in this
eccentric fashion. "Nothing matters," Bierce dogmatized, and
people actually had the audacity to question him! From
his viewpoint, there was no other possible conclusion. Mrs.
Bertha Clark Pope, in her introduction to the "Letters of Ambrose Bierce," published by the Book Club of California, 1922,
finds it highly unreasonable of Mr. Bierce to state that "this
is a world of fools and rogues, blind with superstition, tormented with envy, consumed with vanity, selfish, false, cruel,
cursed with illusions—frothing mad!" It would seem that there
would be more cause to wonder about the character of a man
who had undergone such experiences and not found life "frothing mad,—*cursed with illusions.*" This was precisely what life
had been for Bierce. The fine tension of the Civil War was
succeeded by a flood of miscellaneous filth, a débris of ideas, the
flotsam and jetsam of a world broken away from its moorings.
Who that fought in 1861 could do other than curse when con-
fronted with the spectacle of Grant's administration? He could
hardly be expected to smile.

The Army of the Cumberland had now routed the Rebels
and the campaign that ensued was a duel of strategy between
General Sherman and General Johnston. Engagement after engagement followed in which the two wily old foxes tried to
cut each other's throats. For the most part these affairs were
sudden, swift, and contested with the perfection in deadliness
that came with four years' training. It was a hundred miles in a
direct line from Chattanooga to Atlanta and Sheridan was now
en route, marching along in circus style. In May there was a
vigorous exchange of arms at Resaca and Bierce saw gallant
Lieutenant Brayle meet death in the manner described in "Killed

at Resaca." Years later, Bierce called on a lovely lady on Rincon Hill in San Francisco and presented the Russian-leather pocket-book which had been found among the effects of Herman Brayle. It contained a letter from this charming creature in which she accused Brayle of cowardice. His insane, breath-taking heroism at Resaca had drawn every eye to his figure until he fell mortally wounded. The expatiation was superfluous. The lady attempted to toss the letter into the fire as she noted it was stained with blood! "The light of the burning letter was reflected in her eyes and touched her cheek with a tinge of crimson like the stain upon its page. I had never seen anything so beautiful as this detestable creature. 'He was bitten by a snake,' I replied."

*   *   *

BIERCE played a rather important part in the famous charge at Missionary Ridge. As topographical engineer, he had surveyed the field and outlined the strategic points of attack. Then, too, as staff officer, he carried the order to Colonel James C. Foy, of the 23rd Kentuckians, in Wood's Division, to make the charge. A few months previous, Foy had got lost with his command during a minor engagement, and Bierce was sent to locate them. As he told the story: "It was found about one-half mile away, utterly isolated and marching straight to kingdom come. Foy had not the slightest notion of where he was going to. 'What are you doing here, Colonel?' I asked, biting my lips to keep from laughing. He looked at me for a moment in a helpless and bewildered way, then pulled on a grave face and replied: 'Oh, I'm sort o' flankin' 'em.' " *

As staff officer, Bierce had a splendid chance to observe, at close range, some of the great figures of the war, and it is a pity that he did not write more extensive memoirs. During one battle he was stationed for about six or seven hours at general headquarters. To be seen around camp, on that occasion were General Grant, and Generals Thomas, Granger, Sheridan, Wood and Hazen. These worthies were not entirely absorbed in the study of military strategy. War must have its anodyne and "They looked upon the wine when it was red, these tall fel-

* "Prattle," November 14, 1888, San Francisco *Examiner.*

lows—they bit the glass. The poisoned chalice went about and about. Some of them did not kiss the dragon; my recollection is that Grant commonly did. I don't think he took enough to comfort the enemy—not more than I did myself from another bottle—but I was all the time afraid he would, which was ungenerous, for he did not appear at all afraid I would. This confidence touched me deeply." In the same issue of "Prattle," Bierce summed up his impressions of Grant as follows: "When the nation's admiration of Grant, who was really an admirable soldier, shall have accomplished its fermentation and purged itself of toadyism, men of taste will not be ashamed to set it before their guests at a feast of reason." *

The Army of the Cumberland continued south in its march of destruction. The enemy crossed its path at Kenesaw Mountain and a battle raged throughout one day in the forests and along the slopes of the hillside. During this engagement, which occurred on the 23rd day of June, 1864, Bierce was wounded. In an affidavit, General Hazen related the circumstances in this manner: "I was ordered by my division commander, Brigadier General Thomas J. Wood, to advance my skirmish line, which I attempted to do, sending my topographical engineer, Lieut. Bierce, to direct it and cause it to be done. While engaged in this duty, Lieut. Bierce was shot in the head by a musket ball which caused a very dangerous and complicated wound, the ball remaining within the head from which it was removed sometime afterwards. This wound caused Lieut. Bierce to be unfit for and absent from his duties for a considerable period of time, when he joined his command and reported for duty."

Bierce was dangerously wounded. A bullet had entered the scalp near the temple and had coursed its way around the side of his head. He was carried back from station to station to Chattanooga, where he was confined in Hospital No. 1 until he was discharged from care, sometime in July, and given a leave of absence. He never forgot the journey of that hospital train back to Chattanooga. They were loaded on flat-cars, covered with tarpaulin and left alone for hours with only the moon to commiserate their agonies. He once told his daughter that he always retained a vivid and unforgetable picture of that

* "Prattle," *The Wasp*, February 13, 1886.

trip. Would they never reach the hospital? The skies were over-
cast at times with clouds, but a turn in the road would reveal
the moon shining down with its cold, ageless clarity. The train
cautiously made its way over miles of doubtful tracks; it barely
managed to keep in motion at times; its movement was almost
imperceptible. The journey was made at night and the heavy
summer humidity finally condensed in a drizzling rain.

After being discharged from the hospital, Bierce left immediately for Elkhart. Before his enlistment in 1861, while
at Elkhart, he had written some romantic lines of verse to one
"Fatima," ending with the phrase:

> "Fatima is divine,
> For I have kissed her twice
> And she is surely mine."

He had sent them to his love, unsigned, thinking the lovely creature, who probably had freckles, pigtails and a penchant for
long flannel drawers, would name the writer with that unerring
accuracy born of an immortal affection. On his furlough, he
called on the lady and asked if she had received the verses. She
replied: "Oh, was it you!" According to the sentimental psy-
choanalysts, this thwarted passion was probably the cause of
his cynicism.

"Gus" Bierce said that Ambrose rode out to his farm one
day for a visit. He remembered that his brother's head "was
all tied up" and that soon after the visit he left for the front.
Wherever he went he probably did not remain long in Elkhart.
He saw the country thereabouts with a new eye. It was flat,
and dull, and unbearably warm. The farms were rundown; the
towns were deserted; and even a returned hero had a hard
time to find amusement. He scoffed at the place very indignantly
and left to spend the rest of his leave in more congenial sur-
roundings. He was through with Elkhart; quite finished with
Indiana, for, as will be shown in a later chapter, it is doubtful
if he ever returned to his home after this furlough. He went
back to the front with a feeling rather akin to eagerness. It was
better than the unnameable desuetude of an Indiana farm in
war-time.

In October, after his return to headquarters, Bierce still

complained of his wound. As he wrote: "In truth, I had done no actual duty since, being then, as for many years afterward, subject to fits of fainting, sometimes without assignable immediate cause, but mostly when suffering from exposure, excitement or excessive fatigue." * During the time he was injured, when his head was "broken like a walnut," he did not draw any pay from the government. There was a period of approximately five months during which the government exacted the last cent for the price of his clothing but refused to pay him a wage. There were, of course, many instances of such oversights during the war. In later years it was proposed by his friends in Washington that he recover compensation for this period of inactivity under the provisions of an Act of Congress permitting such special cases to be investigated and relief granted. The sum to which he would then have been entitled would have been quite a considerable bonus. His reply, addressed to Congressman Hepburn in the basement of the Hotel Willard, was: "When I hired out as an assassin to my country that wasn't part of the contract."

When he reported back for service at East Point, Georgia, on September 30, 1864, General Hazen asked W. C. Whitaker, Brigadier-General, again to transfer Bierce to his staff. To this request for transfer is affixed the report of a physician that "from effects of wounds Lieutenant Bierce is disqualified from marching on foot." Bierce served throughout the remainder of the war with General Hazen, in the command of Sherman, who was sweeping up the Atlantic coast towards Richmond. There are fragmentary notes in Bierce's war book that one can wish had been amplified into regular diary entries, such as, "Beaufort, S. C. January 21, 1865. Then marched to Whitehall. Ward's plantation, aristocratic secesh," or "Guest of plantation—overseer." He must have seen some interesting sights during these last months of the war.

In October of 1864, after he had rejoined the army a few weeks, he became bored with the tedious nature of life around camp and crossed the Coosa River, in the vicinity of Gaylesville, Alabama, for a look at the enemy. He was captured but finally managed to make his escape, and in November he witnessed the last great battle of his military career at Franklin.

* "Collected Works" (Vol. I, Page 297).

His description of Franklin, published first in "Prattle" and then in his "Collected Works" (Vol. I, page 321), is a good illustration of the association that beauty and horror came to have in his mind. One passage will suffice:

> "Sleep was in the very atmosphere. The sun burned crimson in a gray-blue sky through a delicate Indian-summer haze, as beautiful as a day-dream in paradise. If one had been given to moralizing one might have found material a-plenty for homilies in contrast between that peaceful autumn afternoon and the bloody business that it had in hand."

He was finally mustered out of the army at Huntsville, Alabama, at the expiration of this term of service, on January 16th, 1865.* There seems to be a wild divergence of opinion as to this date. Mr. Grattan would have it February 16th, 1865, at Huntsville, Louisiana, but the reliable "Atlas of the World" discloses that Huntsville is not in Louisiana. Dr. Danziger has the place correctly stated, but fixes the date as "June 22, 1867," which is obviously inaccurate. Bierce was in San Francisco in the spring of 1867. I have been unable to locate any text that would support the statement that Bierce was mustered out of the service in Louisiana or that the date was in 1867. Bierce was brevetted major in August of 1865, by President Andrew Johnson, for "distinguished service during the war," and the brevet was made, *nunc pro tunc,* as of March 13th, 1865. The brevet was, of course, purely honorary. The power of appointment in such cases rests with the President, and the rank assigned is merely nominal. On October 22nd, 1866, J. C. Kelton, Assistant Adjutant General, at Washington, signed a commission for Bierce as Brevet Major. The character of Bierce's service during the war was really "distinguished." He was mentioned in the dispatches for gallantry about fifteen or sixteen times; I have referred to only a few of the occasions for lack of space. General Hazen, who was not given to egregious praise, always spoke of Bierce as "that brave and gallant fellow." †

* "Official Register of the Volunteer Forces of the United States," 1861–1865.
† "A Narrative of Military Service," by W. B. Hazen, Ticknor & Company, Boston, 1885.

Bierce was brought up in a military tradition; his early ambition was to enter the army. General Hazen had taken the place of his uncle, Lucius Bierce, as the ideal type which he desired to emulate. After he was in the service, he thoroughly relished his soldiering. He took a lively interest in the soldiers under his command and even wrote sentimental pieces for their annual reunion pamphlet. It was the nearest he ever came to a feeling of solidarity with people and, even then, the democratic impulse was checked by a system that admits of little informality. His association with the fellows in his command was always a real pleasure. He once wrote that:

> "It was once my fortune to command a company of soldiers—real soldiers. Not professional life-long fighters, the product of European militarism—just plain, ordinary, American, volunteer soldiers, who loved their country and fought for it with never a though of grabbing it for themselves; that is a trick which the survivors were taught later by gentlemen desiring their votes." *

His observations about the nature of war were exceptionally keen and sharp. To be sure, his writing was spoiled by the attitude of the professional militarist, but even with this limitation he seemed to divine the nature of the focalizing forces at work in the Civil War. There were times when he perceived the true significance of that terrible welding, that profoundly revolutionary war, born in smoke and blood and the high cries of battle. The sense of sharp precision in a battle thrilled him, probably because it suggested form and order and symmetry in which his early experience had been so deficient. He envisaged this tendency to concentration and order in one of his stories as follows:

> "An army in line-of-battle awaiting attack, or prepared to deliver it, presents strange contrasts. At the front are precisions, formality, fixity, and silence. Toward the rear these characteristics are less and less conspicuous, and finally, in point of space, are lost altogether in confusion, motion and noise. The homogeneous becomes heterogeneous. Definition is lacking; repose is replaced by an apparently purposeless ac-

* "Prattle," August 17, 1890, San Francisco *Examiner*.

tivity; harmony vanishes in hubbub, form in disorder. Commotion everywhere and ceaseless unrest. The men who do not fight are never ready." *

The tension of the battle line, its suburb orderliness, gave Bierce a feeling of definiteness and a sense of harmony that the hopeless disorder and endless confusion behind the lines could not possibly have given. The strange elation of battle was dear to his heart, however much the details revolted his sensitive nature. The war acted in a two-fold manner: it liberated him from the trivial, and brought him face to face with the great dark music of death; and it stung him into an awareness of the dull edges and slothfulness of life. He sensed the duality of the experience in one of his stories, when he wrote:

> "The exhilaration of battle was agreeable to him, but the sight of the dead, with their clay faces, blank eyes and stiff bodies, which when not unnaturally shrunken were unnaturally swollen, had always intolerably affected him. He felt toward them a kind of reasonless antipathy that was something more than the physical and spiritual repugnance common to us all. Doubtless this feeling was due to his *unusually* acute sensibilities—his keen sense of the beautiful, which these hideous things outraged. Whatever may have been the cause, he could not look upon a dead body without a loathing which had in it an element of resentment." †

Most of his war stories are romantic but occasionally he would become horribly facetious, writing of death in a manner that would shock the cruelest jester. His heartlessness on such occasions would indicate something of the great resentment he felt towards death; his unwillingness to be reconciled to experience. This resentment, growing out of the war, took two forms of expression: a sharp, pungent criticism of the world of corruption and emptiness that grew out of the collapse of idealism, and, second, a resentment at the gruesomeness of the struggle itself. There is really nothing contradictory about his writing; the stories and his satire both sprang from the same experience. With particular reference to his stories, the war created in his mind an image of beauty as being, in some strange

* "One Officer, One Man."
† "A Tough Tussle."

way, an aspect of horror. The thrilling exultation of a far-
flung battle line with the sweet assembly call running like
music down the ranks of blue, was always shattered by the
unforgetable image of the burning bodies at Shiloh. This vision
came to be fixed in his imagination and he wrote of beauty
and horror as one.

The other type of resentment was purely mental and found
expression in his satire. He keenly resented the bombastic
heroes of peace: such men, for example, as General W. H. L.
Barnes and General Salomon, and the other "Generals" and
"Colonels" whose very presence made one feel ashamed of
having been a soldier. One of these gentlemen actually claimed
to have been the true hero of the charge at Missionary Ridge,
and it remained for Bierce to point out, in his "Prattle," the
nature of a lie. Of General Salomon, who was always making
speeches, he wrote: "General Salomon drew his tongue, marched
against the Confederate dead and laid down his honor for his
country." And when Salomon spoke against the fallen rebels,
Bierce wrote:

> "What, Salomon! such words from you
> Who call yourself a soldier? Well
> The Southern brother where he fell
> Slept all your base oration through.
>
> Are you not he who makes to-day
> A merchandise of old renown
> Which he persuades this easy town
> He won in regions far away?"

Illustrations of the same sort of satire may be found in all his
journalism. His abuse of scoundrels, of the whole period of
stagnation that followed the war, is traceable to this same influence. The war gave him a background against which to measure the petty puppets of peace. The violence of his satire was
a survival of pre-war idealism.

Only a few of the more important influences of the war
on Bierce's character have been traced. It would be impossible
to catalogue the ramifications of this experience. One cannot
overestimate the importance of those years of soldiering; they
must be kept constantly in mind. He was only nineteen when

he enlisted and his services extended over practically six years, considering his post-war work in the South. During these years, he witnessed some of the hardest fighting of the war. He was captured and seriously wounded. He had actively participated in four of the most important engagements of the war: Shiloh, Stone River, Chickamauga and Franklin, not to mention a list of other engagements. Moreover, he had seen the show from a very interesting viewpoint, that of a staff officer, which permitted of some objectivity. He was always a soldier.

During these wild, mad years, Bierce was leading a life of intense action. There were few intervals for rest or reflection during his enlistment. The rhythms that such a life stressed became unalterable. Bierce was always restless when physically inactive; he longed, in old age, for the unrestricted, strenuous, and unpredictable life of a military campaign. It meant movement, new scenes and excitement. He had soldiered in the mountains of West Virginia, along the Mississippi, and had marched through Georgia. It was his initiation into life, for his soldiering came when he was a fit age for preparatory school. There was no preliminary schooling in irony: his awakening came like a slap in the face, the irritation and shock of which were unforgetable. Overnight he became a soldier and remained such for six impressionable years. Fetid swamps and ambling fences and the indescribable despair of makeshift farming, were replaced by the crimson precision of battle. It was an experience that made him restless and impatient under physical inactivity; leisure annoyed him; he sometimes wrote, like he had soldiered, for excitement and danger. His sentences were neat, orderly and obedient. There was, literally, a swordlike thrust to his wit. His column of "Prattle" sounded, on occasions, like it had been written under fire. After he had reached sixty, Bierce's views were easily recognizable as those of an "old soldier" (a very intelligent old soldier, of course). All that was most distinctive about the man in after life was a carry-over from his military career. There was something of the cold informality and unquestionable finality of the court-martial in his judgment on men and events. It is interesting to compare his writings of the war with Harold Frederic's "Marsena and Other Stories of the Wartime" and Francis Grierson's "The Valley of Shadows." The difference is that between a

soldier and civilians. Frederic and Grierson were young men
who caught the distant rumble of war behind the lines: naturally
their work was slow, rather mystical, and full of the soft lights.
Bierce never thought of war without becoming excited.

The war was a troubling memory. It never left him; he
mused and puzzled about it all his life. He was still thinking
about it when, an old man over seventy, he made that last inspection of the old battlefields. Reading his journalism from its
inception to the day of its last appearance, one is impressed
with the frequency of his references to war, the constant presence in his mind of its images, and the color that it gave his
thinking and even his vocabulary. On more than one occasion,
he would drop the castigating of rascale long enough to write,
in that ornate poetic style of his, such lines as:

> "Along the troubled valley
>   The evening shed its rest;
> A last faint troubled gleam of day
>   Sank slowly down the west.
>
> The river of the valley
>   Crept sighing to the sea;
> And crimson with the red, red blood
>   That ran for victory.
>
> The stars lean'd from their chambers,
>   And through a rain of light
> They quiver'd, shiver'd, in amaze
>   And watch'd the dead all night."

He suddenly ceased, in the days of the Spanish-American
War, from lambasting Sampson and the other militarists of the
day, to sigh: "Jo Wheeler!" A news dispatch had mentioned the
name of General Joseph Wheeler, late of the Confederate Army.
Suddenly the Spanish-American fiasco was forgotten; gone,
too, were the memories of London, of San Rafael, of San
Francisco. Everything slipped away into the obscurity of time
and only that one experience stood forth, and he exclaimed:

> "Is it not all a dream—all these thirty-odd years of peace
> and reconciliation, ending in a fantastic Federal-Confederate
> War with Spain? Shall I not be waked in a few hours by the

shuffling feet of the men as they form silently in line and
stand at arms in the dark of the morning to repel an expected
attack by Jo Wheeler?" *

The war was a great emotional adventure that carried
Bierce from his early life on an Indiana farm deep into the
darkest recesses of experience. It was an adventure that swept
him to the stars and then left him on a high note to drift in a
narrowing circle of small things, petty details, withering and
fetid atmospheres, down to the zero hour of his final jest with
death in Mexico. It was a long span of years that stretched
like a miraculous bridge from the homely, earthly prose of
Abraham Lincoln, to the majestic nonsense of Dr. Woodrow
Wilson, at whom Bierce sniffed suspiciously, and, with great
good fortune, escaped into Mexico as though he had some pre-
monition of the maudlin days to follow. There was much in
the years 1914-1918 that would scarcely have made him smile.
"Ideas run recurrent on an endless track," he once said, and it
was an act of divine justice and grace to spare him the agony
of witnessing Warren G. Harding enacting the rôle of a latter-
day Rutherford Hayes. His friends should rejoice in his disappearance into Mexico in 1914. He saw enough of this world in
seventy years for an eternity of sleeping, and Bierce was "sleepy
for death" when he turned his back on his country, with magnificent disdain, on the eve of its adoption of prohibition, Wil-
sonian idealism and the doctrine that silent men are inevitably
wise, and went south to see what death was like among the
operatic scenes near Chihuahua. If he had lived to compare
"The Backwash of War" by Ellen N. LaMotte, with his "Tales
of Soldiers and Civilians," it would only have increased his
loneliness and impressed him more deeply with the nature of
man's sorry plight. It was better that he should forget the
endless mimicry of man and turn to the "sacred steep uncon-
sciousness" of Robinson Jeffers, "the great kingdoms of dust
and stone, the blown storms, the stream's-end ocean."

* "Prattle," August 20, 1898, San Francisco *Examiner.*

CHAPTER IV

NEW SCENES

I⊤ has been frequently stated that Bierce returned to Indiana after the war and that he remained there until he left for San Francisco and the West. But the known facts would indicate that he never revisited his home after the war. When he was mustered out of the service, he immediately accepted a post in the Treasury Department, as a minor official, in charge of captured and abandoned property. He was stationed in Alabama, but the headquarters of the division was in New Orleans.

At the close of the war there was, of course, no semblance of government in the South. Military officials took charge of the situation and attempted, after a fashion, to restore order. The national government had placed treasury officials throughout the South to take charge of "captured, abandoned or confiscable" property. In the last days of the war the Confederacy had floated a Produce Loan in which huge quantities of cotton had been pledged to the government. This property was, of course, subject to confiscation. It was the duty of the treasury agents to seize all confiscable cotton and to collect a duty of twenty-five per cent on all sales of cotton made by owners after the war. The commissions of the agents were paid out of the proceeds of sales. Naturally a most deplorable condition resulted. Practically all of the confiscable cotton was centered in Alabama, where Bierce was stationed as a treasury agent. It was found in the reports of the Ku Klux Klan that millions of dollars were filched and stolen from southerners by dishonest treasury agents. To show the value of such posts as Treasury Inspector, prices as high as $25,000 would sometimes be paid for the appointment. Huge quantities of cotton were actually stolen and spirited north to Mellen, a large broker at Cincinnati. Two treasury officials in Alabama, T. C. A. Dexter and T. J. Carver, were actually indicted by Federal grand juries. S. B. Eaton, the inspector in whose division Bierce was an agent, was moderately honest, but even some of his accounts to the government are rather amusing. One reads:

Cotton sold $15,963.01
Total Receipts 27,799.48
Total Expenses .... 27,799.48 *

Such clever accounting can only be described as ingenuous and typical of the time. The conduct of these inspectors resulted in a grave scandal; every report that was made, as, for example, the report of Ben Truman to the President, only darkened the guilt of these unscrupulous agents. Of course, much of the damage was done by men who merely represented themselves to be treasury agents, so that it was difficult to fix responsibility. The life of even the honest agents was most exciting. A state of actual war existed between the agents and the cotton planters. Agents were driven out of Choctaw County and had to receive the support of cavalry units. It was this régime of irresponsible, disorderly, and chaotic administration that Bierce had to witness and to help enforce. It gave a fatal pause to his idealism.

Not only was the entire system of the treasury agent wrong —for the government profited nothing by the system, as the rascally agents stole the revenue collected—but it kept the South in a state of delayed and arrested reconstruction for years. It would have been difficult enough to rebuild the South under the circumstances that existed at the close of the war, without the handicap of this system of espionage and graft. Selma, Alabama, where Bierce was stationed for a time, had been the scene of a raid by General Wilson's cavalry in the last days of the war. Wilson had sacked the valley. The disorderly conduct of his drunken soldiers was a scandal even in war time. His raid was eloquently denounced in every history of reconstruction in the South. He not only destroyed the town of Selma but he

* "Civil War and Reconstruction in Alabama," by Walter L. Fleming, Columbia University Press, 1905.

drove 800 horses and mules into the town and killed them, so that the roads leading into the village could not be traversed for months because of the dreadful stench. The trail of his raid could be marked for years afterwards by the charred ruins of villages, burned stumps that once were homes, and the miscellaneous débris of destruction. Bierce lived in this valley of death at a time when the fires kindled by the union raiders were still smoldering. It is small wonder, then, that he wrote such a story as "An Inhabitant of Carcosa," which might have been a memoir of his experiences in Coosa County, Alabama. It is the story of a man who returns to his homeland and finds it empty of life:

> "No signs of human life were anywhere visible nor audible; no rising smoke, no watch-dog's bark, no lowing of cattle, no shouts of children at play—nothing but *that dismal burial-place,* with its air of mystery and dread, due to my own disordered brain. Was I not becoming again delirious, there beyond human aid? Was it not all an illusion of my madness? I called aloud the names of my wives and sons, reached out my hands in search of theirs, even as I walked among the crumbling stones and in the withered grass."

During his occasional trips to New Orleans to report to his chief, S. B. Eaton, Bierce had occasion to see something of the notorious "Ben Butler" régime, an experience that never ceased to cause him mortification and annoyance. He once remarked that, at the outbreak of the Civil War, his imagination drew him irresistibly to the Union cause and that he was convinced beyond doubt or skepticism of the ideals of the anti-slavery faction. After witnessing the depredations of Ben Butler in Louisiana, he regretted his zeal in fighting so strenuously for the North. His understanding of the carpetbag régime in the South came as the first shock to his illusions about the war. He was to see the soldiers whose lives had been devoted to "principles" loot the people their comrades had offered their lives to bring back into the Union. Some died that others might rob. Bierce once expressed his feeling in his column of "Prattle": "Time was, in that far fair world of youth where I went a-soldiering for Freedom, when the moral character of every thought and word and deed was determined by reference to a

set of infinitely precious 'principles'—infallible criteria—moral
solvents, mordant to all base metals, and warranted by the manu-
facturers and vendors to disclose the gold in every proposition
submitted to its tenets. I have no longer the advantage of their
service, but must judge everything on its own merits—each case
as it comes up." *

The period may be summarized in several stories that Bierce
told of his experiences. Once, in company with several comrades, a number of whom had been rebel soldiers, he was returning from a tavern. They noticed that a man kept shadowing
them. Not heeding their warning to stop, he kept on following
the group and was shot dead by one of Bierce's companions. A
Justice of the Peace heard the complaint and at once dismissed
the charges against all defendants except as against the man
who fired the fatal shot. He was fined five dollars and costs!
While bringing some confiscated cotton down the Tombigbee
River, Bierce was fired upon from ambush and a battle royal
ensued in which he narrowly escaped with his life. His days
were full of such adventures and the experience was not
altogether unpleasant, yet the tenor of the reconstruction period
disgusted him beyond measure.

Bierce continued to work as a treasury agent throughout
the spring and summer of 1865. His duties were not arduous
and he was seeing new scenes and experiencing new adventures
daily. The monotony of the work was broken by frequent trips
to New Orleans. The old St. Charles Hotel was a special delight; it was his first introduction to the grand manner of living.
Even if New Orleans suffered from post-war depression it
yet had certain charms which one cannot associate with Elkhart,
Indiana. It was not the New Orleans that Walt Whitman visited in 1848, but the outline of its loveliness still lingered about
the town. To the young treasury agent it was probably as
exotic as Tahiti.

In the fall of 1865, while he was in New Orleans on a
holiday, he suddenly decided to take a boat to Colon, or Aspinwall, as it was then called. The trip was a vital experience; he
saw such scenes as his imagination had never conceived. His
interest was aroused, and, with the instinct of an artist, he
began to draw sketches and make notes. In the back of his

* The *Examiner*, May 9, 1897.

Civil War notebook are a few pages of notes about this expedition, into which he crowded his impressions. The notes are written in a legible script but reveal a meager education. Because it is perhaps the earliest specimen of his style, it will be quoted in full:

"After witnessing some of the phenomena of a tropic sea, we arrived at Aspinwall on the 10th day of September at daylight and found ourselves at once in the heart of the tropics. The first object that attracted my attention after going ashore was a groop of Cocoa Palms with the nutes thick upon them. The next thing that impressed me was the free and easy impudence of the native black boys asking to carry my luggage. I noticed the gardian of the Washington full of roses and briliant blossoms. Coming out of the companies grounds I could glance down the main street of the town. It was filled with a throng of natives, mostly women, peddling fruits and confctionory. I walked back and forward through the crowd to enjoy the strange sights and sounds. Buy oranges calls a tall tawny mulatto girl, 'good lemoneed honey,' cries another. Not satisfied with what I saw on the main street, I went round to explore the back part of the town. Aspinwall is built on a coral reef. Hollows in all directions form malarious swamps. Filith universal the rude cleanliness in the dresses of the woman formed a pleasing contrast. The main part of the town is buildt of slovenly wooden houses back of those are Palm hutts. Some pleasant houses are on the esplanade. Palm trees of different kinds I found growing all through the town, unknown plants on every side. The throngs of great black buzzards sitting on every roof and tree, and opping fearlessly about the offal strewn streets was in keeping with the general appearance. The people cut beaf into long stripes and hang it on racks in the sun to dry. One of these racks I noticed the buzzards were watching suddenly a daring old fellow hopped towards it; flapping up amongst the long tempting slices commenced a ravenous attack; at this a half nude old woman rushed out upon him with cries and after repeatedly walloping him over the head with a towl succeeded in dring him off. They have a respectable episcopal Church here. The principal frwit vended in the street were oranges from Jamaica, large and fresh Lemonds, Limes, Alagator Pairs, Pomagranits, Mauva Peirs, Mangos, Cocoa Nuts, Pineapples, Agauvas. I procured an indifferent meal at the Howard House for one Dollar in silver. The train started at 12:30. We went dashing

along through the midst of tropical swamps. Tropical in
earnest. Scarcely a single plant or three had I seen before.
And every thing growing so luxurious and on so jigantic a
scale. From Aspinwall the first 10 or 11 miles of road is mostly
through swamps. Near Panama Hills and Mountains pre-
domenate.

All along the R R the ground is covered with the sensitive plants, prospate, prickley, compound leaved, and very sensitive. Cane grew in the swamps, the same we have in the
South, only it was 80 or 100 feet in length and from 4 to 6
inches in diamiter. Palmettos grow but not plenty. Four different kinds of Palms I noticed. Besides the broad fruit tree with
fruit well matured, I plucked some of the fruit and punctured it, a milky sap jeted out, which rapidly thickened like
starch, tasted like sage. The stevenst—I saw many parots and
one ring-tailed monkey.

Panama is a quaint old town almost crowded into the sea.
By the Mountains, sentinells were stationed at each car as we
halted. They were slovenly negroes and looked quite unserv-
isable. The Bay of Panama is full of Islands—is very shole so
that Steamers have to lie out miles. Passengers are taken out
in a kind of steamferry. The bay is full of large fish, sharks,
etc., that dashing about make a beautiful display of its phos-
phoresence."

If Aspinwall gave Bierce fresh images and new interests,
an even more important adventure awaited him on his return
to New Orleans. There he found a letter from his old commander, W. B. Hazen, offering him the post of engineering
attaché to an expedition of exploration, survey and inspection
that the General was to conduct through the Indian Territory.
The government had directed General Hazen to map the Indian
region, and to inspect the fortresses that gave protection to
settlers and emigrants. Bierce was tired of his work as treasury agent and he welcomed the chance to see new lands and to
seek even more romantic adventures. He was the more eager
to join the expedition, as Hazen suggested that he might obtain
a commission, perhaps a captaincy, in the regular army. Without waiting for the commission to be issued, and, apparently
without returning to Indiana, he left to meet Hazen in Nebraska where the little party was assembling. This is borne out
by the circumstances. His commission, a second lieutenancy in

the Fifth U. S. Infantry, was actually issued. I. C. Kelton, Assistant Adjutant General, wired to Bierce, care of Lafayette Burr, former adjutant to the Ninth Indiana, offering the commission. But the wire was returned to Washington by Burr; apparently Bierce was not in Indiana. It was then sent to Hazen in Nebraska, but by that time the expedition was already on its way west. It did not catch up with Bierce until the spring of 1867 in San Francisco. From these circumstances it is obvious that his family in Indiana did not know his whereabouts, or at least that they did not know his exact address. How Bierce could have been a free-lance writer for the newspapers in Indiana after the war, as Dr. Danziger suggests, is a rather difficult problem to solve.

In fact, Bierce's attitude towards his family and towards his early life is shown by the brusque and peremptory manner in which he dropped all former associations and jumped at the chance to go west. There was no reason why he should return to Indiana. "I was one of those poor devils born to work as a peasant in the fields, but I found no difficulty in getting out," he once remarked. His home life was never congenial. His brother, Albert, was the only agreeable companion of all his innumerable brothers and sisters. One sister early evinced symptoms of the missionary impulse and Bierce knew that it was time to leave before shame took the place of affection. Moreover, Indiana meant a flat country, literally and figuratively, and such an inflated experience was unthinkable. After the glamour of the war, culminating in the starry honor of Brevet Major, and after the levees of New Orleans at dusk, he could never be content with swamps and corn fields and barnyards. The war saved Bierce from Indiana and turned his face westward. He did not follow his brother Albert to the coast, as has so often been stated. Upon receiving his discharge, Albert returned to Indiana and married. He did not arrive in San Francisco until Christmas Day, 1869. approximately three years after Ambrose reached the coast.

When Bierce joined Hazen, the little Nebraska village was dotted with the white canvassed emigrant wagons leaving for the West. The days of '49 were over, and the real westward movement was now in full swing after the interruption caused by the war. The number of stray dogs, herds of cattle, and mule-teams, indicated that the great trek was in progress. Through the unmarked streets of this outpost on the fringe of civilization, General Hazen rode at the head of his expedition. They were soon lost in a brown immensity of earth. The trip that followed was a great liberating force in Bierce's life. The scenes were new, fresh and unknown. The strange atmosphere jolted him out of his habit of complacency and opened new vistas. The trip gave him a chance to recover his health, too, for he suffered from the disease of asthma which he had inherited from his mother. It had not bothered him much during the war, but it had sorely harassed him in the South. No sooner had the expedition started west than he began to feel better with every change in climate.

The expedition was really a camping trip. There were few duties to perform. Bierce made topographical maps of much of the territory through which the party passed, and kept them in a note-book. The first maps were drawn in the Dakotas where the party journeyed to inspect a few forts. Bierce was particularly impressed with the Black Hills country and noted its topography with care. He was interested, too, in the rumors of gold in the hills, but the territory was not then open for settlement. Years later he was to make good use of this information. As the little caravan trotted along its route, they would occasionally see an impromptu grave or the ashes of a hastily extinguished fire. It was like revisiting an old scene for Bierce. As a boy he had devoured the romances of Capt. Mayne Reid and to be actually traveling through the "Indian Country" was as pleasurable as it was "romantic." Along the North Platte, the party passed before the great Court House Rock, the famous landmark of the western emigrants. Of it Bierce wrote in later years, the memory saddened and romanticized: "What a gracious memory I have of the pomp and splendor of its aspect, with the crimson glories of the setting sun fringing its outlines, illuminating its western walls like the glow of Mammon's fires for the witches' revel in the Hartz, and flung like banners from its crest." *

It was not long before the Dakotas were lost and they entered a region that was new, and therefore marvelous, to them all. Something of the exuberance of their spirits is indi-

* "Collected Works," Vol. I; page 363.

cated by the sketches and drawings, and data for maps, recorded in the journal that Bierce kept. These blurred lines on fading paper were symbols to Bierce and represented the wild grandeur of the Rockies. Some of them actually look as interesting as pictures. There were penciled maps with notations of the Big Horn Mountains, Crazy Woman's Flat, Clear Fork, Tongue River, Little Big Horn, and a map of the Judith Mountains. Nothing seems to have escaped his eye: the book opens with a large drawing of a bison's head; interpolated with the maps are copies of Indian inscriptions seen on the rocks at Powder River and on the stumps of trees in the Yellowstone Valley. The party moved rapidly on horseback and Bierce had little time to draw, but he captured every significant scene and landmark and tried to express the lovely contour of a hill by hasty shadings in a ten-cent notebook. To him all these lines, dots, and circles were the symbols by which he could recreate the memory of the foaming waters that roared over the Shoshone Falls and drifted into glistening mists that floated soundless to the rocks below, lost in a roar that seemed to come from a distance.

Hard and disagreeable as some of their experiences were, they yet had time for amusement and sport. Just as some of the maps are significant of the romantic glamour in which the valleys were veiled for Bierce, so are the penciled notations interspersed throughout the book full of their own potential amplification into accounts of amusing enterprises. Fort Benton brought this note: "Improvised Program. The Ladies, H. Beveridge, Enthusiastic single man. 'The Ladies, God Bless Her.' Labored effort (painful one) in response by Whatisname Gomer Evans. Song, Mary of Argyle, Sam Mayer. Bloom is on the Rye. encore. R. Kohler, Cornet Solo, The Last Rose of Summer." It must have been a maudlin carousal ending with that music so dear to the heart of the inebriate: a sad cornet solo. But they were marching fast: Fort Fetterman, Fort McPherson, Fort Kearney, and Fort Bridger passed in swift succession. They were stern little outposts where army officers taught Hardee's tactics to the uninitiated. The great log gates rolled back, and the little cavalcade trotted through into the fort. The garrison was prepared for General Hazen's inspection, and the place was a model of orderliness: arms glistened, uniforms were spotless, flags resplendent, and headquarters was decked for the occasion. After the inspection was made, there were moments of entertainment and leisure, and, over the glasses and cigars, reminiscences. These fellows lost in the wilderness guarding Indian braves had been in the Civil War, too. "Orchard Knob? That afternoon? Of course!"

The expedition was ordered to return to Washington, via Salt Lake City, San Francisco and Panama. At Salt Lake, Bierce had an opportunity to inspect the Mormon experiment in colonization, and he was most enthusiastic. He never failed to raise his voice in defense of the Mormons, when, in later years, people still permitted the peccadillo of polygamy to blind them to the undeniable evidence of fine economy, industry and genius in government. One excerpt is sufficient to show how Bierce reacted to the settlement at Salt Lake: "I have no religious convictions. I do not care a copper for the Mormons. But I do care a good deal for truth, reason and fair play; and whenever I cease to be indignant at the falsehood, stupidity and injustice that this harmless people have suffered at the hands of the brutal and harmless mob of scribblers and tonguesters who find profit in denouncing them, I shall have had a longer life than I merit." *

On this western trip he had occasion to see something of Indian warfare, and he always scoffed at the bravery of the pioneer. Part of his denunciation of the pioneer as a warrior, sprang from his deep-seated admiration for the regular army. He once wrote in "Prattle": "I have marked the frontiersman's terror-stricken hordes throng tumultuous into the forts before the delusive whoops of a dozen lurking braves. I have observed his burly carcass scuttling to the rear of the soldiers he defames, and kicked back into position by the officers he insults. I have seen his scruffy scalp lifted by the hands of squaws, the while he pleaded for his worthless life, his undischarged weapon fallen from his trembling hands. And I have always coveted the privilege of a shot at him myself." † This sounds rather like Three Star Hennessy dicta, but it no doubt is based on actual observation.

One of the military posts visited was Fort Phil Kearney.

* *The Wasp*, April 30, 1881.
† *The Wasp*, September 2, 1881.

Shortly after Bierce's party left this fort, some Indians lured a force of ninety men and officers outside and slaughtered them to a man.* From Fort C. F. Smith, the party turned north and swam the Yellowstone. In the Valley they found herds of elk, deer and buffalo. It was a magnificent region. It eclipsed even his memory of the mountains of Virginia. Surely if there was this much grandeur in nature, there must be a similar current in human life, if one but acted magnificently enough to strike the right chord. He began to act on this principle. After leaving Yellowstone, the country was bare and without game. They proceeded to Fort Benton and arrived there a "sorry-looking lot," as Bierce phrased it. Then they went north to Helena, Montana, and back south again to Virginia City, most fabulous of all western mining camps. The last bivouac of the party was on the camping ground of the famous Donner party, where Bierce first heard the story of that memorable expedition.

These months of camping and riding, from Omaha to San Francisco, were for Bierce an introduction to the western manner. He was still young enough to be impressed with the feeling of liberation that the fresh and untrammeled life of the West created. He was essentially a Westerner in many ways. Of late years the influence of the West has been made the subject of sharp comment by Eastern critics. Mark Twain, we are informed by this criticism, was not the splendid fellow that the West always envisaged: care-free, lazy, laughing and full of a great gusto for life, but a hen-pecked journalist, bitter with disappointment. Such criticism overlooks the fact that Twain, if he was ever overawed by social prestige, was victimized in the East. Both Bret Harte and Mark Twain lost their early force and vitality when they went East. But this fact should not obscure the values that the West did create, for, as Mr. George West has written, "it offered a certain masculine freedom and zest and some very genuine values." Many of these values are invariably associated with Bierce's name. The West gave such a character elbow-room and if he became an excessive individualist it should not be too seriously deplored. His enormous energy, personal bravery, forceful directness; his impatience with pettiness and disdain for social fetishes, all these qualities were

* He used this recollection as an incident for a story in "A Man With Two Lives."

Western. Of course it is always difficult, if not specious, to localize a virtue. But the West did emphasize certain values which have come to be called Western. Bierce's best work was done in San Francisco, and it was to San Francisco that he was now journeying.

As the party left Salt Lake and began the last part of their trip, the talk was rife as to the nature of the land they approached. California was a magical word in the fifties and sixties; it was "El Dorado" as Bayard Taylor had written. And what of San Francisco? They had heard nothing but stories about this city since leaving Nebraska. They were so impatient to see San Francisco that they only lingered a few days in Virginia City, and then turned westward again, skirted the edge of Lake Tahoe, and came to the end of their wilderness route at Dutch Flat in Placer County. From this point to San Francisco they could travel along the road-bed of the new transcontinental railroad. Through Placer County they saw marks of "diggin's"; miners were along the hillsides and the creek bottoms. They hastened forward; Sacramento did not detain them long. They visited "The Plains" saloon and admired the paintings of the Wind River Mountains and Fort Laramie that adorned the walls, but they were eager to be gone. The journey down the Sacramento River was one fraught with expectancy. The soft brown hills dropped into bottom lands and finally rose to the last ridge of bluffs along the bay. Monte Diablo gleamed in the distance. They sailed through the Straits of Carquinez and the bay was outspread before them. The picture was sharp, swift and unforgetable. Such a bay!

But what of this fabulous San Francisco? The miners and traders on board, obdurate to the scene, grunted that it was "over across the bay," and pointed to a reach of land veiled in mist. The boat struck the currents of the bay; winds swept in from the ocean; the waves slapped softly against the boat; and the desert was quite forgotten. San Francisco could be seen rising behind the sand dunes: a wind-swept city that sprawled along the water front and climbed up its three hills for a look at the bay. Flocks of white sea birds fluttered about the boat and dove down to ride the slate-colored waves. Alcatraz huddled in the bay like an iron-backed turtle that had risen to the surface with an effort. Dusk came and suddenly the place seemed ageless: full of shadowy sorrows, a mezzotint of dark hills, the spars of ships and the rickety frame houses on the hillsides. . . . He would like to stay here for a while, but his commission undoubtedly awaited him and he would soon leave for Panama. The chatter of the waiting crowd at Clark's Landing interrupted his thoughts. It was the voice of a new mob, a polygot mob, a miniature world with which his destiny was to be inextricably woven. There was surely something lively and envigorating about this city. He had arrived in San Francisco.

CHAPTER V

SAN FRANCISCO

THE San Francisco of 1866 was a most extraordinary city; nothing quite like it was ever seen on this continent. The gold rush of the early fifties had somewhat subsided, but the city was still in an uproar. It was teeming with life and through the entire fabric of the place ran a thread of gold, the gold of Virginia City and the Comstock. It was the supertype of Western bonanza town, but spiced and scented with the orient; Chinese chattered in the narrow passageways of Chinatown, and Kanakas from the Islands worked in the streets. San Francisco had numbered two thousand in the first of 1849; it passed twenty thousand and the white sails of seven hundred vessels had come to port in its harbor by the end of that year. Bayard Taylor arrived in '49 and left on a hitch hike for Monterey. He retured to the city in four months and could scarcely find his way about. By 1866 some of the early turbulence had subsided. Casey and Cora had blasphemed from the scaffold in front of the Vigilante Committee headquarters as they were precipitated into that hell to which, in their last words, they had so warmly consigned their executioners. James King of William was already a legend. Fires had ravaged the town several times, but it had always grown back with weed-like rapidity. The first glorious flush had waned and the period of magnificence had arrived. It was the dawn of the era of the "Great Developer" and there was much talk of Teavis, Fair, Mackay, and Flood. The whimsicality of the "Oh Susanna" mood had gone; colts had been replaced by derringers; the sombrero by the black beaver hat. Judge Terry's famous Texan knife was momentarily sheathed and Leland

Stanford was gazing hungrily at the large estate left by his former partner, Colton.

San Francisco was still tumultuous and gay. It had not as yet settled down to the lethargic mood that possessed it in later years: the sordid days of graft, race-horse gambling and China-town sporting, under the régime of "Boss" Buckley. There was still a great vibrancy about San Francisco in the sixties. It was impossible to live there and not be excited by its keen music. Bayard Taylor wrote that "The very air is pregnant with the magnetism of bold, spirited, unwearied action, and he who but ventures into the outer circle of the whirlpool, is spinning, ere he has time for thought, in its dizzy vortex." * It was a dis-tinctly masculine community and its atmosphere of uncertainty and transiency provided a tireless spur to rowel men out of established ruts. The early commentators noticed the amazing contrasts and swift movements in its social life. Doctors and ministers forgot their callings and turned speculators; profes-sors drove ox-teams; and army officers took minor government posts and married wealthy girls. Taylor, however, in the midst of his first enthusiasm, observed certain "dissipating and dis-organizing" influences at work. By the sixties this whirligig society was coming to a pause and sobering up. The dust clouds stirred by its early rampancy were settling and when they finally disappeared a somber scene was revealed. The big strike was over; hilarity was supplanted by calculation; and the boom was followed by its inevitable aftermath of dark days.

Into this "gray town, prematurely wrinkled, like a woman in whom youth's excesses too long burned, which huddled on a point of sand, scourged with winds, racked by fogs, scintillant with dusty motes in the cold sunshine," came Major Bierce. For him the place was full of novelty and charm. Spring, with its gay light warmth, hovered about the streets that ran up hill-sides to disappear in unseen hollows beyond. With General Hazen, Bierce visited the Presidio, speculating excitedly as to the rank of the commission which he had no doubt awaited him. There it was, neatly sealed and magnificently embossed, but it was only for a second lieutenancy in the Fifth United States Infantry! Hazen cursed and tried to hit upon an explanation for such stupidity, but his young attaché, with characteristic

* "El Dorado," by Bayard Taylor.

disdain, announced that he would refuse even to decline such
a commission. He had come to the coast with no intention whatever of remaining but now that he was here he might as well
stay. It was about all that he could do, under the circumstances,
for he would never accept a second lieutenancy and the fact
that he had even been tendered such a lowly commission made
argument or expostulation unthinkable.

The officers at the post suggested that Bierce try to obtain
a government position. This suggestion was agreeable, particularly as he had been a treasury agent for some months. He
applied to the Hon. D. H. Cheesman, head of the United States
Sub-Treasury, for a position and soon went to work as a night-
watchman. It has been stated so many times that computation
would be difficult, that Bierce was an employee of the Mint in
San Francisco. But the positive recollections of perhaps the only
two men who knew him at that time, and who are still alive,
Emory M. Long and Elisha Brooks, are to the effect that he
worked in the Sub-Treasury. This department was connected,
of course, with the Mint but was regarded as separate and distinct, at least by the employees of the two institutions. During
these days Bierce roomed with Elisha Brooks, who also worked
in the Sub-Treasury, although he was later transferred to the
Mint. His fellow employees were impressed with Bierce's fine
military carriage, his dignified manner and his unbending pride.
Mr. Brooks had also been in the war, and the two of them
spent long hours thrashing out old battles. One trait that Bierce
possessed which they all disliked, since to them it was inexplicable, was his irreverence. The man was frostily ironic; he would
not tolerate piety and found nothing too sacred for satire. To
quote from a recent letter of Mr. Brooks: "Bierce was a very
genial and pleasant man to associate with if you could tolerate
his denunciation of all religions and his habit of using the most
offensive language in speaking of matters that people usually
regard as sacred. He would never allow you to differ from him
in his views of religious or sacred matters. Otherwise people
liked him very much."

Not long after Bierce began to work for the government,
he announced to Mr. Long that he intended to become a writer.
He made this statement with his usual assurance. His room was
soon piled with books from the library; the "heaviest" books,

according to Mr. Long. He cannot recall the titles but he does
remember that Bierce read long passages from Gibbon with
marked approval. He would permit, so his roommates say, no
word to go unnoted; he loved precision and definition became
a mania. He read avidly and with great determination. His style
was as yet but a "diamond in the rough," but he was beginning
to polish it into form. His first compositions were atheistic
tracts. The employees of the Mint had heard of this fellow in
the Sub-Treasury who debated about God. Being more reverent
than Bierce but no less disputatious, they issued a challenge for
an exchange of letters on the subject of atheism. Bierce
defended his position with great vigor. The employees of both
institutions read the letters aloud and were delighted with the
verbal blows that were meted out. One thing they all remembered, however: a cold, sardonic, implacable element about
Bierce. It rather startled them. It was not sophomoric irreverence: it was more a passionate protest against ignorance and
piety. Death had marked him at Kenesaw Mountain and had
left a question in his mind about which he was to puzzle all his
life. Just at this time, he expressed himself by mocking idols.
But the impetus for his iconoclasm was the thought that people
died; always death and death's hand even in the sunlight of
youth.

These fellow employees would have quickly made a devil
of Bierce had it not been for his personal charm. They liked
him. He drew amusing pictures and cartoons for them, which
were posted about the Sub-Treasury and the Mint. They roared
with laughter at the sharp, pointed wit that animated these
sketches. But, strangely enough, they knew and respected
Bierce's desire that his drawings should not be shown about.
The sketches were just for their amusement. He seemed apologetic and diffident. Once, however, a political campaign was
raging in the city. Every one was talking about the merits and
demerits of the candidates. Bierce wearied of the balderdash and
drew a series of cartoons which were posted about the offices.
These pictures are remembered with glee by his friends. They
satirized and gibed at politics in general, ridiculed both candidates, and reduced the entire campaign to the elements of farce.
An ambitious co-employee stole these drawings from the walls
and divided them into two sets, one of which he sold to each of

the respective political parties. The next morning the streets of San Francisco were placarded with these amazing cartoons. Bierce was full of white fury. Who had done this? But the silence was profound. He stormed and raged and cursed, but no confessions were forthcoming. A few days later the culprit went to Bierce and told the story, but he had with him some $800 in cash. A division was made and Bierce felt somewhat mollified. But he ceased drawing pictures.

Bierce was never under any illusions as to the state of his cultural development at the time he arrived in San Francisco. "I came to California in 1866 with a fair knowledge of political economy, and a cast-iron conviction about everything, from the self-evident to the unknowable, both inclusive." * Although he was studying hard, his time was not altogether given over to the reading of Gibbon. He enjoyed the life of the town and no interesting incidents escaped his attention. He was getting the feel of the city; becoming acquainted with its scandals, political and otherwise, and becoming familiar with its chief characters. The very rowdiness of the place seems to have had an attraction for him. Soon after his arrival, he witnessed the hanging of one Juan Salazar in the streets of the town. He told the story in later years and closed the incident with these words: "The sheriff performed his peculiar duties with a skill and dignity that made one rather covet the distinction of being hanged by him. Salazar assisted with intelligent composure, and the spectators, who had repented of his crime, endured his death with Christian fortitude and resignation." *

*   *   *

Bierce did not take his duties at the Sub-Treasury office too seriously and devoted all his spare time to writing. He attempted to write ironic pieces much in the manner of his early drawings. He would select some local happening, write of it in an elaborately ornate manner, and then puncture the bubble of his own rhetoric. This was a favorite trick of the early humorists and it was humor that most interested the early San Franciscans. One could not write critical essays or philosophic tracts or rondels for the amusement of gamblers, miners, prostitutes and ladies of fashion. They wanted something amusing and the

* *The Argonaut*, March 9, 1878.

broader the humor the better. It must not only provoke a smile: it must drum the risibilities of the callous until they burst into guffaws. Bierce began by doing a few sketches in the wildly humorous manner of the times. He had some predecessors in the field, and he did not hesitate to follow their technique. He began to modify it to suit his own needs later, but his first work clearly belonged to the school of Dan DeQuille and Mark Twain. A most interesting chapter in California letters was just coming to a close when Bierce arrived in San Francisco.

The chapter had opened with the publication, in 1852, of the first issue of *The Golden Era* by J. MacDonough Foard and Rollin M. Daggett. The journalists of that day—bombastic old Stephen Massett, young Bret Harte, the romantic Joe Goodman, moody Prentice Mulford, James Bowman, Mark Twain and Dan DeQuille—were a great lot. They developed a typically Western manner of writing, aptly characterized by Idwal Jones as "whimsical and bombastic." The style that came into vogue with them was a child of the marriage of the wildly humorous manner of Mark Twain—the literary equivalent of a barroom story—with the plaintive and sentimental whimsicality of Bret Harte—an etherealized banjo tune. It is perhaps true, as Mr. Jones suggests, that the style dated back to pre-Civil War days. It was in this tradition that Bierce was schooled. He came upon the scene in the sixties when times had somewhat changed; but, along with Charles Warren Stoddard, he contributed sketches to the *Alta California,* and came to know Bret Harte, secretary of the Mint. Up in Portland one C. W. Miller (Joaquin Miller) published his first volume of verse in 1868, "Specimen." But, although Bierce did adopt something of the riotous, Western manner of Twain, it was tempered with some very scholarly instruction that he received about this time from James Watkins. The result was that Bierce soon abandoned his early models and became a close student of the classics. In later years Bierce remarked that he had read Mark Twain "to sharpen lethiferous wit against bovine humor" and the comparison is most apt.

Prior to the work that he did for the *Alta California,* Bierce had sent some sketches to "The San Francisco *News-Letter* and California *Advertiser,"* which were accepted. This interesting publication was founded by F. A. Marriott on July

20, 1858. Marriott was a London journalist, who at one time had edited the London *Illustrated News,* and later the *Morning Chronicle* and *Chat.* These various publications had all failed and Marriott had come to California to start over again. *The News-Letter* was modeled after the London weeklies of the day and was a a rather sprightly journal. Soon after Bierce's first sketches were accepted, he received a neatly written, finely phrased note from James Watkins, the managing editor of *The News-Letter,* asking him to call at the office. Bierce lost no time in accepting the invitation, and met a most charming gentleman. Watkins was a strange, whimsical, scholarly fellow, who had been a journalist in London and New York. His style, rather suggestive of Stevenson's, was delightful. He was, according to Bierce, "one of the greatest writers of English that ever lived," * and while the statement is hyperbolic it does suggest something of the real value of Watkins' style. Watkins was a singularly sweet-natured and lovable character, and he wrote a style that, for the period, was indeed remarkable. It had rhythm, variation and was full of charming cadence. Doomed to the life of an unsuccessful journalist, poor Watkins went from paper to paper, writing blurbs for poultry farmers and irrigation projects on the side, in order to earn a livelihood. Years later he worked on the New York *Sun.*

Bierce and Watkins became the best of friends and, strangely enough for Bierce, the friendship continued. Watkins instructed his young protégé with kindness, intelligence and insight. He was a student of Shakespeare and, judging from the copy of "Othello" which he presented to Bierce, he devoted some time to pointing out the values of dramatic blank verse to his young friend. Then, too, he called Bierce's attention to Swift, and Voltaire, and advised him to read over the material that William Thackeray had written for *Punch,* that he might clothe his wit in the silk of a charming style. Watkins' influence on Bierce cannot be overestimated. He pointed out the vulgar and called attention to the best in style with unimpeachable taste. He was, without doubt, the most cultured and intelligent associate that Bierce knew during this period. And it was a crucial time in Bierce's life. Watkins was a rare spirit and he seemed to understand Bierce better than any one else ever did.

* *The Examiner* (San Francisco), January 22, 1893.

Surely Bierce never gave to another the respect and admiration that he always accorded Watkins. They spent many delightful hours together in these first years, and the friendship was never broken.

Many of Watkins' early letters are full of shrewd comment and advice. In one letter, written in 1874, he mentioned La Rochefoucauld, Murger and Balzac, whose works he had praised to Bierce, and then added this comment: "Your method of language is that of these Frenchmen; your method of thought, meanwhile, is essentially different from theirs: it is the real English (or American) thought, and you give us the net result of its processes phrased with the Frenchman's wit and point and epigram."

At the time that Bierce began to write for *The News-Letter* it contained, as a regular feature, a page called "The Town Crier." Bierce did not start this page, which was as old as the magazine itself, but he did take it over, when, in December of 1868, Watkins resigned as editor and induced Marriott to give the post to Bierce. Bierce was editor from that date until March 9th, 1872. In addition to this work, he also wrote for the *Alta California,* along with his friend, Charles Warren Stoddard. He had given up his post in the Sub-Treasury when he became editor of *The News-Letter.*

With Stoddard and "Jimmy" Bowman, and the other young journalists of the time, Bierce kept San Francisco highly entertained. These fellows engaged in some amusing exploits. One night after they had passed beyond the merely facetious state of inebriation, and when their voices were shouting valiantly to be heard above the din and blare of a New Year's Eve celebration, it was proposed that they strike Christianity a fatal blow. They did not propose to go about this work in the methodical manner of Martin Luther, but with anarchistic means. There was a great wooden cross that stood upon a hillside in the region of Golden Gate Park and it had often annoyed them with its attestation of piety. There they journeyed after midnight with ropes and fagots. They roped the cross and tugged and pulled in a vain effort to tear it down. But the cross was triumphant. They then concluded that if they tied the rope about their bodies, the trick could be turned. But their success was no greater. By this time these "eminent tankard" men were exhausted and, in their struggles around the cross, became entangled in the rope and fell down bound to the cross in a manner that would have inspired the faithful to draw an obvious but ironic moral. This story was first related in the chapter on Ambrose Bierce in Paul Jordan-Smith's "On Strange Altars," but its truth has been vouched for to me by a distinguished San Francisco editor whose name would give immediate credence to the story, but unfortunately he was one of the young men at the foot of the cross, and his identity must remain a secret.

In order to appreciate the fame which Bierce soon attained with his "Town Crier" copy, one must keep constantly in mind the significance of "Western humor." The book stacks of London were flooded with wild, irresponsible stories in booklet form about the gold mines of California. The West, particularly California, soon became a fantastic place in the eyes of every Englishman. He was in a mood to believe anything that he heard about the country and its inhabitants. So that the "wild" and "ferocious" satire of Bierce, along with the broad, rough, fun of Twain, was accepted abroad with enthusiam. It will be remembered, too, that Joaquin Miller first attained fame and recognition in England, for none of his countrymen would take the old braggart seriously until England had pronounced him a great poet. Western humor, with its coupling of exaggeration and excessive understatement, found a large audience in England. The copy had great novelty about it then, and it is not surprising to find that Bierce's paragraphs, unreadable as they are to-day, were quoted in the Glasgow and London and New York papers. As a writer once put it in the New York *Arcadian:* "In 1867 or 1868, I forget which, *The News-Letter* in San Francisco contained every now and then queer, irregular paragraphs, each pungent and striking and all pervaded by a *new and puzzling* flavor that was a combination of eccentric wit and utterly unconventional form. All that could be ascertained of their authorship was that a clerk in the San Francisco Mint was the author and that he 'threw them off—just for the fun of it.' "

A few further quotations will suffice to show that Bierce was really attaining a considerable fame with his "Town Crier" work and that it was being appreciated for its true worth. The uncertainty about Bierce, the misunderstanding that has only increased with the years, was largely due to this early interruption in his literary career. The New York *Nation* wrote of his work: "One main quality of the humorist—a Rabelaisian audacity which stands abashed at but very few things indeed—the 'Town Crier' possesses in fullness; if he is not the most impudent and most irreverential person on the Pacific Coast, then he must have the steady assistance of his most admired friends, for a newspaper page that exhibits less respect for constituted authority of whatever kind than his page parades is not printed in English." And *Every Saturday,* published in New York, contained this comment: "It is possible that some of our readers are not familiar with this candid voice of the Pacific Coast, though his fame has reached England, where his homicidal paragraphs are quoted by such journals as the *Saturday Review* and the *Spectator.*" But, just at the height of this early fame, Bierce left for England, and during his absence was forgotten.

As editor of *The News-Letter,* Bierce came in contact with many of the early journalists and writers on the coast. Foremost amongst these were, of course, Mark Twain and Bret Harte, neither of whom had as yet attained to any great national fame. Bierce was fond of telling about the first time he ever saw Mark Twain. Bierce was working one afternoon, in the offices of *The News-Letter,* when a tall, lanky fellow, who talked with a drawl, came into the room. He stood, bare-headed, in the middle of the room and looked slowly and deliberately all around the barren walls, allowing his eyes to finally come to rest on the youthful editor at the desk. "Young man," the voice drawled, "this room is so nude I should think you and the owner would be ashamed of yourselves." Bierce made some comment and kept on working. The man with the drawl spoke again: "Young man, where is the owner?" Bierce replied that Marriott was somewhere about town and would return soon.

"Young man," Twain said, looking intently at Bierce, "are you sure he is not in that next room drunk?"

Bierce was still mystified, but explained that Marriott was actually away and asked Twain what he wanted. Twain explained that he had come in to repay a loan, and Bierce then suggested that Twain pay the money to him.

"Young man," the voice drawled again, and the man fixed Bierce intently with his eyes, his whole expression assuming a grave and serious mien, "look me in the eyes and speak as though you were talking to your God: if I gave you that money are you sure your employer would ever see it?"

In those days Bierce had, I think, a high regard for Twain, whom he later came to know well in London. He had occasion to say of Twain in later years that he had "suffused our country with a peculiar glory by never trying to write a line of poetry." What he thought of Twain's work at this early time is not known, although in later years he was careful to admonish George Sterling to re-read "Huckleberry Finn" and said: "See if you don't find more there than mere funning." He was, however, disgusted when Twain married a rich woman and wrote rather sharply of the matter in *The News-Letter*. In his "Town Crier" page of February 19th, 1870, we find this: "Mark Twain, who, whenever he has been long enough sober to permit an estimate, has been uniformly found to bear a spotless character, has got married. It was not the act of a desperate man—it was not committed while laboring under temporary insanity; his insanity is not of that type, nor does he ever labor—it was the cool, methodical, cumulative, culmination of human nature working in the heart of an orphan hankering for some one with a fortune to love—some one with a bank account to caress. For years he has felt this matrimony coming on. Ever since he left California there has been an undertone of despair running through all his letters like the subdued wail of a pig in a washtub." The sentiment was rather harsh, considering the fact that Bierce was himself soon to marry and to marry, also, a rich man's daughter. Twain never mentioned Bierce except to refer to him in a casual way in his "Autobiography," and his collection of "Humor Stories," and in both cases Twain's references were erroneous. He says in the "Autobiography" that Ralph Keeler, Bret Harte, Charles Warren Stoddard, Prentice Mulford, and Bierce, all contributed to Joe Lawrence's literary magazine *The Golden Era*. This is, in all probability, an error as far as Bierce's name is concerned. In his "Dictionary of Humor" he refers to Bierce as the author of "Bierciana," a collection of wit published in England. In this he was in error also. Later in London, as will appear in a subsequent chapter, Bierce and Twain met often and became quite good friends.

Bierce's relations with Bret Harte are better known. In

The Examiner, March 3, 1889, Bierce said that Harte never thought much of his celebrated "The Heathen Chinee," and that, in fact, Harte offered the manuscript to Bierce for publication in *The News-Letter,* saying he had written it to fill a place in *The Overland Monthly,* but thought it too trivial. Bierce wanted it for *The News-Letter,* but had the unprofessional candor to tell Harte that it really belonged in the *Overland,* and there Harte published it, although reluctantly. Upon its publication, of course, it made the name and fame of Brete Harte.*

The relations of the men were strained, after Harte became a national figure and went east. There was much dissent on the part of his friends, but there seems to have been a general and abiding dissatisfaction with Harte's attitude, which had apparently changed with success. This did not, however, change Bierce's admiration for his style. He would occasionally damn him, in later years, for a careless circumlocution, but he would usually end his remarks with some such statement as this: "The flight of his genius is always in one direction, but it beats the air with as strong a wing as when it first sprang away." He was one of the first to praise Harte's "incomparable humor."

He also had some friendly relations with Harte as contributor and editor, for Bierce wrote the "Grizzly Papers," signed "Ursus," that appeared in *The Overland Monthly,* in Number 1 issue of that periodical in January of 1871, and that followed for the next three issues, down to April of 1871, by which time Bierce had left San Francisco for England. Some of the views expressed in these early papers are interesting, for most of the work that Bierce was doing for *The News-Letter* at this time was nonsensical "funning" that is negligible to-day. In fact, in the issue of February, 1871, we find Bierce setting forth, tentatively, his creed and ambition as a writer which he was to follow so steadfastly in the years to come, in these words: "If any man of true wit shall seriously, sharply and pointedly assail folly, cant, hypocrisy, and villainy in the persons of their representatives, being not too particular in the suppression of names, he shall win for himself a great applause from those who will look coldly on while he runs a tilt against

* "Life of Bret Harte," by Henry Childs Merwin.

a possibly foolish, but certainly insignificant habit of thought
or expression, or impales the inoffensive moon."

As I have said, his *News-Letter* work was negligible,
although it did give him an opportunity to try his wit on the
enemies of the paper and to keep a lively interest centered on
his column of abuse. Occasionally wearying of restraint, he
would have at some local statesmen with a bludgeon. He wrote
of one forgotten unworthy: "Of all the donkeys in our State
Legislature, and the number is limited only by the State Constitution, Mr. Henry of Sonoma can bray the loudest, longest
and with the most elaborate monotony." Once an antagonist
wrote some witty verses aimed at "B*****," which might have
meant Bierce, Bowman, or Barnes. Bierce, not to be outdone,
replied:

> "Young man, when next you wag your pen,
> Discretion should assist it;
> When next you use uncertain words,
> Your B shall stand for Biscuit;
> When next you have an asterisk,
> Think twice before you risk it."

It was after Bierce became editor of *The News-Letter* that
he first met Mary Ellen Day, or "Mollie Day," as she was
known. Mollie Day was the only daughter of Captain Holland
Hines Day, a Forty-Niner, who had crossed the plains from
Galena, Illinois, where Mollie was born. He won his title of
"Captain" as an Indian fighter in the Middle West prior to leaving for California. His brother, James L. Day, was a prominent
mining man in the West, having discovered the "Emma" mine.
He was a millionaire and the famous "James L. Day" steamship was named after him. Captain Day had mined in Trinity
and Placer counties until the discovery of gold in Nevada. He
opened the Savage Mine and was later superintendent of the
Ophir, one of the famous Western mines, and of the Central.
He later became interested in mining properties in Utah,
particularly one mine "The Tintic," and was so highly
regarded in Salt Lake that his name was once proposed for the
office of United States Senator. He was a fine, kindly old gentleman. Mr. Thomas Beer would, however, have called his wife
a "Titaness." She was full of pretense and determination, and

was quite a figure in early San Francisco society. The romance of their only daughter with a nondescript journalist, of whom no one knew anything and none dared ask for information, was not met at first with warm approval. When it became apparent, however, that Mollie was determined to marry "The Town Crier," they offered no opposition to the match.

Mollie Day was a very beautiful girl. She had wit and verve and excellent taste. She played the piano and sang and was excessively romantic. Along with her friend, Miss Riemer, she was one of the most popular girls in San Francisco society of the times. Mollie lived for years in the handsome residence of the Days' on Vallejo Street, but she had spent a great deal of time in Nevada, visiting her uncle and father, and also her friend Fanny Fee at Virginia City. There, too, she came to know the Sam Davis family. Disappointing as the fact will be to those writers who have always referred to her as a "lovely Irish girl," Mollie Day was, on both sides of her family, of Dutch blood. The Days had once lived in New York and came to Illinois from that state. When Bierce first met her, she was an extremely sentimental young lady, as is shown by her letters, and was done up, so to speak, in furbelows and ribbons. A note that she once wrote her mother, accompanying some presents for the latter's birthday, is indicative of her nature: "Darling Mother, this is your birthday, will you accept of these simple presents that I now offer you, with the best love of your daughter, and always think of me as, your loving child, Mollie Day."

Bierce had been stricken with recurrent attacks of asthma soon after he arrived in San Francisco, and had been forced to seek relief in San Rafael, across the bay, in Marin County. It was quite a popular summer resort in those days, and the Days spent much time there. It was thus that Bierce met his future wife. They had a group of friends that went on boating and picnicking expeditions, among whom were Ina Coolbrith and Charles Warren Stoddard. The group was frequently invited to Miss Day's home. Once Stoddard failed to appear to keep an appointment and Bierce wrote him: "I had arranged a nice card party with the ladies and you don't know how much beauty and youth, and virtue, and similar stuff you missed by not remaining another night." * The letter is postmarked from San Rafael

* Collection of Bierce letters in Huntington Library.

and refers to "Miss Day." The Major, after he became editor
of *The News-Letter*, began to be quite well known. He was one
of the organizers of the Lotus Club, the first yachting club to
be formed on the coast, and he used to take Mollie Day for
boat rides around the bay in the yacht of Capt. Moody. At the
time the club was organized there were no by-laws. Later, when
asked to sign the by-laws, Bierce refused because he noticed
that they contained a clause against the use of intoxicating
liquors while on the seas! When they were not picnicking
in Marin County, or boating, they attended such dazzling
affairs (and amusing) as the Sharon Reception and the Calico
Ball. These gorgeous social gatherings impressed San Francisco
as being easily the equivalent to court life on the continent.
Then, too, there were expeditions to Woodward's Gardens to
gaze at sea shells!

It was not long until their engagement was announced and
on December 26th, 1871, the following notice appeared in the
Daily Evening Bulletin: "In this city, married, December 25th,
by Rev. Horatio Stebbins, Ambrose G. Bierce and Mary E.
Day." Bierce had unmercifully ragged this same Horatio Stebbins in *The News-Letter*, and was often to satirize him in the
future. In fact, he once suggested to Rabbi Nieto that he should
have dedicated "Black Beetles in Amber" to Horatio Stebbins
because he had performed the marriage ceremony. But this was
only in later years, after their separation; it was then, too, that
he wrote the lines:

> "They stood before the altar and supplied
> The fire themselves in which their fat was fried.
> In vain the sacrifice!—no god will claim
> An offering burnt with an unholy flame."

A later issue of the *Evening Bulletin* announced that the marriage ceremony was performed at the home of the bride's
father and mother, and that "all of San Francisco attended,"
which probably meant that several friends were present. On
December 30th, 1871, a news story appeared in *The News-
Letter* which purported to be a resolution of a Woman's Suffrage Association announcing their glee over the marriage of
the Town Crier who had always reviled their sex.

The young couple did not leave immediately for England

on their honeymoon, but took up a residence in San Rafael. There is in existence a letter from Bierce to Stoddard under date of January 5th, 1872, from San Rafael, acknowledging in a friendly way Stoddard's felicitations and closing with the statement: "We are living cosily. My regards to Ina," meaning, of course, Ina Coolbrith. They lived in San Rafael until their departure for England in the spring. But on March 9th, 1872, Bierce bid farewell to the readers of the Town Crier page and made this valedictory:

> The present writer's connection with this paper ceases for at least a brief season, with this issue, be the same longer or shorter. Since December, 1868, he has, with one or two weeks' intermission, conducted this page. The Town Crier does not seek a wider field for his talents. The only talents that he has are a knack at hating hypocrisy, cant, and all sham, and a trick of expressing his hatred. What wider field than San Francisco does God's green earth present? Gentlemen,—Ah! and you, too, darlings, we came near overlooking you—a large, comprehensive and warm farewell! Be as decent as you can. Don't believe without evidence. Treat things divine with marked respect— don't have anything to do with them. Do not trust humanity without collateral security; it will play you some scurvy trick. Remember that it hurts no one to be treated as an enemy entitled to respect until he shall prove himself a friend worthy of affection. Cultivate a taste for distasteful truths. And, finally, most important of all, endeavor to see things as they are, not as they ought to be. Then shall the Town Crier not have cried in vain; and if ever again he shall resume the whip of the satirist, it shall fall upon your shoulders as a snowflake settles against the rocky side of Mt. Shasta."

Some of the eastern papers read that The Town Crier was to leave *The News-Letter* and commented on the fact. *The Critic* contained these lines:

> "Noos Lettah, so fierce
> Has lost his Bierce,
> And doesn't know where to find him;
> Left all alone
> He must weep and groan
> And tuck in his tail behind him."

It was not long after the marriage that "Sandy" Bowers, an old friend of Captain Day, gave a reception for the young couple. "Sandy" had been just a common Irish day laborer until he made a fortune in mining. The reception was one of the most unique events in early San Francisco's social life. The Bowers had pieces of Italian statuary through the house and on the figures of some of the models, Mrs. Bowers, with a sense of modesty that has perhaps never been paralleled, had draped pink cloth to hide any suggestion of the improper. In the library old "Sandy" had a picture or bust of the various authors over each section so that he might know whose books he was pointing at since he could not read the titles.

It was about this time that Bierce and his bride left for England on a honeymoon, as their passport was issued on April 30th, 1872. The yellowing document gives an interesting picture of Bierce, rather suggestive of the description of General L. V. Bierce: "Age 30; five feet four; forehead, medium; eyes, grey; nose, large; mouth, medium; skin, medium; hair, light; complexion, florid." The trip was financed by Captain Day and was in the nature of a wedding present. Mr. Marriott of *The News-Letter* fortified Bierce with letters of introduction to various Fleet Street luminaries. And thus, with money and the open sesame to his chosen field of journalism, Bierce left for England. It is undeniable that Bierce personally wanted to go to London. His acquaintance with Marriott and Watkins had fired his ambition to become a "London journalist": all others were as trash; even New York was provincial. He had received some letters from England about his Town Crier work and it had been frequently quoted in the English press, so that he thought he would have no difficulty in securing a place on the staff of some periodical.

These first six years in San Francisco had been interesting and eventful. During this period he had forever abandoned the thought of a career in the regular army and had become, after an interval in the Sub-Treasury, a professional journalist. Then, too, he had married perhaps the most beautiful girl in San Francisco and one of the wealthiest. The young couple had been sent on their way with much ringing of bells, good wishes and prediction of happiness. Along with this good fortune, was a trip to London, London! Bierce's *ultima thule*, the symbol of earthly elegance and perfection.

As they traveled eastward along the line of the railroad that had been completed in 1869, Bierce must have thought that he had come miles in the journey of life since he had ridden westward over these very plains. Indiana was just a memory; the war a vivid recollection temporarily hidden.

From his farewell note in *The News-Letter* it is apparent that Bierce did not intend to return to San Francisco. He had finished with the West and was now going to carve a niche in Westminster Abbey. Farewell, San Francisco! "The marble dream by the Ægean Sea," as his young friend Ina Coolbrith had sung of it. The first great chapter in his life was rounded out: he was on the threshold of fulfillment. And what of Mollie Bierce? Doubtless she was as certain of their success as her handsome young husband. Certainly she could not have been happier. She had a picture taken leaning over the railing of an ocean liner, a diminutive muff raised in a gesture of farewell, her face all laughter and joy. At their age, with money, youth and beauty, happiness was inevitable. Life was an unopened wine bottle.

CHAPTER VI

LONDON

THE Bierces arrived in Liverpool and went directly to London. They found Liverpool "a wildly uninteresting commercial soil" but London was "Paradise" and they were possessed of a "haunting fever of impatience to visit Stratford-on-Avon." They stayed, however, in London for some time. It is apparent from Bierce's papers that he must have had some correspondence with John Camden Hotten, the publisher, before leaving America. Hotten published Mark Twain and Artemus Ward, and doubtless desired to add the Town Crier to his list of Western Humorists. It has been rumored that Bierce was induced to go to London because of a correspondence with Leigh Hunt. This is erroneous, as Hunt died in 1859; nor are there any letters from Tom Hood addressed to Bierce in America. It would seem that Hotten was perhaps the first person to call on Bierce after his arrival in England, for there is in existence a note from Hotten, dated July 29th, 1872, asking for an appointment. Publisher and author seem to have come to terms quickly for, in September, Hotten was writing Bierce that the "proofs" were ready, and he was doubtless referring to "Nuggets & Dust," which was merely a compilation of some of the paragraphs from the Town Crier's page with a few new pieces. It appeared in 1872.

It was through Hotten that Bierce met many of the men with whom he was to be associated during his residence in England. Foremost among these was, of course, Tom Hood, the younger. Hood was editor of *Fun* at the time, and asked Bierce to send in some contributions. They were quickly accepted and

Bierce was asked to become a regular contributor. His first
journalistic work in London was done for *Fun*, a series of
humorous sketches—"Fables of Zambri the Parsee," "translated
by Dod Grile," which was the pen name he used in England.
The first series of these sketches ran from July, 1872, until
March, 1873, and were published in that year, first, by the *Fun*
office in a paper edition, and later in the same year in regular
book form. After his work on *Fun* became known, Bierce was
asked to write for several other publications, and soon became
associated with James Mortimer, editor of *Figaro*. Bierce wrote
regularly for *Figaro* a column called "The Passing Showman."
It is interesting to note that some issues of the magazine are
adorned with the vignette of a handsome woman by Faustin,
who was none other than Mollie Day Bierce. The same vignette
was once reproduced in *Fun*. It has been said that Bierce wrote
for *The Bat* and *The Cuckoo*, two publications edited by one
"Jimmy" Davis, but I have been unable to find verification for
the statement. But his early fame was won with his contributions to *Fun*. His alleged acquaintance with Mr. Gladstone
would seem to be mythical. Gladstone in later years gave an
interview to the press, in the course of which he said that he
had just purchased from H. H. Harley, 21 Park Street, Camden
Town, a copy of "The Fiend's Delight," and that he remembered
reading the book when it first appeared. The story was current
in many papers, and Robert Barr of *The Idler* sent Bierce a
news clipping, and a correspondence with Gladstone resulted.
But that he knew Gladstone in England does not seem likely.
It is difficult to state accurately just how much work Bierce did
for *Fun* during his residence in England. The few things that
were republished can be easily identified in the files of the
magazine, as, for example, the Zambri Fables, which were published in "Cobwebs From an Empty Skull," published in 1874.
But he wrote much besides these fables, as is shown by a letter
from Henry Sampson, in the course of which Sampson said:
"Before you came Tom used to do nine columns, and I one. He
used then to average seven columns a week, the paper holds
ten or less, and the other three were divided between you
and me."

Bierce did not stay long in London. After having interviewed Hotten, arranged for his book and started his work for

Fun, he left for a visit to Stratford-on-Avon with his wife. He was so enthusiastic about the trip that he wrote a long three-column account of the visit for the *California Alta,* under date of October 3, 1872, which appeared in the form of a letter to the editor. Parts of this letter were later reprinted in "Nuggets & Dust," but several significant passages were omitted. Bierce was utterly delighted with Stratford-on-Avon. At last he was before the great literary shrine of the period. He entered the following lines of verse in the Visitors' Book:

> It nothing boots exchanging "saws"
>   With canting dunces who proclaim
> The lightness of the world's applause—
>   The worthlessness of human fame.
> Fame valueless? They'll have it so—
>   They still will teach and preach the same—
> Until by chance they undergo
>   The cheating done in Shakespeare's name.
> Perhaps they then will bow them down,
> And own there's profit in renown."

And he closed the letter with this sentence: "I did not visit Charlecot, where Shakespeare stole the deer, nor did I extend my pilgrimage to the crab-tree under which Will and his guzzling companions lay drunk. For me it is sufficient that he *did* steal a deer, and that he *did* get drunk."

Bierce found during his short residence in London that he could not work well in the ctiy, and that his health was seriously affected by the damp climate. Hence, he went to Bristol to live. He wrote to Stoddard, under date of December 29th, 1872, from Bristol: "I am at Bristol because I fear the London fogs and because my boy so far forgot himself as to be born while I was on tour. He swears he won't travel just yet."* This child was named Day, although in later years, out of vanity, he attempted to rechristen himself "Raymond." Bierce was fond of telling a story about the birth of his first child. It seems that Mrs. Bierce had ardently desired a daughter, and that she was acutely disappointed when the doctor, a bluff, red-cheeked old

* Throughout this chapter all the quotations from letters to Stoddard are taken from the collection in the Huntington Library at San Marino, California.

fellow, announced that her child was a boy. To comfort her, the Doctor said: "Well, Madam, at his age it really doesn't make much difference." Day was a remarkably beautiful child, destined to a short but dramatic life. Always the favorite of both parents, richly endowed with good looks and intelligence, he grew into a handsome, arrogant youth.

While residing at Bristol, Bierce seems to have had no fixed plans. His residence there was born of three necessities: work, his health, and the birth of his son. He wrote Stoddard that he expected to remain in Bristol for only two months and then he would return to London. He did return to London in January of 1873, but he found it difficult to work there, as his accursed asthma troubled him no end, so that in March he had to move to Bath. He wrote Stoddard, from No. 6 Sydney Building, Bath, on March 16th, 1873: "I am doing just work enough over here to pay my current expenses at this somewhat expensive place. It does not require much of my time either. Have not attempted to get any permanent work, and don't suppose I shall, as my object in coming was to loaf and see something of the country—as Walt Whitman expressed it, when the paralysis had, as yet, invaded only his brain, 'to loaf and invite my soul.'" Of course there was a touch of bravura about this letter, as the father-in-law had sponsored the trip, and what Bierce earned as a journalist was a mere pittance. The passage does show, however, what his object was in going to England.

The western journalist was, during this period, something of a *rara avis* in London life. Francis Grierson, in his unpublished memoirs, noticed that London society simply doted on these queer and eccentric fellows. It puzzled him, for, having been born in the Lincoln country, he knew that Joaquin Miller was something of a faker. People had heard fascinating stories about life in far-away California, and it was but natural that they were interested in writers who made a living by telling gorgeous lies about the region. They were never disappointed in these characters, for surely two more interesting and amusing fellows than Mark Twain and Joaquin Miller never lived. Miller was, however, about the only writer of the group who was the complete embodiment of what Europe imagined was a western journalist. He possessed a movie actor's vanity and was wit enough to be vastly amused at the amazement he created. In any

event, Twain, Miller and Bierce formed a great trio and naturally they were well received. The English liked Twain's gorgeous stories and his inimitable, drawling manner of telling
them; they were fascinated by Miller's hip boots, red belt,
flowing locks, and wild west mannerisms; they were puzzled,
but amused by Bierce's studied indifference and his cold, sarcastic turn of mind.

The three were once guests at the famous White Friars'
Club in the winter of 1873. Bierce later, along with Twain,
Miller and Col. Dudley Waring, became an honorary member
of the club. The dinner in question was, however, really in
honor of Bierce, for in the South London *Express* the next
morning this notice appeared: "Last night a personage of world-
wide celebrity dined at the White Friars' Club—as honorary
guest. I refer to the Town Crier, one of the most original and
daring humorists this age has produced." Miller came to the
dinner arrayed in his usual western regalia, with a huge knife
in his belt. Twain and Bierce feigned indifference and did not
so much as comment on their compatriot's eccentric appearance,
giving the impression that such unique costuming was quite
common in America. When Miller picked his fish up by the tail
and swallowed it whole, they did not appear to notice his conduct. It was on this occasion, too, that Bierce was called upon to
make a speech. Thinking to have some fun with Twain, he
told the story of Twain's visit to the office of *The News-Letter*.
But Twain never cracked a smile, and merely appeared to be
bored with the story; Bierce said that his expression of sad
despair was perfectly feigned. No one laughed and it left Bierce
quite stranded. The White Friars' Club was located in Mitre
Court, Fleet Street, nearly opposite Fetter Lane, and the regular
meetings were held on Fridays.

It was about this time that Bierce began to be somewhat
annoyed with Joaquin Miller's irresponsible conduct. An incident occurred which brought the matter to a crisis. Olive Harper, after first seeking and being denied an interview with
Bierce, wrote of him in the New York *Evening Graphic,* that
he had once worked in a brickyard, but now that he had married
a rich woman and gone to live in England he had given himself
airs. Bierce knew immediately that Miller's hand was in this
story. On November 16th, 1873, he wrote a letter, which ap-

peared in several London journals, stating the facts and then quoting the following open letter to Miller:

"Dear Mr. Miller:
"It would be a favor to Mrs. Harper if you would kindly indicate to her, in any way you like, that I hope she will not do me the doubtful honor of calling. Perhaps when she shall have associated long enough with the nobility and tradespeople, her manners will improve, and her conversation acquire a touch of decency; at present she is rather vulgar. I trust this will not offend you; if it does I shall be sorry. Anyhow, it is better you should keep her from calling than to have my servant shut the door in her face."

Of course, Bierce's irritation was caused by Mrs. Harper's taking revenge on him for denying an interview in the manner that she did, but nevertheless he knew that she had gotten her information from Miller. In later years Bierce and Miller tolerated each other in private and admired each other's work in public, but the personal antipathy was quite apparent.

The months at Bath were particularly enjoyable to Bierce. His letters of this period have an unmistakable quality of contentment; they are full of wit, to be sure, but it is never shrill or sharp or bitter. He was entranced with the English countryside, and wrote to Stoddard, who was still in San Francisco: "It is the most charming of all imaginable places. Every street has its history, every foot of the lovely country its tradition. Old Roman, and even Druidic, remains are plenty as green peas. You are aware that Bath was the stamping ground of Pope, Fielding, Smollett, Warburton, Malthus, Beau Nash, Ralph Allen,—who 'did good by stealth and blushed to find it fame'— and a lot of worthies whose haunts I frequent and over whose graves I shed judicious drops and tried to fancy myself like them. I don't succeed."

During the summer of 1873, Mrs. Day came to England from San Francisco to visit her daughter and to see the grandchild. Upon her arrival, the Bierces moved back to London, and took up temporary quarters at 19 Downshire Hill, Hampstead, and it was there that Bierce planned to receive his friend, Charles Warren Stoddard, who by then had sailed for England. Bierce wrote to Stoddard and insisted that he come directly to their home until he was located, and closed the letter with a characteristic touch: "And so God(?) bless you (!) and by-by." To this letter is appended a succinct postscript: "My Mother-in-law is here, wife is well, and baby marvelous."

Just what had been Bierce's reactions to literary London during this first year? The matter is not a subject of speculation, for it is summed up admirably in one of the most remarkable Bierce letters in existence. It is addressed to Stoddard, under date of September 28th, 1873, and posted from the Hampstead residence. In order to get the full purport and meaning of the letter, one must remember the circumstances. Bierce had been in England for over a year as a journalist, and during this time he had seen something of literary London and had come to know its chief personalities. His friend, Charles Stoddard, would have to face the same tests and under the same circumstances that Bierce had previously experienced. Naturally, Bierce would have preferred to advise Stoddard orally, but it so happened that he was leaving England for two months in Paris with his wife, Mrs. Day and the baby. So he wrote the letter, pinned it on the door at the Hampstead residence so that Stoddard might find it when he called and thus be carefully and wisely advised as to how he should conduct himself. With these circumstances in mind, the letter is most illuminating:

"I have told Tom Hood to look after you. Now mark this: Tom is one of the very dearest fellows in the world, and an awful good friend to me. *But* he has the worst lot of associates I ever saw—men who (with one or two noble exceptions, whom you cannot readily pick out) are not worthy to untie his shoe latchet. He will introduce you to them all. Treat them well, of course, but (1) don't gush over them; (2) don't let them gush over you; (3) don't accept invitations from them; (4) don't get drunk with them; (5) don't let them in any way monopolize you; (6) don't let them shine by your reflected light. I have done all these things, and it is not a good plan, 'for at the last it biteth like a serpent and stingeth like an adder.' *I* don't mind biting and stinging, but you would—particularly if done in the dark.

"Remember this: London—literary London—is divided into innumerable cliques which it will require some time to get the run of. Remember, also, that if you fall into the hands of one clique, all the others will give you the cold shoulder. Remember, also, that everybody will profess the most unbounded admiration for you, and not one of them can tell a line you have written. . . . You will, by the way, be under a microscope here; your slightest word and most careless action noted down, and commented on by men who cannot understand how a person of individuality in thought or conduct can be other than a very bad man. Lord! how I have laid myself out inventing preposterous speech and demeanor just to get their silly tongues wagging. It is good fun for me. Walk, therefore, circumspectly, keep your own counsel, don't make speeches at clubs, avoid any appearance of eccentricity, don't admire anything, and don't disparage anything; don't eat mustard on mutton!

"You just 'bet your boots' I know these fellows and their ways. They think they know me, but they don't. I am hand-in-glove with some hundreds of them, and they think they are my intimate friends. If any man says he is, or acts as if he were, avoid him, he is an impostor. This letter is *strictly confidential,* and when I come back I shall ask you to hand it to me."

It has been suggested that Bierce was rather flattered and swept off his feet by the reception given him by these Fleet Street journalists whom the London *Spectator* referred to as "raffish celebrities." That such was not the case is shown by the letter to Stoddard. However much Bierce might have been affected by his first exposure to their flattery, it is apparent that one year's experience with them was enough to open his eyes. As a matter of fact, he loved Tom Hood; was very fond of Henry Sampson, editor of *The Referee,* and co-editor with Bierce of a "Dictionary of Slang"; liked James Mortimer; and was amused by George Augustus Sala, but it cannot be said that he entertained a very high regard for his other associates. He did know, however, quite a number of prominent literary figures. The vignette in "The Fiend's Delight" is said to have been done by W. S. Gilbert. Bierce also knew Barry Sullivan, G. R. Sims, Henry S. Leigh, who wrote some charming songs and died a pauper; Austin Dobson, and quite a host of others, including William Black, the novelist—Capt. Mayne Reid. Bierce denied that he ever knew Clement Scott and once gave him an unmerciful pummeling in "Prattle."

But he did have, however, a real affection for Tom Hood. Of Hood's personal charm, so much has been written that it may be assumed. Naturally Bierce was fond of him. Hood's letters to Bierce, very few in number, are touched with the most delightful wit and grace. After the birth of Day, he wrote Bierce that he was coming down to Bath to see the new "Day-Man who is the real Fiend's Delight." And, again, on New Year's he wrote: "A happy new year to you—and to the dawning Day—I suppose you'll want him made a Knight, your republican tendencies of course being aristocratic as shown by your signature 'Bierce' as our Dukes and Earls write 'Wellington' or 'Derby'—are you sure you are not the real Tichborne?" Throughout their correspondence there is not the suggestion of a quarrel or a misunderstanding: a rare experience with Bierce.

Bierce used to visit Hood in Penge, a suburb of London, beyond the Crystal Palace. "Back of his odd little house was his odd little garden, and here we were accustomed to burn our cigars after which we commonly passed the entire night in a room upstairs, sipping grog, pulling at our pipes, and talking on all manner of things. . . . Tom had in him a vein of what in another I should have called superstition, but it was so elusive in character and whimsical in manifestation that I could never rightly assign it a place, nor determine its metes and bounds. It may have been an undeveloped religion, a philosophical conviction, a sentiment—for ought I know a joke." * During many of the nocturnal visits they talked of ghosts, and one night they made the usual death pact with each other that the one who first should die would attempt to communicate with the other. Bierce left London shortly after this for a trip, and during his absence Hood died (1875). One evening after his return to the city, he was walking to his home in Warwickshire, when he felt the presence of his friend rush past. "I need not attempt to describe my feelings; they were novel and not altogether agreeable. That I had met the spirit of my dead friend; that it had given me recognition, yet not in the old way; that it had then vanished— of these things I had the evidence of my own senses. How strongly this impressed me the beating of my heart attested whenever, for many months afterward, that strange meeting

* *The Argonaut*, April 6, 1878.

came into my memory." He was to make use of this incident
when he wrote "The Damned Thing."

Aside from Hood, Bierce was on more intimate terms with
Henry Sampson than with any of his other associates. They
became the best of friends. Sampson seems to have been of a
somewhat quarrelsome nature, and was constantly talking and
writing about his "enemies" and their "blackguard tactics" in a
most saturnine manner. Along with Bierce, he cherished a particular and special antipathy for Sir Henry Lucy. When Hood
died in 1875, Sampson took over the editorship of *Fun*. Both
Hattie O'Connor, Sampson's only child, and Mrs. Croston (formerly Julia Sampson), knew Bierce well. In fact, they visited
the Bierces in San Francisco on a return trip from Australia
years later. Mrs. Croston's slight memoir of Bierce may be
found in the London *Evening Standard*, September 15th, 1922.

Bierce once related an amusing story about himself. It
seems he was in the bar of the Covent Garden Theater with
Henry Sampson one evening. Sampson had a habit of practical
joking which was well known by all his friends who had been
its victims on numerous occasions. Bierce was aware of this
trait, and, like the other members of their circle of friends, was
constantly on guard. Henry Irving entered the room and saluted them, and was by Sampson introduced to Bierce. "Our
foremost actor," Sampson added by way of showing off his lion.
But, as Bierce said, "I mistook the lion—I thought the remark
was addressed to Mr. Irving, a bit of fun suggested by the
spirit of the place. Still, one does not care to have one's profession misstated. Looking Mr. Irving gravely in the eye, I said:
'Mr. Sampson is facetious.' Irving said nothing, but I soon began to gather from his manner that he did not think Mr. Sampson facetious; and it was not long before I renounced that view
of the matter myself. The silence was shocking, but in the
midst of it, Sampson managed to signify a sense of thirst. We
drank, and at the conclusion of the rite, Mr. Irving said good
evening with a considerable *vraisemblance*. I thought him a good
actor." *

Bierce and his family soon gave up their residence in
London and returned to Bath, where they spent the winter of
1874. During this period, Bierce was still writing for the weekly

* San Francisco *Examiner*, September 3, 1893.

and monthly humorous magazines of London. By this time he
had published three books: "The Fiend's Delight," published by
Chatto & Windus as successors to John Camden Hotten; "Nuggets & Dust"; and "Cobwebs from an Empty Skull." The first
two volumes were negligible and were compiled at the suggestion of John Camden Hotten. In "The Fiend's Delight" is one
section of "Aphorisms," many of which Bierce thought well
enough of to give them a place in Volume XVIII of his "Collected Works." Aside from these few aphorisms, Bierce did not
entertain a very high regard for the work printed in these early
volumes. Referring to "Cobwebs from an Empty Skull," he
said in a letter to Stoddard (December, 1873): "I am pleased
that Mark likes my fables, but your idea that they ought to
create a 'furor'—I think that is the word—amuses me. I don't
create furors. The book in question has never, I believe, been
sent to a single journal for review, is not published in anybody's
list, and is not even advertised—If I had one of Mark's cocktails I would finish this letter; as it is I have not the spirit to get
through it, and if anything else strikes me I'll telegraph." And
in still another letter to Stoddard (January, 1874): "Do you
know I have the supremest contempt for my books,—as books.
As a journalist I believe I am unapprochable in my line; as an
author, a slouch! I should never put anything into covers if I
could afford not to." This is a singularly revealing statement,
not so much because it shows that Bierce had a clear-headed
conception of his faults, (one would expect that of such a man),
but because of his calm assumption of supreme worth in "my
line," i.e. journalism. Bierce knew that as a satirical journalist
he really was "unapprochable." He remained a great satirist all
his life, and it is to be seriously doubted if so immensely effective a journalist, in his own manner, ever wrote in this country.
To some it may only be "journalese," but others will find in
"Prattle" such mordant satire, such utterly annihilating sarcasm
and abuse, as cannot easily be paralleled.

But, regardless of their value, Bierce was too modest in
his letter to Stoddard about the reception of these early books.
As a matter of fact, they were quite well received. Tom Hood
was enthusiastic about them; so was Henry Sampson. Hotten,
who published them, was pleased and asked Bierce for more
copy, suggesting, however, something a "trifle less bloody—

less swinging of the meat axe. I am sure you must have written plenty of delightful conceits not entirely of a gory character." His English associates knew that Bierce was simply amusing himself with these "awful" stories; they were not compelled to convert him into a sadist but were willing to accept his statement, made in "The Fiend's Delight"—(Page 75)—"One of the rarest amusements in life is to go about with an icicle suspended by a string, letting it down the necks of the unwary. The sudden shrug, the quick, frightened shudder, the yelp of apprehension, are sources of pure, because diabolical, delight."

One reviewer in mentioning "Nuggets & Dust" made this comment:

> "If Artemas Ward may be considered the Douglas Jerrold, and Mark Twain the Sydney Smith of America, Dod Grile will rank as their Dean Swift. There is a grimness and force in him which place his humor far above anything of the kind ever attempted. The New York *Nation,* a literary authority of ability, is struck with Dod Grile's wit and delightful badinage, every line of which is written in the most forceful English."

When "The Fiend's Delight" appeared, Bierce reviewed it himself, under a *nom de plume* in *Figaro,* and said that it was: "A piece of exasperating blackguardism, begot of comprehensive ignorance and profound conceit. But it is useless to chide this animal; the wise man has said of the fool that though brayed in a mortar yet his folly will not depart from him. Still, it is a grateful task to bray him, anyhow."

In the spring of 1874 the Bierces moved to 20 South Parade, Leamington, Warwickshire. In a letter to Stoddard dated April 26th, 1874, Bierce said: "You will want to see Kenilworth, Warwick, and Stratford-on-Avon again. You have no notion of the beauty of the country now when it is green." He made innumerable trips through the English countryside and never ceased to praise its beauties. In "Nuggets & Dust," he tells about a visit to Kenilworth Castle one Sunday. On his return he stopped at a little inn on a hillside.

> "As I sat in my little ten-by-twelve parlour, looking upon the gigantic hot joint gracing my table, flanked with a jug of nut-brown ale, and then backward across the remnants of the old priory in the valley, to the solemn Ruin, the westering sun

struggled from behind one of those mountains of tumbled
cloud which I have never seen but in an English sky, and set
the giant pile afire with a great glory. The light burned and
flickered upon the angles like the flame of molten iron; broad
banners of it seemed flung from every summit; it poured in
jagged torrents through the rent sides, and shot in long straight
beams through the narrow fissures, ribboning with gold the
blue-black shadows darkening broadly about its base! Anon
the glow crept athwart my own windows, streamed in, and
gilded the brown joint upon the board with a radiance all its
own."

Stratford-on-Avon and Warwick made similar impressions.
Bierce never wrote in this manner about any other experience.
It was his introduction into an orderly life in which chaos was
but a faint rumble; all the futile landscapes of his youth were
replaced by this loveliness of Old England. Memories of Horse
Cave, Ohio, were crowded out of mind by the glitter and
warmth of the Mitre Tavern. He was happily married; he had
an established reputation as a man of letters; he was the comrade of many distinguished writers. He was tasting the sweets
of life. The disquieting sense of futility which he had experienced soon after the war, was almost forgotten as he gained
confidence in the possibilty of orderliness in life.

Mrs. Day was still living with her daughter at this time.
She had traveled to London to gaze upon one grandchild and
stayed to witness the birth of another, for in May, 1874, the
second son, Leigh, was born at Leamington. Shortly after the
birth of this child, Mrs. Day departed for America. It has been
bruited about that she returned to America with her daughter.
This, of course, is untrue. Bierce never liked his mother-in-law,
but this antipathy had nothing whatever to do with the estrange-
ment with Mrs. Bierce which occurred at a much later date.

The summer that followed on Mrs. Day's return to America, was far from pleasant for Bierce. Much of the worry of the
household fell on him, and he was scarcely the type of man to
be delighted with domestic cares. He wrote to Stoddard from
Leamington (July 4th): "I have had a deal of worry—having
more work than I can do, and Mrs. Bierce having two babies and
nursemaid to look after.—Then, too, I have been, and am, up to
my ears in work, grinding stuff for five publications: one semi-

weekly, two weeklies, one monthly, and one 'occasional'—a pizen thing of which I write every line. If some of these don't die of me I shall surely die of them." The exile was broken by visitors from London and one or two callers from San Francisco, such as Belle Thomas and Prentice Mulford. Belle Thomas visited the Bierces on her way to Paris to study music. She was a great favorite of the Bierces. Mrs. Bierce once remarked that the most delightful evenings in England that she could recall were spent "toasting crumpets with Prentice Mulford." Later Mulford anticipated Dr. Frank Crane with his catchy, optimistic "White Cross Library," but with all the inconsistency of the professional smiler he was found dead one morning in a boat at Sag Harbor. He could smile cheerfully through all life's cruel disappointments, but when "Josie," the inspiration of Miller and Charles Warren Stoddard also, deserted him he found his philosophy of no assistance. Through these occasional visitors Bierce maintained some contact with San Francisco, but he had ceased to correspond with any of his old friends with the exception of James Watkins. Stoddard was, at the time, in Rome, attempting to see "the Holy, if somewhat eccentric, Father," as Bierce phrased it; Miller was gone; Twain was no longer in London. The only California newspapers that he read were *The News-Letter* and the Santa Cruz *Sentinel*. He had definitely abandoned America in his own mind.

One of Bierce's close associates at this time was James Mortimer, editor of *Figaro*. Mortimer had had a varied experience as journalist in England, America and in France, and was typical of the profession at that date; hard-drinking, witty, irresponsible, and lazy. He had perfected the technique of polite blackmail, then so much in vogue among struggling journalists. He had immediately recognized in Bierce a writer with a genius for satirical expression, and had given him all the work he could do. He kept nagging Bierce for copy, writing "Go at it again, try to be exceptionally bitter," or "Be as cynical and disagreeable as you like, which is saying much." He made endless sport of Bierce's enigmatic initials "A. G.," referring to him as "Aaron," "Abner" and whatnot. Along with Sampson, Sir Henry Lucy and others of the time, Mortimer belonged to a class of journalists that disappeared about 1890. Their work is hard to read to-day because the personal allusions have been forgotten, and the innuendoes are no longer comprehensible. They specialized in personal abuse of the most scurrilous variety, and often had to flee across the channel, as Mortimer did more than once, to evade the harsh criminal libel laws of England. Bierce was of a much finer caliber than any of these men, but they did instruct him in the art of verbal fencing.

Mortimer, during the time that he had lived in Paris, had become an intimate of the Emperor and Empress. After they fled to England, he had been able to render them many courtesies and had performed many valuable services. It was but natural that they should consult him when it was announced that Henri Rochefort was coming to England. In order to appreciate fully the significance of what follows, it is necessary to know something about this amazing Rochefort and his relation to the royalty of France.

Henri Rochefort, Victor Henri, Marquis de Rochefort-Lucay was the scion of a very aristocratic family in France. After first failing very ignominiously as a medical student and later as a clerk, he became a revolutionary demagogue of great rhetorical violence. In 1863 he was one of the editors of *Figaro*, and soon afterwards began the first of his mordant attacks on the Napoleonic régime. But these early writings were mild indeed compared with the diatribes he began to publish in 1868 after the more arbitrary restrictions on the press were relaxed in France. It was at this point that Rochefort launched his famous weekly, *La Lanterne*, which immediately upon its publication enjoyed an enormous circulation. In the columns of *La Lanterne*, so-called because, as its editor said, "A lantern may serve both to lighten the day of the honest men and to hang wrongdoers," Rochefort left nothing unsaid about the Emperor or the Empress. He even went to the extreme of denying the legitimacy of the Prince Imperial! This abuse continued for some months, but finally Rochefort was convicted of "disrespect against the government" and fled to Brussels, where he joined Victor Hugo, also in exile, and continued the publication of *La Lanterne* from that retreat.

In 1873 Rochefort was sentenced to the penal colony at New Caledonia, and it was generally held that a good riddance had been made of bad rubbish. The man was really a most remarkable firebrand. His memoirs, "The Adventures of My

Life," in two volumes, published by Edward Arnold in 1897, is a most interesting account of a life devoted to intellectual carnage, riot and excitement. His days seem to have been entirely taken up with duels, quarrels, plots, and scurrilous attacks on people of the highest estate. And, as might be expected of so violent a temperament, his nights were rarely given over to meditation.

Aside from the memoirs, the best account of the man to be found is that by John F. MacDonald, published in the *Contemporary Review*, August, 1913. According to this observer, Rochefort was Baudelaire turned politician. He was known throughout Europe as "Rochefort the Lurid" and "Rochefort the Vicious." Of his personal appearance MacDonald says: "Pale, steely blue eyes lit up cruelly, evilly at times, a face seamed, sallow and horse-like in shape; he had a harsh, guttural voice; and large, yellowish hands with long, pointed finger nails." That Rochefort was capable of pithy utterance when aroused is shown by some of the epithets he hurled. He called M. Jaurés "a decayed turnip"; M. Georges Clemenceau, "a loathsome leper"; M. Briand, "a moulting vulture"; President Loubet, "the foulest of assassins"; and President Fallières, "a fat old satyr." He dallied in the cafés of Paris with a toy lamb on his table, making cruel sport of the people that he met. He was utterly capricious and entirely mad. Purporting to be a liberal, he pursued Captain Dreyfus with relentless vigor and even allied himself with such rank militarists as General Boulanger and Paul Derouledè. For some fifty years he was "a holy terror," as Bierce would say, in French journalism. His papers, notably *Figaro, La Lanterne, L'Intransigeant,* and *Patrie,* were renowned for his vicious, scurrilous, vulgar abuse.

The Empress Eugénie had come to fear Rochefort's diabolic attacks during the days when she was in power in France. It is small wonder, then, that she trembled in exile whenever his name was mentioned. She had fled to England after the collapse of the Empire and settled at Chislehurst. Although England was gracious enough to Marie Eugenie Ignace Augustine De Montijo, it was quite a problem to determine just how royally a nominally republican government should treat a fugitive monarchist. Eugénie had fled from France, however, with most of the loose gold of the realm, and with this in mind

England was amenable to the ever-pleasant conviction that the rich must necessarily be the just.

It was about this time, 1874, that the ubiquitous M. Rochefort escaped from New Caledonia and was, via Australia and the New World, en route for England and Eugénie. Rumors reached the Empress that this inhuman scourge was coming to invade her sanctum for the express purpose of humiliating her, and at this Chislehurst began to erect barricades. Rochefort, on arriving, announced that he would publish *La Lanterne* in London for a time, printing one edition in English and the other in French, the latter edition to be smuggled into France, where Rochefort was still *persona non grata,* and the former to be used in tormenting Eugénie. The prospect of such a state of affairs, particularly at a time when public support was sorely needed, must have worried the Empress exceedingly. She had no way of knowing what Rochefort the Lurid would say; why, for all she knew, the fellow might even question her chastity!

When Mortimer was consulted by the Empress as to what course of action she should pursue, he recommended that she found a journal to be called *The Lantern,* and beat Rochefort at his own game. Mortimer saw a fine opportunity to make some money and to win the favor of the Empress, and it could all be done cheaply, for he would hire Bierce to write the copy, and it could be printed at the regular offices of *Figaro.* Thus it came that Bierce wrote every line of the two issues of *The Lantern* that appeared: one on May 17, 1874, and the other July 15, 1874. It was a most interesting publication and boasted that it was the first newspaper in the world printed in six colors. Whether this is correct or not, the journal was certainly a handsome publication for the time, and it is interesting to note that *The Wasp,* a periodical Bierce edited in San Francisco, was remarkably like *The Lantern* in makeup.

Bierce, in his account of *The Lantern,* intimates that Rochefort left London immediately upon the appearance of the magazine. It would seem now that this was not altogether the fact. Rochefort, in his memoirs, tells about his amusement over the derisive welcome given him in *Punch* and other "local magazines," and comments upon the fact that he was followed by jeering mobs through the streets whenever he left his hotel.

He states that it was his intention to publish *La Lanterne* in England, but adds that he actually published one or two issues there. However this may be, he left England soon and went to Geneva, where *La Lanterne* waved for a time in 1874.

The Empress was delighted with the work of her kept satirist. She invited Bierce to call at Chislehurst, but unfortunately her invitation was worded in the form of a "command," and he refused out of an avowed deference to republican habits! As a matter of harsh fact his refusal can only be designated as another of his studied gestures, because he would always be "republican" when he could at the same time be grand. The Empress being gracious if not "republican," accepted his rebuff in good part and sent him a beautiful ivory card case as a gift.

With the spring of 1875, Mrs. Bierce had decided to return to America and visit her mother. There was no other reason at that time for her return. Contrary to the rumors that have circulated for years, she did not leave Bierce at this time. There is abundant evidence to show that she merely planned a trip to America, and that she intended to return to London in the fall or the winter of 1875. Her departure with the babies left Bierce very lonely and despondent. Stoddard had returned to London by this time, and Bierce wrote him on June 2, 1875: "Awfully glad you are back, and want to see you very much, for I am lonely, of course, without the wife and babies. . . . I am struggling with more work than I can manage, and that is partly what has made me ill—for I am ill though I keep pegging away, somehow. Second, I live precariously and abominably. . . . As soon as I feel well enough to travel I'm coming to London till Mrs. Bierce returns, when I shall have a house somewhere in the suburbs. I have heard nothing from Mrs. Bierce since she left New York, but am expecting a letter every day from Salt Lake. I am not so ill as you suppose. It is only a cursed sort of semi-lunacy, I think, from lack of sleep, hard work, and unchristian cooking." This letter is revealing, indeed, and scarcely needs emphasis. But two facts are quite apparent: that Mrs. Bierce intended to return to London and that Bierce intended to remain there; that he missed her greatly. The talk about "cooking" and "abominable living" are the words of a man used to a pleasant home life. They reveal a condition that speaks loudly of his affection for his wife and boys, and are about as demonstrative as Bierce ever permitted himself to become.

Bierce remained in Leamington during the summer of 1875, leaving for London in the latter part of August, 1875. He lived in London for several months, and then in the latter part of 1875 sailed for America, as he had received word from Mrs. Bierce that she was again *enceinte* and he hastened from London, abandoning his plans, work, friendships, and associations, so that he might return and be with her during her confinement. He must have realized that this meant a break in his life: a return to the West which would perhaps be permanent. The trip had, after all, been little more than an extended honeymoon. They had not yet come to grips with life. Bierce had not even been able to pay expenses with his earnings in London. He knew that when he arrived back in San Francisco he would have to go to work again as a hack libelist for some journal of the day. And yet he returned to America. His conduct can scarcely be considered the act of a disgruntled husband. He sailed on the *Adriatic,* arriving in New York Sept. 25, 1875, and the unpleasant nature of the voyage was somewhat alleviated by the presence on shipboard of Madame Theresa Tietjens, the famous opera singer, whose care and well being had been entrusted to Bierce's hands on sailing by a mutual friend. She is the opera singer mentioned in "Bits of Autobiography." Bierce tells about the mysterious foreigner whose civility anticipated Madame's every need and desire. On visiting Madame Tietjens in New York, Bierce discovered that the fellow was her servant!

And so the London residence was at a close and it was the new world again, to be rediscovered, and tried once more. That Bierce liked England immensely cannot be doubted; and that, after his arrival there, he intended to make it his home can still less be doubted. If it had not been for his wife becoming *enceinte,* there can be no doubt that Bierce would have remained indefinitely in England. It was the scene of peace, quiet and order that he instinctively sought; it was the period of rest and pause in his life; a period of work, meditation and study. These years had done much for him, coming late as they had in life. The man had been fundamentally the same at all times: super-sensitive and given by this very fact a sharp, swift, insight into human affairs. He was a man to whom every contact with vulgarity, dishonèsty and sloth brought a reaction so spontaneous and violent that it unbalanced him for the moment. He saw the evasion and he struck. Perception and reaction were spontaneous with him. This gave his wit its force and aptness. Meditation would have brought doubt, and doubt in turn might have resulted in meditation and study, which might have brought about abstract thought and philosophy. But not for a sensitive man. He had not learned, as had Anatole France, "to despise man tenderly." He hated ugliness; detested dishonesty; shunned hypocrisy as the evil one itself. I shall have occasion again and again to emphasize this sensitiveness which bordered on the pathologic in the course of time. In time, too, came a gruff exterior; a layer of cynicism that tended to become coarse. But beneath that exterior the man was almost feminine in his vibrant perception of values. It appeared, this same trait, in his son Day. Mrs. Isgrigg has told me how Day would stand in the middle of the room, at St. Helena in later years, his eyes flashing, quivering with rage, his sensitive nostrils dilated, his whole person flaming with indignation like a Shelley, and say: "I wouldn't think of doing such a thing!" when told about some act of dishonesty or petty cheating. This same sense of values was Bierce's. It was scarcely æsthetic, not philosophic, it was more a poetic intuition, a sharp ability to perceive realities beyond realities, a certain fine quality of perception.

Mr. Mencken has spoken of Bierce's "appalling cynicism" and with this phrase I have no great quarrel. But it stated only one side of the equation. Externally Bierce was a cynic, for experiences had made him so, and, as W. L. George once pointed out in connection with Anatole France, a highly developed human being tends to hold two views upon one topic: the one of his instincts and the other of his reason. Instinctively Bierce was one of the most idealistic men that his generation produced in America, a man of exquisitely balanced perception, intuition, and even a sort of harmony. He maintained mental balance by giving violent expression to his work-a-day views. The core of the man was idealistic: shining, brilliant, forceful. The cynic is the concave idealist. The only utter cynic is the man who mouths platitudes which he knows to be untrue. Compared with the men of affairs of his day, Bierce was a great moral force: he was truth resplendent, for the man would not lie, and truth alone mattered to him. It came to mean more than beauty, always a rather secondary consideration with Bierce; it came to be the paramount value of his life. He could not have willed it otherwise. Sensitive, fine, idealistic, splendid, he was destined to fight hydra-headed monsters of untruth all his life. The rage finally exhausted him. He was devastated by his own apocryphal digust with mankind. Idealism burned itself out in him.

He scorned moderation, philosophic meditation; he would have nothing to do with George Sterling's oft-repeated "implications of infinity"—the assurance that many things were transitory and did not matter; they mattered greatly to Bierce. I want to say again: he was shocked in a manner that is very difficult for us to understand, and to an unbelievable degree, by base things. He has been criticized for his sharp, harsh treatment of friends who sinned against his code; he has been violently assailed by a few personal friends for his harsh treatment of his wife's alleged infidelity. But what I want to force home is that he could not prevent his passionate convictions, his ungovernable, uncompromising determinations. If idealism ever is pathologic sin, it was with Bierce. His violent shots at friends for their shortcomings were boomerangs that took notches out of his own soul: they burned, and hissed, and cut his inner calm to shreds. Ingratitude of friends tortured him as it did King Lear. He suffered from these things. It was not a merely intellectual perception of degraded states of life: he was incapable of such objectivity. He was so shocked by baseness that he froze inwardly, suppressing every natural inclination, suppressing a very great and tender affection. The death of his son, Day, rocked his life like nothing had done before. The slightest suffering or pain tortured him. Inwardly he was so tender, so kind, so idealistic, that when the stimulus came it toppled him off balance in the other direction. It doesn't do any good to attempt to explain this quality: it is difficult enough to describe. He was simply that kind of man. War or no war, sorrows or no sorrows, he was Bierce and an inscrutable destiny had made him what he was.

It has often been stated that Bierce learned his trade as a witty journalist in England. This is inaccurate. In his writing for *The News-Letter* he struck the note which echoed through all his later work. He was fundamentally the same before as after his residence in London. What he did acquire from his years abroad was a manner, an attitude, something of a personal style. It was often remarked in later years by people who knew Bierce but slightly, that he was of English origin. Gavin McNab, the famous San Francisco attorney, once wrote me that he was quite positive Bierce was an Englishman. He had about his person something that suggested the foreigner; his manners alone set him apart from the ultra-Americanism of Twain and Artemus Ward. Even his writing possessed certain qualities that impressed critics as European. John G. Neihardt, writing in the St. Louis *Post-Despatch* (December 31, 1927), suggests that Bierce was a "congenital outsider." Herman Scheffauer wrote of Bierce: "During his short sojourn in England, he adopted many English, not to say Tory, externals. He once told me that his ideal of an aged man's appearance should be a florid face and silver white hair: a color harmony which he realized in his own life." * The London residence was only to make him the more romantic, for on his return to America he felt infinitely superior to all "local" writers. Then, too, the men he had associated with were the survivors of a rather anemic period. Their influence was perhaps more harmful to Bierce than it was helpful. But the years abroad did give him personal poise, polished his manners, and gave him an opportunity to read and study that would have been impossible in San Francisco.

But important as were the years in London from a personal standpoint, they are even more significant when Bierce's views are considered. Before attempting an analysis of his own views on the matter, a personal explanation is necessary. What Bierce actually said and wrote is relatively unimportant to-day. It would be folly to attempt a scriptural defense of his views, although he did possess what François Porché has so finely termed "the essential virtue of judgment: lucidity." One can point out, with sophomoric ease, that many of his views are trite, lack learning, were conceived in excitement and are hastily phrased. But all this is really beside the point when one considers his personal significance. What is important is that such a man lived and wrote.in early San Francisco: a man so

* *Preussiche Jahrbucher*, September, 1926.

forceful and so impressive that he stamped his personality in an indelible manner on every one he came in contact with. He stirred his generation in the West as no one had done before, or has done since, for that matter. His influence was essentially a personal influence. What gave his satire, for example, such tremendous force at the time it was written, was the knowledge uppermost in the mind of every reader that Ambrose Bierce had written it.

Considering his ideas, then, from an objective standpoint, it is apparent that may of them are of English origin. He once wrote a long panegyric about the English system of government in the course of which he said: "For nearly all that is good in our American civilization we are indebted to England; the errors and mischiefs are of our own creation. In learning and letters, in art and the science of government, America is but a faint and stammering echo of England. The English are undoubtedly our intellectual superiors." *

His admiration was genuine and his attitude towards democracy, although influenced by his own personal bias, was essentially the attitude of an Englishman. In pointing out evils in American society, he would invariably point to the superiority of the English custom.

Often, after his return to San Francisco, he would drop his mask as satirist in "Prattle" and write a few revealing lines of reminiscence about the London years. They came in the course of time to be an oasis in his life. He perhaps magnified his happiness and well-being during these few years, because of the aridness of the times that followed. Nothing he ever said on the subject is so significant as this passage from "Prattle" (*Argonaut,* Nov. 9, 1878): "A certain friend of mine, who writes things, is commonly accused by those of whom he writes them of thinking himself a Titan among the pigmies. It can hardly be from vanity, for he frankly confesses that the happiest and most prosperous period of his life was passed where he felt himself a pigmy among the Titans. My friend used to write things in London." To one familiar with Bierce's writing from its inception to its close, such lines, rare as they are for their simplicity and personal quality, speak volumes. "My friend used to write things in London." . . .

* *The Argonaut,* February 9, 1878.

CHAPTER VII

"THE TERRIBLE SEVENTIES"

BIERCE returned in the fall of 1875 and spent most of the winter with his wife and children in San Francisco, where they were living at the home of Mr. and Mrs. Day on Vallejo Street. For a brief holiday in December, he took his wife to Calistoga Hot Springs, then a famous resort. The Napa Valley through which they journeyed was in striking contrast to recent scenes in England, but they were not disheartened at the prospect of living on the coast. Mrs. Bierce, in particular, was delighted at the thought of being near her friends. After the birth of their daughter, Helen, they moved from San Francisco across the bay to San Rafael, in Marin County, where they had lived when they were first married. Bierce found, soon after his arrival in San Francisco, that by living in Marin County he could secure relief from the attacks of asthma which had always troubled him. This cursed disease made him a fugitive from society and his grief was unassuagable, when, one evening as he bent over his son Leigh, he heard that dreaded wheezing, that painful breathing, of the asthmatic. Thenceforth there were two exiles in the family.

One reason that the Bierces had decided to live in San Rafael was the fact that their friends, the Getliffs, who had visited them in England, made San Rafael their home. The two families lived next door and were neighbors for many years. Bierce found life very pleasant in San Rafael. It was a pretty town, only slightly removed from the bay, full of a quiet and restful beauty. He could tramp the brown hillsides with their evenly spaced clusters of green, umbrella-like trees.

He took long walks up Mt. Talmapais where the sun burned down upon the slanting hillsides with warming indolence. Then, too, there were trips across the bay to San Francisco, when the waters were dull with sorrow, full of uneasy restlessness, tugging at the shoreline. He would return home in the evening with his banker friend, Getliff, or perhaps with Judge Boalt as a week-end guest, and they would talk over the affairs of the day. A friend remembers a picture of the three of them standing near the railing, dignified, clear-eyed, but in that state of inebriation that converts every word into a sonorous intonation and makes of every movement a superb gesture. There was still a spaciousness about life, then, that permitted of gestures, verbal violence and magnificent sentiments.

What work Bierce did for the San Francisco journals immediately upon his return must have been under a pen name. There is no mention of him in any of the early journals until June 24th, 1876, when there appears a letter to the editor of *The News-Letter* from "A. G. Bierce" dated in San Francisco, enclosing Bierce's version of the poem "Dies Iræ." He might have done, and probably did do, a good deal of free-lancing during these months in an effort to reëstablish himself in journalism, but whatever work he did, it is buried to-day in a manner that would defy exhumation.

Bierce found, upon his return to the coast, that conditions had radically changed during his absence. The impossible prosperity of the sixties had abated and the spectre of unemployment stalked the state. Thousands had been lured to the coast by fabulous yarns of gold, only to be stripped of their earnings and property. When the boom subsided, they naturally cried for work. But, in the meantime, a new class of laborers had preëmpted the field. The Chinese had been shipped into the country by the thousands to work on the Central Pacific Railroad under the supervision of Crocker, the labor-boss of the famous Stanford-Huntington-Hopkins group. When Bierce left for the West in 1866, he saw the eastern section of the trans-continental railroad at work in Nebraska and he met the western construction unit at Dutch Flats. When the work was well under way, it is said that "Charlie" Crocker had approximately ten thousand Chinese at work on the western division.

This cheap labor was effective at the time, although no one seemed to realize that the Chinese intended to stay in America after the road was completed. There had been slight demonstrations against the Chinese as early as 1854, but popular feeling did not reach its crest until after the railroad was constructed. The situation was somewhat alleviated by the Burlingame Treaty in 1868, which secured certain rights to the Chinese. But with the panic of 1873, there came a serious economic depression and the unthinking immediately attributed this condition to the presence of the coolie, who has ever since been a favorite scapegoat. The economic depression culminating in the panic was due to causes that bore no relation to the fact that Chinese were employed in large numbers; it was simply a period of post-boom depression, a common phenomenon in California. The collapse of the Bank of California, which, under the leadership of William C. Ralston, was the leading financial institution of the state, precipitated the panic. It was most seriously felt during 1876 and was accompanied with a sharp depression in the mining stocks which had driven California wild with the fever of speculation during the late sixties. Out of this period of doubt and misgiving, of economic depression and unemployment, came the figure of Denis Kearney.

This young Irishman had been a drayman in San Francisco, in the early days, and had secured some training in oratory at a "Lyceum of Self-Culture." With this meager background, his demagoguery could not be other than the dangerous, incendiary stuff that it was. Kearney began to whip the crowds of unemployed into frenzies of wrath. So keen did the agitation become that during the winter of 1877 a business men's vigilance committee was formed, analogous to the earlier Vigilante Committee, and headed by the redoubtable William Coleman. This committee was styled "The Pick-Handle Brigade" from the weapon found most productive of orderliness. Kearney, and his lieutenants, delivered their blood-curdling harangues before mobs that gathered on the vacant sand lots near the city hall. Hence the movement was later known as Sandlotism. It was during the first few weeks in 1877 that Kearney led a mob to burn the mansions on Nob Hill, but, like most of Kearney's enterprises, this worthy architectural reform failed of consummation. To make a bad condition worse, several journals of the day, notably *The Chronicle* and *The Call*, seeing a chance to win popular favor, took up the cause of Kearney, and with the aid of these billows the movement was converted into a hurricane. The Workingmen's Party of California ("W. P. C.") was formed and it seemed as though Kearney might gain control of the state.

Something had to be done about Kearney. It was this necessity that gave birth to *The Argonaut*. Its founder, Frank Pixley, was a most interesting character. He was a bit of the soldier and pioneer, and had once been United States District Attorney in San Francisco. Ambitious politically and possessing an overpowering lust for money, he was yet a man of courage. He decided to run Denis Kearney out of San Francisco, and to make the place most uncomfortable for the Irish Catholics generally. With this end in mind, he founded *The Argonaut*. But at the time he established the journal he was scarcely literate. A young man once sent in a poem to the publication which was accepted. A few days after its appearance, the poet met Mr. Pixley and thanked him for printing his "sonnet." Pixley stared at the poet with incredulous eyes and said: "What's a sonnet?" Having no experience as a journalist, Pixley needed an editor. He associated with him a very brilliant journalist, Fred Somers, who went east in later years to found *Current Literature*. Somers, in turn, selected Bierce as managing editor. This selection was inevitable. Bierce fitted every requirement: he had a name on the coast as a great satirical journalist, and, moreover, he possessed the halo of a "London" reputation. He stood far above the rank and file of the profession on the coast and he was, at the moment, unemployed.

The first issue of *The Argonaut* appeared March 25th, 1877, and in this initial number appeared "The Prattler," a column by "Bierce." With almost the first issue, Bierce became virtually sole editor. Much dispute has raged on the coast as to whether Bierce ever actually "edited" *The Argonaut*. It is true that the masthead of the paper, during this period, carried the names "Frank Pixley and Fred Somers, Editors." But Bierce himself once stated that he had edited the magazine, relating the circumstances, and neither Somers nor Pixley denied his statement. Then, too, "The Elite Directory" published in 1879 by The Argonaut Publishing Company, a subsidiary of the press, listed Bierce as "associate editor of *The Argonaut*." It is quite apparent that Pixley was too busy to edit the paper, as was Fred Somers, who was interested in several private enterprises at the time, such as the little journal *Figaro*. Then too, there is the significant fact that one can literally see Bierce's hand, throughout the early issues, in every department of the magazine.

"The Prattler" was the most important feature of the paper and was paraded, for a time, on the first page. The name of "Prattle" had been taken from Rochefort's journal *The Lantern*, but in the first few issues Bierce called his column "The Prattler" and then changed it to "Prattle" and such it remained for practically twenty-five years. Bierce left little doubt in the minds of his readers as to what his editorial aims were, for he wrote in the first issue: "It is my intention to purify journalism in this town by instructing such writers as it is worth while to instruct, and assassinating those that it is not." San Francisco was sorely in need of just this kind of treatment for, in truth, its journalism had fallen to a low level. The quality of its journalism in the fifties and sixties, when presses sprang up by the twenties overnight, was sprightly and full of charm. But, by 1877, this early enthusiasm had waned and "Mike" De Young was teaching his competitors that it was folly to devote any money or time to improving the quality of journalism. De Young belonged to those early precursors of modern journalism who, in an effort to be understood by the mob, talked so barbarically low that they became unintelligible.

These were busy days for Bierce. He wrote his two columns of "Prattle" every week, edited the paper, and wrote in addition numerous poems and articles, besides reprinting from time to time some of his "Parsee Fables." It was about this time, too, that he began to publish those ghastly animal humorous stories of his, in childish dialect, called "Little Johnny and his Menagerie." That Bierce could have written such stupid drivel has always remained a mystery. If Swift had written Boz it could not have been more surprising.

Bierce's work for *The Argonaut* contained some droll remarks. For example, he noted that an insane woman had been found sleeping in a cemetery. The incident drew from him this comment: "Mary's preference for lodging with dead men is, I confess, indefensible,—she may not be demented; she is indisputably unique." He noticed the name Clitus Babcock in the press of the day and had the temerity to remark: "Clitus Babcock—for whose first name might be substituted a work which, it is hoped, no one will have the hardihood to suggest." It was during this period, too, that he wrote one of the most ruthless lines about "lovely woman" that he was ever to pen: "A woman in love is like a pig, which having firm standing ground roots it up, and if cast into deep water cuts its throat with its toes."

There were many amusing incidents that grew out of remarks that Bierce made in "Prattle." Many of these were exciting as well as amusing, and succeeded in keeping San Francisco's more intelligent residents vastly entertained. Sometimes the unfortunate local poet—there was no one Bierce hated so much as a "local" poet—would retaliate. One of them, Hector Stuart, struck back at his tormentor by writing these verses:

> "Here low in the dust,
>   As dry as a crust,
> Lies Bierce, who befuddled newspapers;
>   Well-prized for his nob,
>   Very dear as a bob,
> And noisome as Butcher Town vapors.
>
>   When he lived long enough
>   He belched his last puff,
> And burst like a wad of gun-cotton;
>   Now here he doth lie,
>   Turned to a dirt pie,
> Like all that he scribbled—forgotten."

Bierce did not answer for a week or so and then he wrote this comment: "Concerning my epitaph by Hector S. Stuart, it is perhaps sufficient to say that I ought to be willing to have my name at the top of it if he is willing to have his at the bottom. As to Mr. Stuart's opinion that my work will be soon forgotten, I can assure him that that view of the matter is less gloomy to me than it ought to be to him. I do not care for fame, and he does; and his only earthly chance of being remembered is through his humble connection with what I write." Arrogant prophecy? and yet how extremely true! Bierce was clear headed and knew the worth of some of the things that he was writing, just as he realized very keenly his limitations, as I will have occasion to show a little later.

He returned to Stuart in a later issue,* with these words: "Oh, Stuart, Stuart!—let not these dumb dead bones speak to thy hot blood in vain! In some incalculable distant age, after my scurvy prose shall have been forgotten, and before thy noble verse shall come to be read, how wilt thou like some delving antiquary to spade us out of our little mound—the dunghill upon which we fought and fell—the fingers of thy mouldy frame gripping the neck of mine? there in the blaze of the world's eyes, dead in a deathless feud, two mortals immortally implacable! Why, man, it will look like murder. Stuart, let us be friends; throw down thy pen forever, and give me thy nose." This Stuart, along with one Fred Emerson Brooks, suffered under Bierce's withering blasts for years. Yet nothing could daunt their poetic ardor. They would write verse despite devils and tormentors. Finally Bierce seemed to weary of the chase and wrote:† "Perseverance is, indeed, reckoned amongst our virtues, but then it is also one of the vices of local poets. Have they stopped writing? Have they shut down the back windows of their souls and ceased for even a week to pour a deluge of bosh upon the earth? Who began this thing? As the steel-trap said to the fox."

I have related how men who deemed themselves insulted by some remark in "Prattle," would walk into the office of *The News-Letter* and demand satisfaction. Perhaps the most amusing incident of this sort occurred while Bierce was on *The Argonaut*. It seems that one evening in October, 1878, a man by the name of Henry Widmer, who was an orchestra leader at the Baldwin Theater in San Francisco, entered the office of *The Argonaut* and asked Bierce if he was the author of certain lines in a prior issue of the paper. Bierce replied that he was; whereupon the man slapped him across the face. As well might he have thrown a match in a tank of gasoline,

* April 27, 1878.
† May 26, 1877.

for Bierce immediately drew his gun and would have killed
the man but for the timely intervention of Frank Pixley. Later
Widmer gave an interview to *The Chronicle*, owned by "Mike"
De Young, in which he called Bierce a coward. To this Bierce
replied:

> "Mr. Henry Widmer has not thought it expedient to act
> upon my studiously respectful suggestion that he disavow the
> insulting falsehoods published concerning me in his name.
> Moreover, I can prove him their author,—that he devoted the
> life which I mercifully spared to systematic defamation of
> my character and conduct. I, therefore, take this opportunity
> to remind those who have the misfortune to know him, and
> inform those who have not, that he has the distinguished
> honor to be, not a man of principle, but a ruffian; not a man
> of truth, but a liar; not a man of courage, but a coward.—
> In order that there may be no mistake as to what member of
> the *canaille* I mean, I will state that I refer to Fiddler Wid-
> mer, the charming blackguard." *

Such incidents were not isolated. "Prattle" was a rather exciting experience for the entire community and it remained so
for many years.

As to Bierce's other literary work at this time, there is
little to be said. He was too busy with editorial duties to do
much writing. But he would write an occasional poem and
several stories appeared in *The Argonaut,* among them: "Night
Doings at Deadman's" and "The Famous Gilson Bequest."
Judged even by Bierce's standards, these are not exceptional
stories. They show the obvious influence of Bret Harte in their
effort to be whimsical about the pioneer. Some of his other
work at this time was, however, interesting. He wrote for *The
Argonaut* a series of articles on prosody which revealed an
amazingly accurate and precise knowledge of the subject. The
articles were the primer in versification for many a budding
poet. Then, too, in a regular department, he was publishing
selections of French epigrams, the work of La Rochefoucauld,
A. de la Salle, Stendhal, and others. It is undeniable that he
studied the work of these men with great care and that he
modeled his wit after theirs. Also, Emma Frances Dawson was

* *The Argonaut,* October 12, 1878.

making translations of E. T. A. Hoffman's stories of horror and the supernatural, and that Bierce read these yarns with care is borne out by an examination of his later work.

While on *The Argonaut,* Bierce became a party to an amusing literary hoax. His co-conspirators were T. A. Harcourt, who had formerly contributed to *The News-Letter,* and William Rulofson, a well-known photographer in San Francisco. The idea for the book was largely Rulofson's and he wrote most of the manuscript, which Bierce corrected, with Harcourt participating to some extent in the plot. There have been many conflicting statements about the authorship of "The Dance of Death," but the version I give is based upon Bierce's own account of the matter, published in the San Francisco *Examiner,* February 5th, 1888. The book purported to be a fierce attack on the seductive influence of the waltz, and it created a tremendous furore on the coast. Bierce stirred up considerable comment about the book by writing a vicious review of it in "Prattle" in which he said: " 'The Dance of Death' is a highhanded outrage, a criminal assault upon public modesty, an indecent exposure of the author's mind! From cover to cover it is one sustained orgasm of a fevered imagination—a long revel of intoxicated propensities. And this is the book in which local critics find a satisfaction to their minds and hearts! This is the poisoned chalice they are gravely commending to the lips of good women and pure girls! Their asinine praises may perhaps have this good effect: William Herman (the pen name used by Rulofson) may be tempted forth, to disclose his disputed identity and father his glory. Then he can be shot." *

Such propaganda must have been very efficacious, for "The Dance of Death" sold 18,000 copies in seven months, and was actually endorsed by a Methodist Church Conference! An answer to so provocative a book might have been expected and it was soon forthcoming in "The Dance of Life" by Mrs. J. Milton Bowers. Of this book Bierce wrote in his characteristically tender style: "It is the most resolute, hardened, and impenitent nonsense ever diffused by a daughter of the gods divinely dull." † Vincent Starrett, in his admirable "Bibliography," intimates that Bierce might have written this book

* *The Argonaut,* June, 23, 1877.
† *The Argonaut,* September 29, 1877.

himself and advances some interesting evidence to support the theory. But I see no reason for doubting Bierce's statement, made years later in *The Examiner,* that the book was actually written by the wife of Dr. Bowers. T. A. Harcourt, a fellow member of the Bohemian Club, and Bierce's colleague in this enterprise, was an interesting character. He wrote some admirable verse in his day, and did some early translations of Zola. Shortly after collaborating on "The Dance of Death," his wife deserted him and ran away with another man. Harcourt grew bitter and morose and proceeded to drink himself to death. He anticipated the slow decay of alcoholism by jumping out a window and committing suicide. It was of him that Bierce wrote the lines:

> "Thus my friend,—
> Still conjugating with each failing sense
> The verb 'to die' in every mood and tense,
> Pursued his awful humor to the end.
> When like a stormy dawn the crimson broke
> From his white lips he smiled and mutely bled,
> And, having meanly lived, is grandly dead."

About 1880, Fred Somers, one of the proprietors of *The Argonaut,* resigned from the staff and sold out his interest in the magazine to become editor of *The Californian,* the most ambitious of Western literary magazines. He induced Bierce to write a series of articles on the dance, carrying on the controversy begun by the two books. These articles appeared under the general head of "On With the Dance!", beginning with February, 1880, and were written under the *nom de plume* of "Bashi Bazourk." Later Bierce collected them for republication in his "Collected Works" (Volume VIII). They constitute some of the most downright drivel that he was ever guilty of having written. Along with the regrettable "Little Johnnie" stories, they represent a dark blotch on an otherwise remarkably even record of performance.

This same Fred Somers was a very shrewd observer of life and letters, and Bierce profited by his advice. After he established a considerable reputation as an editor in the East. Somers still corresponded occasionally with Bierce and kept in touch with his work. Its continued bitterness brought forth this comment: "Now if you had not drummed and hunted these literary pismires out of their holes, and bruited them into public sympathy and recognition we should have been free of them. Yet you still continue poling at Windmills, setting them up often yourself—and for a wage—sneering at the industry. Sycophant or blackguard there is little choice." This was exactly the dilemma in which Bierce was so often involved: instead of his satire "lashing rascals through the world," it merely earned them popular sympathy. His remorseless attacks on David Lesser Lezinsky, a young poet in San Francisco, aligned many people, fundamentally in sympathy with Bierce, with the enemy. Ina Coolbrith, for one, turned against Bierce because of his unrelenting satire. Of course, Bierce explained his position by remarking to a friend: "It is perfect rot to say that I am responsible for Lezinsky's death. I never met him and would have refused to do so had the occasion arisen. I never once attacked him personally but only his verse. When he elected to become a poet, he impliedly consented to public criticisms of that which he made public." Bierce's journalistic satire was impulsive and irrational. It was the result of irritation grown chronic. He attempted, at various times, several philosophic justifications for his attitude, but never once did he strike close to the real fact, which was that he could not avoid being indignant. There was nothing eclectic about his position.

His first philosophy of criticism was, and it is still a popular theory, that he hugely enjoyed scourging rascals, and that he did it for entertainment. He once attempted an elaborate statement of this theory in his column of "Prattle":

"I know a chap whose trade is censure; fools are his theme and satire is his song. Knaves and vulgarians, impostors, sycophants, the variously unworthy and the specifically detestable, no sooner draw his eye than he is on to them with bitter abuse. . . . Moreover this fellow's social habits are consistent with his literary: he is imperfectly civil to the rich and distinguished, coldly declines introductions, utters his mind with freedom concerning people's characters, takes an infantile delight in cutting men whose acquaintance he deems no longer desirable, cherishes the most shocking convictions, maintains a private system of morality and is not in sympathy with civilization. From the books and proverbs it is clearly deducible that this person ought to be the most miserable of men, tormented by conscience, baffled by secret and overt antagonisms, hunted by the dogs of hate reared in his own kennels, and roosted on by homing curses thicker than blackbirds on a tree. So far as I can see, the wretch is mainly engaged in more deeply imbedding his kidneys in broader layers of leafy fat, peacefully nourishing an oleaginous and comfortable content, gratifying his soul with a bird's-eye view of human ilfare, happy in the prospect of a green old age and indulging fascinating dreams of a blessed hereafter." *

This was written after twenty years at the trade of hired satirist; it was, at best, an *ex post facto* rationalization, and none are more illusive or unreliable. Properly to analyze his cynicism, one must start at a point prior to his becoming a journalist, for, as I have shown, his first writings were (a) atheistic pamphlets; (b) satirical journalism. From the moment he began to write, he had a satirical bent. Furthermore, it is quite apparent that his satire sprang from no such *contented,* harum-scarum, jolly motive as he suggests. His explanation is mere camouflage. It is impossible to associate such force and energy, with a desire merely to amuse himself. He was rather hesitant about admitting his idealism but he was essentially idealistic and romantic, just as he was always overtly cynical and realistic.

In order to come closer to his motives, one must turn to James Watkins, just as Watkins shall be called upon to explain Bierce's æsthetics. Bierce once wrote Watkins that his cynicism was the great barrier to the development of his creative powers. To this letter Watkins replied, and because the passage answering Bierce's doubt blazes a way to the very heart of the darkness and misunderstanding in Bierce, I shall quote a considerable passage:

"Why, yes, if you read into the word 'cynic' a meaning special to this mode of thought and arrest the meaning at the mode. But this thinking is in fact no more than fetching the images and pictures out of the dim religious light where all manner of unnatural colors are strained upon them through painted windows, and handling them in the light of day. Turn

* San Francisco *Examiner,* September 3, 1889.

them round and about, knock the dust off, see how they are
made, and examine the canvas side, plenty of bugs tumble out,
which excite disgust. But then, as often, you earn a laugh—or
cause for laughter, which is not quite the same thing. Now,
I hold, as an issue of simple propriety in the use of language,
that, allowing this to be the mental process of the cynic, its
motive must be of one special sort before that mind can rightly
be employed. I take it that your cynic must do all this out of
an inborn hate of dirt, which is the reverse aspect of his love
of light and sweetness. But, unless the individual be inspired
by this spirit, the noble word 'cynic' does not apply. There are
folk who raise a dust out of pure love of annoying others,—
out of cussedness—to whom the annoyance is itself an aim
and an end. Many religious folk, for example, make others uncomfortable as a good in itself—self-operative for righteousness, which it is understanding righteousness in their sense, as
one aspect of hatefulness. Or another way, in the overflow and
waste of benevolence turn a ray of light in on abodes of filth
and creeping things, on the chance that the responsible occu-
pant may be led to clean up, and refrain from breeding
typhuses and plagues. Sure, it is using language out of its
meaning to class such a loitering lantern-bearer among the
order of cynics.

Now, it is true of myself—I know that you are mixed
with a more coercive conscience—that I do not care one damn
for the alleged human being who lives in that filth. He is less
to me than the strange dog, of whose race I am really fond.
But I am superstitious about typhuses. It is a distinct superstition with me that, if you keep your lantern slide shut when
passing pest spots, the germs bred there will contrive to lay
hold on you. Hence the blinks of light I aim to shed on such
places, hasting on to something more agreeable. You drag open
shutters and pour in a beam of illumination as from a Drum-
mond apparatus; this attests the love of light which implies
hatred of murk and muck, and wrath against them by whom
these things are maintained. My performance is misprized by
pure cowardice, and accompanied by no sentiment but disgust
for them by whom these things are maintained. You are the
cynic: I am something less.

Because you are a cynic and informed with righteous indignation, you glow and scorn, and distil words that are de-
structive of animal tissue. I would be glad to, for I think it a
fine thing to do, and to be able to do; but my power is limited
to stopping the passersby like the good bishop, to invite at-

tention to the offense—'Observe this grisly beard, Observe, my
friends, this nose': then tillup along over the cobbles with a
conciliatory, if not positively apologetic, carriage. The word
cynic is inapplicable unless to bigger men than me.

The bearing of all this? Dear boy, it is an apology for
not doing anything serious; an apology, and in part a caveat
against misjudgment. Don't think that I think that what I am
doing is serious. That is all. That is the whole meaning of it
all. The day is still as far as ever when you and I are to run
a sheet that is *to lash the rascals as with whips of scorpions,
naked through the world.* But, Oh my God! what larks it
would be!" *

It seems to me that Watkins, with all his kindly insight and
intuition, stated Bierce's position far better than Bierce ever
did himself. And, it is to be noted, Watkins points out the
pettiness of the attitude that would justify satire as a form of
self-amusement, under which theory "the annoyance is itself
an aim and an end." Such a philosophy is, of course, sophomoric.
Watkins perceived the more fundamental nature of all great
satire.

During these years after his return from England, when he
was reëstablishing his reputation on the coast as a writer and
editor, Bierce was living happily with his wife and family in
San Rafael. It has been said that Bierce's subsequent trouble
with his wife was the "cause" of his cynicism. But Prentice
Mulford, who also had trouble with his wife, was the most
saccharine of optimists. Furthermore, the three great tragedies
in Bierce's life all occurred after he was past middle-age. He
was writing in the same vein for *The News-Letter* in 1869,
before his marriage, that he wrote after the separation.

These early years reveal no organic invections; Bierce was
living happily with his wife and children, had many friends,
and was actually quite a popular social figure. He joined
the Bohemian Club when it was formed on March 9, 1872.
After his return from England, he took an active interest in
the affairs of the club and was secretary for the year 1876-
1877. Years later he quarreled with the club. The occasion was
the visit to San Francisco of the Emperor of Brazil. His Maj-

* Letter from James W. Watkins, 1037 Fifth Avenue, February
15, 1891.

esty was received with such sycophancy, particularly at the club, that Bierce resigned in disgust. He said the "flexibility of the republican knee and the arch of his back" were inexplicable.* But while his association with the club lasted, it was very pleasant indeed. Many of his friends were fellow club-members, notably Jeremiah Lynch, the Egyptologist, and author of "Three Years in the Klondike" and "A Senator of the Fifties," and E. L. G. Steele, who published "Tales of Soldiers and Civilians."

Occasionally the paper would print a notice that "Mr. Bierce is confined to his home in San Rafael with a severe attack of asthma." The blight was unconquerable and relentless. It plagued his days and made his nights livid with agony. Sometimes, however, he suffered from minor casualties. In fact, his life was interspersed with semi-humorous accidents: he shot himself in the foot when in the Sub-Treasury; broke a rib at Calistoga Hot Springs when his bicycle went over a bank (old Schram's white wine was probably responsible for this); and had lumbago in his old age, followed with hives! Once while crossing the bay from San Rafael, he was standing on the deck when a barge rammed into the ferry boat. He attempted to jump aboard the other ship and was thrown into the bay and nearly drowned. It amused him for weeks thereafter to speculate on the pleasures of death by drowning over those of asthmatic strangulation. Death was, truly, the last and silliest folly. He had led columns in attack at Pickett's Mill, and now his life was threatened by the most childish disasters.

In San Rafael he had many friends, among others Sheriff Tunstead, a renowned "man hunter" of Marin County. He was a giant of a man, with huge moustachios, and the voice of Paul Bunyan. His pictures are as amusing as anything to be seen on the comedy lots at Studio City. This old fellow went for long tramps and hunting expeditions with Bierce. They both enjoyed the outdoors and were crack shots. Mrs. Bierce detested Tunstead. The vulgar old ruffian was forever poking his head in a window and yelling: "Where's Bierce?" just at the moment when one of the children would run in breathless to announce that Mrs. Charley Crocker's carriage approached. Mrs. Bierce once asked her husband why he associated with such a character as Tunstead who "had no manners." Bierce replied:

* San Francisco *Examiner*, October 15, 1893.

"True enough, my dear, but you should see him shoot!" Bierce and Tunstead would spend long nights over a bottle in the study where the shades of Pascal, Sir John Mandeville, and Thomas Browne hovered, listening to these two old soldiers match stories of hangings, murders and other such humorous tamperings with the life-stream. Bierce, for all his fine rhetoric, liked honesty even when he found it in illiterate sheriffs.

To illustrate the complete honesty and consistency of Bierce, one example will suffice. Pixley launched a movement to oust General O. H. LaGrange from his position as head of the United States Mint. Bierce had known La Grange for many years; in fact, he had induced LaGrange to give his brother Albert a position in the Mint when the latter arrived on the coast in 1869. The attitude of *The Argonaut* was thus putting Bierce in a very embarrassing position. So he went to Pixley and asked permission to state his own private views on La-Grange in a signed article. This request was granted and on September 1, 1877, Bierce's defense of his old friend appeared, cheek by jowl with a biting and accusatory editorial. General LaGrange was befriended by Bierce on more than one occasion. It seems that the General could not, like many another mortal, resist the unscrupulous type of woman. His enemies were constantly producing one of these discarded but revengeful amours to cause the General great confusion and embarrassment at critical political junctures. But when Mr. and Mrs. Bierce separated, the General was one of the first to denounce Bierce, without waiting for an explanation. Bierce never forgave La-, Grange this disloyalty and wrote him a letter in which he said that it was his desire that LaGrange should always remember the hurt and sorrow that his criticism had caused, particularly in the light of what had happened in the early days of their acquaintance. Poor Bierce! He could write the cleverest epigram imaginable on the frailty of friendship, but when he lost a friend in private life it was only with deep sorrow.

In later years Bierce repudiated most of his work written for *The Argonaut*. He acted wisely, for much of it was ephemeral and ill advised. But, realizing that it was written just as journalism, there is an amazing clarity and force to such statements as this: "There was enough of Lincoln to kill and enough of Grant to kick; but Hayes is only a magic-lantern image without even a surface to be displayed upon. You can not see him, you can not feel him; but you know that he extends in lessening opacity all the way from the dark side of John Sherman to the confines of space." Or such cogent reasoning as this: "No man of sane intelligence will plead for religion on the ground that it is better than nothing. It is not better than nothing if it is not true. Truth is better than anything or all things; the next best thing to truth is absence of error." He anticipated Nietzsche by saying: "No one but Jesus Christ ever loved mankind." Not only was he beating some of the sound tenets of skepticism into the gaseous souls of his fellow citizens, but he was pummeling them out of their magnificent rhetoric, their incurable fondness for bombast, which was really the same thing. He made this suggestion to Loring Pickering, editor of one of San Francisco's largest daily newspapers: "Mr. Pickering, I have told you a dozen times that to call rain a 'pluvial dispensation,' is to be a magniloquent idiot, compared with whose style the song of a sturdy jackass in braying his love to a star is chaste and elegant diction."

Bierce had returned from England impressed with the possibility of an intelligent control of life. He reëntered a madhouse in San Francisco; became a partisan in the struggle with and was personally pitted against, Denis Kearney. The experience threw him off balance and forever prejudiced him against anything that even sounded of sociological amelioration. His name for an unpleasant person was always "an anarchist." He elevated sandlotism to universal significance; he magnified it out of all proportion to scale or perspective. The Bay District was the world *in petto,* and Kearney was its Nero. Bierce actually used such historical names as Jack Cade and Wat Tyler in searching out parallels for Kearney. He became slightly prophetical, and, like most prophets, slightly ridiculous. His excitement was justified at the moment: only Anatole France kept his head during the Dreyfus trial.

If the ideas that Bierce championed in later years are to be understood, or rather the psychological states of mind that produced these ideas, one must constantly remember his experience. To illustrate the importance of this relation, take the volume "The Shadow on the Dial." It consists of a number of essays which, when gathered into book form, were not read as they were printed—by the side of news stories of riots, arson and theft. Many of the essays did not carry the date of their appearance as a footnote; hence confusion was inevitable. The title essay itself, "The Shadow on the Dial," appeared in *The Argonaut* as an attack on Kearney, some thirty-two years prior to its publication in book form. When the book was published, Bierce dropped Kearney's name, and generalized an incident into an historical principle. This is apparent in such a passage as the following:

> "The Kearneyism 'episode' is not an episode; it is part of the general movement. Thousands of armed men are drilling all over the United States to overthrow the government. I tell you the good God, Majority, means mischief."

Much of Bierce's writing during this period was simply hysterical journalism, inspired by the moment and forgotten with its passage. George Sterling, who was scoffed at as a thinker, had some ideas on the significance of time that Bierce might have read with profit. George did not agree with Theodore Dreiser's "Hey-Rub-a-Dub-Dub" when it appeared. It sounded specious to one who had heard the roar of the surf at Monterey with its undertone of eternity, so he wrote a little essay "The Implications of Infinity." Bierce, however much he might have appreciated the essay, would never have accepted its philosophy. And, after all, who was the real cynic, Bierce or Sterling? Sterling was wise enough to be cynical of mere intelligence, so-called, and wrote few essays but was careful to be always kind and gentle. Bierce's splendid indignation hardened and crystallized into intolerable prejudice and bias. His violently reactionary views on crime, his merciless attacks on "rose-water penology," are incredible when read apart from his experience. When one learns, however, that in the eighties California had a Governor by the name of Stoneman who pardoned all the most atrocious criminals, a new light dawns. After this experience, Bierce would never listen to reason about criminals.

> "Stoneman at last is made to dwell
> Where pardons do not come;
> O Father, thou dost all things well
> Though rather late with some."

It is interesting to speculate on what might have been the consequences had Bierce stayed with *The Argonaut*. In two years he had made it the foremost weekly in the West. Who can tell what might have resulted if he had remained as editor? He resigned from *The Argonaut* for private reasons and was not discharged as some of his biographers would have us believe. Ultimately he would have either resigned or been discharged, for he could not have endured Frank Pixley forever. They had nothing in common except an aversion to Denis Kearney. But Bierce was swept away from journalism by the excitement over the newly opened mining territory in the Black Hills. He decided to become a miner and *The Argonaut* lost its first, and one is tempted to add, its only editor.

Thus came to a close the first chapter in his life after his return to California. The period prior to that is complete, self-contained and final. With his return to California the years of his journalistic satire began in earnest, for his mining expedition was of slight duration. He had entered the field at a most significant time. The "terrible seventies," as Mrs. Atherton refers to the period, saw the collapse of the artificial and un-utterably gorgeous society of the sixties. In those early years the town had gleamed with gold, and mining speculation became the enterprise of an entire community, with the Nevada stocks alone rising from seventeen millions to eighty-four millions in one year. It was the day of Comstock Lode, Consolidated Virginia, Crown Point, Belcher and Ophir. The mining fever acted as a vortex that sucked into its inexorable funnel all the gold that the forty-niners had discovered, along with all the additional money that the settlers had brought with them. The end of the seventies saw the money being accumulated into the hands of a few, and, while the eyes of the community were dazzled with dreams of gold, the promoters of the trans-continental railroad had very craftily saddled and bridled the state. When people awoke from the trance, they were servants to an empire of monopoly. Radicalism swept in for just a moment, but was poorly generaled by Denis Kearney, and soon failed. The leader of the Sand Lot abandoned the W. P. C. and went back to Boston, where he captured large audiences at·Faneuil Hall with orations that were written for him by newspaper reporters. Bierce saw all these swift and moving events and was conscious only of the particular actors in the drama and the essential pettiness of both sides. The romantic California of the sixties was gone forever: Spanish California, built on a sound, self-contained culture, had existed for years and might have flowered into a fine civilization but for the discovery of gold. With 1849 a new era came into existence, raced through its meager term of years, and expired in 1870. There would be no more cotillions and Calico Balls; Mrs. Fair would now forget her ambiguous origins and become a grand lady. By 1876 the whirligig society of the sixties, in which Mollie Day's hand was open game, was irretrievably gone, and, the pity is, without a record. Bayard Taylor's slight volume, the romantic tales of Bret Harte, and a little of Twain: this alone marks the passage of an immensely important era. With the seventies came a period of horrific solemnity—magnificent, dull and empty.

The period that followed suffered from the excesses of individualism. Mr. Brownell once wrote that "Lack of sympathy with each other; a narrow and degrading struggle for 'success'; a crying competition; a dull, leaden introspection; no community of interest, material or ideal, except of a grossly material religious ideality; duty ignorantly conceived; sacrifices needlessly made; generous impulses leading nowhither, and elevated effort clogged by the absence of worthy ends; the human spirit, in fine, thrown back on itself and operating, so to speak, *in vacuo,*—" * and, to break his sentence, one knows that this is a description of the seventies. Read "Prattle" just as it appeared in the newspapers and note the advertisements, the popular news, the announcements, and, in a word, all the unstudied expression of the period, and you cannot help but conclude that Bierce wrote "in vacuo." Later his steadfast skepticism bore fruit in a tradition, but in the early days his satire was wasted; he might just as well have gone fishing with a copy of Rabelais, as to have written those reams of abuse.

What difference did it make whether rogues were rogues; and why become excited over the fact that the county treasurer was a thief or that there was an occasional murder in San Francisco? Did it really matter so much?

This, then, was the end of an important experience; the high adventure of the war was a memory; the trip across the

* "French Traits," by W. C. Brownell.

plains was forgotten; London existed only in the form of a few witty anecdotes; and he was now nearing middle-age, married, with a family to support, with no position, hated by every powerful lobby in the state. Is it small wonder that during these days when Bierce thought that the firebrands of the sandlot were destroying the nation he had fought to preserve that he exclaimed: "Patriotism? Wouldst thou serve thy fatherland? Cultivate, then, the habit of uttering whatever thou art most reluctant that its enemies should know. . . . Patriotism is fierce as fenur, pitiless as the grave, blind as a stone, and irrational as a headless hen." Patriotism? And every 4th of July saw General W. H. L. Barnes marching at the head of his regiments of valiant peace-soldiers down Market Street!

These were, indeed, bad days for Bierce. The country reeked with the peculiarly fetid odor of money-lust. In all those days Bierce, alone of his generation in the West, mustered a shout against the awful futility of such a society. He stuck by his guns in a most manly fashion, and never once truckled to the molochs of the day. As an editor, his only congenial contributor was Emma Frances Dawson, an old maid who wrote ghost stories for *The Argonaut* and later turned into a ghost herself, living alone for years in a little hut, and dying finally of starvation in Palo Alto. While Mr. Stanford was mouthing delicious platitudes in public and waiting eagerly for the decision in *Colton vs. Stanford,* the decision of the supreme court having been delayed several times to permit of convenient last-minute elections, the artists of the day had turbulent dreams of rattlesnakes and wrote ghost stories. It was the tradition of Poe or that of *Godey's Lady Book.* Of Mr. Godey's magazine Bierce wrote: "It is a publication which from the teens of our grandmothers has poured a thick and slab stream of irreparable and unaffected bosh into the misunderstanding of genderless gents, lettered wet nurses and misses cherishing a blasted hope apiece." One afternoon in a quiet corner of the lobby in the old Belle Vista Hotel, a very beautiful woman, who dressed in charming widow's weeds and had a taste for poetry, asked Mr. Bierce why he never wrote a love story. Her question was, under the circumstances, something of a love poem itself, but he answered: "The world to-day is only interested in love and horror and it is impossible at present to write of love with decency." He was

quite right. The most scandalous book of the seventies in San
Francisco, a volume that rocked the town, was "On the Verge:
a Romance of the Centennial" by Philip Shirley. "Philip Shirley" was the pen name for Annie Lake Townsend, who, *en
passant,* wrote some very tender poems to Mr. Bierce. Her
novel was a sensation. One may open the book at random and
find such delicious morsels as this:

> "He found, beside the concerto, Schubert's 'Wanderer,'
> Spohr's 'Bright Star of Night' and Virginia Gabriel's 'When
> the Pale Moon Arose.' His expression as he looked them over
> was just what she knew it would be and what she had de-
> termined not to encounter; but the thing was done now. She
> leaned back and defied him with flashing eyes."

In 1879, when such a book as "On the Verge" was hailed as a
masterpiece, the only thing for a gentleman to do was to write
a ghost story.

Bierce closed this chapter of his life thinking he was
through with journalism forever: better mining than blasphemy
at nothing a line. This time he left San Francisco under colors
not quite so bright or fair as before. There was not quite such
an atmosphere of hope and triumph about his trip to Dakota
as there was to the London adventure. Mark Twain tried his
hand at the publishing business; Ambrose Bierce became a
miner. "The Gilded Age" claimed them momentarily, and when
it "panned out," both were left to do some prospecting in their
souls.

CHAPTER VIII

THE BLACK HILLS

"GOOD memoirs," Max Beerbohm once wrote, "must ever be the cumulation of gossip." If the truth of this statement be assumed, it is not surprising to find that Bierce's fragmentary memoirs are so disappointing. The manner in which a man writes about his own life, the details which he selects as illuminating, the attitudes he stresses as important, constitute a good measure of his capacity for honesty. Bierce, who was so frightfully honest about others, was not publicly truthful about himself. In his letters there are moments when he is off guard, but his "Bits of Autobiography," found in Volume I of the "Collected Works," are most significant in their highly romantic version of several major happenings of his life. He never related a mean experience about his life; he selected only the "grand" episodes and wrote of them after the manner of an elderly gentleman entertaining a circle of excited ladies. One can detect in the manner in which these experiences are narrated, the dramatic and studied gesture, the carefully planned pause, the shock and surprise, and then the murmur of laughter and approval as the delighted audience of faithful admirers subside in quiescent rapture. His "memoirs" are told in the manner of a professional *raconteur,* and were selected solely for their dramatic possibilities as stories and for the romantic halo which they cast about his own life. He bows, in these memoirs, more than once to the galleries.

In none of these episodes was he more misleading than in the few paragraphs which refer to his experience as a miner in the Black Hills. He prefaces the episode with a note about the melancholy that enshrouds the life of a "sole survivor." Then he announces that he was once on his way to Rockerville,

Dakota, with "thirty thousand dollars on my person, belonging
to a mining company of which I was the general manager.
Naturally, I had taken the precaution to telegraph my secretary, etc." The story follows about how one of his hired des-
peradoes, Boone May, shot a bandit who attempted to rob the
manager of his money. This is the only record that Bierce left
about his year in the Black Hills of Dakota. There are reasons
why he would not particularly care to discuss this period in
his life, and why he permitted it to be veiled in obscurity. Even
his own family did not know much about what happened, and
his only advisors in San Francisco were Judge Boalt and
"Charley" Kauffman. It was surely not the romantic interlude
that he infers in the episode mentioned.

The entire matter may be traced to Bierce's trip across
the plains in 1866. Hazen's expedition had passed through the
Black Hills on its way west, and Bierce had made numerous
sketches for a map to be made of the entire region. When,
after his return to San Francisco from England, there began
to be much excitement about the Black Hills territory, which
was then being thrown open by the government for settlement,
Bierce made these notes into a map which was published by
A. L. Bancroft & Company, in 1877, under the title: "Map of
the Black Hills Region, Showing the Gold Mining District
and the Seat of the Indian War. Drawn by A. G. Bierce from
surveys ordered by the War Department." The gold fields of
the Far West had been thoroughly exploited by then and the
floating, migratory, mining population was looking for new
regions in which to prospect for gold and silver. Naturally
Bierce was interested, particularly as he was familiar with the
Black Hills region. He was, moreover, beginning to be rather
disgusted with Pixley.

Mining as an adventure exercised a great sway over the
popular imagination from 1849 to 1890; the period of the
supremacy of mining as a popular ideal probably lasted until
after the collapse of silver mining which perished with the
repeated defeats of William Jennings Bryan. There was scarcely
a Western family during these years that was not affected in
some manner by mining. The extent of the widespread popular interest in mining is reflected in the Western journals of the
day. These newspapers were full of mining news, mining stock

quotations, rumors of strikes, the fabulous escapades of Tabor and the rise of Leadville. The habits of the miner became Western traits of character, and the jargon of the mining camp colored the stream of our vocabulary. It is an amazing experience to check over the lists of publishing houses during this period and to note the flood of books, pamphlets and tracts about mines or mining life. The list of "homely" philosophies of life inspired by queer mining characters would alone make a considerable bibliography. The three foremost figures in Western literature, Mark Twain, Bret Harte and Ambrose Bierce, were intimately associated with mining life. The poems, stories, and novels that came out of the west during this period centered about mining life and, towards 1898, one can trace the sweep of the mining hordes to Alaska and the emergence of a new group of writers who attempted to record that phase of the movement. It is not, therefore, surprising to find that Bierce resigned his position with *The Argonaut* to become a miner.

The matter was even more personal. Bierce had a natural interest in mining; it was a vocation to which many members of his family gravitated. Several Bierces are to-day prominent mining engineers: H. C. Bierce, of Los Angeles, is a hydraulic engineer; and Herman Bierce Waters and Lucius Fuller are well known in their profession. Albert Bierce showed this same interest. Ambrose had some engineering training. Moreover, his work at the Sub-Treasury, which was in effect the United States Mint, put him in contact with mining and mining men. Several of his best friends, such as Capt. Nichols, who married the beautiful Belle Thomas, and O. C. Miller, were miners. Then, too, his wife's family had been miners for two generations.

Dr. Danziger intimates that Bierce's mining expedition into the Black Hills was, in some strange manner, connected with the Southern Pacific. But this, of course, is nonsense. And, contrary again to the doctor's vivid imagination, Bierce did not quarrel with Frank Pixley prior to leaving for Dakota. Bierce was not discharged from *The Argonaut*. Both Pixley and Fred Somers are, of course, long since dead. The only person who perhaps recalls exactly what happened at the time is Jerome A. Hart, an early contributor to *The Argonaut* and its owner and publisher after the Pixley-Somers régime.

As a journalist in the early days, Mr. Hart came to know Bierce, Pixley, Somers, James Watkins, and the other figures of the San Francisco press. According to Mr. Hart, who was on the staff at the time, Bierce ceased writing for *The Argonaut* in April of 1879, and was absent from the office until November of that year. This coincides with the circumstances, for Bierce's copy disappeared from *The Argonaut* in May of 1879. There were a few items throughout the summer; and one series of "Fables and Anecdotes" and "Little Johnny" appeared on October 11, 1879, but it is apparent that this was copy which had been left at the office. From other records which Bierce left with his daughter, it appears that during the summer of 1879 he was interested in the promotion of several mining companies. There are several letters from O. C. Miller, an old friend, written during August of 1879, indicating that Bierce was associated, in some manner, with the Carrie Steele Mining Company, along with Miller and several other San Franciscans.

What happened after Bierce returned to the office of *The Argonaut* in the fall of 1879, may be related by Mr. Hart. "About this time Bierce grew much excited over the talk of gold mines in the Black Hills, then thrown open by the U. S. Government to miners and settlers. His knowledge of assaying acquired in the United States Mint (*sic*) led to his securing a well-paid position with a mining company in the Black Hills. He resigned from *The Argonaut* staff; I think this was in the spring of 1880. There was no quarrel with Pixley or anybody else; his parting was amicable; everybody in the office wished him well and envied him his potential wealth as a gold miner." * This statement is substantially correct. Bierce secured the appointment because of his familiarity with the Black Hills region, as the publication of his map had made him something of an authority, and not because of any knowledge of assaying that he may have acquired.

The company that Bierce finally became associated with as "superintendent" was The Black Hills Placer Mining Company, which had headquarters at Rockerville, South Dakota. Bierce got in contact with the organizers of this company through an old army friend who was attorney for the project. He was none other than Sherburne Black Eaton, the "S. B.

* From letter of Jerome A. Hart to the author.

Eaton," head of the treasury agents in Section No. 1 of Alabama, who had returned to New York after the reconstruction work and entered the practice of the law under the firm name of Chamberlain, Carter & Eaton. He had kept up his acquaintance with Bierce by correspondence after the war, and when this opportunity arose had naturally tendered the position to his old associate. The company had been organized before Bierce went to Dakota. He was its general agent, with full power of supervision, from July to September, of 1880, at Rockerville, South Dakota.

The company's former agent was one Captain Ichabone M. West. He had resigned from his position, but was fulfilling a contract with the company for the erection of a flume and other structures at the time Bierce took over the management. Some two hundred thousand dollars were advanced to this man under Bierce's supervision on construction work. The company seems to have been poorly organized and soon ran out of capital. Bierce began to write Eaton urgent letters, demanding money to meet the payroll of the mine, as laborers and other creditors were becoming quite insistent in their demands. To make matters worse, Captain West defaulted with the proceeds of a draft from the New York offices, and the local bank refused to pay Bierce the balance of the funds which were on deposit in his name as agent, inasmuch as the bank claimed the right to offset the money West had taken against the amount of the draft.

The situation became too acute for Bierce, and he left for New York in an effort to secure additional funds to carry on the work of the company. But nothing could be done. The Black Hills did not, of course, develop into a great gold mining region and many other companies failed about this time. He stayed on in New York for several weeks, conferring with Eaton and Marcus Walker, and a Mr. Amidon, but it was apparent that the company was insolvent and the directors did not have sufficient confidence in the enterprise to finance it further. So Bierce left New York for California, a very disappointed and disheartened man. His great bonanza had failed and he was in a much worse position than before, since the company even owed him the greater part of his wages for the time he was in Dakota. It was surely not a very pleasant *dénouement* to what had promised to be such an exciting triumph.

Prior to his departure for New York, Messrs. McLaughlin and Steele, the attorneys for the company at Deadwood, brought suit in Bierce's name against the First National Bank of Deadwood to recover the balance of three thousand dollars which the bank would not honor because of Captain West's overdraft. The suit was brought in the District Court of the First Judicial District of Dakota Territory, Lawrence County, and was an interminable piece of litigation. Bierce won in the lower court; the action was appealed and reversed; and was retried again at *nisi prius*. Bierce was merely a nominal plaintiff in the action, inasmuch as the claim had been assigned by the defunct company to its attorneys. These lawyers kept writing Bierce when he was in Auburn during 1884-1885, soliciting his aid. He replied to one of their letters and in the course of his reply said: "My experience with the company's officers has not been such that I am willing to take any steps in matters affecting them without some guaranty that my action will be acceptable to them." * It is indicative of the unpleasant relations that existed between Bierce and the mining company. During this litigation, Bierce was counseled by Judge Boalt. He finally agreed that his deposition might be taken in San Francisco. His answers to the written interrogatories which were propounded are models of clear thinking. Time and again, during the course of this lengthy deposition, Bierce would write down an answer which cut through the irrelevant questions and struck the main issues with very satisfactory directness. The action of "Ambrose G. Bierce vs. The First National Bank of Deadwood" was an apparition of an unfortunate experience that ever and anon reared its head to mock those early dreams of a fortune and independence, for it is quite obvious that Bierce had high hopes as to the success of his mining venture. He had written, before leaving San Francisco, to Henry Sampson, announcing that he was "free" from journalism forever. Sampson, who had probably witnessed several similar revolts in his day, wrote back: "How I envy you when you say that journalism is over with you! But I think I read somewhere once about a dog and

* Letter to McLaughlin & Steele, January 16, 1884.

his vomit which would doubtless apply in my case if it doesn't in yours."

The Dakota episode, and it was only an episode, may have fortified an attitude; surely it did not create one. It only extended over a period of a year and its ultimate effect must have been trivial. But it could scarcely have "sweetened" Bierce's reaction to life. He was always very proud and the rather humiliating circumstances of his return to San Francisco marked the beginning of a new feeling towards the city. He became resentful, and, where he had formerly been satirical in a rather amused manner, he was now vituperative and broad-oathed.

The failure of his mining venture did, however, have one important effect: it was the cause of considerable domestic disharmony. Mrs. Day had always watched over her daughter with an eye that missed no discrepancies on the part of Mollie's husband. There had been some friction between Bierce and Mrs. Day in England and their disagreements now broke out in an open feud. Mrs. Day had always resented the marriage of her only daughter, a daughter so popular and so beautiful, to a mere scribbler, a rowdy fellow who wrote paragraphs for *The News-Letter,* and who had once participated, so the ladies whispered, in a drunken Anti-Christ demonstration. The dear lady was given to social pretense and always annoyed Bierce with her "Great Catherine" attitude towards the world. Once, after she had been in the town of Eureka for some months, the townspeople rented a large hall and held a "social gathering" to bid her farewell, as she was returning to San Francisco. The walls were decorated with "evergreens, pictures and lights. On entering the hall, the first thing that struck the eye was the word 'Welcome' rustically arranged with evergreens directly over the music stand, below which was the stars and stripes extending across the entire width of the hall." During the course of the entertainment, "Mrs. Day was presented with a handsome dressing case, accompanied by a neat little speech from one of the committee of ladies that had selected and purchased the article. Mrs. Day was so taken by surprise, that she said, 'I can't say a word.'" The quoted extracts are taken from a Eureka newspaper clipping. Such things disgusted Bierce, particularly as he suspected that the lady had arranged the social gathering herself. He resented her condescension, and the two of them were never known to agree upon anything. With Captain Day, a genial, fine-spirited old fellow, Bierce was always on the best of terms. Bierce had not consulted either the Captain or James Day, his brother-in-law, before accepting the position with the Dakota mining company. Hence when it failed, he had to return to San Francisco in a rather defiant attitude, and he was precluded from asking or accepting assistance from the Days.

During the time that Bierce was in the Dakotas, Mrs. Bierce and the children lived with Captain and Mrs. Day in San Francisco. The boys, Day and Leigh, attended the old Spring Valley Grammar School, and were great favorites in the neighborhood. After Bierce returned to San Francisco, he rented a home in what was known as the "Fort Mason" settlement. It was high on the hillsides overlooking the bay and was, for the most part, an unsettled neighborhood. The boys organized "gangs," built forts in the hillside and resisted the attacks of the youngsters from the city with great vigor. Day and Leigh immediately joined this "Hill Gang" and became its leaders. Just as their father had flayed Denis Kearney, so would they pummel the dirty youngsters from the city with mud bullets and an occasional rock. Mr. J. G. Hawks remembers the wild battles that used to rage in the afternoons when school was over, and retains a vivid recollection of Day Bierce. Day was a brilliant youngster; he never "seemed to study and was super-normally quick and alert mentally." He was impetuous, valiant, and disdainful in a manner that suggested his father. But in the son the true quality appeared in an uninhibited, undisguised manner, for Day Bierce was something of a Shelley. His genius, and it amounted to that, was vivid and unforgetable and he was impossibly idealistic as shown by later experiences. The other son, Leigh, was talented and clever but lacked the authentic mark of genius that was about everything that Day Bierce said or wrote.

Bierce's manner with his children was most characteristic of the man generally. He was very severe, a Spartan parent, in the matters which he thought were important. He stressed manners rather than morals. He was vehement in his demands that they be individualistic, self-reliant and skeptical of buncombe. Once Day reported to his father that he had slapped an instructor's face who had attempted to chastise him. Bierce not only approved of the rebellious attitude but called on the instructor himself and told him never to attempt a punishment of his son again. Any indication of irreverence in the boys was met with encouragement on the part of their father. Bierce was, as is well known, fanatically neat, one of the most immaculate gentlemen imaginable. His children might be slightly rebellious and harum-scarum, but if they were ever ill-mannered or dirty, they must expect his swift and emphatic denunciation. They could play as they liked; hold such opinions as were agreeable to them; but if they were dirty they must expect the inevitable punishment. He thoroughly approved of his sons' conduct in refusing to attend Sunday school, although he yielded a point to his wife in permitting the daughter to go to church. He thought the experience would do Helen no harm, since, being a woman, it was immaterial what views she held! These seeming peccadilloes of personal prejudice are important, since they show what a remarkably consistent man Bierce was—personally. His ideas might be full of apparent contradictions and paradoxical utterances, but personally he was ever the same. He loathed streets that were named "Twelfth" or "Eleventh," as they were common and unmemorable. He disliked to carry on a conversation over the telephone, particularly with a chance acquaintance, as he could not look his interlocutor in the eye. He would seldom attend a lecture since, according to conventional rules of etiquette, he could not rise and correct some misstatement of the speaker. He abominated vulgarity and the active hatred he entertained for a "common" woman was almost unbelievable. He was always neat, and plain, about his dress, and his tastes were excellent. A typical Bierce letter is alone most significant: it was invariably written on a rather heavy-weight, cream-colored, four-page stationery and folded once, and was written with a stub-pen in a precise and beautiful hand, with never a blotch, a misspelled word, or any hesitancy. The thought was always firm and clear and touched with his personality. The ink tended to become bronzed with time and the old letters when unfolded are a joy to read. On the reverse of the envelope would be the seal, affixed with a scarab presented by his friend Jeremiah Lynch. Bierce was just as fastidious about the matter of cuisine as he was, say, about the structure of the sentence. He had devised some rather tasty dishes, and the Army and Navy Club in Washington was indebted to him for many choice recipes and suggestions, and he is said to have known something about mixing a cocktail.

The Bierces were a memorable couple. An old Frenchman, from whom they once rented a flat in San Francisco, remembers their leaving one evening to attend a performance at the Baldwin Theater. He was standing in the hallway as they descended the stairs with the light shining above them. He says it is one of his most vivid and prized recollections. Bierce dressed in black: tall, erect, his red-golden hair touched with light and energy, and Mollie Day Bierce dressed as though she had stepped from a fashion plate out of *Harper's Bazar*. As they passed out into the night, she turned her head, adorned with a little crimson bonnet and a drop-veil of half length, and smiled *Bon Soir!* with a gesture of delight. He turned indoors sadly, for the picture of this elegant couple had stirred old memories of life on the continent. His recollection is, perhaps, the last record of their happiness.

*   *   *

BIERCE returned to San Francisco in December of 1880. According to Mr. Hart he "applied with confidence for his old job on *The Argonaut*." The owners, Pixley and Somers, after consultation, decided that his prolonged absence proved that he was not indispensable, and therefore they declined to reengage him. Bierce was much chagrined and deeply angered; as Pixley was the "majority owner he held Pixley responsible and never forgave him." * This is an accurate statement, I believe, of what occurred, as it coincides with the facts. In accepting Mr. Hart's version of Bierce's relations with Pixley and *The Argonaut*, I am not unmindful of the fact that Bierce on occasion wrote very sharp notes about Mr. Hart in "Prattle." I make this notation to forestall criticism, but I feel that Mr. Hart's statement is the clearest that has been made and it has the added advantage of being capable of verification in many particulars.

Bierce was, as Mr. Hart says, deeply angered and chagrined

* Letter of Jerome H. Hart to the author.

at his inability to secure a place on the staff of the magazine that he had literally "made." But his subsequent hatred of Pixley, while it may have been colored by this experience, was also inevitable. Bierce did not dislike Fred Somers and he did not dislike the other members of the staff. But for Pixley, there was no phrase too sharp, no comparison too odious. I have tabulated Mr. Bierce's antipathies and the tallies scored after Frank Pixley's name outnumber all the others by a great margin. He excoriated the fellow for twenty years, punctured every editorial bubble that he blew, and traced the ulterior motive in his every change of policy. He would write such incisive sentences as this: "Pixley is as good as it is possible for him to be, has all the dignity he needs in making a back for all the rich to play at leap frog, and as much amiability as is not incompatible with an assassination of character." War was declared between these two militarists in 1881, and continued until Pixley's death. His hatred would have survived even Pixley's demise but, as he noted in "Prattle," Pixley had the forethought to be cremated so that there was no grave to be made the subject of caustic and corrosive comment.

During these black days after his return, the journalistic career of Ambrose Bierce hung in the balance. There was not a paper that would employ him on its staff. He was bitterly hated by "Mike" DeYoung, who owned *The Chronicle,* and the editors of the other papers were equally antagonistic. He could have secured immediate employment by agreeing to be a hired libelist, for his talent as a satirist was well known. But he would make no agreement or bargain. About the only thing he could do was to work as a "free lance," which he did for several months, sending in occasional contributions to various newspapers and magazines.

Dr. Danziger relates, as an uncontroverted fact, that Bierce once worked for "Mike" DeYoung. Upon examination, the doctor's story, however, appears to be based entirely on the hearsay of "Petey" Bigelow, an early-day journalist and friend of Bierce. According to Dr. Danziger's story, DeYoung underpaid Bierce for a contribution and Bierce threw the money back in his face. Here, says the doctor, with naive disregard for the principles of historical research, is the origin of Bierce's hatred of DeYoung. Bierce did hate DeYoung, but that he ever worked for *The Chronicle* is a statement which finds no corroboration in the facts. "Journalism in California" by John P. Young, of *The Chronicle,* makes no mention of such an employment, and surely it would not have been neglected if it were a fact. Moreover, the origin of the story, which Dr. Danziger has either deliberately warped to fit his theory or has repeated without investigation a version which is inaccurate, may be traced to an actual occurrence.

It seems that during these days when Bierce was hardpressed for employment, he contributed occasionally to *The Call* under the editorship of Loring Pickering. The company's records showed the fact of this employment, because a reporter for *The Wave* investigated the matter and wrote a news story about the occurrence here related. Subsequent to the appearance of the story in *The Wave,* however, the original records were destroyed in the great fire and earthquake, so that the only evidence to-day is a record of a record, but it is significant that Bierce knew the editors of *The Wave,* read their story, and made no correction. He would most certainly never have allowed the story to go unchallenged if it were not true. It seems that it was customary in those days for all San Francisco companies to pay their employees in silver. Pickering wrote an editorial in *The Call* in which he denounced this practice, pointed out the inconveniences which it entailed, and suggested that all employees demand payment in currency in order to correct the custom. The next time Bierce called at the cashier's window to receive payment for a contribution to *The Call,* he pushed back the silver tendered him, showed the cashier a clipping of Mr. Pickering's editorial and demanded currency in payment of the debt. The cashier was furious, but walked across the street, got the currency, and paid Bierce. It was the end of his connection with *The Call.* Now it is obvious at once that Dr. Danziger's yarn is a variant of this story, but how melodramatic it became in the Doctor's handling! Not to mention the fact that the scene is shifted from *The Call* to *The Chronicle* in a cleverly disguised effort to show that Bierce was mean and personal about all his hatreds, and that he did not act in accordance with principles and ideals, as though one had to dig up or invent a motive for Bierce's hatred of "Mike" DeYoung! There is a significant contrast between the

Doctor's fulsome, nauseating praise of his "great blond God" and the mean, contemptible way in which he attempts to show that Bierce's three great antipathies: Pixley, DeYoung and C. P. Huntington, were the results of purely personal situations. Dr. Danziger tries to make out this case against Bierce so that his readers may assume or infer that Bierce hated the Doctor for some such petty and personal a motive. But just as it may be shown that Bierce's antipathy to Pixley, DeYoung and Huntington, was but an expression of his instinctive aversion to all men who acted as animals, just so may it be shown that Dr. Danziger was on the "black list" for certain definite and very understandable reasons.

With the doors of *The Call* closed as irretrievably as those of *The Argonaut* and *The Chronicle,* Bierce was driven to the wall. His position was as isolated as it is possible to imagine, and there seemed to be no escape. He could not go east because his wife refused to leave the coast where she was at least assured of the support and care of her family. Moreover, Bierce disliked the East, and was under the mistaken belief, for many years, that his health was better in the West. Then, too, he was without funds to finance such a move. It was under these circumstances that he finally secured a position with *The Wasp* and once more came into control of a journal in which he could flay San Francisco with a wrath that had about it now something of the vindictive and revengeful spirit. The mining days were over and "The Prattler" was once more at work.

CHAPTER IX

THE WASP

ⒷIERCE's new home for "Prattle" was one of the most interesting journals that printed his copy. *The Wasp* (a singularly appropriate name), was said to be the first colored cartoon magazine published in this country. It resembled in many details *The Lantern,* having the same large, full-page colored cartoons; much the same format; and it printed the same sharp comment on men and affairs. Two cartoonists who did excellent work for *The Wasp* were Keller and Backhaus. Backhaus was a boy, only seventeen, and with little education. He was a great favorite of Bierce's. Later he went to Germany, which, as Bierce said, "was right, but he died there, as was wrong." Bierce was, *en passant,* a talented newspaperman. His knowledge of the craft was more accurate and better informed than the second-hand acquaintance of the average columnist. *The Wasp* under his editorship was a most unusual magazine, and its files remain interesting to-day. In 1881 it must have been a minor sensation, and it was in January of that year that it began to publish the first of his work, part of "The Devil's Dictionary." He soon became its editor and published "Prattle" in his pages from 1881 to 1886. But it is apparent to even a casual reader that *The Wasp* was never self-supporting. It must have been a costly publication, there was scarcely any advertising in its pages, and its general tone was surely not such as to have attracted a wide audience. How, then, was this interesting journal financed?

It seems that, unknown to Bierce, *The Wasp* was really owned by Charles Webb Howard, an official of the Spring Valley Water Company, a large public utility corporation operating in the Bay District. To keep Bierce, and others, in ignorance of the true ownership of the paper, a dummy was employed to play the rôle of "publisher." So far as Bierce knew, the paper was owned by one Harry Dam. But Mr. Howard was at all times the real owner, and he made a nice profit by forcing the Spring Valley Water Company to buy about all the advertising space that the paper sold. This condition existed for quite a number of years, even after Bierce became editor, and until he learned the facts as to its ownership. When he discovered the deception that had been practiced upon him, he was furious and could not be placated. "I was more obstinate than ever; and now when I remember the lofty scorn with which I greeted every overture of my employer, I am filled with admiration and convinced afresh that I was born to be Rear-Admiral of a trade-union." * He threatened a public exposé of the fraud, and in order to prevent this calamity Howard was forced to sell the paper to E. C. MacFarlane, an old friend of Bierce's.

From the first issue to which he contributed until he resigned, Bierce was *The Wasp*. He wrote the editorials; conducted his page of "Prattle"; edited all contributions; wrote many poems; and began the publication of "The Devil's Dictionary," perhaps the sharpest and most readable wit that he ever wrote. With the first issue of *The Wasp*, he began the publication of this dictionary of wit, beginning with the letter "P," and continued down the alphabet until March 5th, 1881, when he started the dictionary all over again, apparently with the thought in mind of rewriting and enlarging the original plan. The idea of such a dictionary was, of course, old with Voltaire, but it owed its immediate origin to some work that Bierce had done for *The News-Letter* in December of 1875, after his return from London, called "The Demon's Dictionary" and which ran for only a few issues. It was a convenient frame for a professional wit to use, as it gave him a constant pattern, and all that was needed was to select new words on which to direct his satire. Much of his wit was the result of a formula, a mere verbal juggling with ideas. In the early issues of the magazine appeared, also, "The Wasp's Book of Wisdom," containing many epigrams and aphorisms rather suggestive of the "Smart Set Birthday Book" that Mencken and

* *The Examiner*, January 6, 1889.

Nathan published several years ago. Bierce reprinted in *The Wasp* a great deal of his London work; many of the fables from *Fun* and a few stories first used in Tom Hood's *Comic Annual.*

"Prattle" was the same sprightly page that it was in 1869. There were no exceptions to Bierce's scorn; his abuse was universal and lovely. It was sharpest when directed at a local poet or novelist, as though he resented even the thought of a San Franciscan attempting to write. In many instances his satire abruptly terminated the creative impulse. During the time that Bierce edited *The Wasp,* a fellow journalist, Harr Wagner, was editor of *Vanity Fair,* a continuation of Joe Lawrence's famous magazine *The Golden Era.* Mr. Wagner is an optimistic fellow, and he was even more cheerful and sentimental in 1881. He once published a novel called "The Street and the Flower," which tells the story of a young boy of the streets and the sweet, flower-like maiden who redeemed him. Bierce pounced upon this book hungrily and with joy. For weeks on end he poured abuse into Wagner that would have shamed a Turk. Mr. Wagner was good-natured about the matter, and was shrewd enough to reprint some of Bierce's unkind gibes. They immediately provoked a reaction in favor of the novel and its author, for it was quite obvious that Mr. Bierce was unfair. But, good-natured as he was, Mr. Wagner never wrote another novel. Lillian Ferguson contributed occasional verse to the press during the eighties under the name of Lillian Plunkett. Bierce seized upon this name with sadistic glee and made endless sport of her verse by puns on the word "Plunkett." The recollection of these early burlesques still rankles in the memory of several writers who survived his satire. Charlotte Perkins Gilman remembers him very vividly, as is revealed in this statement: "He was the Public Executioner and Tormentor, daily exhibiting his skill in grilling helpless victims for the entertainment of the public,—for wages. He was an early master in the art of blackening long-established reputations of the great dead, of such living persons as were unable to hit back effectively, and at his best in scurrilous abuse of hard-working women writers. He never lost an opportunity to refer to the cotton-stuffed bosoms of the women writers." * But Mrs. Gil-

* From a letter, April 3, 1929, to the author.

man errs in saying that he struck only those who could not hit back effectively. As a matter of fact, there was no reputation, living or dead, that he was afraid to attack, although his blasts have the unmistakable indication of bravura about them at times.

In a single page of "Prattle" he would excoriate as many as fifteen prominent San Franciscans. Some he never wearied of flaying. General W. H. L. Barnes could not walk abroad but that Bierce would snip at his heels; Loring Pickering never split an infinitive or mixed a metaphor but that Bierce hit him with a longshoreman's swing. Mr. W. C. Bartlett must have hesitated to write his art criticism, for Bierce would wait until he had reviewed an exhibition and then make some such comment as this:

> "The old he-hen who makes the *Bulletin's* art criticism has been in full cackle ever since the opening of the Spring exhibition—Everything about the Exhibition is, to Mr. Bartlett, great and excellent. Furthermore, he has executed this identical prostration of his spirit every spring since Californian art began to defy the law against indecent exposure— Doubtless the senile and unhaired wretch can now show as many little notes of gratitude from the ladies (weirdly malographic and uncannily mispencilled) as he has mentioned names which will visibly enhance the superiority of his smile and endow him with fat sleep and free dreams."

It was an amusing page of malice and the number of victims preserved in its yellowing pages is startling, for it reads like a directory of San Francisco! Poor Pixley was ever and anon made immortal in some epitaph starting, as one did, with the line: "Here lies Frank Pixley as usual." A wretched druggist was once a candidate for Supervisor. He had cards printed with the words: "William J. Bryan, Druggist, for Supervisor 12th Ward." Bierce quoted the card in his "Prattle" and then wrote:

> "Oh! William, such a thrifty trick,
>   Closely on genius verges;
> Your candidacy makes men sick
>   So to your pill-shop double quick
> They fly for pukes and purges."

The collapse of the seventies had given the railroads a magnificent opportunity to gain control of the state, and by 1881 they were so bold about their dominance that it seems incredible that the citizenry could have endured the situation. But they did, and the universal corruption became really laughable; every one was a kept lobbyist for the railroad. The legislatures at Sacramento were a disgrace even for the State of California. Such political corruption and bribery were perhaps never witnessed in an American commonwealth as occurred in California during these years. The supremacy of "Boss" Tweed was localized and trifling when compared with the state-wide control of the Southern Pacific Railroad in California. The railroad took no chances: it owned both major political parties: it controlled the press with scarcely an exception. Bierce became so annoyed with the apathy of his fellow-citizens that his abuse grew shrill and hysterical. "If nonsense were black, Sacramento would need gas lamps on Monday. . . . So scurvy a crew I do not remember to have discerned in vermiculose conspiracy outside the carcass of a dead horse,—at least not since they adjourned." The national scene did not seem much more inspiring: "The frosty truth of the situation is that we are a nation of benighted and boasting vulgarians, in whom the moral sense is as dead as Queen Anne, at her deadest; that we are hopelessly floundering and helplessly foundering in a sea of public and private corruption as offensive as that upon which the Ancient Mariner saw the shiny things that 'did crawl with legs'; that we are a laughing stock to Europe and a menace to civilization." *

Not only was Bierce frantically annoyed with the stupidity of the people of a great commonwealth who permitted thick-browed gentlemen like "Uncle Colis" Huntington to loot them blind, but his feeling of resentment was deeper and more personal. He was lonely for the society of civilized people. The society of San Francisco, at the time, was slightly grandiose and ornate. Some French architects in the sixties imported a psuedo-classic type of design that quickly became a grotesque pattern in the hands of the natives. Greek porticos with Corinthian columns led up flights of wooden steps, and inevitably a "bay window" bulged out over the street. The type gradually became even more pretentious. There were conical towers, ec-

* *The Wasp*, May 21, 1881.

centric steps, Queen Anne flourishes cheek-by-jowl with some
one's idea of Renaissance style. This uneven, quixotic society
ranging from Nob Hill to the Barbary Coast, was shot through
and through with barbarous hatreds and currents of greed that
annihilated even the possibility of good work in the arts. A
satirist could survive, if he were willing to lend his pen to
verbal butchery; but the life did not permit of the same work
that was just coming to flower at the end of the fifties with Joe
Goodman, Bret Harte, and Mark Twain.

It would be impossible to trace the pattern of all the ran-
corous hatreds and scandals that were a part of the life of those
days. The Rev. Isaac S. Kalloch, politician and preacher, called
Charles DeYoung, founder of *The Chronicle,* a bastard.
Threats were made, and a Kalloch killed Charles DeYoung.
Crowds surged in the streets; the saloons were rife with loud
pronunciations of vengeance; and for sixty-five days San Francisco milled around the court room until Kalloch was acquitted.
Judge Terry, who began to "knife" people back in the Vigilante
Days and who killed David Broderick in a duel, fell in state and
became the pawn of the dramatic Sarah Hill. Majestic Stephen
Field, once alcalde of a village in Spanish-California days, but
on his way to the U. S. Supreme Court, offended Sarah during
the course of a trial. Terry made threats. Later he tried to kill
Judge Field and was shot down by United States Marshal Nagel,
who became a famous precedent in *In Re Nagel,* but was saved
by the reasoning of the future associates of Judge Field. The
railroad sent armed thugs into Mussel Slough to oust settlers,
and their pet gunman, Walter Crowe, slaughtered farmers
from ten in the morning until the last hours of the afternoon, when he was shot dead. Sharon sued Sharon through
forty volumes of California decisions, and Mr. Colton's widow
still complained of Leland Stanford. The heirs of James G.
Fair, of Virginia City fame, quarreled about a trust. The case
was appealed to the Supreme Court. The first decision of the
higher court was in favor of the trust's validity by a four to
three decision, Henshaw voting with the four. Judge Henshaw
wavered. After all, he mused, amidst a dusty stack of reports,
"man lives but once," and the next decision found Henshaw
voting the other way. The final opinion shattered the trust, and
Judge Henshaw received $400,000, as shown by the affidavit

of a co-conspirator who saw the light of divine revelation from
a "fake-healer" and rushed to Fremont Older to confess. Hate
and lust and abuse . . . It was a furnace of anger which affected all classes in the commonwealth. In such a society, Bierce
was kept at a boiling temperature for years; naturally when the
hates ran their course, his white fury crystallized in adamant
prejudice and opinion.

It is not surprising to find that during this time Mr. Bierce
was still offering to give satisfaction to the offended. There was
one occasion when two army officers had given affront in crossing the bay one evening. The next morning he addressed this
note to the two unknown culprits:

> "That you are cowards I have not the dimmest doubt, but
> you can hardly afford to prove it to one another by withhold-
> ing from me the power to call you so by name,—which I engage
> to do; my name, Ambrose Bierce, being, I hope, a sufficient
> warrant that the purpose will be executed in good faith and
> to the letter." *

The eighties was not only the era of the false front in
architecture, but it was the age of just as studied an avoidance
of simplicity in the other arts. The literary gentlemen such as
T. H. Reardon, wrote essays about Petrarch, or brought
out editions of Heredia's poem, as did E. H. Taylor, or
wrote Byronesque poetry, as did the sad-eyed Richard Realf.
"On the Verge," the favorite novel of the period, abounds in
French quotations in every other paragraph. And when stories
were written at all, they were generally of the highly artificial
ghost-type that R. H. Milne and E. H. Cloud wrote. They did
not look at life; Mark Twain and Bret Harte had done so
thirty years previously, but these latter-day fellows were too
elegant for this earth. Bierce, during these first years on *The
Wasp,* was too busy to write much besides his regular journalism. "What I saw of Shiloh," appeared in the Christmas number, 1881, and there were reprinted stories from his London
days, but the time had not yet arrived for him to write the
stories which have since become so celebrated.

But whether the society was charming or not, and however
boldly the rascals looted the money-bags at Sacramento, one

* *The Wasp,* July 14th, 1883.

thing remained to console Bierce: the untrammeled, gloriously independent American saloon. If he was poorly paid, middle-aged, ambitionless and weary of the scene, he could always quit work and sojourn along the cocktail route, that commenced on the southwestern corner of Kearney and Bush and proceeded along Kearney to Market, and continued on the northern side of Market west as far as Powell, and "return or not, as the devotee wished or could daily afford," as Major Ben C. Truman once phrased it. As early as 1880 there were nine drinking places between the two ends, not counting Joe Parker's place on the northwestern corner of Bush and Kearney, or the bar at the Baldwin Theater. Business adjourned at about 4 o'clock, and the Latin holiday spirit that ruled in San Francisco in those days was released. There was a stream of men following this cocktail route, ending up at the point of beginning about 8 o'clock in time for dinner. It was not a raucous scene: Hacquette & Hageman's Crystal Palace was conducted as a high-class club. Along this route Bierce would journey, and when he, too, was ready for dinner, the lights of the city were gleaming and San Francisco was not the putrid, foul-smelling den of vulgarity that it had been before he commenced the journey. Booze was a great consolation, a spiritual solace, amidst such scenes. Mr. Upton Sinclair, who, for reasons that it is difficult to understand, called George Sterling foul names because he got drunk at a Ruskin Club banquet (who wouldn't?), has also berated Bierce as "an eminent tankard man." Of course Bierce drank. "Water," he once remarked, "has one merit—it is cheap; and one disadvantage—it is not good."

With the cocktail route, Chinatown and the Barbary Coast, San Francisco had its faith charlatans, and religious intolerance was not unknown. In 1881 Sarah Cooper was tried for heresy. Her chief persecutor was Rev. J. B. Roberts. Of this man Bierce wrote:

> "Dim-pinnacled in the intense shame of his theological environment, he sits astride his evil eminence of personal malignity, breaking the seals that close that pestilence, his mind, and its insupportable rain of red ruin falls alike upon the just and the unjust, the while he cackles his unholy glee till the lute-strings of his larynx are aweary of their work. Look at him—the hideous apparition perched between the

world and the light, flinging his ugly shadow athwart the
scene to fray the souls of babes and sucklings. O, but he is a
bright and beautiful bird-of-paradise, a-ripening for the gun.
Some Christian sportsman fill him a tempest of shot and compile him a bag. He is game by God's unwritten law—and he
shall take himself away from Sarah Cooper's burrow, or I,
for one, will make him wish he were another and better dog."

Finally Bierce wearied of the entire collection of holy idiots
that were constantly creating disturbances and prosecuting the
weak, and in tones of exasperation wrote of them:

"What a procession of holy idiots we have had in San
Francisco—hot gospellers and devil-pelters of all degrees!
Thick-necked Moody with Sankey of the nasal name; Hallen-
beck, Earle, Knops and all their he-harlotry of horribles. And
now this grease eating and salt-crusted Harrison from the
pork regions of the northeast, thinking holy hog-and-hominy
and talking his teeth loose for the dissuasion of sinners from
their natural diet of sin, without which they would be sick!
Can we do nothing to rid us of the periodical incursions of
these scale-bugs—these leaf-worms—these phylloxera of the
moral vineyard? May the devil smite them with a tempest of
sulphuric acid from his Babcock extinguisher!" *

During these early years after his return, Bierce lived in
a flat at 1428 Broadway, San Francisco. He lived with his family when his health permitted, but there were long intervals
when he would be absent, away in the hills seeking relief from
his asthma. Nicassio was his favorite retreat during this period.
It was then quite a pretty resort in Marin County, near San
Rafael. But, in a few years, it became apparent that he could
no longer live in San Francisco or make a pretense of keeping
a residence there. His absences from his family were increasing
in frequency and duration. Contrary to his legendary cruelty,
he was almost sentimental about these trips away into the hills.
He would write his daughter, Helen, charming letters about the
pines where he lived, the rumble in the storm clouds which was
like the "roar of great cannons," tell her in a wistful manner
that he missed her very much, and then always end his letters,
as he did with all his children, "Your Father, A. G. Bierce."

* *The Wasp,* October 21, 1881.

But, before the family moved away from San Francisco, he determined to try one further resort for his health, and this time he went to Auburn, in Placer County, in 1883, where he lived for a number of years.

Prior to leaving for Auburn, however, there had been considerable trouble between Bierce and his wife. It was a rather subtle antagonism. He complained rather bitterly of the "Holy Trinity," meaning his wife, Mrs. Day and James Day, his brother-in-law. These three were always of the same opinion on every question, and the two Days would sometimes succeed in swinging Mrs. Bierce into line with them against her husband. As already mentioned, Bierce had disliked Mrs. Day since his return from London, and his sharp antipathy to his brother-in-law dated from about the same period. The circumstances of this quarrel were well known to members of the family at the time. James Day had fallen in love with the daughter of an aged clergyman, who, strangely enough, was a good friend of Bierce and, for that matter, of the Day family. The affair was a rather sordid one, and the old clergyman was so humiliated and chagrined by the experience that shortly afterwards he committed suicide. It was the breach of friendship that nettled Bierce. The revulsion which he experienced against James Day could never be overcome. He froze into an attitude of contempt. Hence he never forgave him. But, although he was estranged after a fashion from his wife while living at Auburn, there had been as yet no separation. The cause of their ultimate and final separation had not occurred. Many people who knew Bierce at Auburn strenuously insist that he was separated from his wife at that time, but such is not the case. They lived apart a great deal, because of Bierce's health, and there did exist considerable misunderstanding, but they were not separated in any legal sense of the term, nor for that matter, in the sense that they had agreed not to live together.

In Auburn, Bierce lived at the old Putnam House, a ramshackle hotel, the pride of that sleepy village. He rather liked to satirize Auburn, in verse and prose, and on one occasion he wrote of it these lines called "The Perverted Village":

"Sweet Auburn! liveliest village of the plain.
Where Health and Slander welcome every train,

> Whence smiling innocence, its tribute paid,
> Retires in terror, wounded and dismayed—
> Dear lovely bowers of gossip and disease,
> Whose climate cures us that thy dames may tease,
> How often have I knelt upon thy green
> And prayed for death, to mitigate their spleen!"

It was at Nicassio and then at Auburn that Bierce began that long, interminable vagabondage of his, a constant moving about from one country hotel to another in search of a "breathing place." First it was the Putnam House at Auburn; the Cranes Hotel at Sunol; Angwin's on Howell Mountain; the El Monte at Los Gatos; Wright's in the Santa Cruz Mountains; at the Jeffreys Place at Wrights. They were all small, unattractive hotels, sequestered in unbroken solitude. He lived, for the most part, without companions and without care in his periods of illness. That he missed the civilized, social life of London cannot be doubted. He wrote once that:

> "I would rather dine in a receiving vault of a cemetery than in an American dining-room. I mean the dining-room of a hotel where ladies are admitted. The awful hush, the peculiar ghastly chill, the visible determination to be proper and avert the slow stroke of the rebuking eye that awaits the miscreant who laughs or speaks above his breath—these things overcome me. I can't breathe in that atmosphere of solemn stupidity. I choke my food and strangle on my drink. The waiter carries me out." *

Many amusing incidents took place at Auburn that illustrate what a provincial place it was in the eighties, and, still is, I have no doubt. During one of Bierce's most violent attacks of asthma, nearly every woman in the town came to the hotel and advocated some special remedy. One woman, however, did not come to the hotel. Her reticence intrigued Bierce. When he recovered sufficiently to be about, he called on this lovely but adamant lady and asked why she had not proposed some remedy for his asthma. Her cold and professional reply was: "Oh, that's easy to explain: I'm a physician."

There lived in Auburn, at that time, a handsome and attractive widow. She shocked the town considerably by her efforts

* *The Wasp*, July 8, 1881.

to keep far in advance of the times, and Bierce was amused by her antics. One day she proposed to him that they have a picnic in the woods: a bottle of champagne, some verse, and woodland intimacy. He assented and set aside, at least the volume of verse, for the occasion. The lady started to drive down the main street of the town towards the Putnam House, when the horse she was driving ran away. The buggy with the picnic-lady came careening up the street, turned a corner and upset. The contents of the picnic basket, including several bottles of champagne, spilled out in the road in the gaze of the usual crowd of village loafers and gossips, much to the lady's discomfort. But Bierce rushed to the rescue, picked her out of the wreckage, and they picnicked just the same. Perhaps he had this woman in mind when, in after years, he defined a "widow." He was present at quite an interesting gathering in Oakland, and some one happened to mention the word "widow." Immediately Bierce became pensive and sad. "A widow," he mused, "God's second noblest gift to man." There was a pause and then the expected inquiry: "And the first, Mr. Bierce?" Another pause, and then leaning forward in an atmosphere of hushed expectancy, he whispered very softly: "A bad girl."

During the latter part of 1885, and into 1886, E. C. Mac-Farlane, or "Ned" as he was called, began to have great difficulty with *The Wasp*. MacFarlane was a personal friend of Bierce, who had induced him to purchase the paper. But he really had a secret motive in doing so, unknown to Bierce, and this motive soon became apparent. He had a brother, George MacFarlane, who was a wealthy sugar planter in the Hawaiian Islands. The status of the Islands was then quite unsettled, and the sugar planters were anxious to secure favorable rights under the terms of a treaty being drafted between the United States and Their Majesties. To further this cause, the MacFarlanes thought that it would be good policy to own a newspaper in San Francisco, as the measure required considerable publicity.

It was during 1883 that quite a group of people who were interested in the Islands, including a number of newspapermen and their families, went to Hawaii to attend the coronation ceremonies. Among Bierce's effects is an invitation, dated February 12, 1883, in which "Their Majesties the King and Queen request the presence of Major and Mrs. A. G. Bierce in Iolani

Palace for the coronation ceremonies." Mrs. Bierce actually went on this trip, but her husband remained at home and cabled to his friends, in response to their inquiries as to why he was not present: "Why should I bother to see a negress crowned queen of the fly-speck Isles?" This invitation was, of course, the work of the MacFarlanes, and, also, of E. L. G. Steele, who was another San Franciscan vitally interested in the development of the Islands.

After he had moved to Auburn, Bierce surrendered the active management of *The Wasp* to Ned MacFarlane. But MacFarlane, who was quite inexperienced as a journalist, soon began to have difficulty with the management of the paper. It was not so much the matter of money, for the MacFarlanes were wealthy people and could arrange to finance the paper, as it was in the field of politics that the trouble arose. MacFarlane would take flying week-end trips to Auburn for consultation and would return to San Francisco measurably calmed, only to write eight- or ten-page letters the next day to Bierce, exclaiming: "Oh, what shall I do!" He was quite quick tempered and actually feared that he might be overcome with frenzy and kill some of his enemies. His chief tormentor was none other than "Mike" DeYoung.

DeYoung began to attack MacFarlane and Bierce in *The Chronicle*. The main point of attack, and it was insidiously planned, was that MacFarlane had not actually purchased *The Wasp* from Howard, its former owner, but that he was just another dummy, such as Harry Dam had been. This infuriated both Bierce and MacFarlane, but they were powerless to check the effects of the insinuation. They could shout denials and their very vehemence was taken as an admission of guilt. DeYoung was immensely clever about such things, and he knew that nothing would infuriate Bierce so much as this constant intimation that the editor of *The Wasp* was just a puppet for large corporate interests.

Then, too, MacFarlane was caught in the toils of a political dilemma. His brother began to make strenuous demands that *The Wasp* give its unqualified support to the treaty with the Islands. To do so, at the time, required a change in the politics of the paper, as the national party which *The Wasp* had always endorsed was opposing the treaty. Furthermore, the change had

to be made in the midst of a presidential campaign. DeYoung
was gleeful, and, after the change had been made, he pointed at
the apostasy with scorn. The real situation was that DeYoung
had tried to bribe the sugar planters into purchasing the support
of his paper, but he had run foul of Adolph Spreckels. He had
announced that Spreckels, another large plantation owner, was
corruptly influencing the press of California in favor of the
treaty, and, particularly, that he had purchased *The Wasp*. Old
Spreckels stood for this quite some time. But he finally turned
berserk and chased DeYoung into his office and gave him a good
caning. But DeYoung's blow had struck, just the same, for
there could be no denial that Ned MacFarlane, newspaperman,
and George MacFarlane, plantation owner, were merely playing
a game.

"Mike" DeYoung was, without doubt, the most interesting
journalist on the coast. He was unscrupulous but had the courage to be frank in his demands. Every interest had to subsidize
his press if it wanted his support; he was selling influence and
was quite willing that people should know the rates. He could
not be insulted and was adamant to abuse. He outlived all his
enemies and became a millionaire. His impassivity before epi-
thet was amazing. He was called, at one time or other, practically every variety of rascal that the dictionary of abuse could
define. But he would only smile and make more money. Occasionally, in later years, Bierce would hit too hard, and DeYoung
would start out in the morning, after a few drinks, to "kill
Ambrose Bierce." But his nerve always waned or perhaps his
cynicism reasserted itself. Bierce once called him a murderer to
his face, and he still refused to fight. He knew when to smile.

The Wasp was essentially a political journal, and its pages
reflect imperfectly the strident and vigorous manner in which
political issues were debated in the eighties. Full-page cartoons
shrieked blasphemies at the enemy, and editorials blasted the
very foundation of the opponent's platform. Naturally, Bierce's
views began to take color from such violence. The issues were
somewhat obscure, the forces were imperfectly aligned, but political corruption was the rule. "Politics," he once wrote, "is
a pitch that defiles, a tope that endrunkens, a poison that pene-
trates the bones and gets into the hair." In the midst of such
scenes, Bierce despaired of his fine theory about "lashing ras-

cals through the world," and became cynical even of his scorn. He wrote of the press:

> "Newspapers—conducted by rogues and dunces for dunces and rogues, they are faithful to nothing but the follies and vices of our system, strenuously opposing every intelligent attempt at their elimination. They fetter the feet of wisdom and stiffen the prejudices of the ignorant. They are sycophants to the mob, tyrants to the individual." *

No doubt Bierce's views on journalism and journalists were affected by his association with MacFarlane. He thought that his friend was buying *The Wasp* out of a disinterested desire to give him a journal in which to purge the city of its vices, when, as a matter of fact, he was buying the paper to further his own interests. And Bierce had to acquiesce in MacFarlane's wishes, and consent to the ignoble change of policy midstream, and all for a personal consideration. Nothing but the greatest necessity would have made him do so.

In December of 1885, MacFarlane finally admitted that the fight was too much for him, and he left for the Islands, writing Bierce a long letter from the Bohemian Club explaining his motives and, also, advising him that "Charley" Kauffman would make provision for the journal. He also promised to secure Bierce a government position in the Islands, which he never did. Shortly thereafter MacFarlane sold his interest in the paper to Jackson, and the doors were closed on another interesting chapter in the history of "Prattle." Bierce was probably glad that the episode was over, although it left him in a precarious position. It had never been a satisfactory arrangement; he had been underpaid; had worked too hard; had become involved in distasteful alliances; and had been repeatedly disappointed in MacFarlane. But now there was no journal left in San Francisco that would accept his work. He was hated like a rattlesnake. By the spring of 1886, "Prattle" ceased to appear in *The Wasp,* and when "Prattle" was discontinued it invariably meant that Bierce was sick, or fired.

His work on *The Wasp* had not passed unnoticed. Parsons, one of the strongest editorial writers and journalists on the Pa-

* *The Wasp,* March 26, 1881.

cific coast, once wrote a long editorial in the Sacramento *Record-Union* (December 28, 1881), praising Bierce for his fine fearlessness; the Stockton *Evening Mail* (Dec. 30, 1881) was equally enthusiastic. Journalists on the coast read Bierce with indefatigable zest. A writer on the Visalia *Delta* (Jan. 6, 1882) had apparently seen Mr. Bierce in San Francisco, for he wrote: "He is a young man (apparently little over thirty), dresses in fashionable clothes without any affectation or eccentricity, and in bearing is always a polite, considerate, refined and scholarly gentleman." The article then proceeded to analyze Mr. Bierce's journalistic methods and came to the conclusion that his central merit was "absolute honesty." This was, of course, close to the facts. It was Bierce's theory that if you took the personal out of journalism nothing was left. He once asked: "Is it blasphemy to hold the mirror up to the blasphemer?"

But studying his journalism from the perspective which time gives, one is impressed with its futility. Of course, if journalism had to be followed as a trade, and it did during these years, for Bierce had no other means of support, then his fearless candor is no doubt commendable. But what did it matter if "Mike" DeYoung was a rascal, or that politicians were liars, or that local poets were ridiculous? Viewing his work during the six years that he wrote for *The Wasp,* the conclusion is inevitable that it was a waste of effort and that the devastating effects of his rage, reacting upon his own temperament, did incalculable injury to his thinking. To be personal inevitably provoked a quarrel, and when men quarrel they are absurd. The difficulty was, again, Mr. Bierce's idealism. He wrote that "the belief so dominant in the last generation that human events occur without human agency is a captivating absurdity." But was that belief so absurd? The corollary of his proposition, namely, that by human agencies man's nature can be changed, leads to positions which it is difficult to defend. He secretly believed that his satire might be immensely effective in correcting the evils it berated. But this belief, which did not take into consideration the possibility that there are agencies at work in society more important than the merely personal, was rather naïve. For as Remy de Gourmont has written, "The position taken by man outside the world to judge the world, is a factitious attitude." He was hampered and kept ineffective by his lack of information. Mr.

Bierce felt the need of the times; he sensed the situation; and he was correct in his conclusions. He anticipated modern thought, but he lacked the assistance which modern investigation could have given. Because of this inadequacy in equipment, he was sometimes quite incompetent in the personal affairs of his life, and quite ineffective in his criticism of public events. He came to realize this in later years, but in 1886 he was still the victim of his own courage, caught in the mesh of his own idealism, but quite undeceived about the life of his day and writing with a vigor and directness which command modern admiration. "Men are mad," said Pascal, "so unavoidably that not to be mad would constitute one a madman of another order of madness."

CHAPTER X

"SIR ORACLE, INDEED!"

A FTER he ceased to write for *The Wasp* there was an interval in which Bierce was sorely pressed for a livelihood. He was past middle-age and had accomplished none of the work of which he knew himself capable. Then, too, he was ill with asthma and had to find a home in the mountains where he could live. About this time, some one told him that if he would go and live among the pines on Howell Mountain for a year or so, that he would be cured of his asthma. So he decided to move his family from San Francisco to St. Helena in order that they might be near. St. Helena is a charming little town, situated where the north end of Napa Valley is blocked by Mt. Saint Helena, and Howell Mountain runs a long, blue, pine-clad ridge to the east. The Napa Valley is the Rhine Valley of California; the warm sun-baked hillsides are covered with vineyards and the old Graystone Winery, on the outskirts of the town, is a silent spectre of a noble past. It was but a few hours to Oakland, when Bierce wanted to make a foray into civilization. But, for the most part, he lived at Angwin's Camp on the top of Howell Mountain, about seven miles from St. Helena.

St. Helena, in the days when the Bierces first moved there, was a rather popular resort. Many prominent San Francisco families had country places nearby, such as the Polks and Fullers. Capt. Grant was an old friend of Bierce, in the early days in San Francisco, and he it was who suggested Angwin's as a health cure. He even offered the Bierces his cottage on Main Street in St. Helena, which they accepted. There they were to live for several years, in the little white cottage with a special roost built above, for Leigh to sleep in as a haven from asthma. Bierce lived at Angwin's on Howell Mountain, but he would return once or twice a week to his home, and would sometimes take Mrs. Bierce, with one or another of the children, back to his mountain retreat. Life in St. Helena was not altogether unpleasant: the valley was beautiful, many interesting people came there, and tucked away in the north end of the valley was old Schram's winery, where Bierce used to get his wine.

A great friend of both Mr. and Mrs. Bierce lived at this time in the Napa Valley. Her name was Lillie Coit. "Lil" Coit was the first "emancipated" woman of early San Francisco. While returning home from school in San Francisco one day, she noticed the Knickerbocker Fire Engine Company No. 5 stalled on a hillside. She discarded her books and rushed to the aid of the firemen. For this act she was made an honorary member of "No. 5," and the number became a fetish in her life. She had it carved over the door of her room and, so rumor hath it in St. Helena, the sacred symbol appeared on her nightshirts. When the fire alarm rang, she would rush to headquarters and might be seen atop Fire Engine No. 5 careening madly down the streets of San Francisco. She was extremely wealthy and equally handsome, and had a beautiful estate near St. Helena called "Lonely." Her home was the scene of many gay and interesting week-end parties. She was a great favorite of Mr. Bierce and they used to go hunting together. Lillie Coit is a character in several of Mrs. Atherton's better known stories, and she surely deserved to be made immortal, for no more interesting character lived on the coast. She used to drive a tally-ho coach that went whizzing around the Napa Valley, to the amazement of the natives and the delight of her friends. There were barbecue feasts at "Lonely," and, occasionally, "Lil" would drive up to Angwin's, wearing scandalously short skirts and hunting boots, to take "Bierce" out for a tramp in the woods. Her mad escapades were the talk of her generation, but never once was there any personal scandal about her name. " 'Lil' Coit," Bierce once remarked, "is a real woman."

But with the petty townspeople, Bierce had no traffic whatever. They quickly made a legend about the "blond god" who lived on Howell Mountain. On the occasion when he was in the town he would stalk around with all the hauteur of an officer in the imperial guard. There were few people in the town who were on speaking terms with him. The editor of the St. Helena *Star* once crossed verbal swords with him, and Bierce answered the fellow in "Prattle" in his usual terse manner and referred to him as the editor of the "St. Helena Liver-Complaint." But for the most part, the St. Helenans read his column of "Pratttle" and whispered awesomely among themselves. He seldom came to the town, and when he did it was at night, or to catch a train, so that they quickly concluded he was divorced from his wife and the legend became established. But of the lovely Mrs. Bierce, who was tall and dark and most kind, they had no illusions; they adored her without reservation. She would play the piano at their parties, help them with their "receptions," and entertain them, at Mrs. Hunt's home, with stories of London and the great world.

One day the minister came to call on Mrs. Bierce when Bierce chanced to be present. Leigh came running in from the garden shouting, "Oh, Daddy, Day just said 'Damn God.'" The minister and Mrs. Bierce were quite horrified, but Bierce only remarked: "Go and tell Day that I have repeatedly told him not to say 'Damn God' when he means 'God Damn.'"

When Bierce would go to Oakland, he would quite often stay several weeks, sometimes several months, particularly in the winter when he would take an apartment. But even after his family had been established at St. Helena, he would make trips to Auburn and other resorts, moving from one to another as his health required. It was while he was in Oakland, on one of his visits, that an incident occurred of the utmost moment and importance in his life. One afternoon there came a gentle tapping on the door of his apartment, and he went to find who it was that called. Let him tell the rest of the story: *

> "I found a young man, the youngest young man, it seemed to me, that I had ever confronted. His appearance, his attitude, his manner, his entire personality suggested extreme diffidence. I did not ask him in, install him in my better chair (I had two) and inquire how we could serve each other. If my memory is not at fault I merely said: 'Well' and awaited the result.
>
> "'I am from the San Francisco *Examiner,*' he explained in

* "Collected Works," Vol. XII, page 305.

a voice like the fragrance of violets made audible, and backed a little away.

"'Oh,' I said, 'you come from Mr. Hearst.' Then that unearthly child lifted its blue eyes and cooed: 'I am Mr. Hearst.'"

He had come to interview Mr. Bierce. Just a few weeks previously, in March of 1887, his father, Senator George Hearst, had given the San Francisco *Examiner* as a plaything to the former editor of the *Harvard Lampoon*. The young editor showed amazing shrewdness in selecting his staff; the principle behind his choice was invariably the same: he wanted the best. He had determined to commit the unspeakable heresy of making his paper interesting and readable, and wanted the brightest men he could obtain for his staff. He had F. L. H. ("Cozy") Noble; E. H. Hamilton; A. M. Lawrence—one of the best reporters he ever employed—and Sam Chamberlain, a great editor; Alfonso Murphy, Annie Laurie (Mrs. Bonfils), "Petey" Bigelow and Arthur McEwen. It was a formidable array of talent. McEwen was rated as one of the strongest journalists in the West; Mrs. Bonfils invented the "sob" story; and the best of "Jimmy" Swinnerton's cartoons have seldom been equaled. What Mr. Hearst needed was a little elegance for the editorial page, as he wanted to make it a memorable feature of his newspaper. Accordingly he turned to Ambrose Bierce; the choice was inevitable, and the bargain was soon sealed. But before they came to terms, Mr. Hearst was given to understand that there were two inviolable conditions: 1st, "Prattle" was to appear on the editorial page, next to the regular editorials; 2nd, it was to appear exactly as written. Perhaps Mr. Bierce did not define "exactly" at the time, but Mr. Henderson, and the other *Examiner* men, soon came to have a vivid understanding of his peculiarly exact definition of exactness. Bierce was to write two columns, if possible, of "Prattle" once a week for the Sunday edition, and if he did any additional work he was to be paid at space rates. The relationship established was of the greatest importance for both men, and should be, at least, an important footnote in any history of American journalism.

The significance of the incident to Bierce is quite apparent. It was the beginning of his great fame on the coast. It is true that he had a considerable local reputation with his work on *The News-Letter*, *The Argonaut*, and *The Wasp*, but the circulation of these weeklies was rather limited, and in them "Prattle" did not carry the same weight as did the two signed columns in *The Examiner*. And then, again, it gave Bierce leisure to do other writing, and it was high time, for he was past middle-age and had, as yet, done little writing of any moment. From now on he was to be well paid for the rest of his life, and was liberated from the burden of editorial detail. It is a shame that the opportunity did not come earlier in his life. To appreciate the fame that Bierce soon attained with his work on *The Examiner*, one must constantly remember that the Hearst papers in the West (it was then *the* Hearst paper) occupied a far different standing than they did in the East. In the West *The Examiner* was read by every one, including the people of influence and power and social position. *The Examiner* was not the rowdy sheet for the hoi polloi that some of the Hearst papers quickly became in the East. It has been variously estimated what the number of "Bierce readers" was during *The Examiner* days, but it must have been very large indeed. And no one knew this better than did Mr. Hearst.

The association of the two struck many people as being slightly incongruous. But they had several common interests; or, at least, they had certain mutual antipathies which they both desired to eliminate, although from different motives. Moreover, both of them loved a good fight. Mr. Hearst thoroughly enjoyed "Prattle" and never complained of his columnist, no matter how abusive he might be on occasion. It is altogether probable that Mr. Hearst was acting on the defensive when he employed Bierce, on the theory that such a dangerous satirist would be a powerful ally but an implacable foe. But then no one knew what Mr. Hearst's motives were and few do to this day. To build circulation? Perhaps; but there were quicker ways. At times, particularly in the early days of his career, one can easily detect different motives at work in Mr. Hearst's journalism. But he did love *The Examiner*, and he took a great interest in all the members of its staff, including Bierce, whom he pampered, mollified, and befriended at all times.

The sense of power that Bierce now experienced from his work on *The Examiner* added measurably to the quality of his satire. Theretofore it suffered from the impotency of futility, or hysteria. There was something rather harsh and blunt and ungraceful about his work on *The Wasp*. In fact, the years 1881-1886 represent a low-ebb in his satire, probably for the reason that he was overworked during this period. He could concentrate on his "Prattle" alone. Now that he was with *The Examiner*, he took up a rapier instead of the bludgeon which he had used on *The Wasp*. And, now, too, he began to write his stories.

There is much current discussion as to Bierce's actual merits as a satirist. Mr. Vincent O'Sullivan wrote in *The Dublin Magazine* (April-June, 1929), of some of Bierce's satire, that

> "such writing is sheer abuse and too ponderous to get home. The reader's attention is kept on the way it is written, and he feels the man who wrote it is showing off; so the victim, the man who is knocked out, is lost sight of. . . . Bierce's piece has the pomposity, the slow movement and the rotund phrase of rhetorical orators or oratorical rhetoricians."

There is much force to this criticism. Bierce's style was acquired in an age that specialized in the wide gesture and the oratorical flourish. The great styles of the eighteen-fifties were those of Webster and John C. Calhoun; it was the period, as Mr. O'Sullivan writes, of the "beaver-hat." Much of this rhetoric, influenced by ideas of "elegance" acquired in London, crept into Bierce's manner of writing. Even in the best of his writing, that is, the simplest, he could not resist the temptation to intersperse "purple patches."

But with these reservations in mind, it is yet undeniable that "Prattle" was most amusing, and certainly the best written journalism in the west. And the amazing bulk of it! From 1887 until 1899 in the San Francisco *Examiner* alone, it would comprise volumes. Of Senator Vrooman, who was always making a "dying" speech, in "the shadows of the other world," Bierce once wrote:

> "Step lightly, stranger, o'er this holy place,
> Nor push this sacred monument aside,
> Left by his fellow-citizens to grace
> The only spot where Vrooman never died."

Bierce's definition of "retribution" was: "The Vigilance Committee prosecuting the crime of a prominent citizen." His idea of a painting to be entitled "A Bold Bluff" was "Colonel" J. P. Jackson bringing a suit in a court of law to quit his title. Of the famous epitaphs so many have been quoted that it is difficult to make a selection. They were all similar in structure and this one, written for Dick Hammond, is typical:

> "Pause, stranger, and let fall a tear;
> Dick Hammond has been dead a year;
> This is the sacredest of spots:
> At its antipodes he rots."

But, for the most part, his satire was too "ponderous." He was dealing with hoodlums and had to hit hard. The times admitted of no other satire. He once summed up the matter in a fable: "A Rattlesnake came home to its brood about to die— I have been bitten by the editor of a partisan journal, it said." * And such was the case in the early days of California journalism. Much of Bierce's work was the outgrowth of this heavy-witted, hard-hitting Western journalism; it was the sort of writing that delighted the blood-thirsty old scoundrels who loafed around saloons waiting for a fight.

Too much of his writing was abusive, but his power of invective was tremendous and goregous. He once wrote of the secretary to the chief of police in San Francisco:

> "This hardy and impenitent malefactor—this money-changer in the temple of justice—this infinite rogue and unthinkable villain, of whose service Satan is ashamed and, blushing blackly, deepens the gloom of hell—this brilliant malversationalist—this boundless and incalculable scamp, enamoured of his own versatility of unworth, invests the moral atmosphere with an audible odor that screams along all the visible ramifications of his influence among the noses of souls." †

"Mike" DeYoung was a "chimpanzee," "Sir Simian," a "credulous liar." Senator Frye was "that incarnate lachrymosity and slavering sentimentaler"; of another he said that "the very fat

---

* *The Examiner*, December 25, 1887.
† *The Examiner*, September 18, 1887.

on his entrails belongs to the widows and orphans he has
robbed;" and of yet another he wrote that he was "a whimper-
ing simpleton—a hebetudinous hypocrite." Such a column of
abuse was never penned in the West. It was upper Billingsgate;
poetic abuse, vituperation raised to the standard of a high art.

One Robert Morrow, a San Franciscan, was tried for the
crime of embracery, or jury bribing. Of this man Bierce left
nothing unsaid. For weeks on end in "Prattle" he excoriated the
wretch. "Morrow," he would write, "is a rich man and can
afford every comfort and luxury. Yet he chews the cheapest
toothpicks and is not above robbing the poorest widow in the
land." The matter reached such a degree of civic comment
that Hall McAllister, attorney for Morrow, made a motion
in Judge Sullivan's court for a change of venue, and his
motion was based on an affidavit which set forth all of
Bierce's comment and abuse. McAllister said that the satire
in "Prattle" had incensed the entire community to such
an extent that it was impossible for his client to have a fair
trial. He called the court's attention particularly to these verses,
which had appeared in that day's issue of "Prattle":

"The devil felt a sudden thrill
Of course to defy God's will.

Then Morrow spoke: 'As sure as fate
Their witnesses I'll indicate

Or if that prove expensive sport,
I'll—whispering—I'll fix the court.'

Sing, Muse, the subsequent events,
Arraignment, trial and defense.

Alas! their footing simply fell
And all were tumbled into hell." *

"Of course, that really did not include this court," Mc-
Allister is reported to have explained to the judge. Morrow,
who was present in court, paid Bierce the compliment of grinning in appreciation of the laughter that greeted the reading of
the verses. After no lengthy consideration, Judge Sullivan

* *The Examiner,* November 17, 1887.

granted the motion for change of venue and Bierce's only comment was to correct a slight mistake that appeared in the verses as reprinted in the newspaper. He continued to abuse Morrow with unabated ardor.

The incident illustrates something of the enormous power and fame that Bierce acquired in the Bay District. He was a Titan and Cyclops in San Francisco for a quarter of a century. As Joseph Lewis French said in *Pearson's Magazine*, 1918, "he was Sir Oracle, indeed! Seriously I doubt if ever there has been in all the history of letters a more complete dominion." This fame had an important effect on the man. It solidified his early prejudices; stiffened him into an attitude of mental immobility; and made of him a colossal egoist. The people who knew him during these grand days simply worshiped him, and he came to have a sense of unerring vision and sublime divination. The constant applause of his friends and disciples made him always conscious of an audience; the intensity of this local fame lifted the entire scene in his mind to the level of universal experience. He lacked perspective; this was not simply a Western city, in a few years of its development, but it was the drama of the world, and he was the Zeus who stirred the elements. He might not be the artist he wanted to be; he might be enraged at times when he realized the inadequate use he was making of his talent; but he could always burst forth in "Prattle" with splenetic energy, unseating the despot and sending the political alley rat scurrying for cover. It was predestined that he should play this rôle, that he should be warped into this figure of legendary grandeur and power, for, unknowingly, he was establishing a tradition. He could not have escaped had he tried. But the fame was not displeasing. It brought him young disciples, a horde of female admirers, and a comfortable livelihood.

"Prattle" became a gospel for the younger generation in the West. Its influence was more far reaching than is generally realized. A tramp wrote Bierce from Butte, Montana, that "your work on *The Examiner* became a religion to me, fir (*sic*) I believed it." In 1883, Charles H. Phelps, publisher of *The Californian*, while in New York, had shown Godkin of *The Nation*, Bierce's sharp exposé of the historical method of Hubert Howe Bancroft, who farmed out all the research work is his establishment for the manufacture of histories on a "big business" basis. Godkin was most enthusiastic and added a few words of comment himself on the Bancroft technique. Bierce received letters from Australia, Mexico, England and from all corners of the world. A. D. Temple wrote from Mexico: "Every week the Indian mail carrier packed the copies of *The Examiner* across the Sierra Madre and down to the deep canyon at Van tanas, where we, working in the silver mines, had no other communication with the outside world, and we read the latest news from Frisco, sometimes not over three weeks old, and it was your articles in your enchilada manner that we liked best." Herbert Thomas, editor of *The Cornishman,* Penzance, wrote Bierce in later years that he had received his first literary impetus from reading "Prattle" while he was in California during 1889-99. Fannie Charles wrote from San Francisco: "What one has loved as a child and idealized as a girl and respected as a woman gets to be part of one's nature after awhile," having reference to "Prattle." This was literally true: people grew up on "Prattle" for, with the interruptions here noted, it appeared in print from 1868 to 1900 in San Francisco.

Bierce was, of course, a romantic and fascinating figure. San Francisco was rife with stories of his amazing brilliancy, his tremendous versatility, and his sharp wit. He was handsome and courageous and, personally, quite charming when he wanted to be. He had a very gallant manner with the ladies, and the men admired his frosty wit and superb poise. People never forgot this man: he remained a most vivid experience in the lives of innumerable Westerners. It was like coming in contact with a dynamo. Twain amused and flattered them at the same time; Charles Warren Stoddard wrote "pretty" verses for emasculated magazines; and Bret Harte's sentimentality brought tears to the eyes. But this fellow Bierce jolted them out of their lethargy and made them aware of the world. He was a gadfly, a torment and a delight. The secret of his success, the explanation of his fame, is that his influence was always a personal influence. It was not so much what he said in "Prattle," as the fact that the column carried the great moral potency of having been written by Ambrose Bierce. Compared with his contemporaries, he was flawless and impeccable; there were no loopholes in his armor. He blazed indignation and there was a great force to his work that was hard and brilliant and cold. George Santayana has written that "Men of intense feeling are not mirrors but lights." Such a man was Bierce. And it is really unfair to judge him by his work, although his work was never commonplace or trivial. For him simply to have stood out against his times, when the difficulties of independence were unbelievably greater than to-day, was no little distinction. You can pinch his work from the beginning until the end and not find a soft spot. It was brittle at times, sharp and metallic in some places, but it never lost its headiness, it never drooped or drooled or driveled. What is quite apparent from an examination of his journalism with reference to its *milieu*, and the circumstances under which it was written, is that Ambrose Bierce was the most original, forceful and important literary figure of his generation in the west.

*   *   *

DURING the first years of his newly acquired fame as the Sir Oracle of journalism on the coast, he lived for the most part at Auburn, although he made frequent trips to visit his wife and family at St. Helena. He entertained quite a number of guests at Auburn. Jeremiah Lynch came to visit him; as did E. L. G. Steele; and "Charley" Kauffman, one of his closest personal friends. It was at Auburn, too, that a committee from San Francisco asked him to write a "Fourth of July" poem. He disliked the idea, but finally accepted, as he said that he did not always want to be regarded as a "refuser." He spent considerable time over the "Invocation" and read stanzas of it to a friend who owned and published a newspaper at Auburn. Bierce would drop into this man's office in the afternoon and would read a few stanzas that he had written that day, and they would discuss them. The matter is important only in the light of Dr. Danziger's statement that he saw Bierce sit down and write the ode, just as he might write out a check, or sign his name. The poem was the product of quite a period of effort and thought. Much of its tone of dire foreboding and its prescience of dark times ahead may be attributed to the fact that the famous anarchist bombing in Chicago occurred in 1886, and the excitement engendered by the episode had stirred many minds. The poem was read at a mass meeting in the Grand Opera House in San Francisco on the evening of July 4th,

1888, and was reprinted in *The Examiner* the next day with this note: "The poem is not one of the made to order kind. It is not perfunctorily written up to the occasion. It is appropriate, but not with the ephemeral appropriateness that loses its flavor when immediate occasion is past."

The poem was written for the occasion and it has lost something of its flavor because the government was not overthrown by the anarchists. This poem had an interesting history. One of Bierce's great admirers in later years was Louis Dupont Syle, of the department of English at Berkeley. Bierce showed him this poem and Syle hung a copy of it on a bulletin board in the university, with a note attached in which he said: "Several years before Mr. Kipling wrote the Recessional there was published 'The Invocation' by Mr. Ambrose Bierce, on a subject no less worthy than Kipling's and a treatment no less superior." This was in 1899, ten years after the poem was published. Immediately the word went out around the world, from a bulletin board at the University of California, that Kipling had stolen his poem from Bierce. The story, by heaven knows what mysterious channels, was printed and reprinted for years. It is apparently without the slightest foundation in fact. The list of those who have plagiarized Bierce is not as voluminous as some of his admirers would have us believe. In fact, James Huneker in his "Steeple-jack" intimates that Bierce once appropriated an idea himself. But this same idea ("The Man and the Snake"), of a man who dies of fright inspired by a snake with buttons for eyes, if not original with Bierce, was appropriated from his work by Harris Merton Lyon, in a short story called "An Unused Rattlesnake."

Along with these regular friends that came to Auburn, followed the usual stream of visitors. It was at Auburn that Bierce met one of the first of his "pupils." Ina Peterson, niece of Ina Coolbrith, was in Auburn on a vacation with her brother and happened to show Bierce some of her work. He was enthusiastic and instructed her in writing for quite a period of years. Her work began to appear in *The Wave,* a publication edited by two of Bierce's young friends, Hugh Hume and J. O'Hara Cosgrave, and in collaboration with Mr. Bierce she wrote "An Occurrence at Brownsville." A poem that she wrote about him at about this time is indicative of the manner in which he was revered by his many "pupils" who were constantly writing poems to him, such as this:

"Almost has ceased the royal reign of sun;
  Low on his gilded bier the Monarch lies,
  Leaving to Shadow Earth's vain panoplies,
And the long patient Day is nearly done.
Into the West there creepeth, one by one,
  A band of glittering stars, their steadfast eyes
  Filled with the light of a new Paradise,
And of a consecration fairly won.
So will thy Soul, thou glorious, grandly shine
  When the long day hath deepened into night;
  And as thy spirit threads the roseate bars
Of Heaven, midst God's supernal hosts, be mine
The boon to view thee: Thou wilt wing thy flight
  Crowned with a halo radiant with stars."

One can only imagine what Bierce thought of this poem, particularly about walking the "roseate bars of Heaven"—which he so despised—and being one of "God's supernal hosts." He once wrote: "Heaven is a prophecy uttered by the lips of despair, but hell is an inference from analogy." Nevertheless he was secretly much pleased by such pathetic adoration, and being quite romantic, treasured these many mementos.

At Auburn there were few places to take his guests to visit. About the most attractive spot was the cemetery, and there he would repair with his friends to converse about the matter of ghosts, wines and whatnot. He would invariably take his guest to one tombstone, in a far end of the graveyard, on which was inscribed just the single word: "Eulalie." Such an inscription was Poe-esque and "romantic" and he speculated much about the mysterious "Eulalie," until some local historian informed him that she had been a servant girl of a German family; large, bony and unattractive. It was probably this disillusioning experience that provoked him to write of the Auburn cemetery in his story "The Realm of the Unreal": "It was a dishonor to the living, a calumny on the dead, a blasphemy against God."

He was in Auburn on the eve of the election of Benjamin Harrison as President. A celebration was planned at the Putnam House, and through the lobby that evening a miniature parade was led by young Bouthwell Dunlap, later to become quite well known as an historian. Bierce was amused with the shouting, high spirits and nonsense. During the course of the "parade," he was conducted across the lobby and introduced to a beautiful lady in widow's weeds. She was handsome, and stately, and most charming. It was his "Mona Lisa" lady; the beautiful widow who never ceased wearing black because she had worn it when she first met Ambrose Bierce. She was known in San Francisco as the "widow who never ceased mourning," and years later, when Benjamin Harrison was just a name for school boys to mumble, she was sometimes seen on the streets of San Francisco, in widow's weeds, but worn they were, and dusty, and wrinkled, as though her grief had grown old.

It was during this period that he began the group of war stories which first brought his name into national fame as an artist. The stories appeared in the Sunday Supplement, sometimes taking the place of his column of "Prattle" and sometimes being in addition to this work. Some of the stories also appeared in *The Wave.* "One of the Missing" appeared in *The Examiner* early in 1888, and the others followed in succession, nearly all of the "Tales of Soldiers and Civilians" having appeared in print in *The Examiner* before they were published in book form. When Bierce thus set about the task of writing a book of short stories he was forty-six years old, and had acquired some little fame as a journalist—a craft in which he had been actively engaged for sixteen years. His achievement is all the more remarkable in view of these facts. But the war was only a memory when he began writing the stories, and when he did finally write them he romanticized the situations and warped the facts to fit his highly artificial theory of æsthetics derived from Poe. As will be shown more in detail in a future chapter, Bierce set down deliberately to write these stories according to a previously worked out formula. He thought that the world was separated into neat, compact departments, such as Art, Satire, Law, and whatnot, that clicked precisely into place, and that were operated according to the principles of immutable law. Bierce never identified his art with life or with the vital creative impulses in himself. Art had nothing to do with reality; ergo, the more unreal a story was the better story it must be. He was always on the edge of experience; he never penetrated to the essence of things. His failure as an artist was his tragic inability to work out a problem that balanced his enormous energy. He shot all his force and vitality into the obsolete, arbitrary pattern of the short story and toppled it over with the force of the blow. The only form that his expression could take was to make his stories unreal and dramatic, which he did in the extreme. But the worthy protagonist never appeared: he could not envisage a problem that measured up to his power. He was like a giant playing with a toy and generally he broke the toy. The short story form with Bierce was a bracelet on the wrist of a Cyclops. He could get more adequate expression in his satire, but even there he went wide of the mark and became merely abusive in his impetuosity.

Several shrewd observers noticed this quality about Bierce's stories, but jumped to the too hasty conclusion that he was creatively impotent and that his satire was a result of his failure as an artist. This, of course, does not fit the facts, for he was a satirist before he thought of writing stories and his first writings were sardonic. Mary Austin, wrote of Bierce:

> "Never having seen Bierce but once, at Sterling's house, and having known him only through young people who had passed under his hand, I juged him to be a man secretly embittered by failure to achieve direct creation, to which he never confessed; a man of immense provocative power, seeking to make good in other's gifts what he himself had missed, always able to forgive any shortcoming in his protégés more easily than a failure to turn out according to his prescription. I thought him something of a posturer, tending to overweigh a slender inspiration with apocalyptic gesture." *

And she further amplified this thought in a letter to me, in the course of which she says:

> "I do think that he was to a certain extent conscious of lack and failure in his own life which he was never willing to admit. Much of his venom grew out of this secret disappointment. He kept forcing the note of savage irony because what he really wanted would not come. In fact the whole flavor of the man to me was one of alternate high confidence in himself and puzzled bewilderment over the failure of his genius."

* *The American Mercury*, May, 1927.

Now this is fine comment, and it is accurate enough from the standpoint of those who approach Bierce's work from a late date without knowledge of his early life and experience. The "bitterness" or the "idealism," because I insist that with Bierce the ideas cannot properly be dissociated, existed from the moment that he began to write. There could have been no disappointment over the failure of his artistic ambitions at that date, for he had none. There was a failure of his genius as a writer of fiction, but the cause was more obscure. While he was amazingly sensitive in his reactions and had a fine appreciation of values, when he went to weld these elements into a work of art, he found himself in a state of chaos. To extricate himself, he reversed the process, thought out a formula, and then wrote stories to fit the pattern previously devised. Naturally the stories were not superlatively great. That they were excellent for their time, cannot be doubted, and that they have survived this long is proof enough of his power. Whether he was a great artist or not, he was indubitably a great man. He once wrote Scheffauer: "Maybe, as you say, my work lacks 'soul,' but my life does not, as a man's life is the man." And he spoke truthfully.

*　　*　　*

MEANTIME, Mr. Hearst was making progress with *The Examiner,* and had moved it into new quarters. He was so excited about the pretty new habitat for his latest toy that he wrote his elderly critic:

"I will come up this next Saturday, if agreeable to you. Thanks for the fables last Saturday. They were particularly bully.

"We are in the new building at last and Gosh! I wish you could see my room. It has a blue ceiling striped with red, gilded windows and yellow marble decorations 'till your eyes are on edge. I won't tell you any more about it or you will be down before I can get up to see you."

Bully fables and a blue ceiling striped with red! "Gosh!"

CHAPTER XI

"NOTHING MATTERS"

During these middle years when Bierce was traveling from Auburn to Angwins in search of a "breathing place," his family continued to live in St. Helena, a small white bungalow on "Main Street." As Bierce was quite famous on the coast by this time, the presence of his family in such a small town provoked an inordinate amount of comment and discussion. For the most part, this talk centered about Day Bierce. He was a remarkably handsome youngster, with the head of an Apollo. With all his father's pride and energy, he was naturally arrogant and rather contemptuous of mediocrity. He would write and draw with facility. As early as 1883, his father's letters would return certain sketches and poems which had been submitted for approval. Bierce once remarked that his son "seemed to know things intuitively" and this was his definition of genius, for he once said: "Genius knows what it has not learned and apprehends before it has examined." The villagers at St. Helena would stare at Day as he walked about the town; the perfection of his features was that of art rather than nature. To quote these old neighbors, they "marveled" at his beauty. He was a blond, with his father's piercing blue eyes, but his features were much finer. Fifty years after his tragic death, friends and neighbors in St. Helena still retain a vivid impression of his beauty and charm.

One summer Day announced to his father and mother that he was going to be a "newspaperman" and that he was "sick of school." A quarrel ensued. But there was as much determination about Day as there was about his father and neither would yield an inch. It was a case of steel upon steel, and the tears of Mrs.

Bierce were as nought. As a result of this quarrel, Day packed his bag one night and left home. Bierce did not attempt to pursue the runaway, as he thought the experience would prove to be of value. Mrs. Bierce continued to write to her son and once sent him some money, which he returned promptly, with elaborate disdain. It was the prelude to a series of tragedies in Bierce's life.

The first had to do with his wife. Prior to this time, that is, about 1888, there had been considerable disharmony between Mr. and Mrs. Bierce. This friction can be traced, in most instances, to unfortunate circumstances, such as, the Black Hills mining episode, the failure of *The Wasp,* and other misfortunes which made Bierce subject to the criticism of his wife's family. He had not accomplished all that he expected to accomplish, or all that he was expected by others to accomplish, and his intolerable pride resented the slightest criticism. Marriage to such a man as Bierce could not be other than an irksome experience at times. That he realized this clearly is shown by his insistence in later years that adults be frank about marriage. He once wrote: "We shall continue to have marriage, and its dead-sea fruits will grow no riper and sweeter with time. But the lie which describes them as luscious and gratifying is needless." In fact, his entire review of "The Kreutzer Sonata," written in August of 1890, is a rather sharp and acrimonious attack on marriage as an institution.

But despite these minor disharmonies, Bierce lived quite happily with his wife until their separation. If their marriage had not been entirely a "success," they were far from unhappiness or incompatibility. Their friends knew that a great tragedy had occurred, for only a tragedy could have parted a couple otherwise so attached to each other. Bierce was not the type of man who would have permitted a trifling irritation, a merely selfish annoyance, to disrupt his family life. The cause of their separation was a bitter and tragic misunderstanding, the details of which are unimportant. But the matter was the subject of such protracted discussion in San Francisco, and so many conflicting and discreditable stories have been told, that in fairness to both Mr. and Mrs. Bierce some explanation is necessary.

The great tragedies are those of misunderstanding, in which it seems that an unrelenting fate has determined to baffle all the characters and to send them broken from the stage. In such dramas "misunderstanding" is the impalpable marplot at work putting evil potions in every glass, so that all the puppets are left with the fall of the curtain in disconsolate agony. Mr. Bierce once wrote, in the course of a letter: "I don't take part in competitions—not even in love." That he meant what he so casually had written cannot be doubted by those familiar with the facts of his life. A more proud or sensitive man than Bierce never lived. By chance he learned that a man, whom he did not know personally, was enamored of his wife. This man had written Mrs. Bierce letters, couched in the rather ornate and egregious manner of a foreigner, for such he was, and the letters had been discovered. To Bierce these facts were an insurmountable barrier: he would not, he could not, forget.

But the tragedy was two-fold for Mrs. Bierce. To the tragedy of separation was added the torturing realization that she was, strictly speaking, responsible for this misunderstanding. For such it was, without doubt. Mrs. Bierce was guilty of no serious impropriety and her subsequent conduct was a beautiful, eloquent and passionate demonstration of her affection and fidelity. She passed through some harrowing experiences, but always with the most admirable grace and courage. She never whimpered or sniffled or bowed her head. To the day of her death, she would not murmur a word of complaint against her husband, nor would she permit others to do so. It might appear to some that he had acted harshly and unreasonably, but she would never permit such comment to be made in her presence. Her devotion was so whole-hearted that, in later years, when she heard that her husband secretly wanted a divorce, she filed an action so that he might have his liberty. As a matter of fact, nothing was further from his desires, and again was misunderstanding fraught with fatality, for Mrs. Bierce died within three months after the decree was granted. Those who knew them both differ in their opinions of Bierce, but there is a convincing unanimity of views about Mrs. Bierce. You may make the circle of their acquaintances and never hear an unkind word about the life which she so splendidly devoted to her husband and family.

Their separation was a great tragedy in Bierce's life. He left the home in St. Helena immediately, but as yet there was no final separation. Mrs. Bierce did not know what would happen and their relations remained in this state of uncertainty until Day's death. The experience was a shadow that enshrouded Bierce's life until his disappearance into Mexico. But it is apparent, and immediately observable, that it was entirely a personal tragedy. It affected his own happiness, but it had no appreciable influence on his thinking. By the nature of things it could not have been other than a personal sorrow, for Bierce was past middle age and had written the great bulk of his satire by the time of the separation. It is impossible to use this domestic unhappiness as a lens by means of which to interpret his life. It was but an incident, perhaps the most serious, in a chain of tragedies that were predestined. His own nature made such sorrows inevitable. An extremely sensitive man cannot be other than indignant about life, but he may express his indignation variously. It may escape in the flight of lyric verse or religious inspiration or mordant satire. With Bierce the movement was centripetal rather than centrifugal. He was as idealistic as Shelley, but it was an indirect, perverse and disguised idealism. It involved him in contradictory situations and he could rationalize his position only with great difficulty. He recoiled from experience in a swift and startling manner. If doubt once crept into his mind, no evidence or logic could remove it. He knew that Mrs. Bierce was guilty of no wrong, but it was the fact that she had permitted him to discover such a situation that made a reconciliation impossible. His impressions were quick, sensitive, and unforgetable.

Bierce had an uncanny ability to "sense" situations and he was capable of the most intense suffering. Dr. Danziger is correct in stressing Bierce's horror of pain or suffering. In his walks through the woods near St. Helena, he would bring back pigeons, whose wings had been broken, and he would nurse and heal them in his study with the tenderness of a woman. For all helpless and unfortunate creatures, he had a marvelous compassion. He would take his daughter, Helen, for long walks through the mountains. She remembers that he would have her wait while he strode forward into the center of a glade or clearing. There he would stand perfectly still and erect, the sunlight touching his hair into a blaze of gold, while he called wild animals. It was a soft call, half a whisper and half a cry, and birds would come and light upon his uplifted arms, perch on his shoulders, and jump about on his hands. Others report the same experience. He always possessed this power and he was never without a "pet" in his study, be it a squirrel or a lizard. The central fact of his personality seems to have been some quality which invariably suggests such hackneyed expressions as "electric" or "vital." It was this quality which charmed the people he knew, for energy is eternal delight. As with William Blake, "there was for him no evil, only a weakness, a negation of energy, the ignominy of wings that droop and are contented in the dust."

This acute sensitiveness was really pathological with Bierce. He was not amenable to reason once he had received a definite impression. He had a habit of freezing into an attitude of perfect immobility once he was disappointed. Within this shell, he was simply unapproachable. He would not quarrel about such matters, nor discuss them, but with him the doors once closed were closed forever. So it was with his wife. Their separation was as cruel and disheartening an experience as he was ever to know, but that it could have been prevented or that a reconciliation could have been effected is a conclusion that sounds chimerical to any one familiar with Bierce's character. From that date forward, there was no communication with his wife; no letters were exchanged; no words spoken, with the exception of two interviews later noted. If there was a message to communicate, it was conveyed by one of the children, generally by Helen.

But even darker days were ahead. . . . After leaving home, Day had wandered about northern California, going from one town to another, until he came to Chico. There he was employed on a country newspaper, of which he was editor, manager, and virtually proprietor. One reason that had drawn him to Chico was the fact that the previous summer he had met Eva Adkins at an "A. O. U. W." picnic at Red Bluffs and learned that she lived in Chico. When he came to Chico, he boarded at the home of the girl's mother, Mrs. Barney. She had remarried and her second husband was a drunkard. On one occasion Day threw him out of the house. As a result he had caused Day's arrest on a charge of assault and battery, but Day was admitted to bail, one of the bondsmen being his friend,

Neil Hubbs. At the time of the trial, Day was acquitted, so to speak, with honors.

Shortly after this occurred, Day and the Adkins girl became engaged. They were to have been married on July 22nd, 1889, and Neil Hubbs was selected as best man. Of course, no word of this proposed marriage had reached the ears of either Mr. or Mrs. Bierce. The night before the marriage, the Adkins girl and young Hubbs ran away to Stockton, where they were married. They returned to Chico a fortnight later. In the interim, the "practical jokers" of the village had been making unmerciful sport of young Bierce. He was made the butt of sharp gibes in the country newspapers. Such cruelty seems incredible, the more so as the audience seemed to think it amusing. Any one could have foreseen the consequences. It was unthinkable that young Bierce, who had been schooled to have the loftiest regard for personal dignity, would permit such an affront to go unpunished. Moreover, the perfidy of his best friend and the cruelty of his first sweetheart, had made him insane with rage and humiliation. When the young married couple arrived at Mrs. Barney's home, Day awaited them. No sooner did young Bierce and Hubbs catch sight of each other than they began to shoot. They were both mortally wounded and died within a few hours after the duel. Day's last words were: "Send for my father—send for my father!"

The story of Day's death is given in detail for the reason that it has been bruited about of late in a shameful manner. George Sterling unthinkingly remarked that Day had been "killed by a gambler in a sordid love affair." Subsequent accounts have been equally careless of the facts and now it has become quite common to refer to the affair as a "drunken brawl." The entire story appeared in all the San Francisco newspapers; the facts have never been inaccessible. It seems surprising, indeed, that writers enough interested in such a personal tragedy to make public reference to it, would not take the trouble to verify the facts. There is no intimation that either boy was drunk, and, at least from Day's viewpoint, the affair was scarcely "sordid." It must be remembered that Day was a mere youngster—seventeen years old. He was extremely proud and sensitive and he had been hard hit. The brutal laughter of a swinish community was ringing in his ears for weeks prior to the meeting. The Oroville *Mercury* made this comment, which illustrates the general feeling about the tragedy at the time: "At first it seems that Bierce was disposed to forego the matter, but for the sake of sensations the reporters continued to lacerate his wounded heart until the young man actually believed he was the laughing stock of the country." Whether he was mistaken or not, Day could not smile about such a situation, for he was the son of his father and neither ever learned to compromise with life or to discount their ideals.

Bierce was mortally hurt by the death of his boy, the son he always spoke of as "another Chatterton." It was one of the greatest shocks of his life when Day's death was announced. But, again let it be remembered, this occurred in 1889. Bierce was then at the height of his fame as a satirist. Like the matter of his separation from his wife, it was exclusively a personal tragedy. It did not make him "bitter." It saddened him, made him weak with grief, but it did not mold his thoughts.

Two stories are told as to what Bierce did on learning of his son's death. Both stories shall be given, since it is as impossible to discredit either as it is to bring them into agreement. According to one account, Bierce went to Chico, with his friend "Charley" Kauffman, and made an investigation of the facts and then returned to San Francisco. George Sterling seemed surprised that "Bierce did nothing" about the affair. But what, indeed, could he have done? Assuming vengeance to be the duty of a father under such circumstances, where and how was it to be obtained? When he arrived in Chico, he went to the funeral parlor where the body of his son lay naked on a marble slab. He approached the body, bent over, and, speaking as though to one at a great distance, said: "You are a noble soul, Day, you did just right."

By the other version of the facts, Bierce sent Kauffman alone to Chico. A friend recalls that Bierce was stricken with grief and sorrow. "Nothing matters" came to be a phrase born of grief and converted into a philosophy by necessity, but just then something had mattered tremendously. "No words can express his grief," Mrs. Cecil says. It was not the stereotyped blubbering of "Little Nell," but it possessed all the elements of real tragedy. Had not the young and beautiful again been struck down by a brutal and shocking violence? At Shiloh the same

tragedy had seemed splendid and fascinating; but there was
something so gray and so ashen about his feeling over the loss
of Day that he could not see or reason his way to any point of
consolation. So needless, so stupid, so brutal! As he wrote in
one of his stories: "Would one exception have marred too much
the pitiless perfection of the divine, eternal plan?" When Mrs.
Cecil sailed, a few weeks later, for Japan, Bierce came to the
wharf to bid her farewell. He was pale and depressed and ill;
she had never known him to look so ashen. He handed her
Day's ivory-handled revolver and asked her to take it away. He
had been carrying it around for weeks, so he said, and could no
more throw it away than he could forget about it.

But, however dark and cold might be the realm of shadows
that Bierce traversed on a recurrent track during these days of
his sorrow, the world was still as indifferent and brutal as ever.
The two bodies came out from Chico on the same train. At
Sacramento the road branched: young Hubbs was carried to
Stockton; Day was placed on the train for St. Helena. The
Adkins girl stood on the platform of the station, one ear
chipped by a flying bullet from the revolver of one of her lov-
ers, and remarked to the newspaper reporters: "Now ain't that
queer? One goes one way and one goes another, but here I am!"

Bierce came to St. Helena to attend the funeral. He was accompanied by Charles Kauffman and Judge Boalt. After the
services a few friends returned to the Bierce home before de-
parting. That evening one of them recalls that Bierce asked his
wife to step into the parlor of their home, where they were alone
for about an hour. The subject of the interview remains a mystery. But after Bierce left that evening, his wife remarked that
she knew that a reconciliation was impossible. Many of their
friends had hoped that Day's death would bring them together,
but it was impossible. Later, in Mrs. Bierce's divorce suit, she
fixed the date of the separation as "July, 1891." This was obviously incorrect, as far as the year was concerned, although the
month was probably accurately stated. She would have been
more likely to forget the year than to forget the month or season. There is no question but that they were finally separated
after 1889. Just how long previous to that they had been separated cannot be determined, save that it was after Day left
home. Thus the date can be fixed as about 1888.

These twin blows staggered Bierce. Beauty and horror, were their images always to be laid, one upon the other, in his mind? Sensitive and fine natured man that he was, these sorrows must have hit him harder than any one realized. Yet no one was to know the truth. To display grief was vulgar; therefore he froze into an imperturbable calm. It was over and "nothing mattered." He seldom spoke of Day's death afterwards and then only to a few friends. Of his wife he never spoke: not even to friends.

*   *   *

BIERCE returned to Auburn, and, after a two weeks interval, resumed his column of "Prattle" in *The Examiner*. But during his absence old Frank Pixley had not been inactive, as he saw in the tragedy an opportunity to strike Bierce a fatal blow. It seems incredible that even Pixley could have written this editorial, but he did:

> "If it be true, as alleged, that the jibes and jeers of the local press so worked upon the *weak* mind of a young man, maddened by passion and crazed by jealousy over an *unworthy* woman, that he should have resorted to murder and suicide to terminate his unpleasant and ridiculous predicament, may not the incident teach a *moral lesson* to those writers who indulge in such cruel and inhuman satire? May not the death of the younger Bierce teach the older man, his father, how sinister have been the bitter, heartless, and unprovoked assaults which he has spent his life in cultivating that he might the more cruelly wound his fellow-men? Might not an intellect so keen, a taste so critical, and a pen so caustic, have been wielded to some higher and nobler purpose? Might not a life, now growing nearly to its close, have been passed more profitably to humanity, more happily to himself, than in indulgence in the practiced use of a pen more cruel than the most destructive and death-dealing of swords? Does there not rest upon his father the shadow of a haunting fear lest he may have transmitted to a sensitive and tender soul an inheritance which resulted in *crime* and death, while he was cultivating the gift of wounding natures just as sensitive and tender, who had not the courage to end them in murder and self-destruction, but were driven to hide their sorrows in secret? Perhaps this man with the burning pen will recall

the names of those whom he has held up to ridicule and shame; the men and women whom he has tortured and humiliated; perhaps he will analyze the *moral code* which has governed him, and review the relations he has held toward men of whom he might at least have remembered that *gratitude* was something other than merchandise and payable as a debt. Perhaps this man may recall the time, when a boy younger than his, with brighter hopes, folded his wings in a more peaceful death, leaving in his flight a mother's love and a father's fondest hopes; and, while they were in sorrow which could find no relief, how cruelly he wounded and tortured them because there had been said over the last remains of the son they loved words too eulogistic for his hard, incredulous stoicism. We are *too sincere an admirer* of this gifted writer not to regret that when his remains shall have been gathered for entombment in the grave of literature, nothing will be found worthy of preservation, and that if his writings shall find a publisher, they will contain no bright saying that was kindly meant, nor aught that was not cruel and cruelly intended. Upon his tomb may be carved the inscription: 'He quarreled with God, and found nothing in his creations worthy of the commendation of Ambrose Bierce.' " *

It took Frank Pixley to write as mean an editorial as that, for Bierce seldom struck where there was no provocation. If he whipped rascals unmercifully, there are few who would care to contend that his victims did not richly deserve the beating that they received. Pixley croaking of "gratitude" was, indeed, a ridiculous sight. Moreover, the charge that he impliedly makes that Bierce had taken a similar advantage of another, is not borne out by the facts.

Bierce took a long walk with a newspaper friend at Auburn. He carried a copy of *The Argonaut* and after they had completed quite a stroll through the woods, they came to the edge of a clearing. While they were sitting perched high on a rail fence, Bierce read the editorial and said that he had not decided just what he would do. They were just starting back towards Auburn, when the sun suddenly underwent an eclipse and for a few seconds they stood in a world of shadows and strangeness. As the light came back through the trees, it

* *The Argonaut*, August 5, 1889.

seemed as though "the mountains were stained as with wine, and as wine were the seas."

But when Bierce resumed his "Prattle" he lost no time in replying to Mr. Pixley.

> "You disclosed considerable forethought, Mr. Pixley, in improving the occasion to ask for lenity, but I see nothing in the situation to encourage your hope. You and your kind will have to cultivate fortitude in the future, as in the past; for asuredly I love you as little as ever. Perhaps it is because I am a trifle dazed that I can discern no connection between my mischance and your solemn 'Why persecutest thou me?' You must permit me to think the question incompetent and immaterial—the mere trick of a passing rascal swift to steal advantage from opportunity. Your *ex post facto* impersonification of *The Great Light* is an ineffective performance: it is only in your own undisguised character of sycophant and slanderer for hire that you shine above." *

And when some friend wrote in an indignant letter to the press, complaining of Pixley's editorial, Bierce answered him:

> "C. H. L. Your letter in my defense was referred to me. I thank you for your kind intention, but there was no need. The swift revenge of my enemies that God had stood in my path was natural to their degree of intelligence and required but a congenial mood to be amusing. It hardly deserved your stern arraigning." †

Bierce's reply came as near to a confession as anything he ever wrote in "Prattle." He bowed ever so slightly when he made that concession to sentiment: "I am a trifle dazed." But he did not fully realize how hard he was hit. As he wrote of a character in one of his stories: "He had no experience with grief; his capacity had not been enlarged by use. His heart could not contain it all, nor his imagination rightly conceive it. He did not know he was hard struck; that knowledge would come later, and never go."

* *The Examiner,* August 25, 1889.
† *The Examiner,* September 1, 1889.

CHAPTER XII

THE MASTER

SHORTLY after the death of Day, Bierce went to live at the Sunol Glen Hotel at Sunol Glen, California, managed by Mr. and Mrs. H. R. Crane. Like the proprietors of the other small country hotels in which Bierce lived, they were greatly honored by the presence of such a distinguished guest. Indeed, he was quite an attraction, for no sooner was he established than the usual flock of sycophants, admirers, pupils and friends began to haunt the hotel.

His attacks of asthma were very acute at this time. Ina Peterson, with her brother, was visiting Mr. and Mrs. Crane, during a vacation. She saw a great deal of Bierce one summer and has written me that "on more than one occasion we sat with him all night administering chloroform to him to assuage the terrible agony he suffered in his attacks of asthma. He often would say between his gasps, 'Do you think I should stand this?' And then for days would suffer from the effects of the chloroform." She recalls, too, that Bierce was sick and ill for weeks after the death of his son and that he remarked to her one day: "I am just beginning to forget for a moment, and then the memory rushes back worse than ever!"

But his work in "Prattle" reflected none of this despondency. In fact, his journalism was at its best from 1887 to 1890. It had more point and force and cleverness. It seems that Bierce had offended one H. Prescott Belknap, a young Naval officer, and that this gentleman had issued a challenge to him in *The Argonaut*. It was the beginning of an amusing series of notes in "Prattle."

"A chivalrous patriotette which signs its name variously as 'H. Prescott Belknap' and 'Prescott Belknap' complains in *The Argonaut* that I will not join it, a minor, in committing a felony on the 'field of honor.' The Belknaping justified the disappointment by quoting in solemn faith a long forgotten Hibernicism of mine inviting challenges from all persons conscientiously opposed to dueling! When setting that un-baited hook I could hardly have hoped that it would take a sucker—albeit a minnow—so long afterward. Of course the poor creature must not expect to cut a very heroic figure when lifted into its coveted notoriety with a thing like that in its jaw. Ever obliging and willing to assist struggling genius in 'taking the heart' of fame, I hereby cheerfully attest the ex-istence of something calling itself Prescott Belknap or H. Prescott Belknap. I admit that, although in law an enfant, it is thought to have attained the age of puberty, and that it is ferocious, a feeding bottle of gore exciting it like the dickens. But whether it is a boy or girl, I am not informed." *

But more was yet in store and the following note soon appeared, as Belknap kept demanding satisfaction:

"I am in receipt of another ferocious communication from Mr. Prescott Belknap, who, admitting that he is a minor, pro-tests that he is a Man. His letter is addressed to Sunol, where I live, and informs me that the writer is walking the streets of San Francisco, where I do not live, armed with a horsewhip for me. How he is legged for himself he does not see fit to inform me. Mr. Belknap threatens that unless I come up to be horsewhipped he will tell the public of my disobliging dis-position. I shall have to give him the trouble of doing so, for I really do not wish to be horsewhipped if I have to pay the railway fare to enjoy that blessing. The expense of the per-formance ought, I think, to be assumed by the chief performer. I am still persuaded that Mr. Belknap is a girl." †

While he was at Sunol he received one day, not a challenge to a duel, but a request to look over the manuscript of a young author. He consented and found that the manuscript showed considerable merit. He returned it with his suggestions and cor-rections. Further correspondence followed and then, one day,

* *The Examiner,* October 19, 1890.
† *The Examiner,* October 26, 1890.

he received a note from the young authoress asking if she might come to Sunol to see him. It was rather an unusual performance, but Mrs. Atherton never made any compromises with contemporary opinion. Her first meeting with Mr. Bierce was rather disappointing. He was recuperating from a bad attack of asthma and was in an ill humor. To all her fine compliments and tributes to his "greatness," he replied, rather savagely, "No, I'm not a great man. No one is better fitted to judge of greatness in men than I am, and I know that I am not great. I'm a journalist, past middle-age, without ambition, and have written nothing that measures up to my ideals." He told her that it had been a serious mistake for him to return from London, and that he would never have done so but for his wife. Mrs. Atherton and Bierce corresponded for many years, and he had a definite influence on her early work. He became, however, sharply critical of her later novels.

During these years when he was living at Sunol, 1888-1890, Bierce would make occasional trips to San Francisco and Oakland. He was interested in the fate of a little magazine, *The Wave,* that published some good things, including several of his own stories. It was edited by Hugh Hume. Bierce would come to San Francisco nearly every week-end and Friday afternoon would find him in Mr. Hume's office. The time was "devoted to a talk and a walk up Market Street as far as the Baldwin Hotel. Bierce was the mildest and gentlest gentleman I have ever met; there is no writer I have ever known whose pen and tongue delivered such wholly dissimilar thoughts and views. In his conversational discussion of people and events, he was kind, considerate and friendly; it may have been that because his Friday afternoons were play time that he did not permit any of the black beetles to intrude themselves on our holidays. Contrary to the general belief, Bierce was not an unknown figure on the streets of San Francisco. In our rambles from my office on Bush and Kearney to the Baldwin Hotel, and in the many places of resort that we visited, he was well known, and was usually saluted with the utmost respect and regard. He was a flaming figure, and even in San Francisco he was conspicuous and noted." * At the barroom in the Baldwin Hotel,

* Letter of Hugh Hume to the author, April 27, 1929.

which was journey's end for them, they would finish out the afternoon in the manner most congenial to literary gentlemen. Mr. Hume noted, and others made the same observation, that drinking seemed to mellow Bierce, and, strangely enough, that it helped his asthma and seemed to give him momentary relief.

Bierce's fame and influence on the coast reached a high water mark during these years. Quite a group of young writers gathered about him and his influence is reflected in such interesting magazines as *The Wave*. The number of manuscripts that he read and corrected is simply incalculable. On several occasions I have attempted to make a comprehensive list of his "pupils," but have never succeeded, particularly as a definition of "pupil" that would define the degree and extent of his influence over all the young writers who sought his assistance, cannot be framed. Such writers as George Sterling and Herman Scheffauer boasted that Bierce was their "Master." Others deny that he helped them. With many, notably with Mrs. Atherton, his influence never amounted to more than general and casual advice. Moreover, his influence was not restricted to creative work, as he had a marked and decisive influence on many young journalists. Naturally the people that he helped spoke of him to others and wrote blurbs about his books, augmenting his already considerable fame. But, as one might have expected, the praise of these pupils was uncritical and excessively enthusiastic. It came, in time, to be a source of considerable confusion.

To appreciate fully Bierce's eminence on the coast, it must be remembered that in the eighties and nineties, San Francisco was the only western city that made a pretense of culture. Between Chicago and San Francisco there was a dreary wasteland. The position of San Francisco was thus rather isolated and self-contained. It was a complete world in itself. It became self-centered and a survival of the old reckless spirit of the early days served to make it rather contemptuous of the rest of America. It fostered its own groups and its own magazines; devoted considerable attention to local artists and writers; and turned a cold shoulder on the rest of America. Under such conditions, Bierce naturally gravitated into a position, if not of active leadership, at least of proud example. He was the most interesting and fascinating literary man in the West and young writers were irresistibly drawn under his wing. He rather liked

the rôle of "Master," but was not the despot that legend has
made him. It is necessary to remember the position of San
Francisco in order to appreciate the extent of Bierce's influence,
and conversely, in order to understand his slightly pontifical
attitude, one must keep in mind that in San Francisco "Ambrose
Bierce" was a name that quickly became a legend. When he
went east in later years, Bierce struck at random. There was
no direct reaction to his satire; he floundered in vacuity. In
San Francisco he aimed directly and personally at the malefactor and had the satisfaction of watching the arrow pierce the
target. His aim was unerring and his courage superb. But, in
later years, when he attempted to generalize his prejudices, he
was not effective.

On his occasional visits to Oakland, Bierce would sometimes
stay with his son Leigh, who had rooms in the old Blake Block
with Roosevelt Johnson and George Sterling. His residence
would alternate between Sunol and Angwins and Oakland.
While temporarily a guest of his brother Albert, at the latter's
camp on the shore of Lake Temescal, he met an interesting
group: George Sterling, the Partington family, and quite a
host of others who foregathered in the woods for a good time.

Sterling came to California in 1890; two years later he
met Bierce. In the East he had lived at Sag Harbor and had
been a roguish youngster, his fun-making activities ably sec-
onded and championed by his friend, Roosevelt Johnson. The
two of them put a pirate's flag on the top of a church steeple
one night. When Bierce was told of this escapade, he was delighted. He made a trip to Sag Harbor after he went east, and
sent a picture post card to both young men on which he had
drawn a pirate's flag waving in the breeze and had labeled it:
"Roosevelt Johnson's and George Sterling's flag." Johnson and
Sterling were great friends, and after they came to California,
would visit such celebrities as Joaquin Miller and Bierce, although Johnson did not meet Bierce until later. Sterling wrote
of his first meeting with Bierce as follows:

> "I am not likely to forget his first night among us. A
> tent being, for his ailment, insufficiently ventilated, he decided
> to sleep by the campfire, and I, carried away by my youthful
> hero-worship, must partially gratify it by occupying the side
> of the fire opposite to him. I had a comfortable cot in my tent,

and was unaccustomed at the time to sleeping on the ground, the consequence being that I awoke at least every half-hour. But awake as often as I might, always I found Bierce lying on his back in the dim light of the embers, his gaze fixed on the stars of the zenith. I shall not forget the gaze of those eyes, the most piercingly blue, under yellow shaggy brows, that I have ever seen." *

In order to appreciate the influence that Bierce exercised on Sterling, one should really have known Sterling. There was unquestionably a neurotic strain in his life. His father, a physician, had been an early convert to Catholicism, and had been, like both his sons, a heavy drinker. The other son, James, became a priest. He, too, was quite a drinker and died shortly after he reached maturity. George was always excitable, nervous, and extremely impulsive. He was given to strange whims and fancies and was nothing if not capricious. He had attended St. Charles College, at Ellicott City, Maryland, before coming to California. There he had the good fortune to study under Father John Bannister Tabb, but, in 1890, he was scarcely lettered. His lack of a formal education, coupled with his immaturity and his rather weak nature, brought him inevitably under the influence of Bierce. He adopted Robinson Jeffers with just the same enthusiasm years later.

Many of Sterling's friends have bemoaned the influence of Bierce on his life. Mr. James Rorty, for example, writes that Bierce was "the literary Leviathan of the Pacific Coast," and that he was a "cavalry captain in the Civil War." † To this generous show of misinformation is added the statement that Bierce was a miserable satirist, an impossible story-teller, and a wretch personally. The first statement is, of course, a misquotation of a comparison used by Vincent Starrett, but where Mr. Rorty discovered the cavalry captaincy must, perforce, remain a mystery. It is obvious, of course, that some one told Mr. Rorty that Bierce was thus and so, and therefore, the matter is beyond dispute. He also makes the statement that early in life Sterling "discovered socialism, which was excellent. Simultaneously, however, he was discovered by Ambrose Bierce, which was almost fatal." This is almost

* Letters of Ambrose Bierce, Book Club of California.
† *The New Masses,* November, 1926.

as amusing as it is absurd. It is extremely doubtful if Sterling knew what an iambic was until he met Bierce. Moreover, Bierce did not "discover" Sterling. Sterling sought him
out and sat in abject worship at his feet. Just what relation
socialism may have with poetry is, also, a matter which must
remain a mystery. To be just to both Sterling and Bierce, one
must read not only the Bierce letters to Sterling, which have
been published by the Book Club of California, but Sterling's
letters to Bierce, which have not been published. From an examination of the entire correspondence, it is quite apparent that
Bierce did not force themes upon Sterling; he did not attempt
to warp the mind of the poet to fit the bias of the satirist. Nor
was Bierce responsible for the rhetorical quality of Sterling's
verse. Surely there was no one in the west who could have
advised Sterling as soundly as Bierce did. Furthermore, George
Sterling knew this quite well, and never regretted his association with Bierce. Has Mr. Rorty forgotten that Bierce was one
of the first individuals in this country to praise the poetry of
Ezra Pound?

It is difficult to imagine a Master, if one must have a
"Master," more patient, interested, and kindly than Bierce.
Of course he warned his pupil against allowing his heart to rule
his head; and, of a certainty, he pointed out the danger of permitting his muse to become a ballyhoo for every lost cause
and pathetic ideal. But contrasted with the other great influence
in Sterling's life, that of Jack London, Bierce's influence must
be conceded the more fortunate. Bierce advised his "pupil" to
study hard; to work incessantly; to devote his life to his art;
and to be independent and self-reliant. It seems to me that the
strongest and finest work Sterling did was that under the direct
influence of Bierce, and that his weakest verse may be attributed
to his association with certain well-meaning but ignorant friends.
Surely, if Sterling had heeded Bierce's advice, he would never
have published "The Binding of the Beast," that most unfortunate volume of hysterical, frenzied, war-mad poetry. If
Sterling had remembered Bierce's definition of "Bohemia"—"A
taproom of a wayside inn on the road from Bœotia to Philistia"
—he might have spent less time enacting the rôle of poet in
restaurants and cafes. The great criticism of Sterling's verse
was that of Lionel Josephare, who said: "George Sterling's

poetry is a representation of poetic values." This criticism is
unjust but it does indicate the real weakness of Sterling's verse,
for which Bierce was not responsible. Bierce actually instructed Sterling in sentence structure, the selection of words,
simple matters of versification. Sterling submitted the manuscript of one poem to Bierce and accepted every suggestion made
by Bierce, some twenty-one or two changes in all. Sterling was
proud to say, as he did, "I write for an audience of one."
Personally the most lovable and generous of men, Sterling
would have been the first to resent such criticism as that by
Mr. Rorty.

And, great as Bierce's influence was with Sterling, he was
perhaps even a more important figure in the life of Herman
Scheffauer. These two young poets worshiped their beloved
"Titan." And he was immensely fond of them, overlooking many
foibles that another might not have tolerated. Later he became
disgusted with Scheffauer for his insufferable conceit and he
became annoyed with Sterling's irresponsible conduct. Perhaps
he should have been more tolerant; but, reading his correspondence in the light of the circumstances, leads one to the conclusion that he was justified in breaking with them both. To have
Scheffauer write, as he did, "Every distinction I have achieved
has been through hard work, and purely by my own efforts,"
was enough to annoy even a more tolerant person than Bierce.
Why, he had taught the fellow to spell! He had sent his verses
about to the magazines, he had lent him money, introduced
him to interesting people, corrected his work, and praised his
verse in the most flattering terms. It was through Mr. Bierce's
efforts that *The Examiner* published the first of Scheffauer's
work. The same is true with Sterling. The patience with which
Bierce sent "A Wine of Wizardry" from magazine to magazine, facing sneers, intolerable condescension, and rebuffs, is to
appreciate the value of his friendship. Sterling, let it be said
to his credit, was never ungrateful nor was Bierce resentful.
Even after his break with both Sterling and Scheffauer, he continued to praise their work.

Joaquin Miller was also a frequent visitor at the Lake
Temescal camp. Bierce would greet him jovially, but there was
a veiled antagonism that kept them from being personal friends.
Polite as they were to each other, in some ways, Bierce did not

hesitate to call Miller a liar on occasion. In a special article in
The Examiner, Bierce once wrote: "In impugning Mr. Miller's
veracity, or rather, in plainly declaring that he has none, I
should be sorry to be understood as attributing a graver moral
delinquency than he really has. He cannot, or will not, tell the
truth, but never tells a malicious or thrifty falsehood. From his
incursions into the realm of romance he returns with clean but
empty hands." * And he once wrote a most delightful burlesque
of Miller's poetry in "The Mormon Question":

> "I said I will shake myself out of my clothes,
> I will roll up my sleeves, I will spit on my hands
> (The hands that I kissed to the sun in the lands
> To the north, to the east, to the south, and the west
> Of every sea that is under the sun),
> I will go to the land that the Gentile loathes
> As he gathers his one small wife to his breast
> Aud curses and loathes till his life is done.
> I will go to the place of the Mormon: the place
> Where the jackass rabbit is first in the race
> And the woodchuck chatters in meaningless glee—
> Chatters and twists all his marvelous face—
> Twists it and chatters and looks like me.
> And I rose in the strongest strength of my strength,
> With my breast of brass and my hair's full length,
> And I shook myself out of my clothes in the land
> Of the Mormons, and stood there and kissed my hand."

It required but a slight change in phrase and emphasis to show
how dangerously near the absurd Miller's verse sometimes bordered.

Bierce only lived at Sunol Glen for about two years, and
then he moved to Angwin's on Howell Mountain again. It
meant another and longer trip for the Bierce tourists who still
pursued "The Master." One day a lady had made an appointment with Bierce. She drove up to the hotel in a carriage and
came rushing up to Bierce, who awaited her, carrying a dog
in her arms. He bowed and said: "Madame, I do not know
you," and walked away. Dogs were ever anathema to him. To
collect all the pages of abusive language that he devoted to dogs

* *The Examiner,* January 30, 1898.

would fill a considerable volume. He never lost an opportunity to slash at them with his pen, and it is somewhat illustrative of the futility of his satire, as these dogs were no more punished by his abuse than were those other "dogs" who might have read his column had they desired.

He began writing about dogs in Tom Hood's *Comic Annual*, in 1873, with a story: "How I Came to Like Dogs." This was merely facetious clowning. The real anti-dog propaganda owed its origin to an occurrence at North Beach, in San Francisco, when a fierce canine jumped on Bierce one night and bit his hand. Subsequent experiences but increased his hatred. It was not merely a whim, or prejudice, it was a deep-seated loathing. In Oakland, during the 90's, an enormous bull dog bit a young girl and disfigured her face. Bierce learned of the incident, took his revolver and called at the home of the owner of the dog. He asked the owner where the dog was kept, and marched out to the kennel and shot him.

Another incident occurred some years later. Bierce was out walking in the woods with his daughter. A dog rushed at them and began to bark and snap. Bierce saw an indolent looking fellow leaning against a tree at some distance and shouted at him to call the dog away. But the fellow did not heed or notice the entreaty in any manner. Finally Bierce pulled out his revolver and shot the dog, adding another victim to his list of dog murders. He then walked over to the lazy spectator and asked him how much the dog was worth, as he wished to make reparations. The fellow shifted his position, leaned against the other shoulder, and then drawled: "Ah, shucks, the dog wasn't mine—."

In *The Wasp* and in *The Examiner* Bierce would sometimes devote entire columns to abuse of dogs and the people who kept them. He once wrote an article on "Dogs from the Klondike," rejoicing in the thought that the gold rush might draw all the dogs to Alaska. He defined a Newfoundland as: "Not only is his bite more deadly than that of the ordinary snap-dog, but that of the fleas which he cherishes is peculiarly insupportable. The fleas of all other dogs only sadden: those of the Newfoundland incite to crime. His fragrance, moreover, is less modest than that of the Skye Terrier; it is distinctly declarative indeed." He described dogs as "small animated pestilences." He wrote that a puppy was "a clammy-nosed, swell-fronted, dutch-built, double-charged, flea-peopled, immodest epitome of all nastiness,—a whelp of a thousand infragrant smells." And to this brief collection might be added the opening lines of his once celebrated poem:

> "Snap-dogs, lap-dogs, always-on-tap-dogs,
>   Smilers, defilers,
> "Reekers and Leakers"—

The subject of dogs became, indeed, a matter for serious philosophical consideration in an essay in "The Shadow on the Dial." He once wrote S. O. Howes: "Pretty nearly all the anti-dog literature gets to me, as I seem to be recognized as the captain of the cult. I sometimes fancy that even the dogs know me and assume the attitude towards me that is dictated by their feeling and interest."

During these months at Angwin's, Bierce met an ugly, frail girl who was attempting, after a fashion, to teach a country school nearby. Her name was Carrie Christiansen and she was the daughter of a poor emigrant family that lived in Napa. At this time she was about the most abject, scrawny, unlettered individual imaginable, and had never been outside the Napa Valley. Bierce was impressed with her pathetic helplessness. He spoke to her one day and she was so overawed that she could only stammer a response. A few days later he actually called at her "school," and the experience nearly overwhelmed the child. She gradually overcame her shyness and told him about her home life, its squalor and poverty, and the fact that she had to contribute to the support of her parents and an enormous horde of brothers and sisters. Bierce was impressed with her sincerity and determination and he took her down to St. Helena with him. It was the beginning of a life-long friendship. Carrie, or "Norrie" as she was always called, became a member of the Bierce household. Mrs. Bierce was really a mother to her, taught her about clothes, manners and people, and gave her the advantages of civilized home life. Bierce arranged to send her to normal school at Berkeley, and, under his instruction, she became a remarkably well read and intelligent woman. In later years she came to Washington as his secretary. The arrangement was, unknown to Bierce, really at his wife's instance. A more devoted secretary than Miss Christiansen could not be imagined, nor a nobler soul, and the imputations to the contrary have been unjust and malicious. After Bierce's disappearance into Mexico, Miss Christiansen returned to Napa, where she lived for a few years previous to her death.

It was during these years, 1892-1896, that Bierce began to have the first of a long and unbroken series of quarrels with Hearst. The statement is somewhat inaccurate, for the quarrels were never with Mr. Hearst directly, but with his employees. These rifts were seldom over matters of policy, but were more often caused by the carelessness of type-setters. It was always Mr. Hearst who patched things up and mollified Bierce. Reading their correspondence over a period of years, one is impressed with Mr. Hearst's kindness, his good disposition, and his clever flattery, which always drew Bierce back into the fold. A sample note, written with typical Hearstian rush and eagerness, contains this statement: "Write about anything you like if you will only write. I only hope you will write 'Prattle' until you can persuade me to relinquish it. Don't for Heaven's sake stop 'Prattle.' I shall think myself a terrible 'hoodoo' if immediately on my return *The Examiner* should lose what is to me its very best feature. I hope you will continue. I don't want to have to stop my subscription to my own paper for lack of interest in the damned old sheet. Shall I appoint myself a committee of one to come up and persuade you?" There were many of these trips, and they invariably resulted in a reconciliation. Bierce could not resist Hearst's flattery, coupled with the fact that he knew that Mr. Hearst gave him a free rein, asked no questions, let him do as he pleased, and, incidentally, paid him well.

"Prattle," as usual, was quite lively. Several rather amusing incidents should be related. It seems that two men, Phillips and Hahn, had gone to a bawdy house in San Francisco, where Phillips had introduced Hahn to the "Madam" as "Ambrose Bierce." They had gotten quite noisy and had been arrested later in the evening, and the ladies of joy announced to the police that one of the culprits was the great Ambrose Bierce. Of course San Francisco's Fleet Street was roaring with mirth the next day. It took all of Sam Chamberlain's ingenuity to pacify Bierce who was out for blood. But the matter was finally smoothed out, much to the satisfaction of all concerned, as both offenders were quite well known in San Francisco. Bierce, in accordance with his invariable practice, would flog a man on trial if he thought the fellow was guilty. A man was tried at Fresno in the Nineties for a particularly atrocious crime and Bierce abused him in frightful terms. His satire provoked the following ditty in a Fresno newspaper:

> "What a brave man is Bierce
> And how very fierce
> This fellow who fights with his pen,
> But when there's a foe
> Of Ambrose you know
> He gives them the slip to return, when?"

Attorney Foote protested to the court at Fresno that Bierce was stirring up too much public discussion but the judge ordered the case to proceed.

It was during this period that Bierce attempted to arrange for the publication of a volume of his short stories, many of which had appeared in *The Examiner* and *The Wave* during the years from 1887 to 1891. The date of the composition of all these stories cannot, of course, be verified. But it is quite apparent that they were practically all written after he began to write for *The Examiner*. If they were written previous to that date, they would have found a place in some of the journals, as Bierce was frequently requested to submit copy to various magazines. The stories that comprised his first volume were thus written during a rather sad period in his life, but one should not be misled by this fact. Many of the stories can be traced into *The Examiner*, and under dates that were prior to Day's death and prior to Bierce's separation from his wife. But the nature of these stories will be considered in the following chapter, as so much discussion has centered around them that it becomes a temptation, even in a biography, to attempt an explanation of their quality.

The first volume of stories, "Tales of Soldiers and Civilians" was published in 1891 by E. L. G. Steele, a San Francisco merchant and friend of Bierce. In a foreword to this volume Bierce wrote that: "Denied existence by the chief publishing houses of the country, this book owes itself to Mr. E. L. G.

Steele, merchant, of this city. In attesting Mr. Steele's faith in his judgment and his friend, it will serve its author's main and best ambition." Now this statement is slightly extravagant. There is nothing to show that the book was "denied existence by the chief publishing houses," nor, for that matter, that it was ever submitted to a publishing house. The circumstances prove that Bierce had made little or no effort to get his stories published. Andrew Chatto wrote from London, immediately upon the publication of the volume, arranging for the English rights, and asked: "Why have I not heard from you all these years?" Stone and Kimball were writing for copy at an early date. Bierce once admitted in a letter to Sterling that he had been "lazy and indisposed to dicker with publishers." Practically all the stories that appeared in his first volume had been published in newspapers or magazines and had been paid for at good rates. If Bierce had shown the slightest disposition to "dicker," as he said, even with Pacific coast publishers, the publication of the volume could easily have been arranged long prior to 1891.

Another myth that has grown up during the years since 1891 is that "Tales of Soldiers and Civilians" was a failure and that Ambrose Bierce was a "neglected" author. Nothing could be more absurd. His first three volumes had received wide comment in England, for books of their type. "Tales of Soldiers and Civilians," if one may take into consideration the edition of 1895, as well as that of 1891, was reviewed in over four hundred newspapers and periodicals. Surely this would not indicate neglect. Moreover, with scarcely a single exception, the reviews were enthusiastic. The fact is that Bierce was never the "struggling" artist; in truth, he was never the artist, save incidentally. The stories were written late in life and simply as a divertissement. Bierce always realized that his "trade was abuse," as he wrote Mr. J. H. E. Partington. That the stories struck such a high level of excellence is only another indication of his remarkably forceful, brilliant, and provocative personality.

It was with the publication of "Tales of Soldiers and Civilians" in 1891 that Bierce attained his national fame as a writer of the short story. "Success," said Remy de Gourmont, "is a fact." Opinions may differ, comments may vary, but if a book is ever once a success, that success is a fact which cannot be forgotten. The truth of this psychological observation was never better illustrated than in the history of this remarkable volume of stories by Bierce. It has been extravagantly praised, violently denounced, and hopelessly mauled, since 1891, but the fact is that in 1891 it was a success. Comment invariably centers around a book that has been a success, particularly if that book be as remarkable a book as "Tales of Soldiers and Civilians." One cannot judge this volume, with justice, by applying the æsthetics of to-day. But when the stories are read in comparison with contemporary collections, their excellence cannot be denied. Bierce's stories were hard, brilliant, cold, and, whatever their limitations, they were never commonplace. But more of this anon. . . .

There was surely nothing about the reception that the book received of which Bierce could complain. It was praised in almost every journal in which it was reviewed. But this comment, particularly in the American newspapers, was stupid and trite; one review was as like another as two peas. "Suggestive of Edgar Allan Poe," "dark stories of death," it was always and eternally the same. Occasionally some reviewer would write intelligently, as did E. H. Clough in the Oakland *Times*. He said, *inter alia,* that "The best modern fiction is not in realism; neither is it based wholly upon the romantic incidents of life and its possibilities. The absolute horror of 'The Mystery of Udolpho' is no longer permissible." This was sharp comment, particularly in light of the analysis made in the next chapter.

As soon as the volume was published, Andrew Chatto arranged for its publication in England under the title: "In the Midst of Life." Chatto suggested this new title, for the reason, as he wrote, that English readers did not like collections of stories unless they had some unifying theme. The English reviews were equally enthusiastic although more intelligent. The *Spectator, Daily Chronicle, Scotsman,* Glasgow *Herald,* and *Scottish Leader,* were all enthusiastic. One reviewer, however, held out against the general praise. He was an anonymous reviewer writing in *Literature,* and he wrote of Bierce that he was "another writer, the unfortunate victim of extravagant and uncritical laudation," who, "has written a number of clever, violent, vigorous battle-notes, which were heaped together between book covers; but crude, unshapen impressions are no more a book than a collection of New England sermons are the 'Scarlet Letter.' " This was much better than the American drivel about a second Edgar Allan Poe, etc.

Not only was the book remarkably well received in the press, but private opinion was equally enthusiastic. Opie Read wrote to Bierce on its publication: "Had you lived two hundred years ago you would be alive to-day, and living to-day, you will be alive when two hundred years have come." Walter Blackburn Harte wrote letters of high praise and devoted an article to Bierce in the *New England Magazine*. Percival Pollard reviewed the volume with a fine frenzy of eulogistic adjectives. Sam Davis called it "a stride in literature." Soldiers in New York State read the book at a reunion meeting and wrote to tell Bierce what fine war stories he had written. And that shrewdest of all Bierce enthusiasts, James Watkins, wrote from New York, where he was working on the *Sun,* with calm and fine assurance: "Probably you will derive only a meager spiritual consolation from the reflection that you are to become a classic, and that in time a test of a critic's acumen and fitness will be his attitude toward Ambrose Bierce. *Yet this thing shall be, and there will be limited editions, and artists straining to disfigure you with cuts.*" And all these things have happened. The pity is that Bierce, who had taken Watkins' advice in nearly everything, did not take the advice with which Watkins closed this letter: "Go on living, old man; you have only to live thirty years to be allowed the foremost workman of your period, if you continue with your work."

Even Bierce's old enemies reviewed the book well, as did Arthur McEwen, in the Oakland *Tribune*. He told a story about being at breakfast with Bierce shortly after the publication of the book. Bierce asked him how he thought the book would sell. McEwen replied: "I won't be surprised if it makes a world hit or falls as dead as a landed salmon. You haven't, in all you write, a trace of what we call sympathy. The pretty girl never appears." To which Bierce replied: "Darn the pretty girl," and McEwen added: "That's what is the matter with you." And this was correct, from the standpoint of sales in 1891.

There was one review that rather nettled Bierce. It appeared in the New York *Sun,* and was written by Mayo Hazeltine. In the course of this review, Hazeltine intimated that Bierce had once been a failure as a journalist in New York, and that "he is a scoffer and scorner and he writes his tales of horror with a sort of fiendish delight." To both of these statements, Bierce replied (*The Examiner,* Jan. 22, 1893) : "In all my life I have submitted but one little piece of my work to an editor of a New York newspaper; and that was accepted and printed in the *World.* No other eastern publication, daily, weekly, or monthly, has, to my knowledge, ever had a line of my manuscript." This, mind you, from the "neglected" Mr. Bierce! Replying to Hazeltine's other remark, Bierce said: "I wrote my tales of horror without reference to the nerves, or even the existence, of the innocent, and in the belief that they are good and true art—a belief in which I have the obstinacy to remain."

T. H. Rearden, an old personal friend, wrote Bierce that his stories of "human beings in a mass, groveling in the horrors of impossible wounds, and yet sentient and acting, though beyond the reach of help, while wishing and hoping for it, stir one with terror," and suggested a French translation. In this suggestion there was a sound psychological observation, as is borne out by the subsequent history of Bierce's stories in France. M. Victor Llona published "Un Incident au pont d'Owl Creek" in *La Nouvelle Revue Française,* and it immediately attracted a great deal of attention. Jacques Rivière and his successor, Jean Paulhan, kept asking M. Llona for more stories by Bierce. He later brought out a collection of stories published in France as "Aux Lisières de la Mort," which enjoyed a considerable sale. Such stories as "Un cas de conscience" have even reached the popular press and have appeared in such papers as *Adventure* and *Excelsior.*

These were the active publishing years with Bierce. "The Monk and the Hangman's Daughter" appeared in 1892; "Black Beetles in Amber," which some wit suggested should be called "red peppers in vinegar," in 1892; and "Can Such Things Be?" in 1893. Did Bierce select the title of this last volume to complete the thought suggested by the title of the English edition of his first volume of stories: "In the midst of life, can such things be?" Whether he did or not, he was annoyed to discover that "Can Such Things Be?" had been used as the title of a book by Keith Fleming, published by George Routledge, in London in 1889. He was to be similarly chagrined about "The

Shadow on the Dial," a phrase which Ruskin had previously used as a title.

In connection with "The Monk and the Hangman's Daughter," a fine, ironic romance, and "Black Beetles in Amber," those tersely written lines of doggerel, it becomes necessary to discuss Bierce's relations with Dr. Adolphe Danziger. This is a duty which, had it not been for the tremendous notoriety and publicity that the Doctor has attained by forcing the association of his name with Bierce as that of a "collaborator," and for the misstatements that he has made, would be pleasantly ignored. In the first place, Dr. Danziger (he now calls himself DeCastro), claims that he is entitled to all the credit for "The Monk and the Hangman's Daughter." In a letter to me he made this statement: "at present no one but myself has any right to the story or the name on the title page." This is, indeed, a most extraordinary claim. To begin with, the story was only a translation of a story by Dr. Richard Voss, originally written in German. Danziger made the translation, but admits that at the time he was not sufficiently familiar with the English language to do the story justice, and that he took the manuscript to Bierce and paid him to rewrite it. Whether he paid Bierce or not, the fact remains that Bierce rewrote the story and that Danziger had nothing whatever to do with the revision. Compare the chaste, simple style of the book as it now appears in print with the style of Dr. Danziger in books admittedly of his entire authorship, to wit, "In the Garden of Abdullah and other Poems," a volume of verse privately published in Los Angeles. It would be doing the Doctor an unpardonable injustice to quote these verses, but any one who takes the pains to read them, along with Dr. Danziger's collection of stories "In the Confessional," will never be in doubt as to the pen that wrote "The Monk and the Hangman's Daughter" as it now stands.

The Doctor, who has been at various times a dentist, a lawyer, and Rabbi of Congregation Bikur Cholin of San José, was once a publisher. He organized the Western Authors Publishing Company, in which enterprise, so he says, Bierce and W. C. Morrow, were partners. The plan of this company, according to the Doctor's own explanation, was to charge poor, illiterate hacks who wanted to "write" an enormous sum to pub-

lish their books. That Bierce was ever a party to such a scheme
is incredible and there is nothing in all his entire correspondence
and papers that gives the slightest credence to such a statement.
It clearly appears from Bierce's correspondence that Dr. Danziger's partner was one William Langton; that Bierce suspected
both of them and that he dealt with both at a considerable
fish's pole distance, making copies of even the slightest note
addressed to either, and trying, in every imaginable way to
shield himself from the very charges that Dr. Danziger has
made of recent years. It is significant that these charges were
never made during Bierce's lifetime.

Early in their acquaintance, Bierce had defended Dr.
Danziger from a vicious attack by Dr. Jacob Voorsanger in the
Jewish *Times and Observer*. Bierce soon came to rue the day
that he made such a foolish gesture as the article he wrote in
defense of Danziger. As a matter of fact, Bierce was always
gullible about people. If they would flatter him, he would listen
and then smile. The inevitable disappointments that followed on
the revelation of unworth were among the saddest experiences in
his life.

But, to return to Dr. Danziger, it seems that about 1893,
the Doctor wanted to publish a collection of his own stories,
"In the Confessional," and that he greatly desired to have this
book illustrated by J. H. E. Partington. To pay for this service,
Dr. Danziger went to a very dear friend of Mr. Bierce, and,
on the strength of his acquaintance, borrowed some three hundred dollars. When Bierce discovered what had been done, he
was furious. Dr. Danziger has sniffed disdainfully at George
Sterling's statement that Bierce once broke a cane over the
Doctor's head. Were it not for this fact, omission would be
made of what is, after all, a rather trivial and personal affair.
Personally I did not see Bierce apply the cane, nor did Sterling.
But Bierce did save the fragments of a broken cane, to remind
him, so he said, "of the nature of friendship." Moreover, he
discussed his quarrel with Dr. Danziger in print and no denial
was made, at the time, of his version of the facts. It would seem
that these quotations state Bierce's views rather clearly:

> "I have not the conceit to suppose the public is interested
> in the business affairs which Dr. Danziger gratifies his nature

at the expense of his welfare by lying about. It cannot make any material difference whether I swindled him or he swindled me; commercial usage and the proprieties of business were sufficiently observed if some one was swindled. Nor with reference to 'The Monk and the Hangman's Daughter' is it important whether he or I had the larger hand in spoiling the work of a better man than either. These matters are trivial and dull, even to me, except in so far as they show (as doubtless Heaven ordained them to do) how far a man may be willing to go in procuring food for the conceit in him. For nourishment of his insatiable inner dog, Dr. Danziger would steal any bone of recognition that he could not get by cheating. What is really amusing is his solemn censure of me for *assaulting with* fist, *stick* and pistol (he seems to have forgotten the cannon) an inoffensive 'minister' who desires to do his lying in peace. As to that, I beg leave to explain that having had no voice in Dr. Danziger's choice of a profession, I do not feel compelled to suffer inconvenience from the abuse of it.

"As a matter of fact, the wretch is a 'minister' in the same way that Jonah, after being spewed ashore, was a part of the whale. I never was ashamed of being an infidel until Dr. Danziger assured me that he was one. For ten minutes I was an easy prey to any strolling exhorter that might have passed that way, cadging for souls.

"In Dr. Danziger is a dual individuality like that of a two-headed calf; the natures of saint and sinner are so intimately interblended as to make him preëminently a man of parts. He is a layman for lying and a minister for fighting. He carries his sacerdotal character in his hip-pocket and pulls it only when his face is slapped. He carries a pistol there, too, but when invited to pull that he says it is the proudest moment of his life, but family reasons, largely hereditary, compel him to decline. But, Lord, Lord, you should have heard this holy man of God swear when tapped upon the nimbus! And dance!—why, not a curly young worldling in San Francisco's entire 400 ever footed it so neatly! O, a fine and serious minister he!—isn't he, Dr. Voorsanger? By the way, Voorsanger —shake." *

Dr. Danziger has written that George Sterling was lying when he told the caning episode; furthermore, he says, the story was absurd since he could have "broken Bierce" with his hands. To

* *The Examiner,* July 23, 1893.

this the answer might very conceivably be that in 1893 he had a perfect chance to do just that thing, and there is no record of his having done so. Moreover, he could have passed over the incident in his "Portrait of Ambrose Bierce" without calling George Sterling a liar and "irresponsible drunkard." But since the issue has been raised, as suggested by Mr. Harry Hansen in the New York *World,* it should be met. It is not, perhaps, so trivial as might be assumed. If a biographer was once caned by his subject, it is submitted that the fact has at least some significance, from a critical standpoint.

In a subsequent issue of *The Examiner,* Bierce gave the public a further explanation:

> "I wrote every word of 'The Monk and the Hangman's Daughter' as published. Until Dr. Danziger saw that it was a creditable book he never, so far as I know, professed to have done more than translate the German story by Dr. Voss upon which it was founded. I have never seen that story and do not read German; what changes he may have made I do not know, nor care. If there was as little of Dr. Voss in his version as there is of him in mine, I am unable to conjecture what the original yarn was like. It was for lying about that and other matters that I punished him; and apparently he is not yet reformed." *

Mr. Hansen, and those interested, can make such definition of the word "punished" as they desire; I make my own definition, and doubtless George Sterling made his.

*   *   *

WITH these years an important chapter in Bierce's life came to a close. The violent and impetuous days on *The Wasp* had kept him in a perpetual bad temper about a number of things that were of no ultimate importance. The close of the eighties had seen him swept to prominence with the publication of the three volumes of fiction upon which his reputation as a story-teller rests. With his work on *The Examiner,* he had attained an undeniable position of ascendancy on the coast. He was thus converted into a Master and a Prominent Figure. His picture was prominently displayed in "Men of the Pacific

* *The Examiner,* August 13, 1893.

Coast" published at this time. *Munsey's Magazine* (April, 1896), had announced that "Mr. Bierce" was an author of great importance, and a number of other periodicals had voiced similar views. On November 18, 1889, the Hon. Henry Highton had lectured on "Bierce as Satirist" in Honolulu. Bierce was made a member of the American Social Science Association in 1899, for "service in literature and journalism." He became quite a grand figure with the publication of his stories. William Dean Howells announced in a lecture at Columbia University that "Mr. Bierce is among our three greatest writers," to which Bierce had made answer that "I am sure Mr. Howells is the other two." J. H. E. Partington painted his portrait which was exhibited at the World's Fair in 1893 and won a gold medal. In this picture Bierce is shown standing by the side of his writing table, on which is a skull. Perhaps people would not have admired the portrait so much had they known that the "Skull," when it was a "head," had been a friend of Mr. Bierce! Several palmists came to study Mr. Bierce's hand as painted by Partington, as it was thought to be a most interesting hand. It was announced in the newspapers that the "hand" was a masterpiece. One of these experts gave an interview in which he announced that: "the hand shows that Mr. Bierce has not had many love experiences."

During these halcyon days, when nonsense was at its height as a national characteristic of our letters and art, that perennial lark of California song, Ella Sterling Cummins, was in charge of the "California Room" in the fine arts section, at the Fair. To those eager to learn about California in letters, she would gracefully suggest that they purchase: "A Story of the Files," which she had written under the auspices of the World's Fair Commission. In this interesting book all the grandees of California verse, song, and story are made immortal. Here, in the covers of one book, all the enemies came together, kissed, and for the honor of California, wrote flattering blurbs about each other. Mr. Bierce waived his acklowledged right of first slaughter and became a lamb of praise. He wrote of Joaquin Miller's verse: "And here I wish to say, and upon the assertion stake whatever reputation for literary understanding I may chance to have, that in all the work of all the red planet's victims there is not a larger, nobler, more purely poetic conception than this (of Miller's) of their surviving brother, whom, in gratitude for the delight he has given me, I beg to warn that the menace of Mars burns implacable in the skies, 'a still and awful red,' etc." To which the only response is: "Ambrose, you are a talented, gorgeous, and slightly inebriated liar." It is incredible that Bierce wrote that blurb unless he was in his cups. I shall not quote it in its entirety: the experience would be unbearable. But turn about was fair play, for Markham, E. L. Clough, W. C. Morrow, Adele Chretien, Arthur McEwen, Mrs. Atherton, J. O'Hara Cosgrave, and George Hamlin Fitch joined in the love feast and showered the giant of Howell Mountain with an abundance of bouquets. Mr. Markham delved deep in his library and produced this morsel: "His is a composite mind—a blending of Hafiz the Persian, Swift, Poe, Thoreau, with sometimes a gleam of the Galilean." To which might be added, with equal exactness, John Brown, Christopher Columbus and Florence Nightingale. It was the year of portraits and fairs, of compliments, bows to the gallery, and hand kissing. The spirit of Victoria's Jubilee had permeated the states.

* * *

To-day Angwins' Hotel has been removed and the spot where Ambrose Bierce wrote countless reams of "Prattle" is adorned with the pure and stately columns of the Pacific Union Theological Seminary: where "Bitter Bierce" sent forth his weekly thunderbolts of wit, the Seventh Day Adventists now perform their strange rituals and carry on their clandestine whispering with God. It is a circumstance that should be significant to those who believe, as did Bierce, that satire has a peculiar efficacy, and that nonsense can really be confounded by sharp wit and noble example.

Down in the Napa Valley, during these years when Bierce was fast becoming an Olympian, Mollie Day Bierce was reading "Trilby" with Mrs. Hunt, as it appeared in Harper's *Magazine*, and kindly but firmly declining to see old friends. She lived quietly alone, at the foot of Howell Mountain, waiting and hoping that some day a reconciliation might be effected. She dressed invariably in black, but she would not permit even her unfortunate separation from her husband to make her gloomy or melancholy. When asked to play the piano for the "young people," she would straighten out the folds of her dress, pin a flower from her shoulder, and play as long as they liked. One day she consented to go on a picnic in the mountains with some friends. The carriages toiled up the mountainside and came to a pause in a clearing. A man strode through a bit of brushwood and stood for a moment in the sunlight, as if puzzled and annoyed at the sight of the picnickers. He was tall and straight and handsome and many people called him a god. Mrs. Bierce hastened from the carriage and walked to his side. They stood apart from the others, whom Bierce did not recognize, and talked in low syllables for a few moments and then parted. They were never to see one another again.

CHAPTER XIII

BIERCE AND THE CHARNEL HOUSE

THE publication of "Tales of Soldiers and Civilians" in 1891 and of "Can Such Things Be?" in 1893, provoked the beginning of what has since become the most irregular body of critical opinion devoted to an American author of any prominence. The only parallel situation is that involved in the work of Edgar Allan Poe. Difficult as it is to analyze these stories, it is still more difficult to explain the interest that has always centered about the two slender volumes of fiction. Bierce only wrote, in all, about sixty-five short stories and this estimate takes into account the stories of two and three paragraphs collected under such topical heads as "Bodies of the Dead." Of this group of short stories approximately eighteen are war stories and the rest, with one exception, are tales of the supernatural. And yet since 1893 Mr. Bierce has been hailed as a "bitterly realistic" writer, although by a simple mathematical calculation one can demonstrate that forty-seven of his stories are admittedly pure fancy and even the other eighteen are subject to close scrutiny on the same charge, as will be shown.

It is immediately apparent, upon the most casual examination, that many of Bierce's stories are commonplace. Some of them are actually unreadable to-day. Yet it is upon this fragile foundation that his fame as a man of letters rests, since criticism in this country has always centered about his fiction with remorseless persistence and to the neglect of his great talent as a wit and satirist. It is quite a difficult task to explain why Bierce's short stories have always attracted such an inordinate amount of interest and comment. It is not sufficient as an explanation to observe that, at the time they were first published, his stories were unusual. They had a quality, to be sure, but it was not a novel quality after Poe. What fascinated most readers was perhaps the thought that these stories represented a disordered mentality. Without the aid of modern psychology, it was a simple deduction from the short stories of Poe and the work of Maturin to assume that they were neurotic. And, since Bierce's stories bore a superficial resemblance to the work of these men, was it not logical to assume that he, too, was the victim of some hallucination? The question has always been, whether openly stated or not, a personal problem. In other words, were Bierce's stories subconsciously motivated?

That such has been the basis of the critical interest in his stories is apparent from an examination of some of the more serious comment about his work. Dorothy Scarborough, in "The Supernatural in Modern English Fiction," first stated the issue and it has been raised by many writers since, including a specialist in psychiatry, Dr. Louis J. Bragman. Miss Scarborough wrote of Bierce's stories: "The carrion ghosts of Bierce, animated by malignant foreign spirits, surpass the charnel shudders produced by the Gothic. . . . Bierce's stories beat upon the mind like bludgeons and his morbid plots are among the most dreadful in our literature. One wonders what *abnormality of mind* conceives such themes, evolves such situations." The inference that Bierce was mentally disordered has been echoed in a great portion of the criticism devoted to his work. The normal mind is interested in the spectacle of a man preoccupied, or seemingly preoccupied, with the macabre. A sound instinct makes such men suspect. And so it was with Bierce.

This problem of motivation is one which is germane and pertinent to a biography, because it is really a personal, rather than a critical, problem. At the outset, one is impressed with the fact that there is not a taint of abnormality about Bierce's life. He was vigorous and healthy and possessed none of the symptoms of the neurotic. To be sure he was an asthmatic, but this of itself cannot be given great importance. It caused him considerable pain and was a constant annoyance, and it is true that frequently he had to take chloroform to obtain relief from his suffering. But personally he was far from "bitter" or "morose" and there is nothing in his life that one could hit upon to explain his work in the same manner that Mr. D. H. Lawrence and Dr. Joseph Wood Krutch have psycho-analyzed Poe. Bierce's physician and an eminent nerve specialist who was his friend, have assured me that it would be a far stretch of the imagination to attribute the somber quality of his work directly to the fact that he was an asthmatic. Moreover, the stories are as nothing when compared with the enormous bulk of his satire. There are surely no clouds of abnormality enshrouding his satire. Bierce had a rather sharp perception of the limitations involved in the critical habit of moving from an author's work into his life, as is shown by a note on Carlyle:

> "I had supposed that when Carlyle died his dyspepsia would die with him, but his death seems to have rather aggravated the disease. His disobedient gastric fluid formerly disordered only his own literary work; it now tinges with ghastlier green the work of those who write about him. . . . Carlyle—more Carlyle—*toujours* Carlyle! I fall poisonously indisposed of too much Carlyle. The man is dead; shall he not be permitted to enjoy the rotting? Has the long-waiting graveworm no rights, that we balk his mandible till we have had our will of the corpse? Let there be surcease of Carlyle. I hate him." *

But, examining Bierce's work closely, it is apparent that one does not need to chart his life to come to the conclusion that he was not abnormal. The same conclusion is warranted by close critical attention to his style, by a knowledge of the origin of many of his stories, and by a study of his theory of æsthetics. These considerations will be discussed in order.

His style itself throws considerable light on the problem, as becomes immediately apparent when it is contrasted with that of Edgar Allan Poe. Mr. Thomas Beer has written that "Bierce erected his mortuary filigrees with traceries from the style of Poe." Bierce denied this charge in his lifetime with a vehemence with which one can sympathize. The one thing he did not derive from Poe was his style. As will be shown, the terror-romance tradition was old with Poe, who contributed little to its technique. This Bierce realized and he did not hesitate to adopt many of the devices used by Poe, but he was always careful to

* *The Wasp*, April 16, 1881.

safeguard his position on the charge of having aped Poe's style. If Mr. Beer had compared, let us say, "A Son of the Gods" with "The Fall of the House of Usher," he would have noticed the sharp difference in style. The method, in so far as it attempted to produce a "dominant impression," might be the same, but the styles were of two worlds. Bierce's style has nothing of the sonorous, rhythmic sweep of Poe's best prose. On the contrary, Bierce aimed at clarity, precision, and simplicity.

This difference in style represents the difference in men. Dr. Krutch clearly recognized this fact in his book about Poe. To quote an illuminating passage: "Even Ambrose Bierce, who seems, at first glance, more nearly related than any other writer to Poe, will be found upon analysis to be different in an essential particular. He too depended largely upon horror. But unlike Poe he would often base that horror upon the exaggeration of *a normal emotion*. . . . His bitterness, unlike Poe's, is the result of a sense of the world's cruelty and is thus essentially social as Poe's is essentially individualistic." Poe, as Mr. Brownell observed years ago, was *sui generis*. He was a "case" for the psychiatrist from the start. The same can be said of the work of M. G. ('Monk') Lewis and Charles Maturin. There is a feverish quality about the work of these men that is unmistakable evidence of neurotic temperaments. But even in the most "awful" of Bierce's stories, he marred their effect by his "unpardonable facetiousness," which always snickered at his own grisly yarns.

In a previous chapter the origin of several of Bierce's famous war stories has been traced to actual occurrences. When he used an actual incident in a story, however, he invariably warped the facts to fit his theory of the elements of a short story. In every instance, he treated the story in a romantic manner. He once rode forward at the head of a brigade brandishing a sword. It suggested a story and he wrote "A Son of the Gods" about the heroic young soldier who is killed under the gaze of two armies drawn up in line of battle. The story can be seen to be pure romance. Other instances of a similar transposition, from real to unreal, have been previously observed. The matter of "Mysterious Disappearances" is also illuminating. Bierce was always interested in such cases and, in fact, he made a fine disappearance himself in later years. But his method of writing the stories grouped under that phrase was to collect newspaper clippings and then rewrite them in story form. It can thus be observed that the process was entirely conscious and deliberate. He was not dominated, as was Poe, by an inexorable personal necessity.

As a matter of fact, the genuine moments in his stories are the moments of tenderness and the "horrible" situations are used merely as counterpoint for his own feelings. As Mr. Alfred C. Ward has written: "His war stories frequently represent a cry from the heart, such as should inspire us to veil pained ears and eyes, rather than to hide grinning mouths." This is true even of the stories that cannot be traced to actual occurrences. Bierce invariably used a horrible incident for a dramatic purpose, which, of itself, shows the clearest deliberation. He placed severed legs, slashed heads, and broken bones about his canvases in a manner bordering on the melodramatic.

It would be difficult to compute the number of times that it has been suggested that Bierce's war stories are so "grimly realistic" that they should be compared with Tolstoy's "War and Peace." There is nothing in common between the methods of the two men. This should have been immediately apparent by the examination of a single story by Bierce. Take, for illustration, "The Occurrence at Owl Creek Bridge." Technically it is one of the best of his stories, but it is not a war story. He wrote it as a psychological experiment and discussed his method very frankly with Dr. J. M. Robertson. It was pure romance and had no relation to the war, except incidentally. The same is true of many of his war stories. When, as in his sketch "What I Saw of Shiloh," he did come to grips with war, it was in an admittedly personal vein. If he had been a genuine realist, he would never have permitted the dead to die so dramatically. A realist, Mr. Harold Frederic, wrote a collection of stories about the Civil War: "Marsena and Other Stories of the Wartime." In one of these stories, he told all that there was to tell of war in a simple picture of a group of country people behind the lines standing about a bulletin board reading the casualty lists.

One has only to image the many war incidents that Bierce might have used, and then to examine a few of the situations he selected, in order to understand the essential character of his

work. Captain Graffenreid, a brave man who has been used in
drill work behind the lines, is suddenly shifted to the front and
terror besets him. He jabs a saber through his body and an
officer in the rear notices, with calm interest, the sharp point
of the sword coming through Graffenreid's coat as he sinks to
the ground. It develops that the attack which so frightened Graffenreid was just a false alarm. In a word, a man was killed by
terror, the oldest trick of the terror romance. The manner of
Graffenreid's taking off rather irritates one: it is unnecessarily
dramatic. One hears offstage the clanking of the chains as the
technician pulls his events into a dramatic order. It should be
obvious, too, that the incident was purely imaginary. Outwardly,
all of Bierce's stories are objective, as though he had mistaken
the origin of the creative impulse.

Take, again, the story of George Thurston, a brave man
because he is a coward. He fears his cowardice to such an extent that he is unnecessarily heroic to beat down his terror. But
he meets death in a swing. The swing soars too high and he is
thrown out and his body crashes to the ground. "Then there is
an indescribable sound—the sound of an impact that shakes the
earth, and these men, familiar with death in its most awful
aspects, turn sick. Many walk unsteadily away from the spot;
others support themselves against the trunks of trees or sit at
the roots." It will be observed that the objective act of falling
from the swing is deliberately *used* with the purpose in mind
of inspiring horror. It is another ancient trick, old with Horace
Walpole. The story was clearly manufactured. Deeply imbued
with this theory of his art, which failed to identify appearances
with an inner reality, Bierce was forever in quest of some
"strange" or "unusual" incident to use as a story. This accounts
for the meagerness of his stories and their essential uniformity.
He was a romantic figure himself and he carried over into art
some of the strangeness which he felt inhered in his own experience. He would write only of the "unusual" or the "strange,"
because art had nothing whatever to do with reality, and where
could he find the "unusual" save in the realm of the unreal in
which horror exists solely for the reason that it cannot be explained. Manfred parades his melancholy; Poe announces that
loveliness is sad; Mr. Bierce speaks tenderly of the dead.

If further argument were needed to demonstrate the real

nature of Bierce's fiction, one has only to refer to the incidents
he used in his stories of the supernatural. Some of the details
of these stories have greatly perturbed Dr. Louis J. Bragman.
Writing in the *Welfare Magazine* of the Illinois State Re-
formatory (June, 1928), he said: "Other chilling and unnerv-
ing topics Bierce develops in his mad search for the macabre
are ghosts, the return of the dead, spirits, and spirit-rappings,
haunted houses, mysterious disappearances, visual hallucinations,
amnesia and delirium tremens. On what strange philosophic
food did he nourish himself to produce such gloomy creations?"
The answer is not as difficult as it might appear. Dr. Bragman
must realize that the details, which have so horrified him, have
been the common property of romantic terrorists for centuries.

To understand Bierce's theory, one must keep constantly
in mind the fact that there has always been a definite tradition
of the terror-romance. The tradition dated, to be arbitrary and
therefore inaccurate, with "The Castle of Otranto: A Gothic
Story" by Horace Walpole in 1764. The terror-romance from
this early romance to the present date has always been a
romantic outburst. The Romantic Movement, so-called, has
been traced to the work of Walpole, Ann Radcliffe and M. G.
Lewis, I am informed by the academicians. Mr. Lascelles Aber-
crombie in his series of lectures on "Romance," denies that the
Lake poets had much to do with the movement, and, specifically,
that Wadsworth was ever a part of it.

It would require a volume to summarize the methods by
means of which Walpole and Mrs. Radcliffe succeeded in
achieving their aim, which was to suggest a spirit of place that
would dominate their romances. They deliberately set out to
make the scene other than it was in fact. In other words, they
used purely objective tricks to attain a mood that satisfied some
secret yen in their own natures. To attain this end they invented
the "haunted house" and so typical did the castle or house become in the work of such writers that Mr. Eino Railo entitled
his capital study of English Romanticism, "The Haunted
Castle." This type of romance released the imagination from
the commonplace; it was an efflorescence of the romantic temperament. The most interesting of the early terrorists was M.
G. Lewis. He was well read in German romanticism and, under
its influence, wrote a book the title of which has an ironic ring

in connection with this study: "Ambrosio, or The Monk." It appeared in 1795 and was an enormous success. The title was shortened to "The Monk" and Lewis quickly became "Monk" Lewis. It is well known that Byron was deeply influenced by this book, just as Shelley was under the spell of similar romantic terrorism for a time. Poe, with his inventive intelligence, liberated the terror-romance from its fixed locale. He also added certain details of his own, such as old manuscripts, miniature portraits, and similar devices, which he used as objects upon which to liberate his romantic rhapsodies. Then, too, Poe used pseudo-scientific data to bolster up his work, just as he used the first person.

It was this tradition of the terror-romance, softened by the poetry of Southey and Coleridge, made fanciful by Hawthorne, and broadened by Poe, that Bierce inherited. Bierce became familiar with the tradition as early as 1874. It was a tradition characterized by its fanatical avoidance of the commonplace and its yearning for the strange, which is in effect a form of disgust with the obvious. It was a flight away from life. Naturally the tradition had much to offer Bierce. He became familiar with it at an early period in his life and he was inducted into its mysteries by his first and only mentor, James Watkins. It must be remembered that an adventurous and independent American, coming into the world of art in 1869, would inevitably fall into the tradition of Poe. Bierce had not passed through many phases of experience at the time and he assumed that Poe's principles were true. All his life he labored under this misapprehension and frittered away his splendid energy and ability accommodating himself to a set of principles which did not align with his own feelings. He was basically ironic and quickly outgrew the tradition, but he never abandoned its principles in his work in the short story.

That he worked in the tradition of the terror-romance may be proven with ease. All the clichés of the tradition were used by him time and again in his stories. Like Poe he used the pseudo-scientific to bolster up his tales and to give them a ring of probability that they would otherwise lack, thus avoiding the errors of Mrs. Radcliffe. He read queer books in an effort to get this data. He quoted Denneker's "Meditations" in "A Psychological Shipwreck," in "Stanley Fleming's Hallucination" and in "Charles Ashmore's Trail." He quoted from Dr. Hern's "Verschwinder und Seine Theorie." He speculated with Hegel's doctrine of Non-Euclidian space, suggesting Poe and his Eureka talk. Bierce's "Moxon's Master" is suggestive, too, of Poe and his automatic chess player, which in turn relates back to the frequent appearance of the Frankenstein monster in German and English fiction. Then, too, Bierce used the incident of a severed part of the body to inspire terror, a trick which is at least two hundred years old. He wrote a group of stories about "haunted houses" and "mysterious disappearances" which were favorite subjects with all the terrorists. It will be noticed that Bierce contributed nothing to this type of story save, perhaps, his style. Practically every incident he used as the framework for a story had been used before. His was not the febrile intelligence to invent such schemes in the first instance. He was personally at antipodes from Poe, whose theory of æsthetics he adopted because it was more adaptable to his purposes than any other. The greatness of Bierce's best stories is that they transcend this very tradition; that they break the bonds that his mind placed upon them.

But, to prove his alliance with the terrorists of fiction, one need only quote his own words. Writing of the tradition in his "Collected Works," he said: "Tapping, as they do, two of the three great mother-lodes of human interest, these tales are a constant phenomenon—the most permanent, because the most fascinating, element in letters. Great Scott! has the patrol never heard of *The Thousand and One Nights,* of *The Three Spaniards,* of Horace Walpole, of 'Monk' Lewis, of DeQuincey, of Maturin, Ingemann, Blicher, Balzac, Hoffman, Fitz James O'Brien?" * As a boy he read *The Three Spaniards* and was fascinated with the story. Years later, in 1910, he asked Mr. Roosevelt Johnson if he might borrow the book, as he had not examined it since childhood and the memory of it still pleased his fancy.

Writing of the work of Emma Frances Dawson, he said, of a certain "light" about her work, that "it is a light such as falls at sunset upon desolate marches, tingeing the plumage of the tall heron and prophesying the joyless laugh of the loon. That selfsame light shines somewhere through and under Doré's

* "Collected Works" (Volume X, Page 286).

long parallel cloudbanks along his horizons, and I have seen it, with added bleakness, backgrounding the tall rood in the Lone Mountain cemetery in San Francisco." * How Mrs. Radcliffe would have applauded that outburst!

Bierce was interested in the supernatural just as he was interested in the dead. He specialized in cadavers. He used to prowl about the old Yerba Buena cemetery in San Francisco, particularly during the time when it was being removed to make way for the new city hall. But he wrote of these incidents only to shock the readers of his "Prattle." He would write such stuff as this: "I love the dead and their companionship is infinitely agreeable. It was one of those half-dark nights of the wintertime. There was a moon somewhere—I am uncertain if I saw it or heard it." (*Examiner*, June 26, 1887.) If the legion critics who every now and again lift their voices to proclaim that Bierce liked the macabre because he lost his wife and boys, will reflect upon this statement, from *The News-Letter*, (April 22, 1871), months before his marriage, it might arrest their fine psycho-analysis before its full flowering in puerile fancy. Bierce was writing of the Yerba Buena cemetery: "Some rare old corpses have been turned out; among others one which had been bottled up in spirits and seemed as sweet and clean as a pig naked for the oven. One of these fellows was stuck into the dirt twenty years ago and his immortal part hasn't done moving out yet: it still rises 'like the strain of a rich-distilled perfume.' No man with a normal nose can stand above that carcass and doubt the solemn mystery of a spiritual existence." But it is important to observe that he was always mildly ironic about such matters and never wrote of death in the excited manner that was Poe's.

He once summarized his æsthetics in a note on painters in the *Examiner* (May 15, 1887) in this manner: "The great artist makes everything alive; he gives to death itself and desolation a personality and a breathing soul. . . . We are not all equally sensitive to the joyous aspect of a tree, and the sulking of a rock, the menace of the benediction that may speak from a hillside, and the reticence of one building and the garrulity of another, the pathos of a blank window, the tenderness and the terrors that smile and glower everywhere about us. These are

* "Collected Works" (Volume X).

not fancies. True, they are but the outward and visible signs of an inner mood; but *the objects that bear them beget the mood*. No true artist but feels it; and all feel it alike. To discern, to feel, to seize upon the dominant expression "and make it predominant in his picture,—this is the artists' function." (Italics mine.) This, of course, is romantic theory. It shows how deliberately Bierce selected and stressed objective facts on the theory that they created the mood. He sensed a relationship between fact and fancy but he looked outward instead of communing with the Holy Ghost within.

And, if still further proof should be required of his advocacy of the romantic impulse in art, there is the significant passage in his "Collected Works" (Volume X, pages 244-5) which Mr. Wilson Follette wisely quotes in his book *The Modern Novel*. In this passage Bierce said: "It is to him of widest knowledge, of deepest feeling, of sharpest observation and insight, that life is most crowded with figures of heroic stature, with spirits of dream, with demons of the pit, with graves that yawn in pathways leading to the light, with existences not of this earth, both malign and benign,—ministers of grace and ministers of doom. The truest eye is that which discerns the shadow and the portent, the dead hands reaching, the light that is the heart of darkness, the sky with 'dreadful faces thronged and fiery arms.' The truest ear is that which hears

> 'Celestial voices to the midnight air,
>   Sole, or responsive each to the other's note,
>   Singing,'

not 'their great Creator,' but not a negro melody, either; no, nor the latest favorite of the drawing room. In short, he to whom life is not picturesque, enchanting, astonishing, terrible, is denied the gift and faculty divine, and being no poet can write no prose." This reads like it was written with one eye on Bierce's own work and as an apology. It is full of the slightly exaggerated statement of the man who would emphasize a quality to cover a deficiency. It was all right to insist that the artist look sharply at life, for, in truth, it is always picturesque and astonishing to the real creative genius. But to insist that "the objects that bear them beget the mood" is a dangerous theory, since it is but one step to the next proposition, that is, by the mere object one can conjure up a lost feeling as a ghost of the genuine impulse. This cannot be done. It was a trick that Bierce tried on himself time and again, as will be noted in the later chapters. He would visit an old battlefield and feel pleasantly sad. He would return two months later and be bored. Therefore, "nothing mattered" because the illusion was gone. The entire process was the result of a mistaken assumption that values were outward, detached, and objective facts.

Mr. W. C. Brownell wrote of Poe that "he is distinctly so much the most, as to be almost the only, romantic figure in our literature; and his romantic interest has greatly influenced the critical estimate of his work." He might just as well have been writing of Bierce. Bierce was, as George Sterling once remarked to me, "incurably romantic." This fact has disturbed and excited many an otherwise calm critical pen into flurries of nonsense. His pupils, for example, were so fascinated by his romantic personality that they threw their critical senses overboard. While the ladies . . . but one need only read Ruth Guthrie Harding's article. . . .

The inner relation of Bierce to this romanticism is easy to trace. He was an immensely sensitive man and his reaction to life was twice as quick and as violent as the man in the street. But he began to read and think only at a rather late period in his life. Hence he was past middle age when he outgrew his romantic ideas of art, which are usually among the first theories that the novice adopts. He recoiled from the utter futility and fatuousness of existence. Evidence of such futility inhered in his experience. His first great shock, the crash of his idealism that followed after the war, subverted his balance. He swung out of alignment, philosophically. He was in revolt against his environment at all times; not merely his immediate environment, the visible circus-world that he satirized in "Prattle," but also against pain, horror, futility, chaos and death. In his revolt against death lies the germ of his interest in the supernatural. He deliberately "leads us out into an occult realm whose shapes and happenings give us 'zero at the bone,'" as Edwin Markham once wrote. There is something of George Thurston's steely resolve about Bierce's determination to leave no field unexplored. He had a constant prescience of death; the real might be the unreal, for he had seen strange things; hence he wrote rather rhetorically of ghosts.

* * *

THE greatest formative influence on Bierce's work was unquestionably exercised by James Watkins. It was a close, intimate, personal influence. Watkins and Bierce thrashed out the problems of æsthetics, as they saw them, and in nearly every argument Watkins gained his point. Bierce, to my knowledge, never accorded to another the deference and respect that he always showed to Watkins. Hence this excerpt from a letter of Watkins to Bierce *in 1874,* is of the first importance in understanding Bierce's viewpoint:

> "The sort of sensation that waited upon Mrs. Radcliffe's and Monk Lewis' efforts affords some hint of the sort of career the new 'Monk' and 'Castle of Udolpho' would run. The work they did in stupid vaults you execute in the secret chambers of the soul; the poor limelight effects they worked on a painted stage, you would *sear with lightning on the face of nature.* Your work would expand the human mind."

This was written to Bierce, let it be remembered, in 1874, long before he had actually started to write any of his stories. And in a later paragraph of the same letter, Watkins said:

> "The supreme art with a pen is to-day, as it has been throughout the history of letters, the art of story-telling,—of telling a story that has no reason for its existence outside of its own interest. It must illustrate nothing, be devoid of moral, make no one think, in fact, it must *paralyze the faculty of thinking:* It must purely and simply entertain. That has been the character of all work that has been permanent from the 'Arabian Nights' to 'Treasure Island.' This faculty you possess in the highest degree, though you have not chosen to exercise it *dissociated from the thinking faculties.* A man puts himself into a novel. He puts nothing but his imagination into a story."

I doubt if there exists a better exposition of Bierce's viewpoint. With these passages in mind, the inference is irresistible that Bierce deliberately sought to be the 'newer Monk Lewis' and to write the perfect short story. In the effort to carry out

Watkins' advice to the letter, he became involved in this anomalous situation: his inspiration was romantic, but his method was almost modern in its realism at times. He could not exercise his "gift," as Watkins said, "dissociated from the thinking faculties." He was a romantic who wrote like a realist; technically his work belonged to the terrorist tradition and yet personally he was an individual utterly different than Monk Lewis. The conclusion would seem to be that Bierce accepted a theory of æsthetics which did not accord with his own personality and his own vision. But so great was his energy and his divination, that a fine light shines through the shadows of his work and illuminates even the worst of his tales of horror.

His entire life was romantic and he lived as though he were quite conscious of the fact. One of the shrewdest comments ever made about his career was made by John H. McGinnis in the Dallas *News*: "The incidents of his life read like a burlesque on the career of Lord Byron, and yet there is a hard, sardonic element that makes clearer and more poignant his drab romances and his essential tragedy." This statement strikes at the facts most vigorously.

CHAPTER XIV

"DAVID AND GOLIATH"

DURING the period between the completion of the trans-continental railroad until 1896, the Southern Pacific Railroad had gradually acquired a stranglehold on the State of California. There had been no word of protest during the first few years after the completion of the road, as the West was so delighted to have a railroad that it was willing to overlook many disadvantages. During the eighties, however, several far-sighted individuals began to call attention to the consequences of Southern Pacific dominance. A few mass meetings were held and a little indignation was kindled, but it was ineffective. Towards the close of the decade, the feeling became more intense as the railroad squeezed harder. It was an octopus bent on the plunder of the West. Every attempt to regulate its activities or temporize its monopoly proved futile. Farmers began to haul their produce by mule teams rather than consent to the Southern Pacific's iniquitous fares. It was thought that steam navigation might prove a remedy, but this was an idle day dream, as the railroad promptly subsidized the steamship lines.

The extent of the Southern Pacific's control of the political machinery in the State of California is almost unbelievable. It dominated the courts, the municapal governments, the county governments, including such petty offices as sheriff and coroner, and practically every newspaper in the state was receiving money from its coffers. When Fremont Older launched his fight against the railroad in 1896, he was amazed to find that the newspaper which he edited, *The Bulletin,* had been receiving a slight *douceur* of $125 a month for years. There was no definite agreement as to just what the consideration was for this sum, but there it was, and Mr. Older's investigation proved that there were few newspapers in the state that were not on the payroll of the railroad. Judges of the State Supreme Court traveled on annual passes; Assemblymen openly boasted of being kept by the railroad. The thought of a prosecution for the acceptance of a bribe was chimerical. William F. Herrin, attorney for the Southern Pacific in San Francisco, was the "boss" of the state. Applicants for positions, petitioners for governmental relief, and citizens in search of "justice," did not go to Sacramento, for they knew that the real governor was elsewhere, and so they waited in Mr. Herrin's reception room. The situation seemed hopeless until the question of the Funding Bill was presented to Congress. Through the lax political economy of Abraham Lincoln, the railroads had been able to borrow an enormous sum of money from the government, upon which they had never paid a cent of principal or interest. It was now proposed, with brazen insolence, that Congress extend the time of payment virtually a hundred years. In the possibility of defeating this bill, California saw a chance to force the Southern Pacific out of business, and to establish a government railroad from Omaha to San Francisco.

Mr. Hearst, clever demagogue then as now, rushed to the attack, and launched a great campaign against the railroad. His agents circulated a petition and obtained 200,000 signatures against the Funding Bill. Mass meetings were held and thousands were turned away. The fight was on. On January 18, 1896, Hearst sent Bierce a wire, which he published in *The Examiner,* "Railroad combination so strong in Washington that seems almost impossible to break them, yet it is certainly the duty of all having interests of coast at heart to make most strenuous efforts. Will you please go to Washington for *Examiner.* I will send Davenport from here and the *Journal* will use whatever power it has to assist." To this wire Bierce responded: "I shall be glad to do whatever I can toward defeating Mr. Huntington's Funding Bill and shall start for Washington on Monday evening next." The incident is typical of the relation between Hearst and Bierce. Here again, in a strange commingling of motives and purposes, the two were allied. Bierce once wrote: "If ever two men were born to be enemies he (Hearst) and I are they." And yet on many questions Mr. Hearst's self-interested journalism ran parallel with Bierce's prejudices, as was so notably the case with the fight that ensued in Washington over the Funding Bill. Bierce left California at once, taking his son Leigh with him. He was faced east again, the first time in sixteen years. He went prepared for a great fight, backed with every facility that Mr. Hearst could command, and with instructions to lead the attack. There is little question but that he was the generalissimo of the California lobby at Washington during 1896, and how effective that lobby was will soon be apparent. Incidentally he went east armed with a letter from his physician, Dr. Cleveland, whose cousin was President of the United States.

When Bierce went to Washington in 1896, he was at the height of his career. The well-known pencil sketch of Bierce by Miss F. Soule Campbell was drawn from a photograph taken by Prince that year in Washington. It has done as much for Bierce's fame, perhaps, as any merit in his work. The picture used in the "Letters of Ambrose Bierce," published by the Book Club of California is an interesting study, showing, as it does, Bierce with a newspaper clenched in his hands as a bludgeon. But Miss Campbell's study rarefies the rather coarse features of Bierce and softens the expression. In her picture his face is brilliant, fine, poetic. Her drawing should have written under it the verses which he originally wrote for his daughter, but a copy of which he gave to Miss Campbell:

> How blind is he who, powerless to discern
> The glories that about his pathway burn,
> Walks unaware the avenues of Dream
> Nor sees the domes of paradise agleam!
> O Golden Age, to him more nobly planned
> Thy light lies ever upon sea and land;
> From sordid scenes he lifts his eyes at will
> And sees a Grecian god on every hill.

The portrait by Partington is more to life, but, as is so often the case, the more imaginative study divined a quality not apparent to the eye. When this drawing is compared with the best known portrait studies of Henry James,—(with his sleek complacent features),—and of Edgar Saltus,—(trying to look like

an American Oscar Wilde),—something of the difference in
men becomes apparent. The two most interesting faces of the
period were those of Mark Twain and Ambrose Bierce, for in
each case it is a face illuminated with the energy of unique
personality. The matter is not altogether trivial: no one who ever
saw Bierce could think him unimportant.

In Washington the fight over the Funding Bill was attract-
ing national attention. The excitement was at its height during
January, February and March of 1896. Immediately upon his
arrival at the battle front, Bierce began to send long dispatches
to *The Examiner,* the first of which appeared on February 2nd,
1896, under the blazing headline: "Huntington Lying in His
Last Ditch." Bierce never showed more keenness than in his
change of technique during this important campaign. In San
Francisco he had early perceived that he must be direct and
personal to be effective, for the scene would admit of no other
technique. As Percival Pollard once remarked with great dis-
cernment: "The impersonal manner is impossible in our present
sophistication," referring to the America of his time. But in
Washington, Bierce realized that he was writing for the country
at large, and that he was assured an audience. He must be clear,
forceful and persuasive about his presention of the case against
Huntington, and so he quickly abandoned the unmodulated satire
of his early journalism. He did not, of course, become gentle.
He started his first article as follows: "Mr. Huntington is not
altogether bad. Though severe, he is merciful. He tempers invective with falsehood. He says ugly things of the enemy, but he
has the tenderness to be careful that they are mostly lies."

If California was ably represented at Washington, it can
scarcely be said that Mr. Huntington's defense was neglected.
He had established a veritable barrage of publicity and was
fighting, with his customary determination, to befog the issues.
One trick of his hirelings was to quote the names of prominent
San Franciscans who were supposed to favor the bill, thus
creating the impression that California endorsed the measure.
Bierce printed all these names at the head of his dispatches and
such pressure was brought to bear upon them in San Francisco
that they quickly abandoned Mr. Huntington. The railroad
was then virtually Mr. Huntington, as his old associates had all
died previous to this time. Every day that the fight continued

it became more and more apparent that the measure would be defeated. Bierce would intersperse his articles with such a remark as this: "Mr. Huntington appeared before the committee and took his hands out of all pockets long enough to be sworn." The old Hearst squadron was functioning to perfection, and a more effective journalistic machine never existed in this country. Swinnerton and Davenport in their cartoons reached a high level of caricature and left not a vestige of pride or respect to Mr. Huntington. In San Francisco "Andy" Lawrence was shrewdly keeping the people in a frenzy of indignation and excitement, and wiring Bierce to "send some of your gems—something Biercy." Bierce's dispatches were featured in the Hearst newspapers and the interview which he gave some Eastern reporters at the Hotel Page was a masterpiece of effective propaganda. It was the beginning of Bierce's vogue among Eastern newspapermen. They did not forget this very impressive and handsome Ambrose Bierce. A young reporter who was covering Washington at the time for some Pacific Coast newspapers told about visiting Bierce one day during a lull in the fight. He closed his interview in this manner: "Be good till I see you again," he said with one of the smiles which let one see behind the ulterior austerity of his bearing and into the real nature of the man himself, which I am sure is the kindest possible. "Be good, if you don't care for happiness, and God will bless you, and finally kill you." *

Bierce received the active coöperation throughout the fight of Senator Morgan of Alabama, who was being groomed for the presidency at the time. One day, coming out of a committee session, Bierce and some other men met Collis P. Huntington on the steps of the Capitol. Previously Bierce had declined Huntington's hand in a committee session. But on this occasion Huntington approached and began to inquire as to how much Bierce wanted to withdraw from the fight. Meeting with a stony rejection of every bid, Huntington finally shouted: "Well, name your price; every man has his price." It was then that Bierce made the famous statement that his price was the amount that Huntington owed the government, and that he might pay it to the Secretary of the Treasury. The story was sent around the world under the flamboyant caption: "The Pen

* *Saturday Press*, March 2, 1896.

is Mightier than the Sword" or, in some instances, "The Man Without a Price." Later Huntington was asked why he tried to shake hands with Bierce in the committee room and replied, with typical callousness, "Oh, I just wanted to see how big he was," and then added, "I know now." *

The experience in the East was not altogether distasteful to Bierce. He was the center of a great deal of attention and he had enjoyed the experience of matching his satire against the wiles of Collis P. Huntington. Bierce had been sent east, as shown by the wire of Mr. Hearst, but his second trip to Washington was at his own request, and was no doubt the result of the pleasant time he had in 1896. One day he was standing in the Senate gallery and chanced to hear Mr. Sherman shout, during the course of an address: "If that is not war, then where in the name of hell does war exist?" A woman standing at Bierce's side asked him if he had heard anything unusual. He replied: "I really do not know whether or not the expression that he used is common in your tongue. I am from Kansas." †
Another incident is rather amusing. One day he chanced to be in a hotel lobby conversing with two very well-known New York society women who were visiting in Washington. An old, shabbily dressed man walked up and spoke to one of the ladies, and she acknowledged his greeting in a courteous manner. After the man had turned away, the other lady said: "Mrs. A——, how could you speak to such a creature!" Mrs. A—— started to explain that the old man had been a former servant, but Bierce interrupted her to say: "It is unnecessary for Mrs. A—— to offer an explanation. *She* can afford to be seen speaking to any one." The "mauve decade" was never more amazing than during these months. At the home of a Western family which had recently acquired a vast fortune, Mr. Bierce was admonished by the hostess to notice her beautiful "spinal" staircase. It was an age of fuss and showiness and Bierce was amused. It certainly offered a bigger scene than San Francisco. He would come back to Washington again.

During the summer, Bierce's old associate E. H. ("Ned") Hamilton was covering the Democratic Convention at Chicago and the railroad issue was an important question during the first

* *The Examiner,* February 22, 1896.
† *Examiner,* August 15, 1897.

days of the convention. But suddenly it was forgotten in the
shouting about "silver." Mr. Bierce did not, however, show the
same enthusiasm for the young, handsome and rhetorical William Jennings Bryan that the other Hearst journalists did
under the instructions of their chief. Mr. Hearst's papers ac-
claimed Bryan as the great savior; the man of the hour; and
destiny's choice. But Bierce with ears that were deaf to the
rumble and roar of the press and the people, paused in his
castigation of Huntington long enough to remark, with characteristic sweetness, "Mr. Bryan's creation was the unstudied
act of his own larnyx; it said 'Let there be Bryan' and there
was Bryan.'" Bierce marched with Mr. Hearst when it was
against some one he disliked, but now he refused to join a band
wagon that he knew was headed by the most nonsensical
buffoon and demagogue of the century. Moreover, it was from
this date that he began to have frequent quarrels with the
Hearst editors. From 1896 on, Mr. Hearst was looking with
lustful eyes on the possession of the White House, and Bierce
knew it and despised him for the ambition. Bierce had some
hopes of checking the tide of empty bombast that he saw captivating the country, but by 1913 he had long since despaired
of the task. But he did recognize a demagogue when he saw one
and later wrote these very sharp lines about Mr. Hearst:

> "With many amiable and alluring qualities, among which
> is, or used to be, a personal modesty amounting to bashfulness,
> the man has not a friend in the world. Nor does he merit one,
> for, either congenitally or by induced perversity, he is inacces-
> sible to the conception of an unselfish attachment or a disinter-
> ested motive. Silent and smiling, he moves among men, the
> loneliest man. Nobody but God loves him and he knows it; and
> God's love he values only in so far as he fancies that it may
> promote his amusing ambition to darken the door of the White
> House. As to that, I think that he would be about the kind of
> President that the country—daft with democracy and sick with
> sin—is beginning to deserve." *

The excerpt is quoted from a manuscript of about fourteen
pages which Bierce wrote to fill out the last volume of his
"Collected Works." He informed his immediate friends that it

* "Collected Works," Vol. XII, page 315.

formed merely an introduction to a longer work which he intended to write about Mr. Hearst, but which he would never
publish during the life of Mrs. Phoebe Hearst, for whom he
entertained a very high regard. The rest of the manuscript was
never found, and it is extremely doubtful if it was ever written,
although there was one trunk which was lost at Laredo in 1913
that might have contained the copy. What a pity that it was
never written! Bierce would have been a writer fitted by temperament and experience to analyze properly Mr. Hearst and to
point out the significance of the appearance of such a demagogue
in the democracy of which Thomas Jefferson had dreamed so
nobly.

The strain of the long fight in Washington began to tell
on Bierce by the summer of 1896. In the early part of June, he
was stricken quite seriously ill and had to go to Gettysburg,
Pennsylvania. He suffered acutely from his asthma and was
confined in the old Eagle Hotel for some time. Wires poured in
from all imaginable sources, messages of condolence, sympathy,
congratulation, and affection. Sam Chamberlain, Mr. Hearst,
Bierce's children, Amy Cecil, were all worried and alarmed by
the reports they received of his condition. The old blight was
upon him again. Never for a cognizable interval had the shadow
of its dreaded hand been lifted from his life. It came at nights
while he slept; and in the sunny moments of the day, it was a
spectre that stalked by his side. During these long nocturnal
trysts with death when he wheezed and coughed and struggled
for breath, bent over the backs of chairs in squalid hotels, alone
and unattended, all the memories of horror and suffering which
he otherwise kept, as Mr. Mumford intimates, under a "mechanism of concealment," were unleased. Death, and death's music,
were with him always. By experience he had come to view death
quizzically and with a sneer; contemplation of its significance
had made even death negligible. But it served, this ever-present
consciousness of death, to beat life into place, to reduce it to
such a lowly level that it was wholly contemptible and unworthy.
Out in that easy, slothful, lackadaisical world morons and
zanies applauded clowns who shouted and roared for their entertainment and the process was known as the selection of a
president. Other lovely mannered "genderless gents" wrote
novels of "local color" or spent their time in idle, ridiculous,

"muck-raking" and were pronounced artists. "Nothing mattered," he said and who, pray tell, would argue with him?

When he was able to be about, he returned to New York, and his copy was dispatched from that city during August and September of 1896. He was not writing very much for *The Examiner* during these months and occasionally his copy would not appear for weeks at a time. In January of 1897 the Funding Bill was defeated and Bierce left for California. The long fight was at an end, and he was glad to be traveling west again. Another circuit of the continent: to England and back; to Dakota and return; to New York and then to San Francisco again; tracks that passed and repassed in an endless repetition of trivial experiences. But always, it seemed, he returned to the coast.

The work that Bierce did towards defeating the Funding Bill, apart from the sensational drama of the Huntington interview, was of the first importance. Furthermore, it was generally recognized and conceded at the time that his influence had determined the battle. Swinnerton pictured him in several cartoons chastising Mr. Huntington with great vigor and skill. The supplement of *The Examiner* for February 22, 1896, during the thick of the fight, was entirely devoted to an account of Bierce's activities. T. T. Williams wired him, "My congratulations on defeat of Funding Bill due to the able and earnest and honest manner in which you fought against it. If you had done no other good than this, your creation as a beneficent influence would be more than justified." * Long before his colleagues, David Graham Phillips and Alfred Henry Lewis, started their muck-raking journalism, Mr. Bierce had fought and won a most decisive victory over one of the worst monopolies that ever disgraced this country. But he had drawn no hasty inferences, and, once the fight was over, it was for him a closed chapter. Would that there had been other journalists as sensible! When Bierce actually arrived in San Francisco, he was given quite a reception and the newspapers were full of cartoons showing "Ambrose Bierce" returning to a city strewn with flowers, etc., to do him honor.

That this account of Bierce's activities in connection with

* May 28, 1896, wire from T. T. Williams to Ambrose Bierce, Page Hotel, Washington, D. C.

the defeat of the Funding Bill is not colored by personal admiration is borne out by the fact that in 1910, when Charles Edward Russell began to publish his well-known series of articles on the "Railroads," and after nearly two decades had passed and public opinion had become somewhat clarified, Mr. Russell made this comment in reference to Bierce's journalism:

> "These articles were extraordinary examples of invective and bitter sarcasm. They were addressed to the dishonest nature of the bill and to the real reasons why the machine had slated it for passage. When Mr. Bierce began his campaign, few persons imagined that the bill could be stopped. After a time the skill and steady persistence of the attack began to draw wide attention. With six months of incessant firing, Mr. Bierce had the railroad forces frightened and wavering; and before the end of the year, he had them whipped. The bill was withdrawn and killed, and in 1898 Congress adopted an amendment to the general deficiency bill, providing for the collection of the Pacific Railroad subsidy debt, principal and interest." *

And, not only was the defeat of the railroad a great achievement in itself, but the consequences of the victory can scarcely be overestimated. It marked the doom of Southern Pacific dominance in California, for in the mayoralty campaign of 1896, Fremont Older managed to get his candidate, James D. Phelan, a liberal, elected mayor of San Francisco. The tide had turned and it did not cease rolling on to victory until Hiram Johnson had been elected Governor. Then, after he had framed the famous act creating the Railway Commission and amending the State Constitution so as to give the newly created commission sweeping powers of regulation and control, the Southern Pacific episode was closed once and for all.

On the way to San Francisco, Bierce stopped at Los Angeles, registering at the Van Nuys Hotel on March 30, 1897. He was the guest of General O. H. LaGrange for several weeks at Soldiers' Home, where the General was Commandant. There were several long visits with the daughter and with other friends, including Charles Fletcher Lummis, editor of "Out West," but there was no word for Mollie Day Bierce, who, in 1896, had left St. Helena to come to Los Angeles to live with

* *Hampton's Magazine*, September, 1910.

her mother. Mrs. Bierce stayed in the North until Bierce had left for Washington, and then, thinking that he was going to live permanently in the East, had moved to Los Angeles. General LaGrange, on this occasion, made the fatal mistake of trying to intercede with Mr. Bierce, on behalf of Mrs. Bierce, to effect a reconciliation. Not knowing the facts, the General had assumed that it was actually a case of "desertion," and had spoken rather sharply to Bierce about the duties of a husband. There was a stormy scene at the Commandant's home and Bierce left in anger for the North. He wrote the General a scorching letter, in which he branded his old friend with disloyalty, not in befriending Mrs. Bierce, but in accusing Bierce without waiting for or requesting an explanation. Under the circumstances, the General was the last person in the world who should have accused Bierce of mistreating a woman, and the old fellow must have smarted under the lashing lines of that parting curse for many days. But, in an explanation to his daughter, Bierce said: "My child, there is only one woman in my life that I have loved and that woman happens to be your mother."

CHAPTER XV

"THE SHADOW MAKER"

ALTHOUGH Bierce was received with exceptional enthusiasm on the part of his associates and the friends of *The Examiner*, still there were intimations of displeasure from the other journals. A writer on *The Call* observed that "the rascal of the sorrel hair" had returned to San Francisco. Doubtless the old offenders prepared for a renewal of the rough treatment to which they had by that time become adjusted. They were not to be disappointed, for Bierce was soon applying his whip with unmitigated zest, writing that "compared with Senator White, Senator Perkins is a clouted suckling. Senator Perkins is a leader only when followed by a line of cows curious to ascertain what else he is, and if he is good to eat." But it is apparent that Bierce was beginning to suffer from mental fatigue. Satire is endless work and ultimately the satirist wearies of his task, as it gradually becomes apparent to him that his sharp comments are lost in a whirlwind of nonsense. The edge of Bierce's wit was blunted with hard usage, and he could stoop to such clumsy abuse as this:

> "Here lies Greer Harrison, a well cracked louse—
> So small a tenant of so big a house."

But it was about this time that the Spanish-American fiasco gave him the material for the last burst of his fine satirical powers.

Prior to his sojourn in Washington he had noticed that "War—Horrid War!—between the United States and Spain has already broken out like a red rash in the newspapers, whose managing commodores are shivering their timbers and blasting their toplights with a truly pelagic volubility and no little *vraisemblance."* * But when Mr. Hearst, with all his gaudy propaganda about Evangelina Cisneros, had forced McKinley's hand and we were at war with Spain, not even the colored flags and patriotic headlines of *The Examiner* deceived Bierce for one moment. In the thick of the excitement he wrote such trenchant statements as these: "We are at war with Spain to-day merely in obedience to a suasion that has been gathering force from the beginning of our national existence. The passion for territory once roused rages like a lion; successive conquests only strengthen it. That is the fever that is now burning in the American blood." (*The Examiner,* July 31, 1898.) "We are not being pushed into the forefront of this bloody struggle for place and power and more of earth by any necessity more imperious than our desire." (*The Examiner,* July 24, 1898.) And what better comment could have been made at the moment than this: "We can conquer these people without half trying, for we belong to the race of gluttons and drunkards to whom dominion is given over the abstemious. We can thrash them consummately and every day of the week, but we cannot understand them; and is it not a great golden truth, shining like a star, that what one does not understand one knows to be bad?" (August 7, 1898, *The Examiner.*)

He was not deceived by the national psychology that had made war with Spain inevitable. Nor was he particularly deceived by all the talk anent the "perfidious Aguinaldo" and the "mighty power of Spain." Mr. Byan and Mr. Roosevelt did not gain his admiration by their obvious play for the grandstand in "raising volunteer" regiments. He suggested that the regiment which Mr. Bryan threatened to organize should be called the "Nebraska Immunes," and that life insurance companies extend to it special policies at low rates. He announced that he did not share "this paper's confidence in the formidable character of the dynamite cruiser *Vesuvius,*" and he did not hesitate to write very pointed criticisms of Sampson's tactics. "Instead of corking Cervera in, Sampson corked himself out. It did not matter: he was held out, anyhow, by the iron hand of his timidity." The miserable triviality of that tawdry drama was an open book for him: the horrible blunders, the *opéra bouffe* charges, the

* *The Examiner,* March 17, 1895.

sophomoric tactics, the race for honors, the petty bickering and
quarrels, the hysteria of the people and the sentiments of the
press, were all recorded with amused contempt in his column.
The spectacle rather fatigued him, but he did correspond with
some of the officers and later read with care the manuscript of
his friend H. H. Sargeant on "The History of the Santiago
Campaign," and in Washington he was a factor in securing
relief for Wolfson, the Confederate rebel who had fought so
bravely in the war with Spain.

During these first months after his return from Washington, he lived at the old El Monte Hotel in Los Gatos. Los
Gatos, situated at the foot of the Santa Cruz Mountains, overlooking the entire Santa Clara Valley, possessed a warm, dry
climate that seemed to give him relief for his asthma. When
the spells were too severe, he could take the train at Los Gatos
and ride a few miles to Wright's station, almost at the crest of
the mountains, where he stayed at the old Jeffreys Hotel or
camp. To Los Gatos and Wrights came the endless hordes of his
"pupils," admirers, and the few faithful but devoted friends.
He was never to have such a list of pupils as he had at this
time. Carroll Carrington wrote him letters of adoration and
called him "Dear Mentor" and reviewed his books with dutiful
reverence in *The Examiner*. Then, too, Mr. Markham's secretary, Jean Hazen, sent some sketches to Bierce which he managed to have published. These pupils were sending him constant
verses and poems, some of which were addressed to the Master,
as this valentine:

"O Sly Reformer in a cynic's guise!
Fools led by love see deeper than the wise;
I see in Prattle sermons for the town;
That spare the sin, but gaily cut the sinner down.

Thy word has been my lamp for several years:
Now take my little song of praise—and fears,
For well I know thy joy is in the feeble line,
And thou wilt even flay poor me, thy valentine."

He would often visit Mr. and Mrs. Hirshberg at Ione,
where Mr. Hirshberg was in charge of the school for incorrigi-
ble boys. He suggested to Mr. Hirshberg once that these boys

should all be sent away to war and shot: that they could never be cured of the disorders that made them criminals. It was to the Hirshbergs, too, that he would come on his bicycle for periodic visits from Los Gatos. Upon his arrival, he would line the young ladies of the family up in stair-step fashion and kiss them all from the tallest to the smallest. It was once suggested to Mr. Bierce that he was inconsistent in liking female, but disliking male, Semitics. To this he responded, and the observation is borne out by his practice, that he "hated Hebrews but adored She-brews." So greatly was he admired by the female side of the Hirshberg family that some irate male had written under his picture the single word: "God." Mrs. Hirshberg, "the best of my best friends," as he once said, would send him food when he was ill in Oakland and could not be about. As soon as he recovered, he would call at their home. It was like, as Mrs. Hirshberg says, "The sun coming out from behind a cloud: he was eager, joyous, splendid." After one particularly severe attack of asthma, he said to her, "Israel has touched me with his wing again." Naturally he was lionized by the women.

Mrs. Hirshberg and Dr. C. W. Doyle had cared for a little deaf girl, Lily Walsh, who worked around in restaurants and hotels, but who seemed to show considerable promise as a poetess. They showed her work to Bierce, and he immediately became interested in the child and sent her to a school for the deaf in Berkeley. She seems to have been a preternaturally wise and solemn child. She would write all manner of verse, stilted romances of knights and ladies, and essays for Bierce's approval. He kept a sheath of her manuscripts; and the kindness that he showed her was but typical of his great tenderness for all weak and pathetic creatures. To those who think, as does Mrs. Charlotte Gilman, that Bierce was an inhuman scourge, perhaps the realization of the kind and patient care that he devoted to Lily Walsh might force the correction of a hastily formed opinion. The brother of Lily Walsh was also a devoted admirer of Bierce, and he wrote from New York: "He, the ideal Ambrose Bierce, Saint Ambrose of Los Gatos, is the measure of my conduct." * One of Lily Walsh's compositions was the following poem addressed to "A. B."

* Letter of Myles Walsh to Ambrose Bierce.

"O! as some pine towers free and far
Above its forest fellows, matchless in height,
Grace, strength and majesty; so in the might
Of his grand intellect he towers. Dwarfed are
All who beside him stand. They enviously mar
The glory of his shining, quench his light
With lie-tipped tongues, pens dipped in ink of spite
(So, have we seen clouds strive to dim a star
And all as vainly.) While pens scratch, tongues wag
He stands serenely on Truth's rugged rock
To which he's rooted firmly as the pine
Is rooted to Earth's bosom. Winds may drag
That forest monarch from his throne. Not shock
Of Quaking Earth can move this friend of mine."

It was just such blind, unquestioning adoration as this that
Bierce inspired in all his young admirers. There were no bounds
to their enthusiasm. While Lily Walsh was attending the school
at Berkeley, she died and her last request was that she might
be buried at Los Gatos where she could be near Bierce, but her
relatives were Catholics and hence she was buried in St. Mary's
Cemetery at Oakland. Bierce was quite ill at the time or else,
as he afterwards remarked, he would have seen that her wish
was regarded. His capacity for suffering is shown by his grief
over the death of this girl: he mourned over her, as Mrs.
Hirshberg says, "like a father." "To parents only," he
wrote, "death brings an inconsolable sorrow. When the young
die and the old live, nature's machinery is working with friction
that we name grief."

On the outskirts of Los Gatos was one of the largest and
most valuable ranches in California. It was owned then by the
Hume family. This enormous prune orchard stretched along
the foothills for miles. Frank Hume, one of the owners, had
started to build a magnificent country place which he called
"Dotswood," but he had constructed only one splendid room
around which he expected to build his mansion. The ranch itself
was named after his very charming wife, Una Hume, and was
known as "Glen Una." At the time that Bierce first went to
live at Los Gatos, Mrs. Hume was a widow, and she entertained
most elegantly for her friends. She and Bierce became great
friends. In fact, Bierce's affection for Una Hume was one of
the reasons that kept him at Los Gatos so long. When their

friendship was broken, he determined to go east. Mrs. Hume was a most attractive woman, talented, gracious, and charming and her home was always full of San Francisco people over the week end.

One day Bierce walked out from Los Gatos to call on Mrs. Hume, who was just recuperating from an illness. He entered the gates of Dotswood, nestling as it does in a little grove backed against the hillside, and was about to ring the doorbell when he was accosted by a very determined and spirited Irish nurse. She informed him that Mrs. Hume could see no one and a battle royale ensued, but Theresa McCarthy was not to be overawed, even by Ambrose Bierce, and so Bierce had to turn around and go back to Los Gatos. He later became quite friendly with the nurse, and they exchanged many hot sallies of wit during the time she was attending Mrs. Hume.

Miss McCarthy liked to set baits for Bierce's rage during his frequent calls at Dotswood. She asked him one day why he always said: "God bless you!" when he did not believe in God. He answered this by saying: "If I actually believed in him, I wouldn't dare mention his name." The other gentlemen who called at Dotswood, particularly certain San Franciscans, were quite jealous of Bierce's position. In an effort to discredit him, they told Mrs. Hume that he had once been expelled from the Bohemian Club for boasting of his conquests with women. Miss McCarthy, anticipating a great burst of indignation, related this story to him. He smiled and sat musing in the twilight for awhile—the warm sweet twilight that came to them through the stained glass windows designed by Bruce Porter—toying with the cocktail that had been served him from the miniature bar in the rear of the room. Then he said, very softly: "Boasting of my conquests with women at the Bohemian Club? Why, my dear, I couldn't have gotten the floor if I had tried!"

There were several women in Bierce's life who occupied positions analogous to that of Mrs. Hume, that is, the beloved friend and confidante, some one to be slightly romantic about, if not actually anchored to by the skeins of an infatuation. These women knew him better than any other people in his life; it was to them, rather than to his immediate family or to his journalistic associates, that he talked most freely about his career, his dreams and his ambitions. Men saw a different

Bierce: an elaborate cynic, a hardened skeptic, and a calloused satirist. But there were sonnets for the ladies, occasionally, and many a note full of soft pauses and waltz rhythms. With men he was often enough a good fellow, a congenial drinking companion, and capable of rabelaisian bursts of humor. The kindly, white-whiskered old veterans of the domino tables at the Family Club in San Francisco still tell amusing stories about the unprinted portions of his "Devil's Dictionary," ending always with his definition of "Heaven": "Copulation without culmination."

Women were really offensive in the manner that they threw themselves at Bierce. His "Prattle" was literally a dragnet that drew innumerable sentimental notes and requests for clandestine appointments. He did not hesitate in later years to write rather sharp letters to these forward ladies; one such suggestion for an appointment brought this sentence from a scorching reply: "Madam: Commonly when one of your sex writes pleasantly to a stranger, it is because she wants something." But while he was in California, it was not at all unusual for him to receive lyrics on pink stationery from Dimond, California, or stately and quivering sonnets from admiring poetesses at Lake Tahoe, opening with such sentiments as this: "You recall? We walked in the woods that matchless day—" But the ladies that he did admire consumed a great deal of his time: several of his friends lament to this day the hours that he loitered and dallied when he might have been at his work.

At Wrights, Bierce stayed at the Jeffreys Hotel, where he occupied a little cabin set off by itself. One day as he was rounding the corner of the hotel at top speed, he collided with a young girl. He assumed a very superior manner and sniffed something to the effect that he "supposed" she had planned the collision in lieu of an introduction. It was the defensive attitude of a fugitive from feminine wiles. But, to his amazement, he was assured, with extraordinary force and emphasis, that nothing of the sort was in the young lady's thoughts. He apologized and they both concluded that it was a fortunate meeting anyway and became the best of friends. The young lady's name was Leila Cotton. She lived with her family in a delightful old frame house with a circular porch, that was called "Bohemia." He was promptly adopted by the Cotton family, and used to take his meals at "Bohemia."

These last years in California were rather indolent and carefree days for Bierce. His duties were negligible and there were several long intervals during which he did no work for *The Examiner,* the result of spirited and periodic resignations. Nor was he writing any stories at this time. There were long tramps in the woods, usually at night when his asthma kept him out of doors, and the usual week-end foray to San Francisco, or a trip down to Los Gatos to chat with Una Hume. At nights the dark forests of the Santa Cruz Mountains were blue with their cool radiance, and the valleys were full of deep soft pools of darkness. There were redwoods and pines, and an infinite variety of ferns and forest flowers, and in the distance the Santa Clara Valley was full of an unnameable magic when, at dusk, the shadows involved it and the lights of San José gleamed like phosphorescent fish in a sea of darkness. But, strangely enough, none of this beauty, none of the splendid stillness of the forests, ever got into his work save by a mischance. It was a strange man who could live at Wrights and at Angwins and be impervious to the natural splendor about him. But he was preoccupied with thoughts of the past, with grisly images of death, with a feeling of strangeness and unreality about the entire scene.

The constant stream of pupils and disciples did not cease when he was at Wrights, but came up the grade from Los Gatos and followed him to his lair with indefatigible zeal. Herman Scheffauer was often at the camp; Edwin Markham came often, too, until that fatal afternoon when he read "The Man with the Hoe" and was furiously denounced as a traitor to his art and a victim of reform. So severely did Bierce denounce the poem in print that a debate was provoked, the last echoes of which did not cease to appear in *The Examiner* for months. But when Cora Case accused Markham of stealing the poem from her, Bierce was one of the first to rush to the defense of his old friend. The battle which raged over "The Man With the Hoe" was only a battle of ideas and Bierce would not have been so severe in his criticism had he not entertained a very high regard for Mr. Markham's non-socialistic verse. When Scheffauer could not be at "Valhalla" at the feet of his "Tor," as he referred to Bierce and his cabin, he would write interminable letters, thirty and forty pages long, written in an indecipherable script and full of the wildest and most chaotic and emotional bombast. When Scheffauer discovered Nietzsche the effect was almost fatal, for he promptly adopted the rhapsodical manner of Zarathustra and no one could understand his ravings. No wonder Bierce wearied of the fellow.

At the other side of the range was Santa Cruz and Bierce could proceed there in search of amusement when he knew that the hostess of Dotswood was not at home. At Santa Cruz Mr. Bierce came to know Dr. C. W. Doyle. Doyle was a scholarly fellow, something of a bibliophile, and a considerable drinker. He wrote several volumes of Kipling-esque short stories, "The Taming of the Jungle" and "The Shadow of Quong Lung," one of which he dedicated to Bierce. While not, except in a very limited sense, a pupil, he was yet influenced by Bierce and would never have published the two volumes without his kindly encouragement and interest. The Doctor presented Bierce with a handsome volume of Sir Thomas Browne's "Religico Medici" which was, along with a diminutive edition of Pascal's "Pensées," the favorite item in Bierce's library. At Santa Cruz, also, Bierce met some friends of Dr. Doyle's, the MacKenzies, Agnes and Margaret. He thought that Agnes possessed a genuine talent as a painter, and, with Margaret to amuse them both, they would take long jaunts through the woods. Bierce would instruct the one in design at the same time that he corrected the other's pronunciation. Wherever he lived, at San Rafael, St. Helena, Wrights, or Santa Cruz, he was almost invariably the "mentor" of some group of artists.

One time while he was at Wrights, a woman came up from San Francisco to interview him on the subject of the proper method of rearing the young. He tried to avoid her, dodged her questions, and fled in panic to a friendly porch to read his newspaper in quiet. But she soon discovered his retreat and came rushing to propound more questions. Did Mr. Bierce know any of the ancients who might be read with instruction on the subject? It seemed that he did, for he answered: "Study Herod, Madam, study Herod." During an early visit of the Markhams, Bierce succeeded in inducing Mrs. Markham to drink mulled claret on his representation that all the alcohol was "burnt out." He was always willing to drop his book and go for a walk, or to visit with some pupil, as when George Sterling or Mabel

Wood (now Mabel Wood Martin) another pupil, would come up to see him. He was rather bored with his work on *The Examiner,* and spent most of his time in the woods; he seemed to have lost something of his former interest in "Prattle" and only on occasions would it show the brilliancy of former years. He sensed a change and he felt the need of new scenes.

Of all his pupils only Sterling and Scheffauer were destined to achieve any fame or distinction in the art. Some of the others might have gone far, indeed, but when he left the coast in 1899, they quickly neglected the duties and tasks to which he had set them and became teachers, nurses, or Christian Science practitioners. It has been intimated that Bierce helped young writers because he sensed his own limitations, and sought to acquire in another's attainments what he had failed to achieve. It is difficult, of course, to analyze a motive in another. But from an examination of his correspondence, it is apparent that he was quite disinterested in the assistance that he gave many of these young people. He surely did not seek them out: in every instance they came to him begging the advice and assistance which he never withheld from a "worthy case," be it Lily Walsh or Herman Scheffauer. Of course he was hurt and offended when, in later years, Scheffauer told tales about him and scoffed at the idea that Bierce had ever been of assistance to the Scheffauer who had visited Prof. Ernest Haeckel at Basle in 1904 and had his picture taken with the great scientist. By that time he had forgotten those myriad letters, the tons of scribbled adoration and praise that he had penned for his "Magister" at Wrights. It was so with many others. But that there was anything parasitic about Bierce's relations with these pupils is too preposterous to warrant refutation.

Mark Twain had gone East; Bret Harte had been an early fugitive; Stoddard was in Europe for years; and Bierce himself had attempted an escape which had failed. While the others were able to make an escape, Bierce stayed on in the West, rooted to the Bay District. It was thus that he became, as J. S. Cowley-Brown said, "a literary Rhadamanthus," making and breaking literary reputations on the coast, its foremost writer and its chief figure. His name became a tradition in the West. Young reporters cherished their sheath of notes from "Bierce," minor poets were grateful of a few kindly words in "Prattle" or a poem that was printed in its columns, or for a book sent them or a picture, or a pressed fern leaf, or an inscription in "Tales of Soldiers and Civilians." The value of such a tradition can scarcely be overestimated. Bierce sent Sterling on his way to fame; Sterling went to Carmel and himself became a tradition in time; and a decade later Robinson Jeffers published "Tamar and Other Poems." It is not so much a question as to whether or not Bierce's influence was always creative, as it is the fact that some one remained on the coast to keep alive the semblance of an interest in the arts. Personally, I think his pupils could not have had a better "mentor." He would tolerate no cheap and specious reasoning, and they must devote themselves unsparingly to their art. He did not rest with this, but proceeded to pound out of them the emotional optimism which infected the times. As Scheffauer later wrote: "The old Spartan over whom a hundred storms of destiny raged, and who had been obliged to arm himself for many hard battles, had become callous. He ducked me in an intellectual Styx which was for me a veritable chalybeate bath. It bewitched me against many threatening dangers of sentimentality and absurdity which frequently steal upon the young American writer."

It was while Bierce was at Wrights that he came to know Josephine Clifford McCrackin. She was the "Josephine Clifford" of the early issues of *The Overland Monthly* and *The Californian*. This old lady wrote Bierce the saddest of letters addressed to "Dear Grossmeister," for her life had been one long trail of sorrow and misery along which she had moved with splendid indifference and unconcern. She tried to remonstrate with Bierce, when, in 1913, he wrote her that "fear of death is the invention of a humorist," and attempted to point out to him the irrationality of the romantic quest for adventure. But he would not heed her advice; his curiosity demanded satisfaction. Romanticism is, of course, as Mr. Eliot has observed, "a short cut to the strangeness without the reality, and it leads its disciples only back upon themselves." Much of the "Werther-like pessimism" that Scheffauer had noted in Bierce was the result of this feeling of emptiness provoked by a habit of questing restlessly about for a sensation that had once been experienced fortuitously. This impatience began to characterize

Bierce very definitely from 1899 until his disappearance into Mexico.

After the destruction of her home, Monte Paraiso Cottage, in the Santa Cruz Mountains, Mrs. McCrackin was left in straitened circumstances, and it was to relieve this situation that Bierce tried to get several publishers to bring out a volume of her stories. Finally it was arranged, but under the management of George Wharton James, the J. Middleton Murray of Pasadena, who brought out a collection of her stories in 1913, for which Bierce wrote an introduction. His introduction is a little masterpiece of evasion, and it rather admits that the stories were unexceptional, although the lady who wrote them was a noble character. Bierce used to stride out of his little cabin, bang the door, and announce to his friends that he was "going over to see Jo," as he called Mrs. McCrackin. God knows what these rare spirits discoursed about, high in the blue-black shadows of the Santa Cruz Mountains!

A change was taking place in Bierce's writing at this time, a change which must have reflected some corresponding change in the man himself. During these years, 1889-1899, he was at the apex of his career as a journalist in California. Popularly he was known as a Hearst journalist who wielded a mighty sword of abuse when in "good form." But the old fiery days of the "Prattler" were over, for it is apparent from his journalism of this period that he had lost something of his old zest for baiting morons. Without interruption, save for the months in Washington, over a period of thirty years, he had lived and worked in the Bay District. Of its feuds, murders, lusts, crimes, wrongs, not to mention minor frivolities, amusements, social and artistic performances, he had woven a gay pattern which was reflected in the crisp elegance of his column "Prattle." But he began to sense something wrong with his attitude. The satirist was too lowly a figure; he had seen vistas of grandeur during those months in Washington. He aspired to the chair of philosophy. A philosopher was to supplant a wit. The old life in San Francisco was over. The demagogic, prosy attitude of Hearst was beginning to have its effect even on Bierce. Those few months in Washington had whetted his appetite for a larger field, and he told Mr. A. M. Lawrence that a permanent change to Washington would be agreeable.

It is apparent from Bierce's letters to S. O. Howes of this period that he was dissatisfied with his position. We find him writing (date of May 14, 1899), "I am not writing much just now. I 'threw up my job' of Prattle because Mr. Hearst let his fools, fakers and freaks do what they would with it in the *N. Y. Journal*—the which I could nowise abide. They yellowed it every way they knew how, and mangled it at will." It was the recurrence of an old, old quarrel. As early as 1893 he was writing to Blanche Partington, "I peremptorily resigned from the *Examiner*, and permitted myself to be coaxed back by Hearst." How many times he resigned from the *Examiner* it is impossible to estimate; his letters indicate dozens of such quarrels. But about 1899, a serious quarrel was brewing. The Eastern Hearst papers were beginning to reproduce his copy, but would do so in any manner they saw fit. There are in existence two letters, one dated October 31, 1898, and the other November 20, 1898, both addressed to the editor of the *Journal* and remonstrating vociferously about this mooted problem. In fact, for a prior infringement of an imperial ukase about his copy, he ceased to write for nearly a year. He was thoroughly disgusted with his manner of life, and yet there didn't seem much that one could do about it.

Bierce was turning philosophical, becoming pontifical; there was a heaviness about his writing that indicated a change of tempo. Bierce began to realize that this cross-pull in his nature had its limiting elements. He was, however, unable to make a clear break with his past. He was already fifty-seven years of age. The only thing left for him to do now was to attempt a rationalization of his past. In other words, his philosophy was to justify his satire. He knew that the other avenue, pure art, if one may use such a phrase, was a closed field. He had ceased, with a few exceptions, to write stories. He planned no romances. In fact, when asked to write a love story at a very remunerative sum for a popular magazine, he said: "Do I look like one who writes for the entertainment of chambermaids?" No, he was too intelligent to attempt such a belated change. He was caught in a vicious circle of cynicism. But his idealistic-romantic spirit continued to make overtures towards that "strangeness" of experience which finally lured him after its phosphorescent gleamings along the Mexican ranges.

It was about this time that an incident occurred which, coupled with the influences previously outlined, was responsible for Bierce requesting a permanent transfer to Washington. During the first months of his acquaintance with the beautiful mistress of "Dotswood," he had occupied a position in that household of the first importance. It was rather a flattering experience for Mrs. Hume to have as an admirer such a distinguished gentleman. This was particularly true at Los Gatos, where Bierce's fame was almost unbelievable. A lady who had merely a speaking acquaintance with him, once entered the same coach on which he was traveling to San Francisco. She was so delighted with the opportunity of vaunting her acquaintance with Ambrose Bierce, that she proceeded to introduce him to every one in the car, beginning on one side the aisle and completing the circle. Naturally Una Hume was not unmindful of the fame of Bierce during the early days of their friendship. But in time even the celebrated becomes but the accustomed in the court of a beautiful woman. Bierce was first annoyed and then peeved at the manner in which he was relegated by slow degrees to the periphery of her charmed circle of admirers. He was getting old and the realization was unpleasant. He would not, of course, tolerate such a state of affairs and soon quarreled and parted forever with the lady of gray eyes and the melodious voice.

It should not be assumed, for in truth the facts will not warrant such an assumption, that Bierce was devoted to Mrs. Hume or that she was other than a very beautiful and charming woman whom he greatly admired and in whose society he spent many pleasant hours. Such relations were very dear to Bierce, who was always a fugitive from society, living in out of the way places, and always rather lonely. He had stayed on in Los Gatos because it was pleasant and because Dotswood was a retreat that mitigated the horrors of life in such a little village. But now there was no longer any reason to stay.

His determination to leave was a great blow to the group of people who had come to know and love him at Los Gatos and Wrights. He was always leaving and moving on in that restless search for an adequate experience, something, for example, that measured up to the best that war had offered. He was always leaving a circle of people behind him who invariably fell into awkward and strained attitudes once he was gone, losing the ambition which his instruction had inspired. It was because of this, and because of the fact that he was always aloof and never unrestrainedly attached to people, that he came to be called the "shadow-maker." George Sterling, who knew the real story of that phrase as well as anyone, could not resist the temptation to use it in a different sense in his article about Bierce in *The American Mercury,* and to forget, incidentally, who had coined the expression.

One day Bierce had gone for a long walk through the woods with Eva Crawford, another of his pupils, and Leila Cotton. They noticed on this, as on previous occasions, the strange mesmeric power that he possessed over wild creatures. In fact, his cabin at Los Gatos was peopled with two pet doves, "Jamie" and "Jippie," and a toad jumped around on his desk as a paper-weight. But when he would call birds to him in the woods, he seemed a different man. His nature was then entirely transparent, open, full of light and free from shadows. There was nothing artificial about his attitude. The girls noticed this and one of them said that she had always thought that Bierce misled women, that they mistook his chivalrous attitude and his elegant sentiments for a more genuine feeling, and that they never seemed to realize that his inner nature was elusive and they were playing with shadows. Bierce said, in answer to this, "But, my dears, the sun makes the shadow." Eva Crawford replied, "No, it is what gets between you and the sun that makes the shadow, and that's what you do, you are a shadow-maker." During the long period of years that intervened between 1899 and his return to California in 1910, many of them came to think that he was truly a "shadow-maker."

He now arranged to go east permanently. On Nov. 29, 1899, he wrote Howes: "In a few weeks I expect to go to Washington, D. C., where I shall probably remain. It is simply a change of duties, excepting that I shall probably do more work for *The Journal* and less for *The Examiner.*" He soon left, this time to stay, and on January 2nd, 1900, was with his son Leigh, in New York. Leigh had remained on in the East after accompanying his father there in 1896.

This trip east must have been disheartening. He left California at Christmas time, always a sad season for him. He was to arrive sick in New York, unable to continue on to Washington for weeks. His position was not assured, and he was in advanced years—a journalistic hack for the now "Honorable" Hearst. There would be no more mountain boozing parties with Dr. Doyle; the admiring circles of ladies was gone for some time. These trips across the continent were like the balls on a billiard table being shoved across to one end and then back again to the other. Life was a dreary dust-heap of bad things that left a taste of ashes in the mouth, a constant grip on the teeth. Analyzed carefully, existence appeared to be an extremely offensive procedure. Human relationships were so softly veiled and intangible that they crashed on the sharp rocks of circumstances; this phantom "Art" was a sickening vice that meant the abnegation of every full-fledged impulse. The clear, high-toned idealism of youth was a beautiful pageant in the mind, but not practically significant. If you wished to appear eccentric, why idealism was all right. About the only attitude left was cynicism. It turned off many an arrow, and as long as one said resolutely that "Nothing matters," why—"nothing mattered." A good stiff cup of spirits and he was prepared to journey on to Washington in the dead of winter to assume his position as the first of the Hearst Philosophers, those gentlemen whose writings are always accompanied with their picture, adorning the Sunday paper, explaining to the lowly the great mysteries of existence. Bierce was never fully successful in this rôle. It remained for Mr. Brisbane to coin the art of the startling platitude.

The years had slipped past without meaning or any definable significance. What, in truth, had it mattered? There were moments of great intensity when fear or excitement or elation carried the soul high, when the valiant audacity of man gestured in the face of an encompassing futility. But afterwards, during the long intervals of mediocre experience, time giggled awfully. For sixteen years he had been baiting louts, fakirs, charlatans, skinflints, petty politicians and poets in the pages of one newspaper. He had to justify these years, but it was a difficult task. As long as the duel lasted, he worried not as to its importance. But in the quiet of old age, the record of his accomplishments seemed inadequate. Just before leaving the coast he visited a cemetery in Oakland. He strolled about ex-

amining the genuine epitaphs of many that he had once crucified
in a couplet or composed a mocking "epitaph" about. And now
they were dead and had "real" epitaphs. And all in such a short
space of time! It seemed incredible. These arrogant gesturers
had only confused the core of experience, and here they were,
their names in stone: libeled and libeler, blackguard and victim,
lover and mistress, father and son. But still he was "cynical"
and blasé: the only record of his thoughts is a brief note in *The
Examiner,* August 13, 1899, that he had visited the cemetery and
was disappointed to find that Pixley had been cremated so that
he could not spit on his grave!

Across the plains again. . . . And did he expect that even
yet he might win to that feeling of winged splendor that youth
had given? But this continent's end was a land of shadows for
him and it palled upon him unbearably. Thoughts of those halcyon days when the Lotus Club gave picnics in the Marin hills
and the bay had gleamed with a brightness that had seemed eternal in its brilliant energy and power; thoughts of the dark hours
on Howell Mountain and of the long walks through the streets
of San Francisco trying to forget the stabbing pains that the
news of Day's death had brought; of lonely pain-racked hours
in barren hotel rooms; of friendly faces in whose eyes he had
seen shadows; of fights and quarrels. . . . But it had not mattered, and since the close of the war he had been proving over
and over again to himself that it did not matter, and trying to
show innumerable fools that the world was not worthy of their
worship. But he would go east and forget about these things,
for it seemed even too trivial to become indignant about.

There were a few visits to old friends and a few notes of
farewell, but there was no word for Mollie Day, who was nursing an aged mother in a lonely old house on Figueroa Street
in Los Angeles, while former friends circulated rumors that she
was immensely rich and would soon divorce her husband! She
must have smiled at these reports as she stole away from the
bedside of her mother, who was demented, and went down to
Mr. Parker's book store to buy a copy of "Fantastic Fables."
The Times that morning had announced that Ambrose Bierce,
the famous Hearst journalist who had defeated the Funding
Bill, had left for Washington where he would live in the future.

CHAPTER XVI

"ALAS, MY DREADFUL INERTIA!"

A T the time that Bierce left for Washington in
1899, *The Examiner* printed his picture, accompanying an article which explained the reasons for his
transfer to the East. The man shown in the picture is an individual remarkably changed from the handsome fellow that Miss
Campbell had sketched three years previously. When age begins
to assert its dolorous claim, it acts with alacrity. He was an old
man when he returned to Washington the second time. The
reasons for his transfer were thus stated by *The Examiner*:

> "The 56th Congress seems to be of extraordinary interest.
> The subjects before it include such matters as the War in the
> Philippines, the adjustment of our new Colonial policy, the
> disposition of Cuban affairs, and, the action that Congress
> may or may not take with reference to the trusts. These are
> all questions of great national importance. For this reason, *The
> Examiner* has sent Ambrose Bierce to Washington, where he
> will remain during the present session." (Dec. 14, 1898.)

Apparently this was simply a public explanation, as Mr. A. M.
Lawrence is positive that Bierce came to him and requested the
second transfer. He recalls that Bierce expressed a desire to go
East and be away from San Francisco; to address a larger
audience and to study conditions at Washington, thinking, no
doubt, that he might make a national name for himself as a
satirist. But his mood had changed, as indicated previously, and
he was becoming more and more the "curmudgeon philosopher,"
rather than the sharp satirist. He might have been equally suc-

cessful in the East had he been equally caustic and witty, but
instead he became sonorous, portentous and grave.

He proceeded to Washington and took up a residence at
603 15th Street. The public questions were, as pointed out in
The Examiner's notice, interesting if not as important as they
were thought to be. These early years of the twentieth century
witnessed a turning point in national affairs, and the significance
of the change even then was vaguely sensed and appreciated.
It was during these years that America began to look abroad
with an insatiable passion for land. A fever of imperialism
possessed the nation; we had received our first experience with
the exhilaration of foreign conquest. The Mexican War had
been a nice and profitable enterprise, but this Cuban fiasco
offered far greater possibilities and stirred the imagination with
dreams of empire.

Strive as one might to cope sharply with the times, it was
impossible to provoke attention by criticism. The more intelligent critics, such as Mr. Bierce, were ruffled by the vacuum of
public opinion to such an extent that they forgot the art of
satire and became merely sarcastic in a stiff and heavy manner.
How attack the bombast of such a man as W. J. Bryan? The
most astute reasoning and the sharpest satire could not hold a
fraction of the public's attention against the roaring syllables
of honeyed nonsense that the Commoner bellowed forth. It
remained for Mr. Mencken, in later years, to annihilate the
reputation of Mr. Bryan in terms harsh, broad-edged and offensive. But in 1899 America actually yearned to be mentally
seduced. The times reeked with tepid thought boomed forth in
demagogic terms. Perhaps the technique of the orators owed
something to the journalism of Mr. Hearst. Bryan had been a
protégé and had been so carefully instructed in the art of boob-
baiting that he achieved an unequaled mastery. America had
taken in Mr. Hearst's wild talk about Evangelina Cisneros without reservation, and had followed him into the war to free the
Cubans and increase the circulation of the Hearst newspapers,
without regard to the rather timid protests of McKinley.
Naturally, in the midst of such a cave of the winds—it is seriously to be questioned if America ever experienced a time
when ideas were regarded with such hostility—men of sense
were driven to desperation. Mr. Bierce's attack on this gaudy

bombast was too contemporary; he might just as well have shouted at the ocean to cease its pounding on the shore. Mr. Mencken's attack was strategic, properly timed, and immensely more effective. Bierce tried his hand at the rôle of critic for several years, and then turned away from the scene with magnificent disgust.

His first dispatch from Washington under date of January 9, 1900, is an interesting bit of journalism. Bierce had been present during the first session of Congress when Senator A. J. Beveridge delivered his famous speech on our policy in the Philippines, during the course of which the "manifest destiny" apology was advanced as an *ex post facto* cure for a smarting conscience. Beveridge captured the imagination of the nation with his bold, dramatic acceptance of the idea abortive in the public mind, to wit: that while there may have been considerable talk about our idealistic motives in interceding with Spain on behalf of the Cubans, that yet, nevertheless, since certain rich and valuable possessions had been acquired, it was nothing less than our "duty" and "destiny" to retain them. The argument was not without historical precedents, it was a perfect expression of a general but taciturn desire, and it synchronized with the pulse of conquest.

Once more in Bierce's experience had a national fact supplanted a national ideal. It was ever the same: our lust was as inevitable and as predestined to fulfillment as that of all young and strong creatures endowed by an inscrutable fate with the energy that must itself ultimately yield to a superior energy. Bierce listened with mock attention while the galleries were carried away by the practiced and professional oratory of the handsome young senator from Indiana. He listened with equal amusement to Senator Hoar's reply which, like most talk of the kind, got lost in the nebulous ether of idealism. Into the public discussion of this debate, Bierce interjected this note:

"I dare say that is the right view to take of it. I am sure it must be wrong for nations to be wicked. But in the larger politics of this worst of all possible worlds it does seem as if ethical considerations had not more weight and influence than that to which their beauty entitles them. According to the principles so dear to the hearts of the worthy gentlemen who lift protesting hands when the rights of weak nations are invaded by strong ones, not a people on earth to-day has a right to be there. All have dispossessed some other people."

He followed this up with a long article in *The Examiner,* January 14, 1900, "The Survival of the Fittest," in which he gave the correct name to Senator Beveridge's elegant idea. In fact, Mr. Bierce came to think that there was much to be said for the theory of brute force, or materialistic determinism. He used the same idea with a vengeance during the Boer War in which he espoused the cause of the British. As an outgrowth of his articles on British strategy during this campaign, he first began to correspond with Lord Kitchener. They exchanged letters for some years afterwards. All of Bierce's journalism written in the East under the head of "The Passing Show" was extremely reactionary and full of a great seriousness about public affairs. But, then, he held the post as philosopher in the Hearst college and it was beginning to mar his thought.

During these years Mrs. Bierce was living in Los Angeles. Bierce never corresponded with his wife directly, and all communications had to be sent through the medium of the daughter. Every month Helen would receive a remittance from her father, which she would send to Mrs. Bierce. Leigh was in New York at this time. He had studied art under J. H. E. Partington in San Francisco, and had contributed to *The Wave.* Later he began to work for *The Examiner* and Mr. Hearst had sent him to the Yosemite Valley to write some feature stories about the wonders of that valley since desecrated by tourists. He later went to Los Angeles and reported for *The Record,* maintaining a studio up on a region known as Bunker Hill. When his father went east, Leigh accompanied him and soon began to write for the New York *Telegraph.* I have a considerable collection of newspaper clippings containing his work up to December 8, 1900, and they reveal the hand of an intelligent writer. For some time Leigh edited a rather interesting journal in New York called *The Bee.* He drew with facility and his decorations and illustrations were excellent. His early journalism reflected the temper of his father, but the great light does not shine about the lines. Yet he was like his father in many ways. He possessed the same mesmeric power with animals. And he imitated the personal manner of his father. One evening while in Los Angeles he happened to be dining at Ahrend's Café. A waiter was discouretous and Leigh, with that sense of affront in the slightest discourtesy which his father always experienced, gave the fellow a thorough drubbing and made him apologize.

Bierce was much pleased with the success of his son in New York, and looked forward to the time when Leigh would try his hand at a book of stories. Of course he made light of the boy's achievements to others, but he was secretly delighted with his good work in the arts. It would have been interesting to watch the development of Leigh's talent, but it was destined to be of short life. Upon coming to New York, he had become involved with the wife of an artist. His father learned of the affair; in fact, it was a continuation of a liaison begun in Oakland, and it was the cause of heated words for several years. Bierce had no particular objection to such escapades, but in this case the woman happened to be married and her husband was, if not a friend, at least an acquaintance of the family. This made Leigh's conduct a form of dishonesty which his father would not tolerate. But once the affair had run its course, a more serious dispute arose between father and son. Upon arriving in New York, Leigh roomed at a boarding-house owned by an aged woman who had a rather pretty daughter whose name was Flora. Bierce had only been East a short time when Leigh and Flora were married. He never approved of the alliance and never ceased to resent Leigh's disobedience. As usual he showed his great incompetence when dealing with human beings; he was never able to comprehend imperfections. There was no flexibility about his judgments; he was not really unreasonable or dogmatic, but he was temperamentally unable to feel relations as well as to think about them. He saw the issues so sharply and his reactions were so sensitive, that he could not tolerate a sensibility not equally as developed. Consequently he shouted at Leigh, argued, dogmatized, and plead, but all to no avail. Shorlty after his son's marriage, Bierce remarked to a friend: "Why should both of my boys have gotten mixed up with trashy women?"

Once Bierce knew that his son was determined to marry, he cut him off and did not speak or write to him until Leigh was stricken ill. It seems that the newspaper for which Leigh was reporting decided to conduct a Christmas Benefit. Leigh accompanied the expedition to write a news story and to supervise the distribution of provisions to the poor. He halted the expedition as it was passing a saloon, and proceeded to get hilariously drunk. When the caravan again moved on its way, he began to give away all the provisions before the destination was reached. Shortly after this affair, Leigh became seriously ill with pneumonia. His father rushed from Washington to be near him. He kept asking his father to send for his sister, and finally Bierce wired for her to come on to New York. She started from Los Angeles, but while she was en route Leigh died. The date of his death was March 31, 1901. The pain which Bierce had experienced on Day's death was sharp, and swift, and almost unbearable. Much had happened since 1889. This time his grief was no less acute, but he was somewhat benumbed with a growing sense of utter futility. There was no pillar against which he could lean; there was no faith to sustain his spirit. Winter, and death, and a horrible attack of asthma . . . the senseless folly and cruelty of human affairs . . . and death giggling in the drop curtains and whispering in the alcoves. Death had paralyzed his thoughts, embittered his life, made him brave and courageous, and finally it would do away with him. It was, as one commentator announced, "his honey and his poison." A few days after Leigh's death, Bierce wrote a friend: "I am hit hard; more than you can guess—am a bit broken and gone gray of it all." A year later he wrote the same friend: "It is just a year ago to-day that Leigh died—I wish I could stop counting the days."

If it was a great tragedy in Bierce's life, Leigh's death was doubly tragic for Mrs. Bierce, who had to stay in Los Angeles and could not attend the funeral. Poor woman, she seemed destined to a rôle of lonely and unattended sorrow. But death, while it affected Bierce very keenly, never softened him. He would not relent towards the family into which his son had married. He still refused to see them or to be near them; and used his daughter as a medium to communicate money to his daughter-in-law. In fact, Helen met Leigh's wife for the first time at the funeral! On this occasion the father acted quite in character. He admonished his daughter not to be ostentatious about her grief, and, above all, to be proud and dignified. A woman of very slight acquaintance made herself quite offensive by a gushing expression of condolence. Bierce cut this creature short with a word, and told his daughter that nothing was so vulgar as a public display of sorrow.

Back in Washington Bierce was stricken ill himself and it was months before he recovered from the combined effects of grief and asthma. If it had been a gray scene prior to Leigh's death, it was black now. Something of the depression that settled about Bierce during these months is reflected in a letter to Amy Cecil, dated January 2, 1901, in the course of which he said: "I'm leading a life of mere waiting—waiting for nothing in particular, except the end of it all. I do no work that I care to do—just the work that keeps me living—for I've no incentive, no ambition but to go on with as little friction as possible. (Why did not God make us with ball-bearings, like bicycles?) I fancy most observers would say that I'm having a pretty good time, and that's what I usually say myself; but may Heaven punish the malefactor who invented that deathly dull thing, a good time." And he closed the letter with this phrase: "May God give you strength to bear the sorrows which He seems to desire to inflict." No wonder that he drifted into a state of complete indifference and despair during these months. His writings of about this time are the heavy, dogmatic opinions of an old and rather weary man. He built up fortresses of dogma behind which he could crouch and evade the chance bullet of cruel truth that might otherwise break through the careful shield of his cynicism.

Another unpublished letter of about the same time (June 7, 1901) to Theresa McCarthy contains similar thoughts. "I thank you for your kind words of sympathy, for I know how sincere they are. When one is in trouble, one likes to know that not all the world is indifferent. I hope you are again well and happy—as happy as it is consonant with the plans of God's universe for any of his helpless creatures to be—or believe themselves to be." It is the note of a sick and despondent man, a man to whom the thought of death was a continuing sorrow. He might write with insouciance such lines as these.

"Done with the work of breathing; done
With all the world; the mad race run

Through to the end; the golden goal
Attained and found to be a hole,"

but when death touched him personally it was a different matter.
Grief was crippling and it benumbed the spirit. Day and Leigh
both dead! It seemed like a monstrous untruth, and yet it was
true and he must endure it. When he recovered he was "cynical"
as ever, but

"Thou wouldst not think
How ill all's here about my heart!"

He was leading an idle life: a little writing for the Hearst
newspapers; and a few magazine articles. The old column of
"Prattle" had long been abandoned, and it was apparently intended that with "The Passing Show" he would adopt a broader
outlook. In any event, his journalism ceased to be good reading
after 1896. He spent his days in Washington, full of petty
duties and trivial tasks, and would invite some of the boys from
"the office" to his apartment to play anagrams in the evening!
He usually began the day by walking down to the Army and
Navy Club for his mail; then he would journey over to his
office in the Washington Bureau of the New York *American;*
then back to the Club for lunch and a chat with his old army
cronies; when evening came he was ready for Roche's where
his "boozing den" as he named it was located. In the evening
he would sometimes have a few guests at the apartment; sometimes Percival Pollard, or Dr. Franklin from Schenectady; or
Justice Harlan. Later a tray with a pot of coffee would be
brought into his study and he would work for awhile, with
"Mr. Dooley," a pet canary bird, flitting about the room and
trying to alight on his penholder. There, across the desk, would
be the famous skull, to which Bierce could address queries and
guess the answers. It was worse than a twilight existence: it
lacked even the poignancy of twilight. It was a vacuum: a
cave of indifference: an empty shadowland of meditation. He
wrote a few ghost stories about this time and thought them
rather good, but he had too many ghosts in his own life just
then to spend much time imagining yarns about them. On the
desk by the skull was the cigar box which contained the ashes
of another friend. He could steel himself by such bravado ges-

tures against the question which the grinning outline of the skull suggested, as though it would tell him some grave secrets but a horrible mirth made speech impossible. Death worried him all the same. For such a romantic temperament, his life was a boresome existence and gradually the seed of discontent bore fruit in a great disdainful gesture.

Meantime he seems to have been amused with people who wanted adventure and excitement, as though the thought of such experiences was rather attractive to him. Theresa McCarthy wanted to go to China as a nurse, and he was finally induced to see Mr. Meiklejohn and secure the appointment for her. "Why under the sun should you wish to go to Manila?" he would write. A few days later he wrote: "I took your application to Mr. Meiklejohn (whom I found at dinner and therefore good humored), and asked him to approve it before sending it to the Surgeon-General. He said the best way to do would be to order the thing done. He put the application in his pocket; so the Surgeon-General will probably not be bothered about it. We then—took a drink. So I think you may hope to go to Manila and die of a fever or marry one of your patients." He was instrumental in getting Margaret McKenzie appointed as a government nurse; and in getting Mabel Wood sent to the Philippines as a teacher. They were young and wanted adventure; well, why not? He had a few adventures of his own about this time. Coming home one night to his apartment, he was attacked by a big burly negro. But, true to form, he gave battle and beat the negro with a walking stick that fortunately had a steel core. He was laid up in his apartment for some time afterwards with a broken rib as a result of the encounter. He wheezed with asthma; fell over cliffs at Calistoga Hot Springs while bicycling; fought with ruffians in Washington; and always lived. As he once wrote to Howes: "I'm happy to announce the defeat of the hives. I'm now ready for cholera infantum and the ills incident to teething." There was a strange exclusiveness about death. Should one seek it out, deliberately?

The young lady he had met by chance at Angwin's, Carrie Christiansen, was now in Washington as his secretary. Since he had met her, Bierce had been a father to this poor girl, sending her to school and helping her in many ways. She had come to Washington, when he finally succeeded in getting her a place in the public schools, and, because it was quite the sensible thing to do, she also lived at the Olympia Apartments. Miss Christiansen's kindly and loving care of Bierce is an amazing story, a refreshing experience in human affairs, particularly as she was quite sensitive to criticism and was made the target of a good deal of abuse during the years she lived in Washington. Bierce had warned her that such would be the case, but she was quite oblivious to the consequences. She adored Bierce with the sacred admiration of a blind affection. Guileless, naïve, and utterly unsophisticated, her presence was yet an unmixed blessing for Bierce. She assisted him with his work, kept his affairs in order (he was impossible as a business man), and nursed him when he was stricken with periodic attacks of asthma. But to assume, as Mr. Neale has done, that Bierce was deeply in love with Miss Christiansen is ridiculous. The inference that Mr. Neale draws from the manner in which they lived, is repulsed by their correspondence, by Bierce's references to Miss Christiansen in other letters, and by the testimony of those who lived with them. The fact is that Miss Christiansen, if she admired Bierce, was perhaps Mrs. Bierce's dearest friend. She was always regarded, even in St. Helena, as a dependent of the family, as an unfortunate child. To assume that Bierce went into Mexico with a broken heart because Miss Christiansen had jilted him, and to whisper of a secret marriage, as Mr. Neale does, is to be unnecessarily ridiculous if not malicious.

Bierce soon began to acquire quite a reputation in Washington as an unusual and striking character. Young newspapermen would "look Bierce up" and have a few drinks. He became the subject of an endless chain of stories; and his bon mots were frequently quoted. One day he was listening to a very ardent suffragette. Suddenly he said to her: "Madame" (it was always "Madame"), "if you desire equal rights it follows that you must assume equal obligations, does it not?" She eagerly assented. "And, therefore, if an army of the Japanese were to land off the coast of Monterey you would be willing to organize an army of women to fight them, would you not?" Oh, yes, indeed she would. "Well, then, did it ever occur to you, Madame, what would happen if an army of women were ever captured by an army of men?" Asked by a group of women's rights advocates to say something about their sex, he replied: "Woman, lovely woman, if we could only fall into her arms without falling into her hands." A very proper lady was objecting, one day in the apartment, on the ground of impropriety to everything. Bierce finally became annoyed and said: "Madame, you are so proper that I would hesitate to call you a woman, for woman is only man with a womb." He once remarked that to be happy a good woman should possess the three B's, and when asked what they were he replied: "She must be Bright, Beautiful and Barren."

George Horton recalls the Sunday morning breakfasts that Bierce used to give in his apartment in Washington for "literary and brain workers, invitations to which were much prized. He specialized in coffee which he made in a peculiar pot that was shaped something like a long melon, and that oscillated like a pendulum, dripping slowly from either end." He impressed Mr. Horton as the "most genial and kindliest of men, although he seemed oppressed by a secret sadness." * Charles Willis Thompson visited him at about the same time, and his recollections are of interest:

> "It is surprising that a quarter of a century later Bierce stands out in my recollection far above nearly all the hundreds of men I was meeting daily, for those were crowded years. I have difficulty in placing many a United States Senator and Cabinet officer, but Bierce is as vividly before me as the day I first saw him; even the day is before me, a sunny afternoon in Dennis Mullany's crazy little bar-room, a place frequented by all the wits, the home of real conversation. There Bierce was a conversational autocrat; and his first look at a newcomer was unflatteringly appraising. It seemed to say, 'Show me your credentials.' He looked straight at you from under his frosty brows with a bright eye and a cynical smile, which said as plain as words, 'Now what kind of ass are *you* going to make yourself?' But, the moment you *did* show him that you belonged, that air was gone and you were admitted to his camaraderie in an instant, and on absolutely even terms, and for all time. Nobody could be more genial or more intellectually democratic. In *The Herald-Tribune* I described him as my most enduring recollection. He had no time and no use for men who had nothing to say, but was hail-fellow with

* Letter of George Horton to the author.

any one who could talk. The recollection of his personal appearance is that of a wonderfully handsome man with talkative eyes and an eagle nose. I can see him at this moment, though I can't conjure up the face of the British Ambassador." *

The Washington *Post*, March, 1902, reported a meeting of the literati at some salon. Bierce was there, and C. W. Stoddard, Maurice Egan, Harriet Prescott Spofford, and many others. The reporter noticed the handsome Mr. Bierce standing in one corner mixing cocktails, and pouring harsh cynicisms into the pink ears of the Hon. Thomas Nelson Page. The Washington *Times*, August, 1902, sent a reporter around to interview Bierce. "Mr. Bierce was found seated in his den, an apartment hung and carpeted in red and containing a Turkish couch piled high with pillows, a table full of interesting books, and a quaint little sideboard filled with a mixture of curious glasses, decanters, and a chafing dish. He is a modest man and declares that the best thing about his work is the part he doesn't write, namely, the checks, and that even they might be better. He says that at present he is doing nothing, and adds, 'except writing.' He vows that he shall never publish another book and that he has no faith in his own or anybody's inspiration. He spends most of his spare time collecting arrow-heads." It is, I believe, a fair picture. He was "doing nothing," and about the only diversion that might be added to collecting arrow-heads was canoeing.

It was about this time that Sam Davis mentioned to President Roosevelt that he knew Bierce. The President was immediately interested and expressed a desire to meet him. A formal invitation was sent at once. Bierce replied that he was exceedingly sorry to decline the invitation, but that it so happened that he had a previous engagement with an old friend from San Francisco, and that he never "neglected old friends to make new." Roosevelt was delighted and sent another note, saying, "I quite agree with you. Come to-night, and let us be old friends." The loyal Sam Davis was present at the meeting, and, true to Virginia City form, introduced the President *to* Bierce. Later in the evening the three inspected the White House, and Roosevelt showed them the famous painting of San Juan Hill

* Letter of Charles Willis Thompson, March 18, 1928, to the author.

with the Rough Rider, well in the foreground, leading the
charge. He asked Bierce what he thought of the picture, and
was informed that it was inaccurate since it depicted Roosevelt
at San Juan when in truth he hadn't been there!

In the fall of 1903, Bierce went to Aurora, in West Virginia, and there spent most of the autumn. It chanced to be the
scene of his early soldiering, and it was during this vacation
that he gathered the information contained in the letter written
to the Ninth Indiana Volunteer Association. He took long
walks through the woods and inspected the Grafton Cemetery with fascinated attention. He was actually walking
around in the woods near Belington! Wasn't there a fellow
—what was his name?—Corporal Dyson Boothroyd! And
Capt. Madden! It did not seem but yesterday, and now he
walked through the cemetery, gray-haired and haunted with
memories, while a bright and childish sunlight smiled and
laughed with delight. He discovered the fallen Confederates
only by accident. They were not housed in a national cemetery.
"As nearly as I could make out there were from eight to a hundred sunken graves, overgrown with moss and full of rotting
leaves. Fewer than a dozen had headstones, fashioned from native slate of the county, with barely decipherable inscriptions
rudely carved by comrades of the dead. These had mostly fallen
into the excavations." *

The swift and changing habits of time! The black ashes
grown into the green freshness of spring and this new life
itself already moldy with decay. It suggested the order of a
vegetable kingdom that mocked, by its silence and passivity, the
thought of dreams and ideals. What did all this idealism
amount to, this "lashing rascals through the world," had it any
greater significance than the valor he had shown that morning
at Belington so many years ago? They had fought around here
for several days; the gentlemen over at Grafton and these fellows beneath the unmarked slabs of slate, and the struggle was
rumored to have had something to do with slavery. Back in
Washington the great world was shocked with accounts of race
riots at Atlanta, and he stood in the quietness of Grafton and
counted the graves of fallen comrades. It was like Hamlet entering the grave. A sleepy feeling of indifference pervaded the

* *The Cosmopolitan,* May, 1906.

valley, and nothing seemed to matter: rotting logs of breast-works; scarred timbers; a few unmarked graves. But he was still "romantic" about the old scenes; he was still capable of self-deception, and he wrote in his letter to those of his comrades:

> "But the whole region is wild and grand, and if any one of the men who in his golden youth soldiered through its valleys of sleep and over its gracious mountains will revisit it in the hazy season when it is all aflame with the autumn foliage, I promise him sentiments that he will willingly entertain and emotions that he will care to feel. Among them, I fear, will be a haunting envy of those of his comrades whose fall and burial in that enchanted land he once bewailed."

On his return to Washington he wrote George Sterling: "They found a Confederate soldier the other day with his rifle alongside. I'm going over to beg his pardon."

In the winter of 1904, Mary E. Bierce commenced an action in the Superior Court of Los Angeles County against Ambrose G. Bierce for divorce on the ground of desertion. It was a simple complaint: the statutory allegations with the statement that the "defendant" was a journalist who resided in Washington. The interlocutory decree was granted a few months later, and on April 27, 1905, Mary E. Bierce died of "heart failure." Both happenings were a great shock to her husband and daughter. No one knew that Mrs. Bierce intended to sue for a divorce, and for many years her motives remained a mystery. But her counsel, who still lives in Los Angeles, remembers that she filed the action because she had "heard that Mr. Bierce wanted his freedom but was too proud to ask for it." It was another tragedy of misunderstanding, as Bierce had made no such request, and the word that had reached his wife was untrue. He never remarried and never had any intention of doing so.

For many years it has been bruited about San Francisco that Mrs. Bierce filed suit for divorce because she was going to inherit a large estate and wanted to eliminate any possible claim of her husband. As a matter of fact, the estate of Captain H. H. Day was probated in San Bernardino County, California, in January of 1891, thirteen years before she applied for a

divorce. Moreover, both she and her mother were in straitened circumstances at the time the divorce action was filed.
The devotion of Mrs. Bierce to her husband is unquestionable:
a perfect record of unbroken care and faith. For years she had
lived in Los Angeles nursing an aged and demented parent,
uncomplaining, cheerful and indifferent to a sad fate. But the
last years had been too much: the death of Leigh, the condition
of her mother, and the memories that were so unnecessarily
stirred into poignancy by that divorce action, these sorrows were
more than even this brave and admirable woman could stand.
In the final reckoning of things it will be hers and not her
husband's fate that will probably be written of as tragic. There
is something about the story of her life that is too tragic to
write about in the casual manner of narration. In the words
of her school-girl friends, now wizened old ladies in St. Helena,
"Mollie Day was beautiful and kind."

Again the lot of attending to the details of the funeral
fell to the daughter. Bierce had left for the South on a military survey with General Ainsworth shortly after his wife was
taken ill, so the daughter had to rush to Los Angeles and care
for her mother. And it was the daughter, too, who took the
ashes of her mother and the ashes of her brother, Leigh, to
St. Helena for burial.

Bierce wrote George Sterling about this time: "Death has
been striking pretty close to me again, and you know how that
upsets a fellow." If there had been a semblance of vitality about
his work in Washington previous to the death of his wife, it
disappeared with remarkable swiftness afterwards. He seemed
to be numb with cold. He tried frantically to regain the sense
of vivid emotions, even if experienced vicariously in the perspective of memory, but it was of no avail. Events did not
seem to touch him; he was encased in death's antechamber.
Even his work ceased to bring him pleasure. He wrote to Howes,
"Alas, my dreadful inertia!" and so it was, for he could not
feel keenly and knew that he had been deceived and that he
was fast approaching the final mystery which would perhaps
turn out to be another empty vault. His days were full of
echoes and shadows; the troubling half-reality of pale reflec-
tions; the memory of vital sensations. His imagination could
not sustain him. He was still looking about him in the world

for the revealing magic. That early shock which had paralyzed his imagination had also bred an irremediable distrust of all mysticism. But he had missed so much!

"So, too," Mr. George Santayana writes of Hamlet and he might better have been writing of Bierce, "his sardonic humor and nonsensical verbiage at the most tragic junctures, may justify themselves ideally and seem to be deeply inspired. These wild starts suggest a mind inwardly rent asunder, a delicate genius disordered, a mind with infinite sensibility possessing no mastery over itself or things. . . . The clouded will which plays with all these artifices of thought would fain break its way to light and self-knowledge through the magic circle of sophistication. It is the tragedy of a soul buzzing in the glass prison of a world which it can neither escape or understand, in which it flutters about without direction, without clear hope, and yet with many a keen pang, many a dire imaginary doubt, and much exquisite music."

He came to feel that something should be done; it was imperative that he overcome that "dreadful inertia" which left him "weak and will-less." He would "go away" and perhaps he could capture again that feeling of "enormous revelry," of which William Blake once wrote.

CHAPTER XVII

"A MAGNIFICENT CRYSTALLIZATION"

DURING the first years that he was in Washington, Bierce's journalism appeared under the caption "The Passing Show" in the various Hearst papers. But Mr. Hearst had written him: "I will have enough magazines pretty soon to keep you busy in the magazine field, and then you won't have to bother with newspapers. I imagine the magazine field will please you better anyway, as it is an opportunity for fuller discussion." (June 24, 1906.) It became quite apparent that it was the policy of Mr. Hearst to keep Bierce anchored to the magazines and that he should write as little as possible for the newspapers. But 1905 "The Passing Show" was transferred from the newspapers into the files of *The Cosmopolitan,* which Mr. Hearst had purchased, and there it appeared until 1909, when Bierce ceased to write for current publication altogether.

But, if Bierce was out of sympathy with the editors of the Hearst newspapers, he was even more at war with the editors of *The Cosmopolitan.* The radicalism of the late nineties began to find expression, about this time, in the sensational muckraking which Mr. Hearst fostered. It was the era of the "progressive," and "reform" agitation. The movement doubtless had a genuine causation but its expression was weak, futile and ineffective. It took the form of emotionalized propaganda. *The Cosmopolitan* soon became a hotbed of excited and hysterical prose. The muck-rakers were a querulous and nervous lot, full of accusations and charges, but suffering from the phobia of reform, shouting without reason and writing without grace. It was during this period that David Graham Phillips wrote a sensational series of articles on "The Treason of the Senate." Ida Tarbell, Ray Stannard Baker, Alfred Henry Lewis, and Emerson Hough, began to chronicle the lives of the industrial barons evolved out of a capitalistic society. Maxim Gorki published his memoirs, which added color to the movement, and Jack London's hastily concocted stories of the road began to hymn the lowly proletariat in flattering terms. It was the decade of Lincoln Steffens, Upton Sinclair and Robert Herrick. Radicalism was unquestionably making enormous gains throughout the country, and "social unrest" was the favorite subject of the Chautauqua platform. By 1914 the movement had dissipated all its fine energies and it collapsed with the first intimation of war. But the first years of the century were rampant with unphilosophic radicalism.

It was quite predictable that Bierce should war with his fellow contributors. He was entirely out of place in *The Cosmopolitan.* He knew instinctively that there was too much sensationalism about the muck-rakers, who were, for the most part, mere youngsters in the ironies. Their radicalism was in essence but an unidentified itch for front page publicity. One need but point to Mr. Lincoln Steffens' relation to the McNamara case in Los Angeles in 1910 to realize the basic inadequacy of such propaganda. Bierce quickly acquired a reputation with these men as a reactionary, because he was skeptical about the efficacy of reform and dubious of unthinking propaganda. Hence there was something quite significant about the round-table debate that Mr. Hearst sponsored between Morris Hillquit, Bierce and John Hunter, for the discussion of the "Social Unrest" at a New York hotel. There is evidence that the meeting was arranged as a deliberate plot to "get" Bierce, by matching him against two agile minded leaders of the unrest. It was heralded as quite a significant debate and Bierce was announced as "a strenuous challenger of the optimists, a thinker whose views are the despair of the social reformer."

John Hunter, who had just published his widely read "Poverty," opened the discussion with some statistics about poverty. Mr. Hunter was then actually concerned with an important problem: this was before he came to live at Pebble Beach, and before he had forgotten that poverty was other than the title he had once given a book. Mr. Bierce immediately challenged his statistics, but then passed them over, admitting with Hunter that there was a great deal of poverty in the country. Hillquit joined in with an "Amen" and for a moment they were in accord. But soon the reformers became excited about a remedy, and socialism was proposed. Immediately Bierce became skeptical: "I don't see," he remarked, "that there is any remedy for this condition which consists in the rich being on top, or rather, the strongest being on top. They always will be. The reason that men are poor—this is not a rule without exception—is that they are incapable. The rich become rich because they have brains." *

Hunter then proceeded to review the thesis of his new book, but Mr. Bierce immediately rejoined: "Now don't understand me as defending that system," referring to the evils of an unregulated industrialism. "I wish I could abolish it. I only say it is inevitable and incurable. Nothing touches me more than poverty; I have been poor myself. I was one of those poor devils born to work as a peasant in the field; but I found no difficulty in getting out of it." The debate continued.

HUNTER: "Well, sir, how important do you conceive William Waldorf Astor to be to the City of New York? He lives in London; but he and his family extract from the people of New York interest on, let us say, four hundred million a year. Is he that valuable to the community? Is this because of his extraordinary brains?" (How immature this sounds to-day!)

BIERCE: "Let us admit that he is not important and ought to be eliminated. Now, why don't they eliminate him? What I mean is this: If the oppressed workingmen—"

HUNTER: "Don't consider only the oppressed workingmen, but say all workingmen, brain workers as well as manual workers."

BIERCE: "In this country every man has a vote. If he is not satisfied with conditions as they are, why doesn't he change them? If the workingman and the poor are in the majority, why don't they get together? Because they haven't sense enough. They can have any laws or any system they want."

Mr. Hillquit then advanced the theory, so dear to the heart of every socialist, that the poor have a monopoly on all the virtues. But Mr. Bierce made neat capital of this point when

* *The Cosmopolitan,* July, 1906.

he said: "The general idea among the sons of discontent is that the prosperous are dishonest and the unprosperous are honest. If that is so, abolition of poverty is a nefarious business."

He continued: "I don't believe in the greatest good to the greatest number—it seems to me perfect rot. I believe in the greatest good to the best men. And I would sacrifice a thousand incapable men to elevate one really great man. It is from the great men only that the world gets any good. What do we owe to the artisans who laid the stones of the Parthenon? What to the gaping Athenians who stared at Plato?'

" 'I haven't any doubt,' Bierce said, 'that a revolution is coming in this country, which may or may not be suppressed. It will be a bloody one. I think that is the natural tendency of republican government. Undoubtedly we have to go over the whole Paris régime again and again.'

" 'Republican government!' exclaimed Mr. Hunter. 'Tsarism has brought a bloody revolution.'

" 'Yes, sir,' said Mr. Bierce.

" 'And a dictator will bring revolution.'

" 'Sure,' said Mr. Bierce.

" 'The people alone are unconquerable.'

" 'The people are always doing silly things,' said Mr. Bierce. 'They sail in and shed a lot of blood, and then they are back where they were before.'

" 'You think civilization has not accomplished anything in recent years,' asked Mr. Hillquit, smiling. (I can see that smile!)

" 'It has accomplished everything,' was Mr. Bierce's ready reply; 'but it has not made humanity any happier. Happiness is the only thing worth having. I find happiness in looking at poor men in the same way that I do in looking at the ants in an anthill. And I find happiness looking at the capitalist. I don't care what he does, nor what the others do. It pleases me to look at them. Each man is concerned with his own happiness.' "

HUNTER: "Mr. Bierce, I gather from your gray hairs that you are a contemporary of John D. Rockefeller." (People were always using John D. Rockefeller as a token in those days.)

BIERCE: "Yes, sir."

HUNTER: "And I should say you were on a par with him in cleverness."

BIERCE: "I think him a damned fool in some ways."

At the close of the luncheon, Mr. Hunter rushed away to keep an appointment, but Hillquit and Bierce strolled out into the lobby and into the bar. Mr. Bierce proceeded to buy him a drink. Just as Hillquit lifted his glass, Mr. Bierce remarked: "You have a lovely neck, Mr. Hillquit, some day I hope to be one of those who will put a rope about it," and he drank in somber satisfaction while Hillquit choked.

What Bierce resented was the attitude of these men, their calm assumption that the answers to life's riddles were very simple, and that every one was absurd who did not agree with their panacea. Bierce was, to be sure, rather stupid about his arguments, but that he bettered the two young Marxians is apparent. Mr. Hunter's subsequent career has been a long and uninterrupted refutation of the principles that he so glibly mouthed in 1906. Was he insincere then, or has he suffered a change of heart since? What happened to all these muck-rakers of 1905? One looks in vain for their indignation. Upton Sinclair still remains by his guns, but John Spargo, Max Eastman, Floyd Dell (of a later vintage, of course), Ida Tarbell, John Hunter, are they to-day in the vanguard of the liberals? What would their answer now be to the stoical indifference of Ambrose Bierce, who, at heart, felt more compassion for the weak and defenseless than they ever did? Because he would not permit his sympathies to drive reason to unwarranted conclusions, they named him an "old Tory" and raced on to calamitous pitfalls. The debate, indeed, reveals the personal superiority of Bierce as a man. He calmly refused to believe in the sophomoric panaceas of his opponents. The debate is not altogether unlike the exchange of letters that took place between Mr. Mencken and Mr. LaMotte in 1910.

The reaction of the younger generation to Bierce's ideas is revealed in the correspondence between George Sterling and Jack London. Bierce had written that, in his opinion, "The Road" was a bad book. Sterling, always eager for a lively encounter of wits, wrote to London quoting Bierce. But he exaggerated and went so far as to inform London that Bierce had demanded that he give up their friendship under penalty of forfeiting the "Master's" benediction. That Bierce ever made such a threat is not borne out by his correspondence with Sterling. Bierce would not be so ridiculous; moreover, he did appreciate what was meritorious about London's work. (See a letter to Sterling published in "The Letters of Ambrose Bierce," on page 105.) But Jack London, always "a good fellow," did not resent Bierce's alleged intolerance; in fact, he wrote Sterling with admirable spirit:

> "For heaven's sake don't you quarrel with Ambrose about me. He's too splendid a man to be diminished because he has lacked access to a later generation of science. He crystallized before you and I were born, and it is too magnificent a crystallization to quarrel with." *

But although one can admire London's spirit, it is impossible to suppress a smile over his superior talk about a "later generation of science." It is particularly amusing when one recalls that Bierce was actually something of a scientist, at least in the fields of astronomy and engineering, and that Jack London was woefully uneducated. What, forsooth, was this mysterious "science," the ignorance of which made Mr. Bierce the subject of condescension, but the "statistics" of John Hunter and the rhapsodies of Lincoln Steffens? Because London had read Mr. Wells' "In the Days of the Comet," he assumed that he was privy to all the dark and unfathomable mysteries of life. In a later letter to Sterling, he made this comment:

> "I wouldn't care to lock horns with Bierce. He stopped growing a generation ago. Of course, he keeps up with the newspapers, but his criteria crystallized 30 odd years ago. Had he been born a generation later he'd have been a socialist, and, more likely, an anarchist. He never reads books that aren't something like a hundred years old, and he glories in the fact!"

And in still a third letter, from Hilo, Hawaii, 1907, he said: "The quotes from Ambrose were great. What a pen he wields. Too bad he hasn't a better philosophic foundation."

It is quite apparent that there is little comparison between the philosophy of the man who wrote "John Barleycorn" and

* "The Book of Jack London," Volume II, by Charmion London.

the author of "Tales of Soldiers and Civilians." Perhaps London would have been surprised had he known that Bierce wrote intelligently of Nietzsche in 1904; praised Ezra Pound's poetry in manuscript before it was published in book form; was immediately enthusiastic about Baron Corvo's "In His Own Image" when it was first published; defended Tolstoi's "The Kreutzer Sonata" at a time when London was teething; praised Anatole France's "L'Ille des Pingouins" when London thought that Voltaire was the last satirist; and was early in his appreciation of such books as John Galsworthy's "In Motley" and Mary Austin's "The Land of Little Rain." London's attitude is the more ridiculous when examined in the light of his latter-day renunciation of socialism and his heated resignation from the party in 1916. The writer of "rough-neck" literature is generally a sentimentalist, and London was no exception. One reference to his maudlin letters to "Mate Woman," signed, "Mate Man," is a sufficient commentary on this "cultured" gentleman who could afford to be gracious to Ambrose Bierce because he knew nothing of "science" and was not well read in the philosophies.

The decade from 1900 to 1910 was a weak and fluffy period. It was rife with undergraduate free-thinking. In a series of articles by different writers, ranging from John Burroughs to Edwin Markham, on the subject "What Life Means to Me," that appeared in *The Cosmopolitan* about this time, is reflected a milk-and-water sentimentality that is quite incredible to-day. Ella Wheeler Wilcox, who was regarded as quite a thinker, summed up the spirit of the times in a glowing apostrophe: "All hail to life—life here, and life beyond! For earth is but the preparatory school for a larger experience, for a greater usefulness." Even Mr. Howells wrote a book entitled: "Between the Dark and Daylight." What chance had Mr. Bierce in such an age?

In his department of *The Cosmopolitan,* Bierce would occasionally review books. The temper of 1905 is suggested by a list of the books he noticed one month: "Mehr Licht" by Prof. Friederich Delitzsch; "History of Southern Literature" by Carl Holliday; "Temporal Power" by Marie Corelli, which sold 150,000 in a few weeks; "The Industrial Republic" by Upton Sinclair; "Pilgrimage" by C. A. Laurence; "Hypnotism and

Spiritism" by Dr. Joseph Lapponi; Countess Von Arnheim's "Elizabeth and Her German Garden"; Florence Wilkinson's "The Silent Door" and a new biography of Victor Hugo. It was a bewildering deluge but to Bierce it was infinitely amusing.

Occasionally he found a book that he could not review, as his critical vocabulary was inadequate. He once wrote the shortest book review ever written, by simply writing down the title of the book, the name of author and publisher, and then adding this comment: "The covers of this book are too far apart." He would sometimes print a typical extract in horrific but silent disgust, as he did when he discovered a novel with this interesting passage:

> "She remained inactive in his embrace for a considerable period, then modestly disengaging herself looked him full in the countenance and signified a desire for self-communion. By love's instinct he divined her purpose—she wanted to consider his proposal apart from the influence of the glamour of his personal presence. With the innate tact of a truly genteel nature he bade her good evening in French, and with measured tread paced away into the gathering gloom."

What comment could be made? In the midst of such a red plush age, Mr. Bierce's silent integrity becomes the more striking and admirable. He was not alone in his position as a reviewer, for a young gentleman in Baltimore was also discovering an occasional gem. As one comrade to another, he wrote to Bierce:

> "Last night I struck one in which the heroine wants the hero to agree to preserve her virginity. He refuses and the marriage is postponed. A rival now sics a voluptuous wench upon him and he succumbs. Result: a hurry call for 606. While he is being cured the rival marries the heroine and convinces her, by a practical demonstration, that she was wrong about virginity. So she divorces him as a reward, marries the hero (cured by now), and the two go to the mat."

Not the least amusing reading of the day were the sermonettes of Benjamin de Casseres, the apt pupil of Elbert Hubbard, who turned out such stuff as: "All rational pleasure is prayer— prayer is an uplifting, a rising of the soul toward the object

of its desire, an elevation of instinct." It need scarcely be observed that Bierce was out of sympathy with the entire body
of opinion during the decade that he lived in Washington.

But, if Bierce's cynicism was a fine guard against nonsense, it failed to forewarn him of the changes that time might
bring. He was resolutely determined to disbelieve, which is
sometimes the easiest road to gullibility. Accordingly when
Langley's attempted flight on December 8, 1903, was a failure, Bierce joined, in fact led, the jeering and derisive "skeptics" who said "I told you so." Why, it was preposterous to
think that aviation was feasible! Simply too absurd. Hence
he wrote "The Rise and Fall of the Aeroplane" as a record of
the limitations of skepticism. His friend Hudson Maxim wrote
an answer in which he asserted, with a confidence that must
have seemed insane in 1903, that aviation was already *fait
accompli.*

Bierce was occupied during his early years in Washington
with arranging for the publication of several books. He wrote
to S. O. Howes, in 1905, giving his sanction to a proposed
volume to be compiled from early newspaper essays and articles. But his interest was apparently limited to publishing old
copy; he had done little creative writing since 1893. "Fantastic
Fables" appeared in 1899, but it, too, was merely a volume
comprised of old newspaper copy. "Shapes of Clay," a volume
of doggerel, was published in 1903. It was financed by George
Sterling, illustrated by Herman Scheffauer, and its title was
the suggestion of Mrs. Atherton who had read "Omar Khay-
yam." Nearly all the scraps of verse in "Shapes of Clay" can,
however, be traced into newspaper and magazine files. This
was the case with all Bierce's books; they were merely compiled journalism. Even his famous short stories had appeared,
for the most part, in newspapers. Occasionally he would stop
and make a book, either of stories, verse, fables or essays, but
in truth he was merely putting his journalism into book form.
He never wrote a book in the sense that he set down to create
a work of art. Even "The Monk and the Hangman's Daughter"
was but an adaptation. Bierce was scarcely a man of letters, as
the term is generally used, but was always the journalist. He
possessed the journalist's habit of writing fragmentary pieces;
in other words, he wrote his column of "Prattle" week by

week without thought of continuity or coherence. It became a mental habit and explains the fact that he never wrote a first rate book, not even a book of satire.

He started to compile another volume from his voluminous collection of newspaper clippings. This time he showed better judgment, for he began to edit his "Devil's Dictionary." It was eventually printed by Doubleday, Page & Company under the title of "The Cynic's Word Book." While editing his work for this volume he wrote Howes: "The publishers doubtless think it a lot of clowneries like the book to which it gave the clue. When they find that it is only sense, wit and good English they will probably turn it down in a hurry." His publishers did force him to use a new title. The former title, "The Devil's Dictionary," was too demoniacal for the America of 1906. But the volume met with little success, and Bierce suspected that it had been shelved by his timid publishers. It contains, in its present edition, his best wit. It was undoubtedly a forerunner of Mr. Mencken's "jazz webster," although the idea of a dictionary of wit is an ancient trick of the satirist. Bierce was in no mood to write books. He was full of grave misgivings about his entire career, and his life was a denial of one value after another. Why write books? The pity is that he ceased to think of making books, even out of old newspaper clippings, at a time when his work might possibly have met with a general interest in this country.

The impetus to Bierce's republishing mania was the enthusiasm of S. O. Howes. It had been Howes' idea that a volume could be made of the early newspaper essays and to this suggestion Bierce had finally given his consent. It started the habit of looking over old clippings with a thought of more books. But surely Bierce did not entertain a very high regard for this material that Howes was editing, for he wrote: "I daresay there are many articles that are duplicated, and I blush to think how many times you'll come upon the same ideas and expressions. . . . Then, too, you'll find much that old man time has falsified, together with some views that I no longer hold, if I ever really and truly did." Writing to Sterling about his early work, he said: "Indeed, my intellectual status (whatever it may be, and God knows it's enough to make me blush) was of slow growth—as was my moral. I mean, I had not *literary sincerity.*" It was a sharp observation. An American, transformed overnight into a journalist in 1866, would have a predisposition for romantic theories. Art would tend to be for him, something strange, remote, and fantastic. He would feel it a duty to be tangential and whimsical in his essays and slightly perverse in his satire. It is lamentable that Bierce did not come to grips with life until he was past middle age.

Despite the fact that he saw clearly the defects of his early work, Bierce yet consented to its republication. It would seem that his chief motive was to see some of his journalism in book form before he died. He did not even take the trouble to re-write the material that Howes selected, nor did he edit it. It was merely a matter of paste and scissors for Howes. Bierce was undoubtedly growing old. In his letters to Howes, he stressed the importance of the worst material, overruled the selections of wit and satire, and included a plethora of solemn stuff about the fall of the republic and the dangers of anarchism. The first title selected for the volume was "The Curmudgeon Philosopher" and such it should have remained. It was later changed, however, to "The Shadow on the Dial." Bierce was rather apologetic about the volume and suggested to Howes, who was writing an introduction, "Maybe you can express a doubt about all these views being my final judgment of the matters treated and the impossibility of accurately drawing the line, always, between seriousness and levity. As I find it some-times impossible, I assume you must." It is difficult to reconcile his distrust of the worth of this material with his desire that it be published. His cynical misgivings about its reception were well founded. The book was sent to Doubleday, Page & Company, Brentano's, Paul Elder, Appleton's, The Century, and refused by all of them. Ultimately it was published by Alex. Robertson of San Francisco.

Some of the contemporary reviews of the book were rather shrewdly written. For example, one reviewer in *The Bookman* (October, 1909) wrote: "Contempt, not prophecy, has always been Mr. Bierce's animating spirit, and it is the animating spirit of these very slashing papers. . . . Anger is an excellent literary motive and the country needs a drubbing and always did; but somehow these wrathful passages seem to have no natural glow —only the steam heat of journalism." It would be difficult to

have selected a more appropriate phrase than "steam heat of
journalism" for, in truth, the papers were written as journalism.
The essays were, at the time they were written, fearless and able
editorials, but as a book of ideas they were, of course, not
representative of Bierce's power and ability. The London *Spectator* (August 28, 1909) expressed the same thought: "Still, to
be honest, we must own that Mr. Bierce's words sound to us
not infrequently to be somewhat wild and whirling." An article
in the St. Louis *Mirror* (May 5, 1904) said: "Mr. Bierce is a
Niagara running to waste," and the opinion was much to the
point. It is interesting to contrast the simplicity and "great good
sense" of his letters with the oracular manner that he unconsciously adopted in writing an essay. Of course, the letters are
of a later date, but this is only a partial apology for the worst
of his editorials. The essay, like the story, must be slightly ultra-
mundane, it must be pitched in a tempo other than the casual.

Yet there was never any clap-trap about Bierce's essays,
and when he was aiming at a specific target he always got
his man,—or woman,—as when he said that Mrs. Humphrey
Ward "suffers from a temporary impediment in her preach,"
and "Mary E. Wilkins Freeman's characters are presumably
male, manifestly middle-aged and prematurely moral." It was
only when he turned "curmudgeon philosopher" in old age that
he failed to be impressive. But, as George Santayana said of
Nietzsche: "We should forgive Nietzsche his boyish blasphemies. He hated with clearness, if he did not know what to love."

*   *   *

THE days that passed were idle and dull. It was a period of
boredom, the age of torpor. Gentlemen wheeled bicycles and
ladies read thrilling accounts of M. Aguinaldo and the iniquitous prison system in Delaware. The years seemed hollow and
bereft of significance. Bierce fell into the mood of sad reveries.
He was irritated by futility, annoyed by misgivings about his
own career. There was no animating principle to save his life
from an unbearable emptiness. He was utterly quiet and inactive but a restless and impatient anxiety tugged constantly, urg-
ing him away from Washington. One illness followed another
in remorseless succession. James Hopper called at his apart-

ment in Washington and found Bierce suffering from lumbago. Another visitor records an impression of a weak and despondent man who had just recovered from an attack of asthma. His letters reflect the same low spirits. He enjoyed only "brief flashes of good health"; "I've got to be sick wherever I am, and prefer to be sick at 'home' among my angel girls who think it good fun to nurse me"; and, from another letter, "This is my birthday. I am 366 years old."

To his sickness and despondency was added the pain of shattered friendships. It was during this period that he quarreled with Scheffauer. The particular details are unimportant. As a matter of fact, they probably had nothing whatever to do with the disagreement which was the result of a growing suspicion on the part of Bierce that Scheffauer was irresponsible and ungrateful. In this Bierce's suspicions were well founded. But when the actual break came, it was a sharp, cruel pain. Scheffauer had written to a "mutual friend" that, in a controversy with Bierce, he had "come out on top." The friend, of course, repeated the remark to Bierce, who replied, "So Scheff thinks he 'comes out on top'—he may have observed scum doing so." But, in a letter to Howes, he said: "I've had a rather disheartening experience with Scheff. Still, I retain some small vestiges of my faith in the existence of a rudimentary gratitude in the heart of man. Don't know about a German." A month later he was still sad and depressed about the quarrel with Sheffauer. "A habit of the heart is not easily overcome. But I've just had to break off personal relations with him—the second time."

Sterling came east for a visit, and he was with Bierce at Sag Harbor for a few weeks one summer. With the publication of "A Wine of Wizardy" in *The Cosmopolitan,* Sterling came into national fame. Bierce had sent the poem to a dozen or so magazines before inducing the editor of *The Cosmopolitan* to accept it. It seems that Sam Chamberlain had read Lord Bryce's remark about the scarcity of poets in America, and had accepted the poem so that he might make it the basis of an editorial devoted to Lord Bryce's shortcomings as a critic of American life. Bierce was furious when he discovered that his "pupil's" poem was accepted only that it might be put to such an inglorious use.

With this notoriety and fame, Sterling began to act in accordance with the best poetic traditions and Bierce was, at first, very tolerant. Writing to Howes, Bierce had occasion to remark: "George Sterling has written twenty-two love sonnets; so he says, but he has sent me only one of them and says that none of them can be printed. Guess he's afraid—he has a wife. Why can't a fellow content himself (as I have learned to do) with a bird and a squirrel?—or (as you do) with a book and a julep? The irrationality of our race is beyond belief." The group of sonnets swelled in the course of time to a bulk sufficient for publication as "Sonnets to Craig," although the wife of a drummer at Carmel received twice as many sonnets as did "Craig." These escapades came to annoy Bierce excessively. He never could tolerate mere "Bohemianism." It impressed him as tawdry, vulgar and unnecessary. Here again Bierce could not overcome his swift apprehension of unworth. He might, conceivably, have been more tolerant. Sterling, in later years, came to realize the truth of much that Bierce had told him. In an essay in *The Overland Monthly* (November, 1926) he echoed the philosophy of "nothing matters" in terms that might have been written by Bierce himself. "Poor dancer on the flints and shards in the temple porches, turn home," so one is moved to cry when contemplating the pain and suffering that Sterling underwent. If Bierce had been able to foresee the future, he might possibly have been less censorious.

While Howes was working on the book of essays, Bierce and Percival Pollard decided to pay him a visit at Galveston. They left Washington in October of 1907, and stopped off at Chattanooga. It was a memorable trip for Bierce. He paraded Pollard around the battlefields with a proprietary interest, pointing out monuments and delighting his guest with the quality of his reminiscences. Bierce was actually excited and the boredom of many idle and fruitless months in Washington was forgotten in this luxurious reveling in the romantic vistas which he conjured up out of memory. The experience had the same satisfactory sadness of that former summer in the Cheat Mountains, only it was more moving and the emotions it engendered were more profound. And what memories flouted his soul! Men had died here, on these sun-illuminated hillcrests, and he had shot some of them. Had it actually happened? Or was it a dream

of his youth? Battle cries and death yells, and murderous volleys
of shot had once torn all this loveliness into a mad medley of
hell and the skies had bled with man's incurable folly. And all
for what? They had not even known precisely what they were
fighting for! Years later he could stroll through these grounds,
with Percival Pollard, and chat casually of divers things! There
was something uncannily light and unreal and shifting about
these masks of appearance. "A persistent hallucination" goes
with romanticism, and Bierce was forever conjuring up seductive dreams of lost glamour and glory.

At Galveston, Bierce had a delightful visit. He met a number
of Howes' friends and found them congenial, admiring and
flattering. Rabbi Cohen took Bierce through his library and
Bierce presented to him a copy of "Write It Right," with the inscription:

"As one who does not hunger is oft bidden to the feast
The author gives this little book to one who needs it least."

Mrs. Schoolfield,—"that dear woman,"—entertained him. He
fought over Chickamauga with Mr. Brown, who had been in the
Southern army. And he shared Howes' enthusiasm for Anatole
France. They were pleasant, idle, days. He spent some time in
New Orleans with Pollard, and then left alone, coming back on
the *Lampasas* and stopping off at Key West.

While he had been in the South, he had talked with Howes
of South America. It fanned an old enthusiasm and the thought
kept suggesting itself that some day he would journey south
again, with finality and dramatic dignity. This first journey had
been quite pleasant, and it suggested another trip, for Bierce
kept repeating phases of experience like a true romantic, always seeking some unique quality describable as "adventure"
and thinking that states of mind can be regained, as though they
were purely objective. Howes had suggested a trip to Yucatan
and it had met with Bierce's prompt approval. A correspondent,
H. A. Moss, who was connected with the American consulate
in Brazil, wrote alluring letters about South America. James
Watkins and Ralph Smith, two of his dearest friends, had gone
to Tepic in 1881 on a mining expedition and had written glorious accounts of the west coast. Roberto Andrade, the Ecuado-

rian anarchist, had made a translation of some of his stories into Spanish, and their publication had provoked considerable interest in his work in Central America. Then, too, there came enthusiastic letters from Benjamin de Casseres, who was writing for *El Diario* in Mexico City. All these incidents tended to fix his attention on the south. He sorely wished he had gone into Mexico, for on his return he found Washington more dreary and uninteresting than ever.

He began to quarrel incessantly with the various Hearst editors: Chamberlain, Norcross and Rudolph Bloch. Mr. Hearst tried to sick his pet bulldog on Pulitzer but found that Bierce was stubborn. "I don't like the job of chained bulldog to be let loose only to tear the panties off the boys who throw rocks at you. You wouldn't like it yourself in my place. Henceforth I won't bite anybody, a quiet life for mine. I'm going to be a literary gent, thank you,—it is nicer, and there is nobody to say me nay." So Bierce wrote under date of July 8, 1907. It followed a quarrel that was soon forgotten, but others came in rapid succession. Finally when Bierce began to compile his "Collected Works" for Mr. Neale, he quit the Hearst papers altogether and his copy ceased to appear in *The Cosmopolitan* after 1909.

The quarrels were really farcical. Since 1887 they had invariably run the same course: heated words, resignation, reconciliation. A characteristic expression is this to Howes: "I'm off Mr. Hearst's payroll—by voluntary resignation. Couldn't stand the monkeying of his editors with my stuff, and had tired of appealing to him. He always decides in my favor, but never enforces his decisions by 'appropriate penalties.' So I'm without any income, but retain my self-respect, which is not a bad substitute. Anything that comes so high ought to be good." He would follow these grand notes with such weak words as: "My emancipation from Mr. Hearst's service was, alas, brief. He did not want it that way, and I can't resist him, for he has been, on the whole, mighty good to me." In another note, this time to Robert Mackay, Bierce wrote: "I'm a wage-slave for Hearst. But then the negro quarters are fairly comfortable, the corn and bacon tolerable and the overseer's whip can't reach me here in Washington. Sometimes I think I should like to be a free nigger, but I dunno'."

Hearst was always good humored in his replies. In one
note he said: "If you will kindly excuse me for saying so, you
have devoted so much of your letter to soaking Mr. Chamberlain and proving that I am wrong in everything that I ever said
or did, that the details of the arrangement have not received
much attention. The Hon. William Randolph Hearst is
quite as anxious to do what is right and what is agreeable to
all as Will Hearst ever was and I wish I could get you to believe that." Bierce met Hearst one day in New York and announced that inasmuch as he did no work for the newspapers
and little for *The Cosmopolitan,* that his pay should be adjusted. Mr. Hearst said: "You haven't heard me shrieking about
that, have you?" and Bierce was compelled to admit that he
hadn't. Mr. Hearst's tether of a liberal salary account bound
Bierce far more tightly than any other means that could have
been employed. Bierce was decent and loyal, and always realized
that Mr. Hearst had been kind, although he was skeptical of
the motives behind this kindness.

But, if Bierce had not desired to write for Mr. Hearst's
periodicals, there were certainly other opportunities. His papers
contain any number of requests for copy from prominent magazines, offering attractive rates for any stories that he might
submit. *Hampton's, The Delineator, Town Topics, McClure's,*
and many other magazines wrote Bierce for copy. Willard
Huntington Wright, as editor of *The Smart Set,* wrote for
material and offered five cents a word. Bierce commented upon
the offer to a friend and said: "One hates to be caught with a
magazine having so hateful a title. It is to be read secretly, as
we commit adultery and murder."

It is quite apparent that he had no new plans whatever
during the period of his Washington residence. He was merely
revising and correcting, preparing for the "Collected Works."
Even the "curmudgeon philosopher" had lost interest in current happenings. He was musing about the troubling nature of
quietness and even "art" seemed trivial and unimportant. His
hours in the apartment were broken with amusement over the
antics of "John Henry Legs," a pet squirrel, and walks in the
park with "my girls." He jotted down in his letters such an event
as a canoeing expedition as though it were of the utmost importance. He would often visit Pollard at Lyme, Connecticut,

and got to be quite a fearless canoeist, causing his friends no end of worry and alarm by his intrepid expeditions. It was indeed a dreary existence. He would flee for a week or so, visit Mr. and Mrs. Martin at West Point and spend long hours on the verandah of the Officers' Club talking about everything under the sun. He read the verse of Ezra Pound, Samuel Loveman and James Elroy Flecker, with interest, when it was sent him in manuscript. But it seemed so useless, trivial and inconsequential when compared with his own sense of despair and boredom. He was so conscious of death that life seemed a dreary and insignificant buzzing. Why was he so destitute of certainty, so fatigued and weary of existence?

In later years his cynicism sounded off key; it had unquestionably a false note. Bierce learned the trick of paradox early in his career as a professional wit. He could twist expressions about in such a manner that the reader would jump with amazement and call this experiment in the dissociation of ideas "wit." But the process with Bierce was more a trick of expression than it was a quest for information. For, as Mr. Eliot has observed, "true cynicism is a fault of the temperament of the observer, not a conclusion arising naturally from the contemplation of the object; it is quite the reverse of 'facing facts.'" And so it was with Bierce. He had really outgrown his cynicism but he did not seem at all aware of the fact. His was the loneliness of the man whose ideas far outran the information of his time. Just as his cynicism had pre-dated modern cynicism by the span of a generation, just so his later reactions found no strengthening verification in the thought of his contemporaries. He always had to trust his "hunches" and "prejudices" against the showy and pretentious information of the period. Naturally he was forced to carry over his early cynicism as a convenient mechanism of protection.

In these last years he worked feverishly on the "Collected Works" edition in twelve volumes. His letters to Mr. Neale reveal how deeply concerned he was with this enterprise into which he was putting money, time, the efforts of his secretary, and the money of his friends who were circularized for subscriptions. He had to have the feeling that all those newspaper clippings were to be converted into neat pages in a handsome edition. His letters of the period are replete with references to the enterprise, discussions of publishing details, plans for prospectuses, and proofs, proofs, proofs. The last four years of his life were taken up with proofreading and little else, correcting proof after proof, and even paying for the privilege of correction. Mr. Neale's chief typesetter annoyed him to the point of exasperation and he wrote long letters of remonstrance, complaining of the "peculiar" variety of such ignorance which was "dark, profound and general." He was determined to have a collected edition of his work. This feeling was indicative of his sense of misspent time and effort. A letter of praise which he received from Theodore Bonnet actually made him sad! After reading the elaborate prospectus which Mr. Neale had arranged, he wrote: "The only thing that saddens me in reading the prospectus is the thought of how I might have merited the praise if I had applied myself more to my art and less to pleasure." This is a strange note, indeed, for the Bierce of legend. His life had been too much an affair of fiery and impulsive battling, jostlings and tournaments,—Sancho Panza and the Windmill.

He was pleasantly contemptuous of the life about him. Mr. Roosevelt's "charlatanism" disgusted him. Moreover, "Washington is now lousy with statesmen, and I stay indoors a good deal to watch my pocketbook." Everywhere about him he noticed mediocrity, sentimental and brummagem thinking. He began to suspect even his friend Percival Pollard who, in truth, was always something of the dilettante. "Elinor Glyn is here being loudly entertained and uttering the most bombastic nonsense, proving herself a vulgarian of singularly cheap distinction. By the way, Pollard thinks her book fine. I begin to despair of Pollard." And, then, came Mr. Taft. "We had a most disgusting inauguration—with blackguardy rampant and to-day the newspapers print page after page of lickspittle adulation of Taft, Mrs. Taft, the cub Tafts, and everybody connected with the administration. I wish I could get the *smell* of my country out of my nose and clothing." He was no longer young enough to be amused by such nonsense, it weighed heavily upon him, and he longed for a surcease from the monotony of mediocrity. "Compared with the Congress of our forefathers, the Congress of to-day is as a flock of angels to an executive body of the Western Federation of Miners."

An occasional "champagne week end" in New York, with a dinner party for Blanche Bates at Delmonico's, helped to break the tedium of being famous but bored. He was not even reading much. "It requires a regiment of Infantry and two field pieces to get me to read a novel.—We have autumnal weather at last and I have resumed canoeing, to the manifest advantage of my temper. Get a canoe and Fate cannot harm you—though you may drown." So he wrote to Howes. He did read one book with which he was in hearty accord; in fact, he thought that its author might have used some of his own newspaper articles in writing the volume. It was "Janus in Modern Life," by Dr. Flinders Petries, a book of reactionary ideas, tracing the parallel between the rise of the Roman rabble and the agitation of labor unions in modern times. Then, too, he was amused by a book on "The So-Called Christopher Columbus," by Goodrich, and his old friend, Col. Willis Brewer, of Haynesville, Alabama, had in "Egypt and Israel" destroyed another myth. To question the histories of Christ and Christopher Columbus was a noble enterprise in America, savoring of unspeakable heroism. He had read John Galsworthy's "In Motley," and when he selected a title for Volume XII of his "Collected Works" he apparently carried the title over unthinkingly. He read many war texts, notably Sergeant's heavy tome on the Santiago Campaign. He had assisted Archibald Gracie somewhat in writing "The Truth about Chickamauga." At the request of General W. W. Witherspoon, Bierce addressed The Army War College faculty and class on October 3, 1908, on the subject of uniform orders and commands in the military service, which he had devised. He took rambles in the park where he made pets of the squirrels and had his picture taken with them in his hands. He wrote Howes: "The squirrel of the picture lives in a public park, but he loves me just the same—rather better with pecans than without." It was a period of Coventry. Squirrels, walks in the park, idle hours, proof-reading, and an occasional book. Would something ever happen? Was he to die in Washington of acute lumbago or be stricken by that old "adversary of souls," his asthma?

Despite a few minor interests, the general tone of his letters is that of unbearable boredom. I refer to the unpublished letters. A few phrases are significant: "Nothing goes on here

but the talk in Congress"—"I'm weak and will-less"—"I'm
older than the iron hills." Even the praise which his work was
beginning to inspire in many quarters, did not interest him.
He was pushing rapidly forward; the currents were quicken-
ing; it would not be long until he was one of the initiated. In
contemplation of death, he began to get an accurate perspective
on his life and career. His "Little Johnny" stories suddenly
became "rot"; his ironic romance, "The Monk and the Hangman's Daughter," was merely a "yarn"—"simple, sentimental,
religious and sensational." What did it all matter compared with
the oppressing sense of futility that belittled every activity and
made vanity seem the most laughable folly. And what was this
writing but "vanity"? He did not go as far as Anatole France
and call it a "lying pretense," but its ultimate importance was
negligible.

He was convinced afresh of the unreality of appearances.
While he was preparing himself for a swift and shocking duck-
ing in the Styx, the most inconsequential and ridiculous talk
imaginable droned in lassitude about him: woman's rights, labor
unions, the whisper of anti-booze propaganda, the "problem"
novel, Spiritualism, Marie Corelli, Elbert Hubbard and the
poetry of Ella Wheeler Wilcox. Why write anything? If he
did, one of Mr. Hearst's ingenious young men would deck it
out with barbaric banners and streamers, and convert it into an
apocryphal revelation. His protests seem futile and almost
pathetic. No one paid any attention to his demands. He wrote
an article called "The Historian of the Future" and Mr. Hearst
had written him: "I thought we might have a sky-line of New
York across the top, and at the bottom your group of skin-clad
savages gnawing a raw bone; or else we might have merely an
imaginative illustration of the Historian of 3940 writing his
history. Do you like either of these, or would you prefer some
sort of mystic cartoon à la Vedder of greed destroying civilization? I suppose you would rather not have anything, but as we
have got to spoil the article in some way, will you not indicate
what would be the least objectionable?" So far as Mr. Hearst
and his men were concerned, Bierce was just an eccentric old
gentleman whose whims must be humored if possible, although
there was no penalty if he was treated with disrespect. He was,
indeed, "a magnificent crystallization."

CHAPTER XVIII

HOLIDAY

BY 1910 Bierce had turned the last corner in the road and realized that his active career was over. He had definitely ceased to write for any of Mr. Hearst's publications, and, so free did he feel from any obligation to Mr. Hearst personally that he began to jot down notes for a proposed biography. Nothing remained but to complete the editing and selecting of material for the imposing "Collected Works" edition, a matter of "adding, subtracting and dividing" old paragraphs into books. He had arrived at the period of rest and pause and yet he did not feel much like abandoning the old life. There were moments when he felt marvelously young and fresh, but it was a deceptive elation. At times his letters would have his early strength and vigor in every line and his wit would be sharper than ever. But there was always a recurrent strain of sadness, the result of an inevitable and disheartening realization that he was but a shell of the man he had been, a shadowy outline of the old "Prattler." In his despair he began to think of California, old scenes and old faces. He was curious about the place; perhaps he might recapture that illusive feeling of splendor if he returned to the scenes with which it had been associated. And so, in the spring of 1910, he sailed for California.

Ten years had passed since he left California. Now that he was returning, he was excited about the trip. It promised to be something of an adventure. He wrote of it with eagerness and his letters counted the days until he sailed. Perhaps San Francisco would not be the same: the fire had razed many old landmarks and the years had taken their toll. But it would be

a pleasant trip, nevertheless. There was surely no reason why
he should remain in Washington. Moreover, he wanted to see
George Sterling again, who was saving some choice bottles:
"The booze that is like the shadow of a great rock in a weary
land." He sold his canoe, said good-by to a few pet squirrels,
and set sail.

He left in April of 1910, sailing to Colon and through the
Isthmus. The Canal Zone interested him immensely as he had
visited Aspinwall in 1865. The voyage stirred the enthusiasm
of that earlier visit to Galveston, and he began to focus his
attention on South America and its alluring "romance" and
"uncertainty." It was the only land left for the adventurous.
He would return to Central America some day and journey
farther south to the Andes. In this way he might be able to rid
himself of all this old baggage of ideas, dreams, blasted hopes,
and sorrows. For at sixty-eight this appalling "cynic" was still
full of a boyish belief that he might discover an *ultima thule*.

As soon as he arrived in San Francisco, he left immediately for his brother's cabin perched high on a bluff overlooking
the river near Guerneville, California. It was enjoyable beyond
his expectations: a fine interval of quiet, unbroken by the annoyance of duty. The scenery about Guerneville was of a breath-
taking loveliness. He wrote to Neale from Guerneville: "I had
a pleasant but rather long voyage. Was three days in Panama
and saw something of the canal work. On arrival at San Francisco, I gathered up my nephew and his wife and came directly
up here to my brother's shack in the mountainside. And, faith!
it is paradise. Right above a beautiful river (we have a canoe)
with a half-dozen pretty villages in sight below, and the woods
already filled with their summer population from the city. One
meets groups of pretty girls in camping attire everywhere—
some of whom say that I held them on my knee when they
were little (I mean to again), although I fancy it may have
been their grandmothers." He paddled up to town every day
for his mail; the mountainside was ablaze with flowers; and he
was to see George Sterling soon as they were leaving for
Yosemite.

At Yosemite he was even more amazed with the beauty
about him. "As to the 'sights' to be seen, they are simply unspeakable. I haven't it in my heart to say a word about it."

Such a pastoral mood is certainly out of keeping with the "Bitter" Bierce of legend, the ruthless satirist of the Pacific Coast. It is more the expression of an old man who had almost forgotten about life. In July he was back in Berkeley, and, at the Key Route Inn in Oakland, was royally entertained by so many hosts that he could scarcely remember their names. Many old grievances were forgotten and even the journals edited by former rivals were quite polite and docile. The era of bloody journalism in California was at an end.

But there were several uneasy situations that he had to face. When he left for Washington in 1899, he had ceased writing to several old friends, whether out of pique or offended feelings or laziness, no one knows. But he had graciously decided to forget about this neglect and wrote several notes arranging interviews. Soon after his arrival in California, he had written pleasantly to Amy Cecil and suggested an appointment, as though the silence of ten years would explain itself. They met and talked quite casually of a "variety of things," but he offered no explanation of his conduct. Finally, as the day came to a close, he admitted that he had failed to write because of "something" which he later found to be untrue. But if he had expected indifference, he was mistaken. Mrs. Cecil, like several of his other friends, decided that such a sensitive and temperamental creature should be left to his own devices.

It was the end of an old and dear friendship. Some trivial utterance, some letter of gossip, had reached him in Washington, and he had frozen into an unearthly reserve that it had required ten years to thaw. He had not written for an explanation. His experience with friends had been so precarious, that an intimation of disloyalty was enough. He was monumentally unable to deal with human nature,—a sublime incompetent. Some weeks after their first interview, Bierce saw Mrs. Cecil in the Palace Hotel. He bowed rather formally and went his way. They never met again. He might understand but he could not, psychologically, act upon the promptings of impulse. People should not allow their hearts to rule their heads, he was always writing his young admirers, to which one is tempted to add: neither should they be ridiculous.

And his parting with Mrs. Cecil was not an isolated incident. He had quarreled with Leila Cotton before leaving California. It had been a petty misunderstanding, compound of unwarranted inference and conjecture. When Bierce returned in 1910, he invited Miss Cotton to lunch and they went for a stroll in an Oakland cemetery, looking for Lily Walsh's grave. They talked of the fine hours at "Bohemia," of amusing incidents, of old friends. He told her that he was "written out" and that some day he "would go away." It was a phrase that he was beginning to repeat,—a preparation for a farewell. But when they parted that day it was to be for all time. There had been no explanation, not a word of apology, not a token of faith. Had he been ashamed of his impulsive repudiation of an old friendship?

In August there was a round of pleasure: the Bohemian Club play on the Russian River. "The finest spectacle that I ever saw," so he wrote to a friend. But, despite the Grove Play, and despite the luncheons, and parties in San Francisco and Oakland, he was seized with impatience. "I don't find San Francisco quite the same," he wrote. He had written to Scheffauer, prior to their severance of relations, that "San Francisco is not the same city that it was. Where are the courageous men of the Vigilante Committee of the old days? Where are those who broke the head of the mob with pick-handles in the time of Dennis Kearney? I mean, where are those like them? It is clear that the business men and the professional men of to-day are no better than the labor unions and not half so brave." In truth, the San Francisco that he visited in 1910 had little in common with the San Francisco that he knew of old, despite the pamphlets, brochures, and novels to the contrary. He was not in touch with the new city; his former associates were now old men, who had retired. It was a region peopled with ghosts and specters.

Towards the end of the summer, Miss Christiansen arrived on a vacation, and Bierce saw her for a few moments before she left for Napa, "carrying my bird—without which she could not live." They corrected more proofs, checked over some business, and then she left. A few weeks later she returned to Washington to sell some of his favorite Mergenthaler stock and wire him the proceeds. In September he was writing Howes, "my health is pretty good, but I'm a bit homesick. Guess I've had too good a time." And in October, he "left California like a thief in the night" in an effort to avoid his friends. He arrived back in Washington on November 4th, after stopping over at the Grand Canyon for a few days.

The apartment was stuffy; he had an attack of asthma; there was an accumulation of proofs to correct and letters to answer; and his pet squirrel had died. Naturally he was irritable and grouchy. The young newspapermen did not visit him for some weeks. He was still furious when he noticed that the manager of the Washington Directory had printed his name "Major" Bierce in the directory. He sat down and penned him a crisp note, in which he said: "I wish to repeat my protest against being described in your directory as belonging to the United States Army, when in fact I am a civilian, and to beg that in the future my name be omitted from the Directory." He quarreled with the Army and Navy Club, resigned, and then permitted himself to be coaxed back into the fold. Of such things were his days composed.

This editing of the "Collected Works" was becoming wearisome. He was devoting his entire time to the tedious work of sorting out all clippings, pasting, cutting, editing. The edition was appearing, volume by volume, and was creating no little wonderment in many minds. There was absolutely no demand for a "collected" edition of his works; the entire project was pure vanity. Bierce knew that much of the material reprinted was worthless; his letters, particularly those to S. O. Howes, reveal this fact unmistakably. But the desire to have that massive set of books on the library shelves of America, was too much for the "curmudgeon philosopher," and he yielded a point to his vanity. Professor Fred Lewis Pattee was rather confused by the edition, and wrote asking Mr. Neale if Bierce was "really a great man." Editors were equally nonplussed. Franklin K. Lane wrote a hasty letter to a New York newspaper denouncing the author as a "hideous monster, so like the mixture of dragon, lizard, bat and snake as to be unnameable." The old query: "Who is Ambrose Bierce?" was setting tongues wagging again. American critics were quite incompetent in reviewing the edition and generally wearied of the task after the first few volumes appeared.

In England the reviewers received the volumes of the "Collected Works" with less enthusiasm and more sense. A writer on *The Anthenæum* wrote an interesting review of one volume in which he said:

> "It might be interesting to consider what are the prepossessions, the constituents of the alienating view of life, which makes such a solecism (*i. e.* Bierce's views on the novel) possible in an intelligence so acute. Lacking space for that excursus, let us say that though our author's other critical pronouncements are tangential enough, none is so flagrantly wide of the mark, and many must have been a distinct mental acquisition to the audience which Mr. Bierce instructs. . . . The great fault or misfortune of Mr. Bierce is that, when he is not kept right by the pressure of an artistic purpose serious enough to inhibit the characteristic sallies of his intelligence, his writing is apt to be punctuated with lapses and excesses, tags of humor or extravagance or verbiage, which bring it into line, for the moment at least, with very common matter." *

What seems to have troubled so many reviewers was the impression that insinuated itself into their consciousness, that Bierce was really an important and vital personality. His force reached them through layers of "lapses and excesses" and the "extravagances of verbiage," and unsteadied their pens. But little was known of his life, so they could only wonder in silence.

Just how much of Bierce's work went into the "Collected Works" is a question that is difficult to answer. A great deal of his "Prattle" may be found throughout the twelve volumes, but a vast amount of his journalism did not commend itself sufficient to warrant inclusion. In fact, Bierce omitted the most extravagantly amusing passages of "Prattle," as they seemed too rowdy for the handsome morocco bindings that Mr. Neale had provided. But it would be impossible to edit the unpublished satire, as it is entirely fragmentary and nearly every incident would require a footnote. It seems unthinkable, however, that Bierce should have omitted some of his sharpest lines in order that he might include those horrible "Little Johnny" yarns of which he wrote Mr. Neale that it pained him to have to kill any of them.

He led a rather lazy existence at Washington during these last years. The monotony of proofreading was broken by an

* *The Anthenæum,* September 16, 1911.

occasional visit with Dr. Franklin in Schenectady and a few days at West Point with the Martins. He would also visit Mrs. Ruth Guthrie Harding at Paterson, New Jersey. She, too, was another "pupil." With some of these friends, Bierce apparently adopted the slightly theatrical attitude of the man overcome with a sense of lost illusions. It is always a pleasant and successful act, as it secretly flatters the spectator, who, inferentially, must be happier than the sufferer, generally a slightly romantic, Byron-esque gentleman "tortured" with sorrows. Such was the Mr. "Boythorn" Bierce that Mrs. Harding knew. "At times," she has written with great ecstasy, "I used to feel as if I were strolling with Francis of Assisi." It is difficult not to blame Bierce for such a line as that: he should have realized the consequences of tenderness on the pen of a romantic lady. It was but another indication that he was more sorely than ever in need of a catharsis that would purge him of "shadow making" and romantic gesturing. He was often on the quest of adventure, dramatic situations, and, it must be confessed, an audience.

The origin of his tangential, quixotic gallantry would be difficult to trace. The world was not to him the tragi-comic spectacle that it was to Anatole France. It was more a matter of sharp distinctions; impassable gulfs; worlds of thought that were complete in themselves. This habit of thought warred against any possible synthesis since it prevented the identification of the thinker with his world. The roots of idealism in subjective experience was a theory that would have been repulsive to Bierce. His idealism was ever a star in the sky. Like his conception of "art" as a world of romantic strangeness and bizarre sensation, his idealism had no relation with the material world. He collected weird incidents from the press as the material for romantic stories, that is, strange stories, when all he needed to do was to look at life. He was thus at a tangent. Even his wit and satire broke into unassimilable fragments, unrelated crystals that gleamed impishly in the sunlight. Yet there was a great force about the lines, since inwardly he felt the impulse to create but his hand was stayed by an archaic tradition. When he stepped out of the realm of his unreal ideas, he was literally a Titan. But, under the baleful influence of his beloved "shadows," he was capable at times of being a Romantic Figure. No man ever takes the trouble to write epigrams about love who is not at the same time slightly romantic. "Disillusion" is not understanding any more than a headache is wisdom. What he needed was to be plunged layers deep in the so-called material world and to be in sympathy with fundamental rhythms. "Idealism," in his sense, was remote and unnecessary. He saw the dilemma at times but it was too late to amend.

There was an interval when he was away at Sag Harbor, "motorboating, autoing, and so forth," with George Sterling, who was visiting in the east. But it was a short vacation, and he was soon back in Washington. "I'm still playing at asthma. It isn't much of a game; I prefer draw-poker. But asthma is cheaper." The great edition of his work was progressing rapidly and he wrote to Neale that "before 'cashing in' I should like to know that some far future edition of my books will be brought out in a little better shape." His ambition was to be fully realized and his vanity appeased, for the complete set was put on the market about this time.

That it might be properly ushered into the world, Mr. Neale and Bierce conspired over a prospectus, which, properly considered, is one of the most amusing documents imaginable. In it they collected all the odds and ends of compliments and opinions that Bierce could cull from his files. Some of these comments were forced, some absurd, some ridiculous, but they were all included. The prospectus when printed was naturally a most bewildering document. What could the uninitiated think of such a magnificent brochure? "He is a literary Rhadamanthus," "He is as interesting as a kangaroo," said the faithful J. S. Cowley-Brown, who wrote blurbs about Bierce in the *Musical Leader* and *Black and White* (London), and occasionally tapped him for a slight loan! Brander Mathews was present with a gentle and diplomatic compliment. Michael Williams shouted, "Hail, Bierce!" Arthur Machen, William Marion Reedy, Richard Barry, and Gertrude Atherton made their contributions. Mr. Arthur Brisbane, with customary grandeur, said that: "Ambrose Bierce is one of the best writers in America, perhaps the best." Joel Chandler Harris was so enthusiastic that if he were "Santa Claus he would give every one a set of Ambrose Bierce's works." Elbert Hubbard, recognizing the fact that Bierce could write a nice sermonette when in the mood, announced that "Ambrose Bierce is the boss of us all," and then added the famous prophecy which Mr. Vincent Starrett quoted in his little brochure but omitted the name of the prophet, fearing (perhaps?) that its association might injure Bierce's reputation: "Some day he will go up on Mount Horeb and forget to come down. No man will see his death struggle, for he'll cover his face with his cloak of motley, and if he sends us a wireless it will be this: ' 'Tis a Grave subject.' " Perhaps it was Hubbard's suggestion that prompted the final melodrama. The prospectus will remain a literary and psychological curiosity. Arthur Machen, Haldane MacFall, Edwin Markham, Franklin Lane, Joel Chandler Harris, Elbert Hubbard, Eugene Field, and the Wellington, New Zealand, *Searchlight!*

Bierce had few close friends in the East. On the coast, "Charley" Kauffman, Judge Boalt, Watkins, and quite a number of others, were always faithful and loyal. But in Washington he had no associates with whom he felt truly companionable, if one may make a notable exception of Percival Pollard. They began to correspond in the early nineties when Pollard was one of the first Eastern reviewers to become enthusiastic about Bierce's work, and naturally they soon met after Bierce went to live in Washington. Pollard's home, when he was not globetrotting, was in Baltimore. He spent much time with Bierce, at Washington and Baltimore, and also during the summer home in Connecticut. The intervals when Pollard was abroad were always noted in Bierce's letters with a shade of regret. They were constantly in correspondence and had many ideas which they shared in common, although Pollard was of a different temperament.

But even this friendship, imperfect as it was, soon came to a tragic end. Pollard died in Baltimore, December 7, 1911. His death was a great blow even to Bierce, whose reaction to death had been dulled by hard usage. He was stubbornly adamant about Pollard's death, as though he would stifle his suffering by the harshness of brusque statement. He wrote to Howes, announcing the fact of Pollard's death, and added: "That is all I feel like writing." A few days later he wrote again to Howes: "You would hardly care to have in memory the image of Pollard that I must carry for life. You'd not have recognized that handiwork of death. Poor Percy! he must have suffered horribly to become like that. *Well,* we put him into the furnace, as he would have wished, and there is no more Percy." He was determined that nothing should matter, but there is a fatal hesitancy about that "well." He attended the funeral in company with Mr. Mencken, who recalls that he wore an "elegant plug-hat," and told some curious anecdotes on the way to the crematory, chiefly of morgues, dissecting-rooms, and lonely churchyards.

The horrible image of Pollard's face, writhed in agony, haunted Bierce for days. The giddy emptiness of life—a buzzing and unnecessary annoyance—outlined against the sharp drop-curtain of death. Nothing remained for him but death, and he had been thinking of it more and more during these last idle years in Washington. How futile and misspent and absurd his life now seemed! A little fame, a little useless and annoying notoriety, and then this awful fatuous existence in an apartment house! It was better when Sherman was marching to Georgia or when Grant was surprised at Shiloh: a life of wild, exciting and dramatic action. How long, Lord, how long? He was "suffering only from life and that would bring its own cure"; "nothin' doin' here—same old dreary round of religious duties tempered by temptations to murder my fool fellow citizens." It was at this time, too, that he wrote Mrs. McCrackin that "fear of death is the invention of a humorist," recalling Beddoes' lines:

> "For Death is more a 'jest' than life: you see
> Contempt grows quick from familiarity.
> I owe this wisdom to Anatomy."

Bierce owed his wisdom to a slightly different experience than that of a German medical school, but it was anatomical in its way. There was material enough for the students of anatomy at Shiloh.

Two letters to Howes of about this time are suggestive of his desire to run away from an engulfing boredom and ennui. In one letter he said: "In your place I'd go west—to Arizona, New Mexico—anywhere west—and do any old thing I could get to do. Even if you should not 'succeed,' it is no hardship to be poor in the west; and you'll not know the joy of living till you 'cut' cities. Sell the books and just *go,* relying on luck. Nobody suffers real privations in a new country." For Bierce this impatient eagerness for life in the "rough" and a return to nature via Rousseau, was strange indeed. He was, again, transposing ideas in his imagination. It was not that he desired a new experience, or a new land, but that he wanted to find the key that would lead him back to the vital current of existence. Another letter to Howes contains a revealing passage: "In the west is room enow to expand the mind and heart. . . . *Even at my age* I feel the 'call of it,' and it is among the probabilities that I shall not 'return to civilization' when I again get out of the reek of it." The letter is dated April 26, 1912. His plan of escape was already completed in his mind. There is no questioning the ominous ring of the passages in quotations marks, particularly that phrase, "return to civilization." How often has it been used with reference to him since 1913!

During the spring of 1912 he made a trip to Richmond in company with Mr. Neale and Miss Christiansen. The south was for him always a land peopled with strange figures of dreams and stalked by spectres. "Richmond," how that name had sounded when whispered or shouted in 1865! Now it seemed quiet and indolent and full of sleep. Could it be possible? It made him question the veracity of his senses. And he wrote to Sterling: "I went to Richmond, a city whose tragic and pathetic history, of which one is reminded by everything that one sees there, always gets on my nerves with a particular dejection. True, the history is some fifty years old, but it is always with me when I'm there, making solemn eyes at me." The fifty years seemed but a slight cæsura: what mattered were the accented moments when life was lifted by chance to the level of great poetry.

He was no sooner back from Richmond than he left for California. How many times had he made this circuit? How many times had hope alternated with despair, and despair with hope, as he journeyed back and forth across this continent! It was a dreary and tedious business, but this was to be his last trip. He was resolved to say farewell. It was really one trip too often for he found that the scenes had changed. He went to Lake Tahoe and met one evening a lady he had known in Oakland. They were driven into her cabin by a harsh and biting wind and they drank to San Francisco as they tried to forget

the disagreeable and deserted lake resort. But San Francsico
was no better. Like his second trip to the battlefields, this return
visit to California was disappointing. He should have known
the psychological inevitability of disappointment under these
circumstances. A sensation may be recaptured by visiting old
scenes that once have been memorable by mere association. But
the experience will not recur a second or a third time.

Moreover, there had actually been quite a change in California since 1910. During his absence, Christian Science had bitten old friends like a pestilence. He would greet people with the
salutation: "Well, are you also a believer in white magic?" The
Hall of Truth in Oakland, conducted by Mrs. Lillitz, had taken
in many an old pupil, admirer, and friend. One evening when
Mrs. Lillitz was asking for names to be made the subject of
prayer an unidentified voice suggested "Ambrose Bierce," and
a prayer was offered for his soul. By 1912 several of Bierce's
favorites were practitioners and even his daughter had joined
the circle. He smiled when she remonstrated with him about
his skepticism. "Bib" (his name for her), he would say, "has
the greatest gift of all: the gift of happiness."

It was not altogether the "white magic" that annoyed him.
A Radical Club had been formed at Piedmont, and even George
Sterling was flirting with the fatal heresy of socialism. As far
as Bierce was concerned, they were all "anarchists." Even his
nephew and niece talked dangerously of "conditions" and he
told them, with calm but definite certainty, that if they became
"anarchists" they would lose a patient uncle and he a beloved
nephew and niece. He was out of tune with things: he was
actually relegated to the armchair in the lobby of his hotel in
Oakland. Sterling added to socialism a harum-scarum theory
about "free love" which disgusted Bierce, who wrote: "I'm
thinking of cutting Sterling—he gets on my nerves." George
sent him a poem from Carmel with the request that he show it
to a mutual friend. Bierce returned it with an angry note, in
which he said that he would not think of showing such a poem
to a lady! It was too fleshly for Bierce. This was followed by
the famous swimming-pool episode in which Bierce threatened
Sterling if he dared go swimming in the nude. He should have
been more tolerant: George was something of a jester and had
an insatiable mania for nakedness. He once created an inter-

national sensation by a midnight plunge in Golden Gate Park after a lily, and he scandalized several masked balls in San Francisco by appearing in a leopard's skin. However amusing this might have been to Sterling, it grated on Bierce's nerves. He could not tolerate sensationalism. He visited Sterling at Carmel for a few hours, and wrote in George's guest book: "Nothing to say." It was literally true.

His friends observed that he had aged noticeably since his last visit. In two years he had become an "old man." One lady remarked that even on his second visit he seemed as alert and manly as ever when he called. But the next day she saw him crossing a street in town, when he was unaware of her presence. She was shocked by his appearance, for he was bent, walked stiffly, and carried a cane. His voice sounded "old" for the first time. He told Eva Crawford that he was "sleepy for death" and that he "was going away." His summer was taken up with one visit after another in which he repeated this message. The details varied to some extent, but generally the message was the same and it was definitely "farewell." He was determined to make this visit the last and he wanted to leave this impression. All his friends seemed to realize that he walked in a constant shadow, but nothing definitely was said about his plans.

One evening he invited Mr. and Mrs. Roosevelt Johnson to his hotel for dinner. They had a very pleasant evening. When they left, Bierce, said "good-by" in a manner that impressed them both with its tone of finality. As they were crossing the street in front of the hotel, they turned and gazed back at Bierce. He was standing in the doorway, the light streaming from behind. His figure, clad in black, with a suggestion of white about the cuffs and collar, appeared as sharply outlined as though it were set in a frame. As they turned, he lifted his hand in a gesture that said "farewell" even more definitely than his last words.

By October he was again in Washington. The journey had been almost disastrous. He was stricken with asthma while en route, and had been forced to make short stop-overs in order to complete the journey. It had been a bad summer, and he returned to his apartment more determined than ever that he must leave Washington and never return. He had made his usual pilgrimage up the Napa Valley to St. Helena. It had been warm and sultry out in that barren cemetery as old "Charley" Jackson had shown him about the ground. The "Bierce" lot had been removed, as he had instructed two years previously. It was now a square plot of raised earth marked with four palm trees. There were no inscriptions, monuments, or stones. Day, Leigh, and Mollie Bierce . . . St. Helena . . . Howell Mountain . . . shadows and echoes. It really had ceased to matter. He was quiet and gray and sad, but he no longer felt the anguish that he had once thought unforgetable. He left hurriedly for Oakland, telling the sexton that he was "going into Mexico" and that the graves were to be attended with the money that he left for their care. There was a finality about this last trip. Every task had been attended; his affairs were in order. The few old friends had been told farewell, and there was nothing more to say or do. He no longer had a single interest in California. The first visit had been pleasant and amusing, but the second was quite disappointing. It was ever the case with Bierce. He was shambling across the continent again, but he knew with the unquestionable certainty of all great determinations, that this would be the last trip. If he was to be deceived by alluring vistas again, it would be in the South, where there was "something new under an old sun."

In Washington, again, he had resumed the same round of puerile tasks. The "Collected Works" were "out of my system" and he took some satisfaction in knowing that the edition was completed before he "passed on." There were spurts of activity, on occasion, as when he wrote to a friend that he had recovered from the "wobbles" and that there was "life in the old dog yet." There was life enough to write several sharp letters about the new régime in Washington. This fellow Wilson wrote better than the others, but he sounded specious at times. As for Walter Hines Page: "He has done some of the loftiest and hardiest lying that has been heard on this orb in many a year anent pensions." He felt restless and read the papers about the situation in Mexico with interest. It looked like a real fight might ensue. It was about time. Every generation had its baptism of fire, and his shadow had stretched far into the second generation. He corresponded with Carranza and announced to friends that he "liked the fellow." He could not believe all the talk that he heard about Mexico. He decided to go down below Juarez and view the scene for himself. The news of war was broken, however, with amusing incidents as when George Harvey invited him to attend a dinner in honor of William Dean Howells. It seemed like a post-mortem laurel for Bierce, who had always been, as Robert Barr observed, "too full of original hell to succeed in a Presbyterian world," and the world was going Presbyterian just then.

Later in the year, Bierce left for a visit with his daughter who was then living in Bloomington, Illinois. When she had first announced to her father that she lived in this city, he sent her a telegram: "Why *Bloomington!*" He brought with him a box of letters, papers and documents, and left a trunkful of unassorted papers. It was a pleasant visit over a period of about two weeks. The daughter was impressed with his excellent health; in fact, he told her that he had never felt better. But, despite his good health, he seemed vaguely uneasy and was determined that he would "go away." Just at dusk one evening they were sitting on the veranda of Mrs. Cowden's home. An old man walked along the street in front of the house: bent, shambling, forlorn. An involuntary grimace passed over Bierce's face. There was a prolonged pause in their conversation, as she noticed that he was disturbed. Then, after a moment, he said: "Bib, did you notice that old man? I'll never be like that! It is not merely the personal humiliation of age that I resent but the fact that it discommodes others. Old people are cranky and fussy and infernal bores." Both Mr. and Mrs. Cowden remonstrated and assured him that he could come and live with them in Bloomington, but he only smiled enigmatically and began to talk of other things. His insouciance did not, however, deceive his daughter.

She had several long chats with her father during this visit. One evening they were discussing some former acquaintance who had disappointed all his friends by his rather contemptible conduct. Mrs. Cowden chided her father about his indignation. Why should he, who was so "cynical," care about what another did, particularly when "nothing matters"? Moreover, she volunteered, the man in question could scarcely have kept from doing what he did. Bierce was immediately serious. "That's all rot! Why, Bib, a long time ago I came to realize that a man could be a gentleman if he once made up his mind. As a youngster before and immediately after the war, I did many things that I would not approve of to-day. But there came a time when I determined that to be a gentleman was one of the few worthy ambitions in a man's life, and I found that it could be done."

He also told her of his plans. "Why should I remain in a country that is on the eve of woman's suffrage and prohibition? You are well provided for and my proofreading stunt—four years of it—is over. In America you can't go east or west any more, or north, the only avenue of escape is south. I'm going back to Washington and make preparations to leave. I'll take some letters along with me and strike the border near El Paso. It will be easy enough to get along. I'm going to buy a donkey and hire a peon. I can see what's doing; perhaps write a few articles about the situation; and then pass to the west coast of Mexico. From there I can go to South America, cross the Andes and ship to England. This fighting in Mexico interests me. I want to go down and see if these Mexicans shoot straight."

There were questions which he did not answer. He seemed to prefer a vague understanding of his plans to any forthright explanation. His daughter knew him well enough not to remonstrate or to argue. She was worried and alarmed, but, as was always the case, she did not, or could not, change his determination. She could see that there was more to his determination to leave than a mere desire to see Mexico. But he was not morbid or pessimistic. He seemed quite cheerful, as though he were humming to himself. And well he might, for he was excited and enchanted with life once more.

One thing she did ask him about. Had he not been happy in Washington? Why should he want to leave? Washington, he announced, was the city of bores and fools. He was sick of the place. It palled on him. For thirteen years he had been a spectator, watching the idle game of politicians masquerading as statesmen. He was thoroughly disgusted with the scene and eager to leave. New York offered no greater divertissement. Why, he had walked the streets in New York, after Leigh's death, gazing at buildings, counting objects, doing anything to keep from thinking about his own personal sorrow. He avoided seeing even his few friends on these occasions, as they were "shameless" about their happiness and reveled "indecently" in their bliss in his presence. No, he had not been particularly happy in Washington.

While in Bloomington, he took a keen interest in Mrs. Cowden's two step-sons, Henry and Victor. One of the boys was interested in drawing and used to show his sketches to Bierce. Bierce was delighted, commented upon them, and, when he returned to Washington, sent the boy a sketchbook and some Japanese prints. He wrote that the prints were in excellent taste: they were simple, full of health, and saw reality as it should be seen,—from a distance.

The visit was at an end. He told his daughter "good-by" in a smiling and cheerful manner and said that he would write from Mexico. When he told his daughter good-by, the period of leave-taking and adieus was at an end. Was it not better that he should leave in this manner? Nothing is ever irrelevant, as one of Mr. Huxley's characters has announced, and that is a great mystery and a paradox.

By the spring of 1913, Bierce began to prepare for his journey. His letters from May, 1913, throughout the summer, reveal a definite determination to go into Mexico, although not all of them are as explicit as the note to Mr. Roosevelt Johnson which closes with the phrase that he was "dressed for death." The trip had been a matter of much thought; he had toyed with the idea of running away from old age as early as 1899. Troubled and annoyed by the thought of a general and gradual atrophy, he resented the casual deadening of the faculties which age used as an opiate. He wanted to meet death while he was sentient. Having rebelled so long against life, he could scarcely have been expected to acquiesce in what is rather facetiously known as a "natural" death.

Much doubt has been cast about the time and circumstances of his departure. This doubt can now be removed, as the details of his trip have been made available. Bierce was in constant communication with Miss Christiansen from the night he left Washington until his disappearance. Mr. Neale has intimated that Bierce went into Mexico because of a quarrel with Miss Christiansen, and he feels "certain that she never received any letters from him after their last personal interview." There are no circumstances whatever to indicate that Bierce quarreled with Miss Christiansen. When he left for Mexico, she was in charge of his affairs. He had made assignments to her of his property, aside from the gold he took with him, and she was in possession of his papers and personal effects. Furthermore, she attended to all the details of his trip. Do these facts indicate that there had been a quarrel? Moreover, Bierce wrote Miss Christiansen the only specific and detailed account of his trip that exists. She knew his fear of the posthumous publication of letters written hastily and without thought of publication. Consequently, she destroyed all the correspondence, but she did realize the importance of the letters received from him during this time and thoughtfully jotted down in a notebook the dates and significant facts which they contained, even quoting an occasional phrase. That the record she made is authentic, admits of little doubt. The notes are specific and definite. Furthermore, there is no reason whatever to question her integrity, and the occasional phrases she quotes are unmistakably from Bierce's pen.

From this record it is apparent that Bierce left Washington, Thursday evening, October 2, 1913, on the 10:10 train for Chattanooga. He was alone, although he had invited one friend to accompany him as far as the battlefields, just as he had taken Pollard with him on the pilgrimage of 1908. The fascination which old battle scenes possessed for Bierce was compelling and irresistible. When he was visiting in West Virginia, he had written to a friend a letter which contains a most significant passage:

"I have told her of a certain 'enchanted forest' hereabout to which I feel myself sometimes strongly drawn as a fitting place to lay down 'my weary body and my head.' (Perhaps you remember your Swinburne:

'Ah yet, would God this flesh of mine might be
Where air might wash and long leaves cover me!
Ah yet, would God that roots and steams were bred
Out of my weary body and my head.')

"The element of enchantment in that forest is supplied by my wandering and dreaming in it forty-one years ago when I was a-soldiering and there were new things under a new sun. It is miles away, but from a nearby summit I can overlook the entire region—ridge beyond ridge, parted by purple valleys full of sleep. Unlike me, it has not visibly altered in all these years, except that I miss, here and there, a thin blue smoke from an enemy's camp. Can you guess my feelings when I view this Dream-land—my Realm of Adventure, inhabited by memories that beckon me from every valley? I

shall go; I shall retrace my old routes and lines of march;
stand in my old camps; inspect my battlefields to see that all
is right and undisturbed. I shall go to the Enchanted Forest." *

He apparently desired to make a complete and final inspection of these romantic scenes, which were so indescribably
enchanting. He was perplexed by the quiet sleepiness of
meadows and parks that were once the scenes of carnage and
gore. It should be remembered that this was a second visit; a
merely intellectual curiosity would have been satisfied by one
trip. It is obvious that he was in a mood for revery. He was
seeking for a lost magic, as though for fifty years he had been
wandering in a world of negligible importance: weary, bored
and disillusioned. Bierce had always been suspicious of the
metaphysician's identification of himself with light, and sun and
stars. But now he rather vaguely desired that "roots and stems
were bred" out of his "weary body" and his "weary head."
Every man to his own talisman.

On October 5th he arrived at Chickamauga, and the next
day he was in Murfreesboro, registering in a hotel named,
appropriately, "The Hermitage." He tramped over many old
battlefields that first day, missing no landmark of former years.
He reported with pride that he had covered fifteen miles at
Chickamauga and ten at Chattanooga. From Murfreesboro, he
proceeded to Nashville. While he was visiting the field at Chickamauga, he made a sketch of the monument erected to his
brother's regiment and sent it to Albert in Berkeley. "Stone
River"—it seemed an impossible dream and yet the experience
was projected through time and its memory troubled him now
that he stood in the center of silent fields and seemed to hear
the call of bugles and to see the flash of brilliant flags.

A few days later, on the 12th, he left Nashville and journeyed up the river to Pittsburg Landing. If the river banks
had been full to overflowing in 1862, on that memorable day
when he had been ferried across to Shiloh, they were suspended
high above the waters in 1913. It was, indeed, a time of low
tide. A phrase from Miss Christiansen's notebook reads: "A
long and tedious voyage by steamboat. Stopped at every landing
to put on freight. Landings are not towns, just roads coming

* The Letters of Ambrose Bierce.

down to the water. River beautiful but so low that the country could not be seen over the banks. The park so abundantly marked that following route of brigade and regiment is easy. Savannah, eight or ten miles below, looked familiar." There was a hollow depression to the right of a clearing, in which men had been cremated in a burning forest—but it was only a green hollow carefully planted to lawn and might have served as a hazard on a golf course. At Shiloh he counted the graves of twenty men who had been in his regiment, but he noted that less than half of the three thousand graves were marked. It was a dreary trip of inspection and not at all satisfying. He was still disconsolate and troubled and eager for the time when this mask of appearances might be torn aside.

The pleasant sun which had blazed down at Murfreesboro suddenly disappeared and was followed on the twentieth by a snowstorm. He was miserably cold and his trip was a disappointment. He arrived at Corinth, after a long drive, so cold that he could scarcely write his name in the hotel register. Corinth was lost in a fog of coal gas from the engines. Clouds of steam, frosted windows, and a driving wind full of sleet—what evil chance had brought this cold upon him? He was cold, and sick; why, he wondered, had he ever started on this dreary trip. The interval of revery was shattered and the next night he "fled south" towards New Orleans. Nothing mattered; nothing ever remained the same. Even the fine sensation of sadness which he had experienced on his first trip to Chickamauga was gone. It was, indeed, time that he went into Mexico. Nothing was left him. Again that fatal cleavage from reality kept him pursuing a phantom of fine feeling and an impossible elation. He had been deceived into thinking that the lost glamour of war days could be conjured forth by auto-suggestion practiced in the midst of scenes rich in associations. Fumbling old letters in his trunk at Washington had given him the same feeling: sorrow and pain and despair. He had burned many of the letters as "old junk" and he now turned from Chickamauga which was suddenly but a "cold and dismal park." He was annoyed with fugitive emotions. But, after all, "nothing mattered."

In New Orleans the interval of darkness in the north was forgotten. It was good to be in New Orleans. A trace of the old raillery appeared in his letters, and he wrote "Norrie" that "the sun shines in evidence, the horses are twittering in the trees and the autos hopping gaily from limb to limb." The place seemed to please him; it was warming as a cordial. He noticed that even the street traffic seemed full of leisure; that the hotel corridors and lobbies were crowded with handsome people who had pleasant voices; men played billiards just as they did "years ago—and the bars—O you should see a New Orleans bar!" And, a few lines later: "The drinks they make, the trays and trays sent upstairs; the general air of leisure and the love of life." It suggested that trip to New Orleans in 1865. This was an admirable mode of living: leisure, drinks, and gestures towards happiness. Not that damned scrambling in New York, or the hollow tediousness of Washington, but a "love of life." These people were saving life and enjoying it, in the same manner that they lingered over a julep.

But, then, if he returned again to New Orleans, perhaps it, too, would have changed. He had no assurance that its charm was more durable than an hour. He was skeptical even of his own emotions, and, in a few days, his doubts were confirmed. "All my old haunts are lost to me, and excepting a few blocks immediately about the St. Charles Hotel, it is a strange city. I can't find even the places where Pollard and I dined and drank a few years ago." Shortly after his arrival he was stricken with asthma, and spent a day and night pacing his hotel room, bending over the back of a chair, gasping for breath, and wondering, as he had wondered for fifty years, why he endured such pain. He was losing weight and noticed the fact with apprehension. Perhaps he would yet die of "disease." He must hurry. It was a lonely vigil with death in a land where "something was doing." As though such a land existed! But the quest was understandable enough and his courage, as always, was most admirable.

He arrived at San Antonio, October 27th. Texas was in the grip of a blizzard. As soon as the weather improved, he spent some days strolling about and visiting the Alamo— "rather interesting with relics, old documents and bad poetry, the shrine of each Texan's devotion." At Fort Sam Houston that week he had a royal good time; why, he was actually treated as though he were a "foreign ambassador"! It was with difficulty that he prevented the Colonel from parading the regiment in his honor. Some of these army men he had known when they were stationed at the Presidio in San Francisco; many of them had exchanged drinks with him in the Army and Navy Club at Washington. Naturally they gave him a fine reception. It warmed him like the first flush of New Orleans had done. But it, too, was only a fragment of deceptive delight, a slight distraction. Death was his companion on this trip, and they hastened forward on their journey.

In November, "All Souls' Day," was clear and bright. The pale sunlight fell softly on a young winter world. Church bells were ringing everywhere and he took a long walk through the town, observing that several of the churches were "old for his country," and reflecting on the contrast between such overt piety and a name like San Antonio. There were letters to write in the evening and then time for another long stroll before retiring. He would be traveling to-morrow—across the line. What was there? Probably another land of guffaws, boredom and chicanery. But if the fighting was trivial, there was still South America. It promised something; at least it offered more sustenance than the Washington of Woodrow Wilson. All these years he had known that he wanted surcease from a mob-mad democracy, a Leviathan of vulgarity that turned his sharpest shafts of satire with the strength of a great indifference. He had raged and stormed and cursed, but all to no purpose. Had he not seen demagogues on bicycles, the one with a hideous grin and the other with the voice of a bull in anguish, romping across the nation, jerking old scarecrows before the people, depicting promised lands, and leading the sheep to slaughter? No, San Antonio on "All Souls' Day," yea, even with Church Bells, was sweet and kind after such a nightmare.

But he must be going. November 7, 1913, saw him in Laredo. Across the river was Nuevo Laredo, held by the Huertistas. He was near now to the scene of the mock battles that were to follow: like an old soldier he was going to direct a sham battle for amusement. He was known even in Laredo. A newspaper man connected with *The Herald*, recognized him in the streets. This chap told an interesting story about a member of Porfirio Diaz's cabinet who had bored his friends by reading "A Wine of Wizardry" on all occasions. Bierce stayed in Laredo for several days, visiting Fort McIntosh and the old Spanish

Settlement, where he puzzled over ancient inscriptions just as he had made notes of Indian signs at Powder River in 1866. He stood on the river bank and gazed across into a "vast expanse of Mexican territory alluringly spread out and inaccessible." He went on minor forays into the "enemy's" territory, piercing that "inaccessible" and, therefore, "romantic" land to the south.

He proceeded on to El Paso and passed across the line into Juarez. Officials received him cordially and gave him his credentials to accompany the army. On December 16, 1913, he was in Chihuahua, Mexico, and a letter from Juarez relates that he had just ridden in from Chihuahua to post it. It was sharp weather but he was enjoying the life. There was much talk of "Jornada del Muerto," the journey of death, and the roads were dotted with groups of refugees. There was a distinctly military atmosphere about the place and it pleased him. Troops were leaving Chihuahua every day and he was expecting to be in Torreon soon.

There had been a little fighting. These Mexicans fought like devils, but they were unsoldierly and addicted to "unseasonable firing." There was the incident at Tierra Blanca, for example. Inquiry had been set afoot about the "gringo" who was accompanying the army. Was he a soldier? To remove any suspicion from their minds, he had taken a rifle, walked to the top of a ridge, taken careful aim and had gotten his man. They were elated: such firing was unheard of, it was an example of Non-Latin calculation and precision. The old Gringo was given a sombrero and questioned no more. But he was curious. He had shot one of the "enemy," but his only sensation was one of dismay. "Poor devil! I wonder who he was!" War, too, had gone the way of all the mysterious, shifting, tantalizing shadows that were constantly disappearing only to reform into half-shapes and then dissolving again into the mists from which they had emerged and into which everything eventually disappeared. He was no nearer "the heart of darkness" than ever and he was troubled by a recurrent thought: was death to be a jest? He had touched it throughout his life. Once it had placed a long white scar through his hair, and it had mowed down thousands in his sight. Now, in old age, he was flirting with it again, but it did not seem much of an adventure. His early experience, then, had been something personal and subjective. All his life he had cherished the thought of the Civil War as the great "adventure" of his life, and now he knew it had been but another wraith of smoke stirred up by the gods of chance to perplex his sight. "To be a Gringo in Mexco—Ah, that is euthanasia!"

The notes ceased, for there were no more letters. It was near Christmas time, always for him a "hateful" season, full of sad memories. The year 1914 was to bring no word of him. His journey with death was over. He had disappeared—into his "good, good, darkness."

CHAPTER XX

"INCOMMUNICABLE NEWS"

BIERCE once remarked that "Death is not the end; there remains the litigaton over the estate." The wildly imaginary rumors that have circulated since his disappearance into Mexico, certainly suggest an interesting parallel. His disappearance did not put an end to the absurd speculations about his life, but, on the contrary, only gave them a fresh and splendid impetus. The old question: "Who is Ambrose Bierce?" was supplanted by the far more perplexing query: "Where is Ambrose Bierce." Just as America was becoming curious about the first question, the second created even more attention and interest. The matter was made the subject of psychoanalysis, crystal gazing, and sensational news stories. The famous "disappearance" became the theme of short stories of the supernatural, prose fantasies, dialogues, detective stories, and editorial comment. Nothing so augmented the interest in Ambrose Bierce as his disappearance. Obscurity is obscurity, but disappearance is fame. It would be an act of supererogation to list all the stories about Bierce's disappearance that have been tossed to a greedy world by those who have glibly promised to tell exactly what happened to Ambrose Bierce, but a few may be considered.

Immediately upon Bierce's disappearance, that is, when his friends ceased to hear from him, his daughter wrote to the authorities in Washington and requested that they make an investigation, which they agreed to do. The Hon. Franklin K. Lane was one of the men who was induced to take an active part in directing the search that the government made in an effort to get word of Bierce. He was apparently ashamed of his famous dunciad to the New York newspapers and was making belated amends. It was known that the last letters were postmarked from Chihuahua. One was dated Christmas Eve, December 24, 1913, and was addressed to J. H. Dunnigan, in the course of which Bierce asked his friend to "pray for me—real loud." The other was mailed two days later. Some further facts are known, as that Bierce had on his person approximately two thousand dollars in gold, that he carried credentials permitting him to pass through the Constitutionalists' territory, and that he was accredited to the Villa forces. He left a trunk in Laredo, which, *en passant,* was never found and could never be traced. From various sources, it is quite apparent that Bierce did not go into Mexico with the thought of actually enlisting with either side. His rôle was distinctly that of an observer; his credentials so stated, and he had told many friends that he was merely "going through to the West Coast and then to South America." So much, then, for the known facts.

The first important "Bierce Disappearance" story was that by James H. Wilkins. Wilkins, a well-known Pacific Coast journalist, was sent into Mexico by Fremont Older to try and find out what happened to Ambrose Bierce. The result of his investigation was a sensational news story that appeared in the San Francisco *Bulletin,* March 24, 1920. Summarized, Mr. Wilkins' story is that Bierce was shot by a firing squad of Villista troops near Icamoli, on the trail to Monterey, in 1915. Wilkins claims that he went to interview Edmund Melero, associate editor of the *Mexican Review* in Mexico City. It was rumored that Melero had known Bierce in El Paso, and that they had been together for some time in Mexico. Up to this point Mr. Wilkins' story is quite probable. But he strains the easiest credibility by the statements that follow. He went to interview a man supposed to have been with Melero, as Melero did not personally know much about Bierce. This mysterious man, unnamed in the story, then told Wilkins that he had been sent by Villa to capture an ammunition train on its way to Carranza's forces. The ammunitions had been captured and two men had been taken prisoners. These two prisoners were shot down by the firing squad. As the man told Wilkins the story, a pictured fluttered to the floor. Wilkins is "without doubt" that it was a picture of Ambrose Bierce. But he never produced the picture or the man.

There are strange things, indeed, in this world and it is within the range of probabilities that Mr. Wilkins' story may be correct. But it sounds so absurd as to repel even a qualified acceptance. The first objection to the story is that Mr. Wilkins would fix the date of Bierce's death at 1915. It seems unbelievable that Bierce could have been in Mexico for two years without having written a word to his daughter or Miss Christiansen. Moreover, it would have been virtually an impossibility for him to have been on Carranza's staff for two years, particularly after the government had started its search, without being detected by American correspondents. Quite a considerable group of correspondents who were in Mexico at the time have been interviewed and none of them report having seen or heard of Bierce. Nor do any of Carranza's aids recall the presence of such a man on the staff of the Constitutionalists' Army.

But even before Mr. Wilkins had reported the firing squad yarn, there was a widely circulated story to the effect that Bierce was in Europe with Lord Kitchener. This story, which had a most questionable origin, was sent all over the world by an excited and unreliable press as an authentic account of Bierce's disappearance. Dr. B. F. Mason, a physician in San Leandro, California, had given an interview to a reporter on the Oakland *Tribune,* in which he said that he had just received a letter from a relative, Col. Henry Charles Mason, who claimed to have seen Bierce with Kitchener's forces. This was the origin of the story. It was promptly reprinted throughout the country, but with the statement that Bierce's daughter had confirmed the story at Bloomington, Illinois. She did nothing of the sort. All that she said, when interviewed, was that she had read the newspaper stories about her father. This casual statement was converted into the definite assertion that she had "received a letter from her father," and that he was with Kitchener's army. As a matter of fact, there was no basis for the story whatever, aside from this circumstantial confirmation: Bierce had corresponded with Lord Kitchener, after the Boer War, and England was the ultimate destination of his trip. But this version of the disappearance, if true, would fix the date at 1915, and it thus becomes immediately subject to the objection that Bierce would certainly have written to his daughter in that period of time. His daughter is convinced that he would have communicated with her, if alive, knowing her terrible anxiety and apprehension. This belief finds the strongest substantiation in his last letters, in which he had promised to write from time to time, as he journeyed south.

Another story about Bierce's disappearance, and a rather probable one, is that by George Weeks. Weeks was a correspondent attached to Villa's forces during the days leading up to the capture of Juarez. He explains how difficult it would have been for Bierce to be on the staff of either Villa or Carranza and to have escaped unnoticed. Mr. Weeks even admitted that he had been unable, personally, to learn a word about Bierce, although he made inquiries at Villa's headquarters. This is important, particularly when Dr. Danziger's story is considered.

After the Revolution, Mr. Weeks published a newspaper in Mexico City, and it was this newspaper of which Edmund Melero was associate editor. Weeks had, in fact, introduced Wilkins to Melero. But Weeks also stated that Melero did not remember much about Bierce. After talking with Mr. Weeks, however, Melero discovered an old Mexican Sergeant who had been with General Tomas Urbina, one of Villa's corps commanders. This old fellow, over a bottle of wine, was induced to tell a story about seeing an American shot down by a firing squad, and, presumably after another bottle of wine, to identify Bierce by a picture that was shown him as the man who was shot. It thus becomes apparent that the Wilkins story was but the story of a story, and that Mr. Weeks, who was personally quite reliable, only stated the story upon the questionable hearsay of Melero, which was based in turn upon the unnamed sergeant's evidence. Such stories surely do not commend themselves. Much publicity has been given to the Weeks-Wilkins story by stating it as an accepted version of what happened to Bierce, but it was never other than a questionable hypothesis. It is far more likely that Bierce was shot during the fighting that occurred at Torreon about the time he was last heard from. No effort whatever was made to identify the bodies of the dead during the Revolution and a disappearance in this manner would be forever veiled in mystery. It would seem that Bierce, if dead, was probably killed during the early days of the Revolution. This becomes apparent when one reads Mr. Weeks' account of the manner in which the correspondents covered both the Villista and Constitutionalists' armies.

Another widespread story about Bierce's disappearance is that circulated by Dr. Danziger. According to the Doctor's version, Bierce went into Mexico with the express purpose of joining Villa's army. Bierce, says Dr. Danziger, was jealous of General Harrison Gray Otis, formerly owner of the Los Angeles *Times,* because the latter, by flattering Diaz, had acquired large estates in Mexico. Hence Bierce wanted to assist Diaz. This is, of course, most characteristic of the Doctor, who, throughout his "Portrait of Ambrose Bierce," goes to the utmost recesses of his fervent imagination to attribute a mean and personal motive to all of Bierce's activities. Regardless of what may be proven or not proven in this controversy, one fact remains clear: Bierce did not go into Mexico with the thought in mind of assisting Villa or because he disliked General Otis.

The Doctor would have us believe that he personally interviewed Villa, and was highly complimented for his courage, the compliment being noted along with several other flattering tributes to the self-narrated glory and heroism of the author of "A Portrait of Ambrose Bierce." He then tells the most preposterous yarn, quoting Villa to the effect that Bierce, by drinking tequila, had become a drunkard. But he never directly states that Villa admitted that Bierce was dead, or that he knew who killed him. He does not offer a scintilla of proof, nor a single circumstance to buttress this flimsy and ridiculous story. Despite the widespread publicity given to Mr. Robert H. Davis' interview with Dr. Danziger, published, let it be known, in 1928, there is scant evidence to support the Doctor's story that he learned about the disappearance of Ambrose Bierce in 1923, but kept the matter a secret for five years. Villa was assassinated July 20, 1923. In 1923, Bierce would have been eighty-one, and in 1928, he would have been eighty-six. It was time for a brilliant revelation.

It has previously been stated that in 1893, Bierce and Danziger had a serious quarrel. This state of affairs was not altered in later years. On July 19, 1902, Bierce wrote Dr.

Danziger a note,—one of the mildest of several similar letters of this time—and a characteristic passage will be quoted:

> "If you come to Washington there will be a few things for you to explain. I have had to pay some bills of yours, for example. And I have reason to think that you have again been 'working' some of the persons whom you knew as my friends. In brief, it is up to you to show, if you can, that you are not an irreclaimable crook."

The Doctor was quite well aware of Mr. Bierce's attitude, for he kept writing and begging for an interview. To quote from a letter of March 28, 1903: "I cannot conceive that you should so detest me that you would not grant my request. Much has happened since we were together that has strengthened my manhood and has raised me above the former level." It is the story of this man that one is asked to believe as to what happened to Ambrose Bierce.

The latest "Mexican" disappearance story is that related by one Edward S. O'Reilly, soldier of fortune. O'Reilly claims to have been an officer on the "staff" of Pancho Villa, in 1914. O'Reilly is firmly convinced that he found the grave of Ambrose Bierce near Sierra Mojada. While in Sierra Mojada in 1914 with General Torivo Ortega, he heard rumors of an old man who had drifted into the town searching for Villa, who had been shot by some local soldiers. Some "scraps" of an envelope were reported to have been found with an Oakland postmark. Of course, none of the circumstances of the story are in any way capable of verification. It is just another story.

Several years after Bierce's disappearance into Mexico, his devoted and faithful secretary, Miss Christiansen, died at Napa, California. Before her death she turned over to Mrs. Isgrigg all her personal effects and the property which Mr. Bierce had given her prior to his departure into Mexico. There was nothing in her papers that throws any additional light upon the disappearance of Ambrose Bierce, other than the notebook to which reference has been made. But her death inspired several new "stories" about Bierce, one of which was quite ingenious. There is a state institution for the insane at Napa. Miss Christiansen lived in Napa several years prior to her death. Therefore, reasoned the inventor of this story, Bierce had been in

Napa all the time and had never disappeared into Mexico. If in Napa, where could he be but in the State Insane Asylum! Of course, the simple fact that Napa, California, was Miss Christiansen's home, would not be a sufficient explanation of her presence there.

But the interest in Bierce's disappearance has not been limited to the reporters and pseudo-reporters. Mr. Edward H. Smith wrote an article about the famous disappearance in a detective story magazine, and later reprinted it in a book devoted to "Mysteries of the Missing." In this volume, with Charlie Ross, Archduke Salvator, and Theodosia Burr, Bierce joins the ranks of the mysterious army of the missing. He had written about these strange folk on many occasions, and now he was of their grisly company. Mr. Smith, trained in the lore of the detective, comes to some interesting conclusions. He rejects, as who would not, the stories by Weeks and Danziger, and makes this sensible observation: "My own guess is that Bierce started out to fight battles and shoulder hardships as he had done when a boy, somehow believing that a tough spirit would carry him through." Indeed, it should be remembered that Bierce had led an inactive life in Washington for thirteen years. He was not a strong man at the time he went into Mexico, although he was well preserved for his age. He had been ill in New Orleans and again in El Paso, as shown by the notes Miss Christiansen made from his letters. He was surely not in condition to undertake the hardships of a correspondent in Mexico during the Revolution.

The labors of Mr. Bierce's bibliographers are incessant and eternal. Any one who has tried to follow all the stories about Bierce's disappearance, will sympathize with Charles Willis Thompson's mild satire on the stories about "the disappearance of Ambrose Bierce," which have been as numerous and as colorful as the stories of Czar Nicholas's death. The writers who have used the disappearance as an incident for pure fiction have been much more successful. Mariam Storm's story "Discovery" which appeared in *The Forum* is much more convincing than most of the news stories. Benjamin De Casseres in "The Last Satire of a Famous Titan" indulges in some pyrotechnic prose, and seats Mr. Bierce in the Café Gambrinus in Mexico City. It would seem that Mr. De Casseres has given a careful attention to details, for in one paragargh Mr. Bierce "tosses off a couple of brandies," and smacks his lips over a third a few lines later. Both the De Casseres and Storm stories are "brandy fiction"; even the few details, such as the old soldier comrade of Bierce and the set of books in Miss Storm's story, are purely imaginary. Mr. Thomas Burke has even suggested a supernatural explanation of Bierce's disappearance! Crystal gazers have been consulted and palmists interrogated, but the mystery remains and the farce continues.

Jay House, writing in the New York *Evening Post,* raised the question as to whether or not there was ever such a man as Ambrose Bierce. Under the circumstances, the question was really quite pertinent. He received some thirty-seven wildly contradictory letters, purporting to tell all that was to be known about Bierce. One correspondent, however, rebelled; he insisted that no such person ever existed! The clipping bureaus have brought in some fantastic stories about Bierce during the last four or five years. He has been seen in out of the way places and has appeared at psychological moments with all Banquo's sense of dramatic values. It is slight wonder that the skeptics ask whether or not such a man ever existed. Was he a salamander, a sadist-masochist, Francis of Assisi, a bat, or an ape? Was he as interesting as a kangaroo and did he have the kick of a zebra? Every semester during the college year some sophomore has discovered the twelve-volume set of Bierce and has written a laborious treatise for the local campus quarterly about this "lonely" figure in American Literature for the edification of the faculty and the bewilderment of the public. One man in San Francisco, who knew Bierce quite well, informs me that he was besieged by four biographers within a space of three months. And so it goes. . . .

Mrs. Isgrigg launched an investigation under the direction of Col. C. J. Velardi, to determine if any new facts could be unearthed as to her father's disappearance. But the mission proved unsuccessful. Will these investigators ever succeed in unearthing genuine clews? The question is unanswerable. But should they succeed? Bierce wanted to find death when he went into Mexico, and his curiosity was justified by a sad experience in human affairs. It was, after all, a personal privilege. Whatever word he may have spoken has, thus far, most certainly

been that "incommunicable news" of which Mr. Markham
wrote, in Bierce's favorite sonnet, "The Wharf of Dreams":

> "Strange wares are handled on the wharves of sleep;
>   Shadows of shadows pass, and many a light
>   Flashes a signal fire across the night;
> Barges depart whose voiceless steersmen keep
> Their way without a star upon the deep;
>   And from lost ships, homing with ghostly crews,
>   Comes cries of incommunicable news,
> While cargoes pile the piers a moon-white heap—
> Budgets of dream-dust, merchandise of song,
> Wreckage of hope and packs of ancient wrong,
> Nepenthes gathered from a secret strand,
>   Fardels of heartache, burdens of old sins,
>   Luggage sent down from dim ancestral inns,
> And bales of fantasy from No-Man's Land."

Events have a strange pattern when viewed by the mystic.
On February 6, 1926, Emma Frances Dawson, one of Bierce's
most brilliant pupils, died of starvation at Palo Alto. George
Sterling wrote me that it was "suicide" and closed his letter
with a stricture to the effect that the only people who committed
suicide were those without energy enough to live. On November 17, 1926, Sterling committed suicide at the Bohemian Club
in San Francisco. When his room was entered, it was found
to be in a state of confusion and disorder. But there was a
picture of Ambrose Bierce on the wall—austere and fine and
handsome. In our last interview, Sterling had said that the
final letter he had received from Bierce had the tone of "God
talking to a gutter snipe." A year later, almost to the day,
Herman Scheffauer committed suicide in Berlin. Both had
chided the "old Titan" about his sternness, but they died with
his name on their lips.

* * *

So great has been the interest in Bierce of recent years
that it is tempting to speculate as to just what his ultimate
position will be in American letters. It is a question which time
will settle in its own impartial manner. But the current discussion about Bierce has been so careless of the facts that

his admirers may well fear that his name is in danger of being dropped in despair by the minority to whom it has always been a byword. Perhaps the ultimate judgment will be that he was more interesting as a man than he was important as a writer. If his name lives, it is within the range of probabilities that it will be as a tradition of wit, courage and decency. Whatever judgment may be passed on his work, it does not affect the important fact that Bierce was one of the most provocative figures of his generation. One cannot reflect upon the facts of his life without coming to entertain an admiration for his splendid courage and indomitable spirit. To those of us in the West who have watched the fate of his reputation with a peculiar and personal interest, it has always been a source of satisfaction to realize that dead, absent or unknown, he has survived his critics and that he has even bettered the enemies who pursued him into Mexico, "to feast on his bones." To some of us, too, whose early enthusiasm for his work has somewhat waned, every light that has been thrown upon the facts of his life has brought a glowing certainty that this man was of the immortals and that around his name has grown up a tradition that we will not willingly relinquish.

Adios!

BIBLIOGRAPHY

THE notes that follow are not intended to serve as a complete and formal bibliography, as Mr. Starrett's "Bibliography" has taken care of that need. The references that are given pertain only to the text of this book. No mention is made in these notes to the various books by Bierce. The notation "Collected Works" throughout the volume has reference to "The Collected Works of Ambrose Bierce," published by the Neale Publishing Company, 1909. "The Letters" refers to "The Letters of Ambrose Bierce," edited by Bertha Clark Pope, with a "Memoir by George Sterling," published by The Book Club of California, 1922.

I
MISCELLANEOUS WRITINGS,
OF AMBROSE BIERCE

The San Francisco News Letter and California Advertiser. Edited by Ambrose Bierce from December, 1868, to March 9, 1872; "Town Crier" page written by Bierce during this period. Sutro Branch, San Francisco Public Library.

The Argonaut. Files from March 25, 1877, to October 11, 1879. Los Angeles Public Library.

The Wasp. Bound files in the library of Robert Cords, Esq., 1881–1886.

San Francisco *Examiner.* Files from March, 1887, to December 3, 1899, thereafter by dispatch from Washington. San Francisco Public Library.

The Overland Monthly. Volume I. January, February, March and April, 1871. "Grizzly Papers," signed by "Ursus."

The Californian: A Western Monthly Magazine. Series of articles entitled: "On With the Dance!" beginning February, 1880, and appearing for several issues. Signed by "Bashi Bazourk."

The Cosmopolitan. October, 1905, to May, 1909. Files in the Los Angeles Public Library.

The Twenty-fifth Reunion Pamphlet, Ninth Indiana Veteran Volunteer Infantry Association, 1904. Contains a letter by Ambrose Bierce.

"Map of the Black Hills Region, Showing the Gold Mining District and the Seat of the Indian War. Drawn by A. G. Bierce from surveys ordered by the War Department." A. L. Bancroft & Company, 1877.

Alta California, October 3, 1872. Letter by Ambrose Bierce.

II
BOOKS ABOUT AMBROSE BIERCE

"Ambrose Bierce," by Vincent Starrett. Chicago. Walter M. Hill, 1920.

"Bitter Bierce: A Mystery of American Letters," by C. Hartley Grattan. Doubleday, Doran & Company, 1929.

"Portrait of Ambrose Bierce," by Adolphe De Castro. The Century Company, 1929.

"Life of Ambrose Bierce," by Walter Neale. Walter Neale, Publisher, 1929.

"Ambrose Bierce: A Bibliography," by Vincent Starrett. The Centaur Book Shop, 1929.

III
BOOKS CONTAINING
REFERENCES TO AMBROSE BIERCE

"California and Californians," edited by Rockwell D. Hunt, chapter by Eric Howard. Lewis Publishing Company, 1926, Volume III, page 59. Article on Bierce.

"Byways in Bookland," by Walter A. Mursell. Houghton Mifflin & Co., Boston, 1914.

"Their Day in Court," by Percival Pollard. Neale & Co., 1909.

"Our Times," by Mark Sullivan.

"More Contemporary Americans," by Percy H. Boynton.

"The Eyes of the Panther," a collection of Bierce stories, published in the Traveller's Library, 1928, contains an introduction about Bierce, by Martin Armstrong.

"The Facts and Background of Literature," by George F. Reynolds and Garland Greever. The Century Co., 1920.

"The Testimony of the Suns," by George Sterling. Contains memoir of Bierce, by Albert M. Bender. The Book Club of California, 1927.

"Among My Autographs," by George R. Sims. London, 1904.

"Ambrose Bierce: Ten Tales." First Edition Club. Contains an introduction by A. J. A. Symons.

"The Testimony of the Suns," by George Sterling. A. M. Robertson, publisher, 1907. Dedication Poem to Ambrose Bierce.

"A Wine of Wizardry," by George Sterling. A. M. Robertson, publisher, 1909. Poem to Ambrose Bierce.

"An Invocation," by Ambrose Bierce. The Book Club of California; introduction by George Sterling, explanation by Oscar Lewis. 1929.

"California: An Intimate History," by Gertrude Atherton.

"Read America First," by Robert Littell. Harcourt, Brace & Co., New York, 1926.

"Essays of Today and Yesterday," by Thomas Burke. George G. Harrap & Co., London, 1928.

"Some American Story-Tellers," by Frederic Taber Cooper. Henry Holt, New York.

"Dictionary of American Biography." Volume II, contains an article about Bierce by Frank Monaghan.

"The Book of Jack London," by Charmion London.

"Ohio and the Western Reserve," by Alfred Mathews, 1902.

"The Supernatural in Modern English Fiction," by Dorothy Scarborough. G. P. Putnam & Sons, 1917.

"The Omnibus of Crime," by Dorothy L. Sayers.

"The Golden Day," by Lewis Mumford.

"Through the Magic Door," by A. Conan Doyle. 1923.

"California Copy," by George Weeks. Washington College Press, 1928.

"The Story of the Files," by Ella Sterling Cummins. 1893.

"Aspects of the Modern Short Story: English and American," by Alfred C. Ward. The Dial Press, 1926.

"California, The Wonderful," by Edwin Markham. International Publishing Company, 1914.

"Modern English Writers: Being a Study of Imaginative Literature, 1890–1914," by Harold Williams. Sidgwick & Jackson, London, 1918.

"The San Francisco Bay Region," by Bailey Millard.

Annals of the Bohemian Club.

"California, Romantic and Beautiful," by George Wharton James.

"Men of the Pacific Coast," published by the Pacific Art Company.

"A Narrative of Military Service," by General W. B. Hazen. Ticknor and Company, Boston, 1885.

The Elite Directory, published by The Argonaut Publishing Company, 1879.

"History of California." Volume V. By Zoeth Skinner Eldredge; contains a reference to Bierce in the chapter on "Literature," written by George Hamlin Fitch.

"Exposition Memories," by George Wharton James.

"California Literature and Its Spirit," by George Wharton James. Syllabus for Lecture IX contains an outline: "Bierce: Last of the Satirists."

"The Social Manual," published in San Francisco, 1884, by E. C. MacFarlane & Company, Publishers.

"Journalism in California," by John P. Young.

"W. R. Hearst: An American Phenomenon," by John K. Winkler Published by Simon and Schuster, 1928.

"Life and Letters of John Muir," by William Frederick Badè.

"The Days of a Man." Volume I; page 461. By David Starr Jordan.

"Autobiography," by Mark Twain.

"American Literature Since 1870," by Fred Lewis Pattee.

"Advance of the America Short Story," by Edward J. O'Brien.

"The Life of Bret Harte," by Henry Childs Merwin.

"California Gold Book," by W. W. Allen and R. B. Avery. Donohue & Henneberry, publishers, 1893.

"Edgar Allan Poe: A Study in Genius," by Joseph Wood Krutch. Alfred A. Knopf, publisher, New York, 1926.

"Mammonart: An Essay in Economic Interpretation," by Upton Sinclair. Published by the author, Pasadena, 1924.

"Mysteries of the Missing," by Edward H. Smith. The Dial Press, 1924.

"The Woman Who Lost Him," by Josephine Clifford McCrackin. (Introduction by Ambrose Bierce) contains a foreword by George Wharton James, publisher, Pasadena, 1913.

"The Mauve Decade," by Thomas Beer. Alfred A. Knopf, New York, 1926.

"A Book of Prefaces," by H. L. Mencken. Knopf, 1914.

"Prejudices" (Series I, II, VI), by H. L. Mencken.

"Anatole France," by W. L. George. Henry Holt, publisher, 1915.

"Emerson and Others," by Van Wyck Brooks. E. P. Dutton & Co., 1927.

"On Strange Altars. A Book of Enthusiasms," by Paul Jordan-Smith. Albert & Charles Boni, 1924.

"In the Midst of Life," by Ambrose Bierce. (Introduction by George Sterling.) The Modern Library, 1927.

"The Modern Novel," by Wilson Follett. Alfred Knopf, Publisher, 1923.

IV

NEWSPAPER REFERENCES

Sacramento *Record-Union*, December 28, 1881. Editorial.

Visalia (California) *Delta*, January 6, 1882. Editorial.

Brooklyn *Daily Eagle*, September 15, 1895. Review.

Oakland *Enquirer*, May 25, 1895. Review.

San Francisco *Examiner*, September 13, 1903. Review by Mr. Bailey Millard.

San Francisco *Examiner*, April 13, 1898. Review by Carroll Carrington.

San Francisco *Examiner*, April 11, 1897. An article by Mr. Bailey Millard.

San Francisco *Examiner*, May 15, 1893; January 7, 1900. Articles about Bierce.

San Francisco *Examiner*, June 30, 1896. Cartoon of Bierce, by James Swinnerton.

San Francisco *Examiner*, February 22, 1896. Large section devoted to Bierce's work in Washington.

San Francisco *Examiner*, February 3, 1929. Article by George Douglas.

Oakland *Saturday Press*, March 2, 1896. Article.

The Transvaal Weekly. Article on Bierce by John Stuart.

Treasure State (Helena, Montana). Article.

The Searchlight (New Zealand), December 14. 1907. Article.

Oakland *Tribune,* July 20, 1907. Letter from Bierce to Scheffauer.

Cincinnati *Gazette,* February, 1904. Review.

San Francisco *News-Letter.* Christmas Number, 1893.

Washington *Post,* March, 1902. News story.

Washington *Times,* August, 1902. News story.

Los Angeles *Times,* March 26, 1899. Review.

Los Angeles *Record,* December 3, 1927. Editorial.

Charleston (West Virginia) *Gazette,* March 10, 1929. Article by Mr. Andrew Price.

Boston *Herald,* September 23, 1928. Article by George Minot.

Galveston *News,* September 28, 1924. Article by F. Douglas Branch.

Dallas *News,* September 20, 1925. Article by John H. McGinnis.

New York *World,* July 1, 1925. Article by Allan Nevins.

New York *Evening Post,* March 29, 1926. Notes by Jay House.

New York *World,* September 23, 1924. Article by Laurence Stallings.

New York *Evening Post,* July 19, 1924. Article by Madelin Leof.

St. Louis *Post-Dispatch,* December 31, 1927. Article by John G. Ncihardt.

New York *Times,* March 24, 1929. Review by Herbert Gorman.

Outlook and Independent, March 20, 1929. Review by Ernest Boyd.

The American Freeman, May 4, 1929. Review.

Plain Talk, June, 1929. Review by G. D. Eaton.

New York *Herald Tribune,* February 9, 1926. News story.

Baltimore *Sun,* May 26, 1928. Review.

Cincinnati *Times-Star,* November 19, 1927. Article.

New York *Sun,* March 2, 1919. Article.

New York *World,* March 1, 1925. "Hiring a Hall," by H. L. Mencken.

New York *World,* April 5, 1925. Article by Charles Willis Thompson.

Times Literary Supplement, April 30, 1925. Letter by Rupert Layard (W. Nichols).

Times Literary Supplement, May 14, 1925. Letter by Herman George Scheffauer.

Times Literary Supplement, May 21, 1925. Letter by Gilbert Dalziel.

New York *Herald Tribune,* February 26, 1928. Mention made of Bierce in an article by Henry Albert Phillips.

London *Evening Standard,* September 15, 1922. Memoirs of Mrs. Croston.

V

MAGAZINE ARTICLES

The American Mercury, "The Shadow Maker," by George Sterling. September, 1925.

The American Mercury, "San Francisco: An Elegy," by Idwal Jones. August, 1925.

The American Mercury, "The California Literati," by George West. July, 1926.

The American Mercury, "George Sterling at Carmel," by Mary Austin. May, 1927.

The American Mercury, "Notes and Queries." August, 1925; July, 1925.

Town Talk, July 18, 1908. Review.

Town Talk, April 18, 1908; September 21, 1907; January 16, 1904. Short notices.

Town Talk, September 7, 1907. Article by Dr. Wolfe.

Town Talk, February 11, 1911. Article by Theodore Bonnet.

St. Louis Mirror, May 5, 1904. Article on Bierce.

San Francisco Wave, September 22, 1894. Article by Georgia Prussia.

The Fra, May, 1909. Article by Elbert Hubbard.

Vanity Fair. August 10, 1910. Article.

Library and Studio, April 30, 1892. Article.

T. P.'s Weekly, September 17, 1909. "A Strange Literary Rebirth," by Haldane MacFall.

T. P.'s Weekly, October 8, 1907. Letter by Herbert Thomas.

Pacific Town Talk, December, 1897. Article by May Lambert.

Pacific Monthly, November, 1907. Article by Porter Garnett.

Pacific Monthly, March, 1908. "In Old Bohemia," an article by Charles Warren Stoddard.

The Outlook, April 1, 1899. Review.

The Journalist, March 19, 1898. Review by S. O. Howes.

Black and White, January 7, 1899. "The American Kipling," by J. S. Cowley Brown.

Black and White, April, 1899. Article by J. S. Cowley Brown.

Chicago Musical Leader, April 22, 1915. Review.

Humanity (St. Louis), February, 1908. "Intimations of Immortality," by Herbert Blake, an article about Bierce.

Chic, June 1, 1895. Cartoon of McEwen and Bierce.

The Wasp, July 3, 1897. Cartoon, "Namby Bierce."

The Wasp, June 1, 1895. Cartoon.
The Papyrus, October, 1907. Article.
Chicago Inland-Printer, February, 1894. Article by Forrest Crissey.
Criterion, April 16, 1898. Review.
Hampton's Magazine, September, 1910. Article by Charles Edward Russell.
New England Magazine, February 22, 1896. Article by Walter Blackburn Hartc.
Saturday Review of Literature, October 13, 1928. Letter from Steven T. Byington, the constant letter writer.
The Argonaut, June 9, 1928. Article.
The Argonaut, August 5, 1889. Editorial by Pixley.
The Publishers' Weekly, May 26, 1928. News story.
The Nation, February 11, 1915. Review.
The Nation, November 23, 1918. Review.
The Nation, August 31, 1918. Review.
The Nation, March 24, 1898. Review.
The Nation, February 11, 1915. Review.
The Cosmopolitan, 1891. Article by Gertrude Atherton.
Congressional Digest, August, 1927. Reprint.
Deutsche Jahrbrucher, September, 1926. Article by Herman George Scheffauer.
The Athenæum, July 3, 1909. Review.
The Athenæum, March 26, 1910. Review.
The Athenæum, July 1, 1911. Review.
The Athenæum, August 26, 1911. Review.
The Athenæum, September 16, 1911. Review.
The Bookman (London), June, 1921. Article by Walter Jerrold.
The Bookman (New York), November, 1928. Article by Wilson Follett.
The Bookman, January, 1925. Review.
The Bookman, September, 1924. Review.
The Bookman, October, 1909. Review.
The Bookman, September, 1925. Review.
The Bookman, February, 1915. "Personal Memories of Ambrose Bierce," by Bailey Millard.
The Smart Set, June, 1921. Review by H. L. Mencken.
The London Mercury, October, 1927. Article by Eric Partridge.
Out West (New Series), January, 1912. "The Literature of California," by Lannie Haynes Martin.
Book Notes, August-September, 1923. Article by Maurice Frink.
Welfare Magazine, June, 1928. Article by Dr. Louis J. Bragman.

The New Republic, March 22, 1919. Review.
The New Republic, "Bitter Bierce," by Robert Littell, October 15, 1924.
The Spectator, August 28, 1909. Review.
Chicago Figaro, May 11, 1893. Review.
The Overland Monthly, April, 1903. Article by Elizabeth Vore.
The Overland Monthly, June, 1915. "Bierce—The Warrior Writer," by H. M. East, Jr.
The Overland Monthly, April, 1921. Reprinted story.
The Overland Monthly, November, 1919. "Ambrose Bierce," by R. F. Dibble.
The Overland Monthly, January, 1927. Note by George Sterling.
Everybody's, October, 1909. Article by Ambrose Bierce.
The Dial, July, 1918. Article by Wilson Follett.
The Double Dealer, January, 1921. Article.
Stratford Journal, June, 1918. Article.
Current Literature, August, 1888; April, 1892. Reprints.
North American Review, May, 1907.
Detective Story Magazine, March, 1919. Article by Edward H. Smith.
The Forum, "Discovery," a story by Marian Storm. November, 1926.
The Smart Set, June, 1920. "The Last Satire of a Famous Titan," by Benjamin De Casseres.
The Mentor, June, 1921. "Mystery of Ambrose Bierce," an article by Richard Barry.
Munsey's Magazine, April, 1896. Short notice.
Munsey's Magazine, June, 1917. "The Mystery of Ambrose Bierce," an article.
Saturday Evening Post, September 22, 1906. Paragraph news story.
Western British American, April 10, 1925. News story.
Sunset Magazine, June, 1904. Article.
The New Age, 1909. Article by Arnold Bennett under the *nom de plume* of Jacob Tonson.
The Scrap Book, April, 1906. Review.
Pearson's Magazine, August, 1918. Article by Joseph Lewis French.
The Critic, March 19, 1892. Review.
The Critic, October, 1898. Review.
The Biblio, January, 1922. Article by Samuel Loveman.
International Book Review, June, 1926. Article.
The American Parade, October, 1926. Article by DeCastro.
South Atlantic Quarterly, July, 1926. Article by Leroy J. Nations.

The Bookman, August, 1925. Article by Ruth Guthrie Harding.

The Anti-Philistine, August 15, 1897. Article by J. S. Cowley-Brown.

Mercure de France, January 16, 1919, July 1, 1919. Mention of Bierce in articles by Vincent O'Sullivan.

The Dublin Magazine, April-June, 1929. Note by Vincent O'Sullivan.

The Reviewer, October, 1925. Article by C. Hartley Grattan.

The New Masses, November, 1926. Article by James Rorty.

VI
GENEALOGICAL REFERENCES

"The Biographical Cyclopedia and Portrait Gallery of Ohio," edited by J. Fletcher Brennan, Cincinnati, 1880.

"Fifty Years and Over of Akron and Summit County," by ex-Sheriff Sam Lane, 1892.

"John Brown," by Oswald Garrison Villard.

"John Brown." Article by Joseph Hergesheimer, *Saturday Evening Post,* 1929.

"Genealogical and Family History of Connecticut."

"Historical Reminiscences of Summit County," by General Lucius Verus Bierce, H. T. and H. G. Canfield, Akron, 1854.

"The Story of Detroit," by George B. Catlin, 1923.

Records of Western Reserve Historical Society.

Records of Miss J. M. Ames and Mrs. Fanny L. S. Meadows.

The Summit Beacon, December 7, 1859.

APPENDIX

BIERCE'S LIBRARY

Samuel John Alexander, "The Inverted Torch and Other Poems."
Gertrude Atherton's "Ancestors."
Richard Edward Boyes, "The Pharisee and the Publican."
Philip Alexander Bruce, "Pocahontas and Other Sonnets."
Paul Carus, "The Gospel of Buddha."
Henry Cohn, "Talmud."
Porter Garnett, "The Bohemian Jinks."
James M. Hopper, "Caybigan."
George Horton, "In Unknown Seas."
Elbert Hubbard, "So Here Cometh White Hyacinths."
Jack London, "The Call of the Wild."
Samuel Loveman, "Poems."
Jeremiah Lynch, "A Senator of the Fifties."
Mrs. Josephine Clifford McCrackin, "The Woman Who Lost Him."
Edwin Markham, "The Man with the Hoe."

Hudson Maxim, "The Science of Poetry and Philosophy of Language."

H. L. Mencken, "The Artist."

William Morrow, "Tentala of the South Seas."

Walter Neale, "The Betrayal."

Percival Pollard, "The Imitator."

G. G. Scheffauer, "Of Both Worlds."

Flora MacDonald Shearer, "The Legend of Avlis."

George Sterling, many volumes.

Edward Robeson Taylor, "Into the Night."

Maria Heredia, "Sonnets from the Tropics."

Thomas Walsh, "The Prison Ships and Other Poems."

Eugene R. White, "Songs of Good Fighting."

INDEX

Adkins, Eva, 191
"Adventures of my Life" by Henri Rochefort, 110
Alta California, 85-98
Amidon, Mr., 145
Ames, Miss J. M., genealogist, 13-14
Andrade, Roberto, 294
"Aphorisms" by Bierce, 106
Arcadian, The, Quotation on Bierce, 86
Argonaut, The, founded 122; history of, 123
Army of the Cumberland, 53
Arnheim, Countess, 287.
Atherton, Gertrude, Impressions of Bierce, 200
Austin, Mary, Criticism of Bierce, 185

Baker, R. S., 281
Balzac, Honoré, 85
Barnes, W. H. L., 61-90
Barney, Mrs. C., 191
Barr, Robert, Work on *The Idler,* 97-315
Barry, Richard, 308
Bartlett, W. C., 157
Bat, The, Contributions to, 97
Bearse, Austin, Ancestor, 13-14
Beatty, General Sam, 44
Beauregard, General, 44.
Beer, Thomas, 90-224
Beerbohm, Max, quotation, 141
Belknap, H. P., 198
Bennett, Arnold, quoted on Bierce, 10
"Between the Dark and Daylight," 286
Beveridge, A. J., 266
Bierce, Ambrose: "Nuggets & Dust," 96
  Books: "The Monk and the Hangman's Daughter," 218-288; "Shapes of Clay," 288; "Fantastic Tales," 263; "The

Bierce, Ambrose (*cont'd*)
  Cynic's Word Book," 289; Collected Works, 230-297-305
  Stories: "A Horseman in the Sky," 31; "The Story of a Conscience," 31; "What I Saw of Shiloh," 38; "A Son of the Gods," 45; "Bodies of the Dead," 222; "A Psychological Shipwreck," 229; "Stanley Fleming's Hallucination," 229; "Charles Ashmore's Trail," 229; "One Kind of Officer," 32; "The Damned Thing," 105; "The Realm of the Unreal," 183; "An Inhabitant of Carcosa," 67; "A Man With Two Lives," 75; "Night Doings at Deadman's," 126; "The Famous Gilson Bequest," 126
  Introduction: paradoxical nature of reputation, 1; work on "Town Crier," 3; reputation in England, 8; Dod Grile, 9; "Prattle," 10; return to America, 10; "Tales of Soldiers and Civilians," 10; Bierce Myth, 3; Starrett Bibliography, 12; disappearance into Mexico, 12; personality, 12; Biographies of Bierce, 12
  Mostly Genealogical: Bearse, Austin, 13; Lucius Verus Bierce, 17, 18, 19, 20, 21, 22; William Bierce (grandfather), 16; Abigail Bierce, 16; James Bierce, 15; Shubael Bierce, 15; Hezekial Bierce, 15; Birth of Bierce, 21; family relations, 23; schooling, 24; boyhood, 25
  War Days: admiration for Lucius V. Bierce, 30; enlists with Indiana regiment, 30; movements of regiment, 31; influence of General Hazen, 48; second lieutenancy, 44; visit to Stone

349